Resistance to Exercise

A Social Analysis of Inactivity

▼   ▼   ▼   ▼   ▼

Mary McElroy, PhD

Kansas State University

Human Kinetics

Library of Congress Cataloging-in-Publication Data

McElroy, Mary, 1952-
   Resistance to exercise : a social analysis of inactivity / Mary McElroy.
     p. cm.
   Includes bibliographical references and index.
   ISBN 0-88011-880-6
   1. Exercise--Social aspects. 2. Physical fitness--Social aspects. 3. Physical education
and training--Social aspects.   I. Title.

   RA781 .M387 2002
   613.7'1--dc21

                                                 2001039260

ISBN: 0-88011-880-6

Developmental Editor: Renee T. Thomas; **Assistant Editors:** Amanda S. Ewing and Sandra Merz Bott; **Copyeditor:** Karen Bojda; **Proofreader:** Myla Smith; **Indexer:** Betty Frizzéll; **Permission Manager:** Dalene Reeder; **Graphic Designer:** Fred Starbird; **Graphic Artist:** Denise Lowry; **Photo Manager:** Leslie Woodrum; **Cover Designer:** Kristin Darling; **Photographer (interior):** Leslie Woodrum (except where otherwise noted); **Art Manager:** Craig Newsom; **Illustrator:** Tom Roberts; **Printer:** Bang

Printed in the United States of America   10 9 8 7 6 5 4 3 2 1

Human Kinetics
Web site: www.humankinetics.com

United States: Human Kinetics, P.O. Box 5076, Champaign, IL 61825-5076
800-747-4457
e-mail: humank@hkusa.com

Canada: Human Kinetics, 475 Devonshire Road Unit 100, Windsor, ON N8Y 2L5
800-465-7301 (in Canada only)
e-mail: orders@hkcanada.com

Europe: Human Kinetics, Units C2/C3 Wira Business Park, West Park Ring Road, Leeds
LS16 6EB, United Kingdom
+44 (0) 113 278 1708
e-mail: hk@hkeurope.com

Australia: Human Kinetics, 57A Price Avenue, Lower Mitcham, South Australia 5062
08 8277 1555
e-mail: liahka@senet.com.au

New Zealand: Human Kinetics, P.O. Box 105-231, Auckland Central
09-523-3462
e-mail: hkp@ihug.co.nz

Contents

▼ Part II
Social Institutions   91

Chapter 4   The Changing American Family   93

Chapter 5   School Physical Education in Crisis   137

Preface

Most people know that they need to include more physical activity in their daily lives. Media images of youthful, attractive men and women actively engaged in sport, bookstores filled with the latest exercise manuals, and a proliferation of home-based fitness equipment serve as constant reminders of the importance of being physically active. Americans have been bombarded with messages stressing the significant role physical activity plays in maintaining good health and preventing disease. During the last decade, several nationwide campaigns have helped people to learn about the many health benefits associated with physical activity. In particular, high-profile public policy initiatives such as the *Healthy People 2000* report (U.S. Department of Health and Human Services [USDHHS], 1990), *Physical Activity and Health: A Report of the Surgeon General* (USDHHS, 1996b), and *Healthy People 2010* (USDHHS, 2000a) have furnished the general public with excellent information about why it is important to be physically active.

Unfortunately, images of fit and healthy Americans and widely circulated health messages have not translated into increased physical activity for most Americans. Findings from a number of large-scale surveys point to the inability of most Americans to participate in minimal amounts of physical activity. More than 60 percent of Americans fall below suggested activity guidelines, and more than one third lead completely sedentary lives (USDHHS, 2000a). Overweight adults are also putting themselves at risk for disease and disability. Medical experts predict from the declines in physical activity that the current generation of children will grow into the most obese generation of adults in U.S. history (Hill & Trowbridge, 1998).

Resistance to Exercise: A Social Analysis of Inactivity examines the current epidemic of sedentary living that has beset contemporary American society. Why do people who know they should be more physically active still fail to do so? What are some of the obstacles to achieving a more physically active lifestyle? Is it possible to transform contemporary America into a more physically active society? Answers to these questions constitute a major portion of today's health promotion efforts. An in-depth exploration of these questions is the principal focus of this book.

This analysis draws information from a wide variety of sources. I have been guided by a number of well-known sociological works, such as C. Wright Mill's *The Sociological Imagination* (1959), Robert Bellah and colleagues' *Habits of the Heart* (1985), and Niklas Luhmann's *Trust and Power* (1970). The works of health promotion specialists, such as Meredith Minkler and Daniel Stokols, and medical sociologists, such as David Mechanic and Robert Crawford, serve as a strong sociological basis for understanding the difficulties in creating a social structure more conducive to a healthier society. I also give attention to some recent critiques of American society, such as David Forbes's *False Fixes: The Cultural Politics of Drugs, Alcohol, and Addictive Relations* (1994) and Robert Putnam's *Bowling Alone: The Collapse and Revival of American Community* (2000). These works provide insight into why many Americans have disengaged not only from health-promoting lifestyles but from active engagement with each other as well.

A large number of critiques of American society, for one reason or another, have not addressed the topic of physical inactivity. The exceptions are works from individuals such as Hal Lawson and Alan Ingham, who have persistently questioned the limitations found in many of the traditional approaches to promoting physical activity. We also should not ignore the works of individuals such as Thomas McKenzie and James Sallis, who have offered innovative strategies to increase physical activity at home, at school, and within the community. These works and the others discussed throughout the following pages serve as a conceptual grounding for what I hope will be a useful framework from which to view the problems associated with getting Americans to be more physically active.

It is my sincere hope that this book will stimulate interest among a wide variety of readers. This book should be useful to those interested in entering one of the growing number of health-related professions. Exercise and recreation leaders, physical therapists, physical education instructors, physicians, and many other health professionals committed to the promotion of healthy lifestyles might benefit from a sociological critique of the influences that affect decisions to start and remain involved in regular physical activity.

This book may also be of interest to individuals who have been unsuccessful in maintaining their own physical activity program. Perhaps after considering the whirlwind of changes associated with living in contemporary America, you may better appreciate the difficulties in starting and sticking with a physically active lifestyle.

You may even be motivated to look within for the wherewithal to overcome the barriers to your ongoing participation, and perhaps you will be able to better distinguish which barriers are under your control and which are not.

From my personal standpoint, the most meaningful, and perhaps most ambitious, objective of this project is to stimulate others to view physical activity as a meaningful commentary on the American experience. Enhancing the legitimacy of physical activity as a topic of sociological inquiry would indeed be very gratifying. To these ends, I hope that health professionals, students, scholars, and anyone interested in the topic of physical activity find this inquiry worthwhile.

Credits

Figure 1.1 Adapted from Centers for Disease Control and Prevention. (1998). *National vital statistics report.* Hyattsville, MD: National Center for Health Statistics.

Figure 1.2 Adapted from Powell, K., & Blair, S. (1994). The public health burdens of sedentary living habits: Theoretical but realistic estimates. *Medicine and Science in Sports and Exercise. 26,* 851-856.

Tables 3.1 and 3.2 Adapted from U.S. Department of Health and Human Services. (2000). *Healthy people 2010.* Washington, DC: U.S. Government Printing Office.

Figure 4.1 and Table 4.1 From Verhoef, M., & Love, E. (1994). Women and exercise participation: The mixed blessings of motherhood. *Health Care for Women International, 15,* 297-306.

Figures 5.1, 5.2, and Table 5.1 From U.S. Department of Health and Human Services. (1999). *Youth Risk Behavior Surveillance System.* Washington, DC: U.S. Government Printing Office.

Table 6.1 Adapted from Crump, C., Earp, J., Kozma, C., & Hertz-Picciotto, I. (1996). Effect of organizational level variables on differential employee participation in 10 federal worksite health promotion programs. *Health Education Quarterly, 23,* 204-223.

Table 6.2 Adapted from Brisson, C., Larocque, B., Moisan, J., Vezina, M., & Dagenais, G. (2000). Psychosocial factors at work, smoking, sedentary behavior, and body mass index: A prevalence study among 6995 white collar workers. *Journal of Occupational and Environmental Medicine, 42,* 40-46.

Table 7.2 Adapted from O'Neil, E. (1995). *Critical challenges: Revitalizing the health professions for the twenty-first century.* San Francisco: Pew Health Professions Commission.

Table 8.1 Adapted from McLeroy, K., Bibeau, D., Steckler, A., & Glanz, K. (1988). An ecological perspective on health promotion programs. *Health Education Quarterly, 15,* 351-377.

Table 8.2 Adapted from Butterfoss, F., Goodman, R., & Wandersman, A. (1993). Community coalitions for prevention and health promotion. *Health Education Research, 8,* 315-330.

▼ ▼ ▼ ▼ ▼

Dimensions of the Problem

Photograph by Tom Roberts

1

Sedentary Living in Contemporary Society

*T*hough **few would argue** *that individuals bear no responsibility for health-related decisions and actions, several consistent criticisms have been leveled at what many see as the dangers of an overemphasis on individual responsibility for health. Foremost among these criticisms is the argument that an overriding emphasis on personal responsibility "blames the victim" by ignoring the social context in which individual decision making and health-related action takes place. In the words of Rob Crawford the victim-blaming ideology both "ignores what is known about human behavior and minimizes the importance of evidence about the environmental assault on health. It instructs people to be individually responsible at a time when they are becoming less capable as individuals of controlling their health environment" (Minkler, 2000:81).*

▼   ▼   ▼   ▼   ▼

Sedentary Americans

People today lead very different lives than their parents and grand-parents did. For the most part, our generation is more educated, better off financially, and geographically more mobile than our predecessors. Although people once were more likely to attend school and to raise their families in one location, individuals today lift up stakes and relocate on average a dozen times during the course of a lifetime (Frantzich, 1999).

People are also affected by changes in the flow of information and knowledge. The transformation from an industrial to an information society begun in the 1960s and fueled by advances in computer technology add up to what futurist Alvin Toffler (1980) more than 20 years ago labeled the "great wave of change." The information age is responsible not only for a dramatic shift in the technological bases of contemporary societies but also for a dramatic social shift as well. Many social and work functions once performed personally in face-to-face settings are being handled through electronic equivalents. One of the greatest challenges that information societies face today is whether they can maintain a sense of *social connectedness* in the face of technological and economic advancement.

Significant changes have also occurred in the composition of the workforce. Particularly notable has been the increased presence of women in paid employment. Starting in the 1960s and 1970s, women entered the labor market in record numbers, and it is projected that by the year 2005, 63 percent of women will be working outside the home, profoundly changing not only the economic roles of men and women but also their social roles (Fullerton, 1993). For example, child care arrangements outside the home, mostly unheard of in our grandmothers' generation, have taken on greater significance not only because increasing numbers of mothers are in the labor force but because relatives have moved away and extended family ties are harder to maintain.

Many of the social changes encountered during the 20th century have also affected matters of health. Considerable stress is identified with moving from job to job looking for a better financial situation or, in many cases, dealing with prospects of unemployment (Ferrie, Shipley, Marmot, Stansfeld, & Smith, 1998). Researchers have also been able to link health-compromising outcomes with the pressures related to the expectations associated with specific job characteristics (Karasek & Theorell, 1990). The challenges associated with balancing work and family life in an age of changing role expectations have also produced heightened levels of uneasiness (Barnett & Rivers, 1998). Even how we get to work can produce health-compromising consequences. Rush-hour commuting has been identified as a source of tremendous psychological stress as those fortunate enough to leave the difficult and expensive living conditions in many of our urban areas now face the long commute to work from the suburbs. According to a report by the American Highway User's Alliance, Americans annually spend more than 100 million hours in traffic jams (Cambridge Systematics, 1999). Thus, the combined negative emotional states associated with work and rush-hour travel spill over into the home environment (Grzywacz & Marks, 2000).

Our changing lifestyles have also had an impact on good nutritional habits. The increased proportion of families with two wage earners has resulted in far less time spent on preparing meals and far greater consumption of precooked or convenience foods (Brinkley, Eales, & Jekanowski, 2000). Although adult consumption of fats has declined slightly in recent decades, there has also been a decline in the consumption of fresh fruits and vegetables and an increase in consumption of refined sugars. Most children exceed national recommendations for intake of total and saturated fats as well (Berenson, Srinivasan, & Nicklas, 1998). Overweight adults and children are putting themselves at risk for obesity and chronic diseases such as diabetes and cardiovascular disease (CVD). One explanation for the increased number of overweight Americans lies in the increased number of calories in the typical American diet. Another explanation lies in the adoption of a sedentary lifestyle.

Today, most Americans participate in little or no physical activity in the course of the day (U.S. Department of Health and Human Services [USDHHS], 1996b). In the past, many of our daily responsibilities involved considerable application of human energy. Before the era of machines that led to many of the conveniences of modern life, people were forced to be much more involved in physical activity and physical labor. People typically spent much of the day in a physically active state, such as walking, lifting, and working with the hands (Fletcher, 1983). Whereas human motion was once an inescapable part of normal daily routines, today people must consciously plan to include enough physical activity as part of their daily practices to maintain good health (Farquhar, 1987).

Technology has given us devices and services that have reduced physical activity both at home and work. Elevators, escalators, computers, and mechanized robots have transformed work spaces into sedentary places. Domestic chores around the home have also been redefined as more passive endeavors. The dishwasher, riding lawn mower, and other mechanized equipment mean that household activities require less time but also less physical effort. One hundred years ago, only 6 percent of the energy used to produce goods was mechanical; the remaining 94 percent was generated by human or animal muscle power (Miller & Allen, 1994). Today, it is estimated that more than 50 percent of the working population does not perform appreciable physical activity associated with work (USDHHS, 2000b).

In an era when home and work patterns require minimal physical exertion, taking part in leisure-time physical activity takes on greater importance. Unfortunately, too many people are choosing inactive pursuits. Stressed from work or the long commute home, many people collapse in front of their television sets. According to the Nielsen Report on Television (A.C. Nielsen Company, 1992-93), U.S. households have their television sets turned on an average of seven hours per day. Increasingly, children are opting for a position in front of the television set instead of a place in the neighborhood pickup game or just shooting hoops in the driveway. A recent national survey reported that 26 percent of boys and 23 percent of girls watch four or more hours of television per day (Andersen, Crespo, Bartlett, Cheskin, & Pratt, 1998). For other Americans, newer interactive forms of entertainment, such as video games and surfing the Internet, compete with the amount of time spent in physically active endeavors. Health professionals fear that with the increased fascination with technological pastimes, sedentary activities are winning out.

Patterns of Sedentary Living

Patterns of sedentary living have attracted the interest of many scientists, medical researchers, and policy makers. During the 1990s, several major scientific and professional organizations issued position statements establishing physical inactivity as a major public health problem. One of the first key statements, released in 1992 by the American Heart Association (AHA, 1992), recognized a sedentary lifestyle as the fourth major risk factor for coronary heart disease, trailing behind only cigarette smoking, high blood pressure, and high cholesterol levels. In an effort to publicize the health benefits of regular physical activity, several professional organizations, such as the American Association of Cardiovascular and Pulmonary Rehabilitation (1995) and the American College of Sports Medicine (ACSM, 1990), issued reports announcing the importance of physical activity. Soon came physical activity recommendations from the federal government, such as the one from the President's Council on Physical Fitness and Sports (1998) and most notably *The Surgeon General's Report on Physical Activity* (USDHHS, 1996b), a joint effort by the Centers for Disease Control and Prevention (CDC) and the National Center for Chronic Disease Prevention. The surgeon general's report endorsed physical activity guidelines that recommend that adults complete 30 or more minutes of moderate-intensity physical activity, preferably on most days of the week.

Unfortunately, widely circulated health messages have not translated into increased physical activity among most Americans. Despite the multiple benefits of physical activity, most people lead sedentary lives, especially as they become middle-aged and older. Information collected from several national surveys reveals the extent of the physical inactivity problem throughout the U.S. population. The first set of data was gathered by the U.S. National Center for Health Statistics as part of the ongoing National Health Interview Survey (NHIS). Interviews were conducted in homes and participants were asked a series of questions about participation in physical activities during the previous two weeks. For each activity, the frequency (number of times), duration (the average number of minutes), and intensity (perceived degree to which heart rate is increased) were determined. Using this information, three categories, which have become relatively standard, were established. The categories are *no physical activity* (no reported activity during the previous two weeks), *regular sustained physical activity* (more than five times per week and more than 30 minutes per occasion of physical activity of any type and at any intensity), and *regular vigorous physical activity* (more than three times per week and performed at more than 50 percent of estimated age- and sex-specific cardiorespiratory capacity).

The NHIS survey—administered on two separate occasions, first in 1986 and then in 1991, to two different samples—uncovered disturbing findings. More specifically, in 1991 only 23.5 percent of adults aged 18 and over reported participation in regular sustained physical activity, and only 16.4 percent reported participation in vigorous physical activity. Nearly one in four adults (24.3 percent) reported no physical activity during the last two weeks (Benson & Marano, 1992).

A second revealing source of physical inactivity patterns among Americans is the CDC's report on health behaviors, known as the Behavioral Risk Factor Surveillance System (BRFSS). Prior to the 1980s, the United States did not have a national health plan. Evaluating the new health priorities meant gathering accurate data on an on-going basis. As part of a federal assistance program to the states, in 1981 the CDC began assisting state health departments in collecting health data, including data on various health risks in the adult population. The BRFSS is a telephone survey administered to representative samples of residents living in participating states. Early surveys included only about half the states, but the more recent data collection provides information from all the states. Physical activity was first included in the survey starting in 1986.

The regular administrations of the BRFSS provided an opportunity to assess patterns of change in physical activity. Participants were asked the question, "During the past month, did you participate in any physical activities or exercises such as running, calisthenics, golf, gardening, or walking for exercise?" If they responded yes, they were asked to identify their two most common physical activities and to indicate their frequency in the previous month and duration per occasion. Intensity was specified using a strategy similar to that used in the NHIS survey. Comparisons of the data from 1986 to 1994, for example, revealed that individuals reporting no physical activity during the prior month remained steady at about 30 percent. Similarly, throughout the same time period, low participation in regular sustained physical activity (19 percent) and in regular vigorous physical activity (11 percent) also remained constant (USDHHS, 1996b).

The BRFSS also provides a unique opportunity to compare physical activity levels across states. The latest round of BRFSS data (figure 1.1) indicates that sedentary living is still pervasive. Most Americans fail to meet minimum levels of physical activity. Although some state and regional differences exist, it is apparent that physical inactivity is a problem occurring nationwide.

National estimates of physical activity have raised another concern: the large numbers of members of racial and ethnic minority and other social groups who participate in little or no physical activity. For example, according to the BRFSS data (CDC, 1992), African-American women (42.7 percent) are one and one quarter times more likely to report no participation in physical activity than their white female counterparts (33.1 percent). Similarly, individuals of both sexes with high school degrees (32.8 percent) were significantly more likely to report no physical activity than individuals who had completed college degrees (17.8 percent).

The disappointing participation rates among racial and ethnic minorities are also confirmed in the National Health and Nutrition Examination surveys (NHANES) (Crespo, 2000). NHANES, admin-

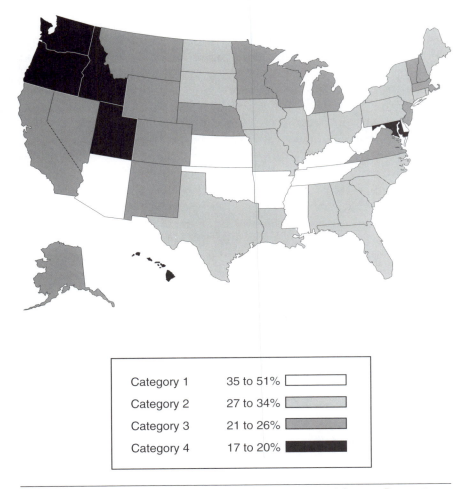

Figure 1.1   Prevalence of sedentary living in the United States. Percentage of survey respondents reporting no physical activity.
Adapted from CDC, 1998.

istered since 1960, uses in-person and telephone interviews to assess health behaviors such as participation in physical activity. The NHANES III sample was designed to deliberately oversample members of minority groups (e.g., African Americans and Mexican Americans) to compensate for their low numbers in some of the previous surveys (Crespo, Keteyian, Heath, & Sempos, 1996). Although the prevalence of no leisure-time physical activity for U.S. adults overall was 18 percent, rates were considerably higher among specific minority groups: African-American men (26 percent), African-American women (43 percent), Mexican-American men (32 percent). Nearly one in two Mexican-American women (47 percent) reported no leisure-time physical activity. For all racial and ethnic groups and for both men and women, persons living below the poverty line had a higher prevalence of leisure-time inactivity than those living at or above the poverty line (Crespo, 2000).

The surveys also allow for a comparison between the trends in physical activity levels and the trends in rates of obesity. NHANES data show that the percentage of obese people has increased from 14 percent in 1976-1980 to 22.5 percent in 1988-1994. Similar results from BRFSS show that the prevalence of obesity increased from 12 percent in 1991 to 17.9 percent in 1998 (Mokdad, Serdula, & Dietz, 1998).

The spread of obesity coupled with little change in physical activity levels speaks to the need to convince Americans to become physically active. In addition to diet modification, initiating and maintaining regular physical activity is an important component of an effective weight-control strategy. Despite the benefits, the proportion of the population that has adopted sound dietary practices combined with regular physical activity has declined rather than increased toward the goals established in the national health objectives (USDHHS, 2000a). Not surprisingly, these alarming statistics have helped catapult sedentary living to a crisis level as one of the major health concerns of modern living.

Diseases of Sedentary Living

Interest in sedentary lifestyles is largely due to the growing recognition that physically inactive lifestyles are related to the major diseases that plague contemporary societies. During the 20th century, heart disease, diabetes, and stroke have emerged as the leading causes of death in the United States. This is quite a turnaround from before 1900, when infectious diseases, particularly pneumonia and tuberculosis, were the primary concerns of public health officials and the medical community. The change in the leading causes of death is partly due to the success of public health and medical advances. The first public health movement gained control over communicable disease by providing safe water and adequate sewage disposal. Achievements in medical interventions, most notably the development of antibiotics, also served to reduce infectious diseases. Today, it is estimated that one in three Americans suffers from at least one health condition that develops slowly over many years. The longer people live, the more likely they are to fall prey to chronic and degenerative diseases. Although people can live with chronic diseases for many years, these illnesses are largely incurable.

Chronic diseases such as cardiovascular disease, hypertension, and diabetes mellitus affect millions of Americans. The American Heart Association (2000a) estimates that nearly 60 million Americans have one or more types of cardiovascular disease, which accounts for more than 950,000 deaths annually or 41.2 percent of the total death rate, by far the single largest killer of Americans. Nearly one in five Americans (and one in four adults) are dealing with high blood pressure. Elevated blood pressure was listed as a primary or contributing cause of death for about 210,000 people in 1997. Diabetes mellitus has also emerged as a significant health problem in the United States. Currently, it is estimated that 15.7 million people have diabetes (American Diabetes Association, 2000). The prevalence of diabetes rose from 4.9 percent in 1990 to 6.5 percent in 1998, an increase of 33 percent (Mokdad et al., 2000). Increases were observed in both sexes, all ages, all ethnic groups, and all education levels. Diabetes today is a leading cause of blindness, kidney failure, nerve damage, and amputations and is the seventh leading cause of death.

The prevalence of chronic diseases today can also be explained by two demographic trends that occurred during the 20th century: a tremendous population growth and an increase in total life expectancy. Prior to 1940, 132 million people were living in the United States. By 2000 the population has more than doubled to more than 280 million. The burgeoning population is also living longer. Since 1900, the average life span of a person in the United States has increased by more than 30 years. The average life expectancy of men has increased from 60.8 to 73.6 years, and for women, from 65.2 to 79.4 years. In 1940 the percentage of Americans more than 65 years old was only 6.8 percent. By 1997, the percentage had increased to 12.7 (AHA, 2000b).

Diseases associated with sedentary living cost the United States billions of dollars each year. Cardiovascular disease in the United States—including its direct costs (e.g., the cost of physicians and other professionals, hospital and nursing home services, medications, home health care) and indirect costs (e.g., lost productivity)—cost more than $326 billion in the year 2000 (AHA, 2000a). Health care and other costs directly related to diabetes runs as high as $98 billion every year (American Diabetes Association, 2000).

The economic costs of physical inactivity are also quite staggering. Colditz (1999) estimated the financial expenses associated with lack of physical activity and its correlate, obesity. According to his analysis, physical inactivity results in the annual loss of $24 billion (in 1995-dollar values). Independent of physical inactivity, the costs for obesity total nearly $70 billion. Not considered in Colditz's analysis are the financial expenditures resulting from reduced physical functioning caused by high levels of obesity or inactivity. Even excluding the loss in work productivity, it is evident that the public health burden of inactivity is substantial and investments in increasing physically active lifestyles would have a large economic payoff to society as a whole (Colditz, 1999).

Particularly important to establishing the role of physical inactivity in disease would be development of more sophisticated measurement techniques. Using population attributable risk (PAR) analysis, Robert Hahn and colleagues (1990) were among the first to provide statistical estimates of the impact of physical inactivity on the death rates for nine common chronic diseases. The PAR technique is a method of estimating the proportion of a public health burden that is caused by a particular risk factor. For example, if we consider physical inactivity as a causal risk factor, PAR techniques allow estimation of the percentage of deaths from a particular disease that theoretically would occur if everyone were physically active. The excess number of cases is the difference between the total that would occur if the risk factor were absent and the actual number of deaths.

The researchers estimate that 256,686 deaths in the United States could have been prevented if physical inactivity were eliminated. Of nine risk factors examined singly for their contribution to deaths from the nine diseases, the largest proportion, 33 percent, was attributable to cigarette smoking, 24 percent to obesity, 23 percent to high cholesterol levels, and 21 percent to hypertension. The total deaths attributable to sedentary lifestyles amount to 23 percent of all deaths. If everyone were highly active, the death rate would be only two thirds of the current rate. Furthermore, as shown in figure 1.2, if 50 percent of the sedentary population became active, potentially 21,800 fewer deaths would result from these health conditions (Powell & Blair, 1994).

Researchers have also been able to link changes in physical fitness levels to the risk of some chronic diseases. One study was conducted as part of the Aerobics Center Longitudinal Study, spearheaded by Dr. Steven Blair and colleagues (Blair et al., 1995). Data were gathered and analyzed from more than 9,000 men who had participated

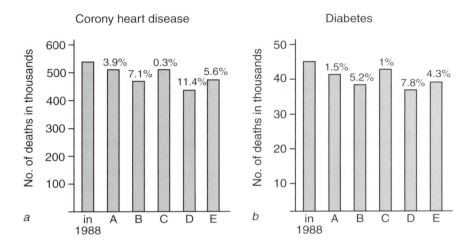

A — Reductions in deaths if 50% of those doing no physical activity become physically active but do not meet minimum requirements

B — Reductions in deaths if 50% of those not meeting minimum requirements begin meeting them

C — Reductions in deaths if 50% of those not meeting minimum requirements begin exceeding them

D — Reductions in deaths if 50% of those in each group move up to the next group (total of A, B, and C)

E — Reductions in deaths if Healthy People 2000 Objectives had been met

Figure 1.2   Reduction in deaths from coronary heart disease and diabetes if exercise levels increased among adults.

Adapted from Powell & Blair, 1994.

in two preventive medical examinations at the Cooper Clinic in Dallas, Texas. Changes in physical fitness were determined by comparing fit and unfit scores from each visit. The highest death rates from cardiovascular disease were observed in people who were unfit at both examinations; the lowest death rates were observed in people who were physically fit at both examinations. Individuals who were initially unfit but became fit experienced a 44 percent risk reduction in all-cause mortality and a 52 percent risk reduction in cardiovascular disease.

Epidemiological studies such as the ones described help quantify the consequences of physically inactive lifestyles in their most visceral terms, the increased likelihood of premature death. These findings also demonstrate that improving physical activity may represent one of the most promising interventions to reduce deaths from chronic diseases, particularly cardiovascular disease. The association between the lack of physical activity and the increased likelihood of premature death has given physical inactivity a prominent place among the other major health risk factors, such as diet and smoking.

Responsibility for Sedentary Lifestyles

A compelling body of knowledge has accumulated in recent years to confirm that regular physical activity has important health benefits. Lifestyle habits such as poor nutrition, excessive drinking, and lack of regular physical activity have been shown to contribute to significant increases in illness and mortality. Although advances in medical and surgical care have contributed to declines in death and disease for most of the population, it is estimated that up to 70 percent of illness today is caused by preventable factors (USDHHS, 1990).

For centuries, writers have warned against the perils of a life without physical activity (Berryman, 1992); however, it was not until the second half of the 20th century that the health implications of sedentary living began to be addressed. Particularly during the 1970s, a growing body of research established a strong case that many health problems were traceable to the living habits of individuals. This position was well chronicled in an essay published by John Knowles (1977). According to Knowles, the greatest enemy to the health of the individual is the individual (Reiser, 1985). Such thinking would lay the groundwork for the health movement of the 1980s and would unite health promotion with the goal of changing risky health behaviors of individuals.

Social scientists have questioned the wisdom behind emphasizing good health through individual lifestyle changes. Social epidemiologists S. Leonard Syme and Linda Balfour offer several reasons for why strategies focused on changing individual behaviors are likely to be disappointing. First, they point to the fact that previous health promotion strategies aimed at changing behaviors have not worked. Despite more than two decades of trying, many Americans have failed to adopt healthy lifestyles. The second reason is that the health conditions of today, such as cardiovascular disease, diabetes, and cancer, involve such large numbers of people that it is impossible to prevent such diseases by simply changing the behaviors of individuals one at a time. Finally, and perhaps most crucial to an understanding of the disappointing results of health promotion efforts targeting the behaviors of individuals directly, they point to how individual approaches do little to address the social conditions that have contributed to the problem. Even if individual health habits are changed, if the wider social and cultural context in which behaviors occur are not altered, there will be the "next generation of people who will suffer from the same adverse social conditions" (Syme & Balfour, 1999).

A number of social scientists have adopted much harsher positions when critiquing the health movement. Among the early social critiques is the work of Sylvia Tesh (1981) who, in her compelling political analysis of U.S. disease prevention policy, describes the situation as one in which the attention to the individual supports a politically conservative position that "brackets off questions about the structure of society." Medical sociologist Rob Crawford (1981) similarly criticizes the lifestyle movement because of its linkages with the more affluent in American society. He argues that by pointing to lifestyle issues that are usually presented as if they reflect the problems of a "homogenized affluent society," health promotion directs attention away from the central underlying cause of illness and disease, that of social class differences. Perhaps the most scathing attack on U.S. health promotion efforts is the book *Dangerous to Your Health*, in which Vicente Navarro (1993) contends that messages and policies of health promotion are cleverly disguised pretenses to divert attention away from the more compelling need to address the social and economic power inequities that divide modern America today. These critiques examine health promotion from different perspectives and come together to collectively criticize the health promotion movement that places the causes of health problems at the level of the individual and not in the social system of society.

Sociologist Stanley Lieberson (1985) suggests that what is important in understanding the challenges of getting people to adopt a healthier lifestyle is to be able to distinguish between *basic causes*, the factors that are responsible for generating a particular outcome, and *surface causes*, which are factors that are related to the outcome, even though changes in these factors do not produce corresponding changes in the outcome. Thus even if we are effective in getting people to adopt health-promoting behaviors such as regular physical activity (e.g., surface cause), as long as the social structure of society remains unchanged (e.g., basic cause) new obstacles are likely to emerge to perpetuate sedentary habits.

Social scientists do not claim that individual behaviors are unimportant. Differences among individuals help some people to take advantage of opportunities that others allow to slip by. But before we can say successes or failures are characteristics of individuals, the sociologist within us must look at the ways in which social conditions affect individuals' opportunities for success.

The Individual Versus Social Structure Debate

Is chronic illness such as heart disease caused by choosing to eat too much fat or participating in too little physical activity? Or are such health conditions caused by social forces in today's society that reinforce the habits of sedentary living? The answers to these questions are at the center of the ongoing debate concerning identifying the most effective strategies necessary to improve the health of Americans and to encourage people to put more physical activity in their lives. The debate can be characterized along the lines of what sociologist Susan Wright (1993) has labeled the individual/social structure dilemma. The individual side of the continuum, according to Wright, is consistent with ideologies grounded in beliefs in individual rights and responsibilities and thus an expectation that individuals are responsible for their own particular circumstances. For example, the failure to maintain a reasonable weight, to drink alcohol in moderation, or to participate in physical activity are perceived as health practices under the control of the individual. The individual in this context has the solutions for dealing with these health problems.

The opposing social structure argument views unhealthy behaviors, including sedentary lifestyles, as acquired within social groups and influenced by powerful social forces. Factors such as unequal distributions of educational opportunities and inaccessible health care services prevent individuals from participating fully in healthy lifestyles. The social structure position assumes that sedentary lifestyles are rooted in the nature of social arrangement and that individuals are seen as subject to conditions that in large part are located outside their control (Crawford, 1981).

The ability to locate situations that affect individuals within the context of the larger social structure of American society is what sociologist C. Wright Mills (1959) termed "the sociological imagination." According to Mills, we can place personal troubles such as poverty or divorce into a larger social context when we view them as public issues. For an illustration he points to the example of unemployment. When relatively few people are unemployed in the midst of a strong economy, the situation can be defined in terms of personal troubles with the solutions lying in the immediate environment of the individual. However, when relatively large numbers of people are out of work, the situation shifts to a public issue and thereby solutions to the problem that focus on the immediate environment of the individual are likely to be insufficient. The sociological imagination implies that many of the things we experience as individuals have to do with how social structures and institutions influence life patterns.

We can extend Mills' thinking to the causes of unhealthy habits associated with living in contemporary society. If unhealthy behaviors such as eating a poor diet, smoking cigarettes, or inadequate amounts of physical activity are confined to only a few individuals, then these lifestyle behaviors can be seen as personal troubles. The effective remedy would be to enact physical activity programming and other health-promotion programs targeting individuals directly. However, when the problem is so pervasive, as is evident by the documented high rates of sedentary living in the United States today, physical inactivity takes on the character of a public problem. The sociological imagination suggests that significant improvements in physical activity for so many Americans requires us to look beyond individuals to the factors in society that lie beyond their control.

The underlying "resistance to exercise" in today's society can be best understood as a struggle between two contrasting ideologies: one that situates explanations for sedentary lifestyles in the failure of individuals to accept personal responsibility for their own health and another that views the cause as part of the larger social, cultural, political, and economic structure of contemporary American society. As we confront a new century, the fundamental question remains: Should the individual or should society be held responsible for changing personal health behaviors such as physical inactivity? A closer examination of how this debate plays itself out among key social institutions in American life comprises the major focus of this book.

Disappointment in Educational Campaigns

Most people recognize the health-enhancing affects of regular physical activity. For example, a recent study conducted by the American

Dietetic Association titled *Nutrition and You: 2000 Trends* (2000), reported that 84 percent of Americans ranked exercise as very important to good health. More than 90 percent also acknowledged the importance of a good diet in conjunction with physical activity. Beliefs and good intentions are often not enough to compel many to establish patterns of physical activity. In a national opinion survey conducted by the President's Council on Physical Fitness (1998) in collaboration with the Sporting Goods Manufacturers Association, 41 percent of those surveyed said that, although they knew exercise was beneficial to their health, they were unlikely to increase their physical activity in the future. Similar results were found in another large-scale study of adults. Most respondents who admitted to poor health during the previous six months—they recognized the beneficial effects of exercise to good health, though they admitted that they did not exercise enough—still failed to increase their physical activity during the subsequent period (Uitenbroek, 1993).

Warnings of disease and premature death are the usual "first rounds of ammunition" used by many health professionals to persuade people to include more physical activity in their daily routines (Kimiecik & Lawson, 1996). Messages found in educational campaigns to "exercise or else" play on the fears of people about developing disease (Bryant & McElroy, 1997). Over the past decade, the mass media have become increasingly popular as a strategy for delivering preventive health messages. Living in an information age in which the concern for health is "hot news," physical activity is the latest in a long list of health topics found in print and broadcast sources. Ranging from the more traditional television and radio outlets to the more recent proliferation of Internet sources, consumers increasingly rely on the media to supply them with a major source of health and exercise information (American Dietetic Association, 2000).

Mass media programs make good sense on the surface, as they appear to have a number of advantages over more traditional health promotion strategies. Media efforts are a relatively inexpensive method to reach a large number of people because they lower personnel costs by reducing face-to-face contact. In an extensive review of media approaches to promoting health messages, Bess Marcus and her colleagues (1998) examined results from 28 studies using media campaigns at the state or national level: 4 were delivered through the health care system, 6 took place at the work site, and 11 were based in the community. According to their review, the recall of health messages was remarkably high, as nearly 70 percent of participants surveyed were able to remember the specific health messages. That is the good news. Although media strategies appear to be successful in promoting physical activity awareness, a number of studies have revealed that most media campaigns are not as effective in altering people's actual physical activity habits (Booth, Bauman, Oldenburg, Owen, & Magnus, 1992).

But why are media approaches ineffective? One reason is that citizens are increasingly encountering an epidemic of large-scale consumer confusion. The public's confusion concerning the many health-promoting strategies is quite understandable as the media hype is spread by media people, advertisers, public relations experts, manufacturers, and members of the health professions. The mass media, well aware that we are now a society obsessed with health matters, often increase our difficulties by attributing a high degree of certainty to new health findings. Health risks are often exaggerated and factual inaccuracies may be relayed to the public, and preliminary research findings are touted as breakthroughs and presented without appropriate cautions (Becker, 1993).

Too many informational campaigns rely on strong messages that are based on the assumption that once people are advised of the health consequences associated with sedentary living they will choose to adopt healthier lifestyles. As pointed out by University of California-Berkeley public health professor Lawrence Wallack, the media tend to present health issues in medical terms with a focus on personal health habits or medical miracles (Wallack, Dorfman, & Jernigan, 1994). Media campaigns promoting physical activity rarely consider the social arrangements that contribute to the problem of sedentary living.

Within educational strategies, attaining healthy lifestyles is seen as a matter of helping individuals to make informed choices. Once individuals understand that their inactive lifestyles contribute to their health condition, and they can identify the obstacles present in their own lives, they will be able to overcome the obstacles to participating in regular physical activity. Education should be viewed as a solution to health problems when it is the lack of information that inhibits individuals from behaving in their own best interests. However, information alone can all too often be viewed as a "magic bullet" that overshadows the need to go beyond educational strategies (Alonzo, 1993). Nevertheless, the belief that informational campaigns alone can do the job still dominates much of our thinking about promoting physically active lifestyles.

There is no question that education is strongly correlated with healthy habits, including participation in physical activity. One of the reasons for the education-healthy lifestyle relationship is that education itself has pervasive effects on health apart from health knowledge. Compared to their higher socioeconomic status counterparts, people with low education face different structural constraints, such as limited occupational options leading to limited access to financial resources and in a growing number of cases limited access to health insurance (Rovner, 1997). Accordingly, efforts to change the health lifestyles of the less educated through informational campaigns to establish health-promoting behaviors without also altering their level of education miss the point. These approaches are not only ineffective but by detracting from the root problems nested in the social structure they are likely to do more harm than good.

Difficulty in Changing Sedentary Behavior

For many people, sticking to an exercise program can be more difficult than starting one. People who join exercise programs believe in the health-enhancing effect of regular exercise, but these beliefs alone are simply not enough to keep more than half of them in the programs for the long haul. Among the many well-intentioned people who set ambitious goals at the start of a new exercise regimen, more than half drop out during the first six months (USDHHS, 1996b). Many people have not been able to overcome the personal, social, and environmental barriers to exercise. People who successfully overcome the initial hurdles to starting an exercise program may later "relapse" back to sedentary living. For example, 41 percent of women enrolled in a year-long exercise program at a local health club, reported one or more relapses lasting three weeks or longer (Simkin & Gross, 1994). A more comprehensive study probed patterns of exercise relapses over a lifetime. In this survey 1,800 residents of San Diego, 41 percent of the adult population, reported frustrations associated with establishing a continuous (6 months or longer) exercise routine and quit for at least three months (Sallis, Hovell, Hofstetter, Elder, Faucher, et al., 1990a).

When people are asked why they do not participate in physical activity, the most common explanation is typically "no time." Business or career responsibilities and family obligations are the usual justifications for the lack of time in a busy day for participation in physical activity. Although certainly important to the explanation, sedentary lifestyles are much more complex than just finding the time to participate. There are as many explanations used to explain why people are not more physically active as there are health promotion professionals who disagree on which explanations seem to be the most credible. In fact, the experts cannot even agree whether people today have more or less leisure time available to them. Juliet Schor in her well-chronicled book *The Overworked American* concluded that the "shrinking of leisure experienced by nearly all types of Americans has created a professional structural crisis of time" (Schor, 1991). Using data gathered by the Bureau of Labor Statistics, she makes a convincing case for the rise of work time among all segments of American workers, men as well as women, the working class as well as professionals, and in all marital statuses and income groups. Since 1970, she estimates that Americans' annual time expenditure in work increased by more than 163 hours.

On the other hand, John Robinson, a professor of sociology at the University of Maryland, and Geoffrey Godbey, a professor of leisure studies at Pennsylvania State University, maintain that Americans today actually have more leisure time available to them than in years past (Robinson & Godbey, 1997). Analyzing information compiled from time diaries kept by thousands of individuals, they found that people had actually gained nearly an hour of free time a day compared with their counterparts back in 1965. These sociologists argued that the change in free time in today's society is due not to a significant reduction in available time but to its form. The diaries revealed that the leisure-time patterns of many Americans could best be characterized by frequent, shorter periods of free time dispersed throughout the day. Free time, for example, is more likely to occur in several 30-minute blocks rather than for extended periods of time. Even with the shorter periods, enough time is available to take a walk or use the exercise equipment stashed away in the corner of the basement. For most people, the inability or unwillingness to engage in regular physical activity is likely due to something more.

The truth of the matter is that participation in regular physical activity is not a simple matter. When we ask sedentary people to become more active, we expect people to do things that they have not done previously and to stop doing things they have been doing for years. The benefits of physical activity may take months or even years, but the discomforts are often more immediate. A commitment to physical activity, as pointed out by clinical psychologist James Maddox (1997), requires much planning and preparation. According to Maddox, participating in physical activity on a regular basis requires constant vigilance to overcome the circumstances that impede participation in physical activity.

Changing Individuals One at a Time

Health promotion specialists have developed a number of models or frameworks in an attempt to understand why some people choose to participate in health-promoting activities and others do not. One of the earliest of these frameworks is the popular Health Belief Model (HBM), first used in the early 1950s by a group of social psychologists at the U.S. Public Health Service (Becker, 1974). Their initial interest was in studying the widespread failure of people to undergo screening for the early detection of asymptomatic diseases, such as tuberculosis. Soon after, the model was applied to prescribed medical regimens. One of the first applications of HBM to physical activity was with a group of individuals at risk for cardiovascular disease (Heinzelman & Bagley, 1970). The basic premise of HBM is that the likelihood of doing health-related actions is influenced by attitudes and beliefs that motivate behavior. According to HBM, the likelihood of performing a recommended health behavior is based on the interaction between one's perceptions of four key factors: susceptibility to disease, seriousness of disease, threat of disease, and the benefits of action when weighed against the barriers. HBM has been the most useful in predicting behaviors that require a specific action, such as seeking immunizations or screening procedures. However, the model has not been as successful at predicting habitual health habits when the goal of the action is related to long-term health (e.g., preventing disease that has not already occurred), or when forces outside the individual, such as economic or environmental, are major barriers to taking some sort of action.

A second popular model that has guided health promotion is the model of planned behavior (Ajzen, 1985). This model asserts that intention or motivation to perform a behavior precedes actual performance. In this model subjective norms, beliefs about the standards or expectations of others, guide acceptable behavior. These normative beliefs determine whether a behavior is perceived as socially acceptable. The personal dimension of the model is reflected in the attitudes of the individual toward specific behaviors and in perceptions of personal control. These factors include whether a favorable attitude exists about achieving a desired outcome, a value of the outcome to the individual, and the perception of ease or difficulty in achieving the desired outcome. Thus for a woman at risk for osteoporosis, participation in physical activity is predicted to be strong if she perceives the activity as socially acceptable, sees it as an important component of risk reduction, believes the program to be feasible, and has a strong desire to avoid osteoporosis.

More recently, exercise professionals have adopted the "stages-of-change" model, which acknowledges that individuals progress through a series of changes as they learn to adopt new behaviors (Prochaska & DiClemente, 1994). Also known as the transtheoretical model, stages of change are measured at six levels: precontemplation (prior to considering need to change), contemplation (thinking about change), preparation (initial consideration of what it takes to change), action (initial efforts at actual change), maintenance (sustaining change and overcoming relapses), and termination (likelihood not to return to old habits). Part of the popularity of the stages-of-change model rests in its utility to assist health promotion specialists in tailoring specific intervention programs for each individual. This approach, by emphasizing the individual's readiness to participate in physical activity, assumes readiness to change resides within the individual and not the readiness of the social environment.

These health promotion frameworks have been less than satisfactory in producing actual changes in physical activity. The difficulty in these approaches lies in a faulty overarching assumption: that is, by consciously activating "cognitive" processes within individuals, changes in their health behaviors will occur. Although there are certainly many examples of successful programs to change behavior, the evidence suggests that behavior change is a very difficult and complex challenge. Numerous factors both individual and environmental moderate the prediction of behavior from intention. Factors such as accessibility to and availability of resources allow the behavioral intentions to be realized. A decision to participate reflects the summed effects of all factors that should be considered in program designs. Unfortunately most health interventions, one way or another, rely on changing attributes associated with the individual.

Individual Responsibility and Social Change

The explanation for why Americans frame social and health issues in such individual terms is in large part explained by the concept of "rugged individualism." Certain values are central to American culture and sustain a powerful presence in American society. For example, Americans widely accept the merits of individuality, success, material comfort, and social advancement. One of the strongest values is the belief system that those who work hard and take advantage of opportunity will be rewarded with a good life of material comfort as well as good health.

The concept of individual responsibility became a dominant cultural motif that values independence and self-reliance and, according to sociologist Herbert Gans (1988), embodies the most widely shared ideology in the United States today. The concept of individualism, as Robert Bellah and colleagues (1985) noted in their extensive study of American life *Habits of the Heart,* lies at the very core of the American character. Americans have traditionally prized success through individual efforts and initiatives. They value the belief that in our social system it is possible for an individual to climb from the bottom to the top. Americans generally attribute failure to the individual rather than to the social system for placing obstacles in the individual's path.

The concept of individual responsibility is prominent in the stories of many cultural icons found in popular sports. Rocky Bleier's *Fighting Back* (Bleier & O'Neil, 1975), which traces his recovery from life-threatening war injuries to the resumption of his football career and ultimately Super Bowl victory with the Pittsburgh Steelers, is an example that typifies the struggle to overcome physical adversity.

Individual athletic prowess is viewed as important in overcoming health problems as well. Take the extraordinary case of Lance Armstrong, one of the world's most talented competitive cyclists. At age 25, Armstrong was diagnosed with advanced testicular cancer. Doctors gave him only about a 50 percent chance of survival. Yet by 1999, less than three years after first being diagnosed, Armstrong rode to victory in the Tour de France. Armstrong's story, one of individual perseverance and triumph over the odds to become a champion in his sport, is just one example among many success stories of modern-day athletic heroes. Gene Littler's *The Real Score* (Littler & Tobin, 1976) and Danny Thompson's *The Diary of a Major League Short-*

stop (Thompson & Fowler, 1976) center on how these two athletes summoned their individual powers to deal with potentially terminal illnesses. Bob Welch's *Five O'clock Comes Early* (Welch & Vecsey, 1982) perhaps most effectively illustrates the pivotal role of individual responsibility in dealing with health issues. Welch's saga is a story about a highly successful young baseball player who is forced to confront his problem with alcoholism. Welch most poignantly shares his coming to terms with his lengthy denial of his drug addiction and his own responsibility for not seeking help sooner. Finally, after a series of personal experiences he comes to terms with himself, engages on an individual journey to overcome his addiction, and of course, in the end against all odds, experiences individual triumph. Welch's story, along with the countless other sport comeback stories, reaffirms that individual traits, such as hard work, perseverance and personal sacrifice, are the necessary ingredients to success.

These stories also give insight into the major shortcomings of the concept of individual responsibility. Although anecdotes about comebacks due to courage and fortitude make for an interesting story, they virtually ignore the significance of the complex social circumstances in which these individual accomplishments are achieved. When outside circumstances affect the individual's comeback, the individual's success is measured by the degree to which the individual single-handedly is able to overcome the forces of the outside world. The message is that people must act in their own best interest and, when they fail to do so, must assume the responsibility for the outcomes. Personal achievement, particularly in resolving obstacles, is the principle underlying individual responsibility and makes clear the idea that social structure is either unimportant or something to overcome, not to change.

Common sense tells us that we should not hold people responsible for something over which they have little or no control; however, this way of thinking occurs all too often. Holding people responsible for things they possess little or no control over is in fact the principle behind the popular euphemism known as *blaming the victim*. The phrase was first used by William Ryan in 1976 to describe the practice of turning circumstances external to impoverished groups in American society into the explanations for their poverty. For illustration, Ryan (1976) applied the concept to the connection between socioeconomic status and beliefs associated with how people judge the importance of a future orientation. A future

orientation consists of recognizing the importance of delayed gratification and the importance of education. Being poor, Ryan argued,
leads to a low future orientation among the many people just strug-
gling to get through each day. The issue is whether future orientation is best understood as a cause of poverty or a response to it.
What may be a response to a condition gets turned around to represent the cause of the condition; for instance, rather than low future
orientation being a consequence of being poor, people are blamed
for being poor because they are less future oriented.

The problem with blaming the victim finds a parallel when we
consider health-related behaviors. The ideology of individual responsibility creates high expectations for people to engage in health-
promoting behaviors, such as eating an appropriate diet and engaging in physical activity. Maintaining a reasonable weight, avoiding
alcohol or drinking it only in moderation, or participating in physical activity are typically perceived as health practices under the control of the individual. Having the right weight and shape and being
fit are important attributes in our culture (White, Young, & Gillett,
1995). Self-management, hard work, delay of gratification, and impulse control are qualities projected on people with the right body.
When the individual fails to maintain the right weight and shape, it
is easy to conclude that the individual lacks the conviction or self-
control to maintain healthy behaviors. The next step is to blame those
with health problems for their predicament. After all, why can't the
individual make choices in relative isolation from the broader social
environment of which they are a part?

A major implication of individualism involves the notion that individuals are able to make choices. When lifestyle approaches are
built around change, but only at the individual level, it fails to recognize the importance of developing policies to lessen societal and
environmental conditions that help generate the unhealthful behaviors people adopt (Ingham, 1985). Although no one should argue
against the importance of physical activity in the equation for good
health, an overemphasis on changing the behaviors of individuals
exaggerates the individuals' capacity to bring about significant improvements in health.

Importance of Social Structure

Social structure is an encompassing term describing many different
factors, both positive and negative, external to the individual that

influence a person's ability to participate fully in his or her social surroundings. The social structure includes interactions with family, friends, and co-workers. It also encompasses social institutions such as families, schools, and workplaces, which help to shape values and attitudes. In thinking about the social structure it is useful to distinguish between proximal and distal social factors (House and Mortimer, 1990). *Proximal social factors* include the readily identified settings and institutions in which we live and participate on a day-to-day basis, such as the family, work organization, schools, neighborhood, and community (figure 1.3). Here the emphasis is placed on the *physical environment,* the material features of the local community that reinforce opportunities to be physically active, and the *social environment,* which includes the way people come together to interact socially, and in some instances, work collectively to promote changes to their physical environments.

Proximal Social Factors	Distal Social Factors
Physical environment	Socioeconomic status
Social environment	Income inequality
Social connectedness	Discrimination
Sense of community	Racism
	Sexism
	Heterosexism

Figure 1.3   Examples of proximal and distal social factors.

Distal social factors consider the importance of large-scale social forces that permeate society and change more slowly over time. For example, positions in the social and economic hierarchies of society and systems of gender and race relations are important to any understanding of the role of social structure.

Role of Physical Environments

Physical activity takes place in specific geographical areas and these *physical environments* can be viewed in terms of the way they promote or restrict physical activity. Physical environments conducive to physical activity provide the infrastructure that contributes to substantial increases in formal and informal sport and physical activity opportunities. These include the presence of exercise classes, health clubs, and work-site fitness facilities, in addition to bike paths, tennis courts, and golf courses.

Not everyone participates in structured exercise programs. Some would prefer more informal activities. For example, walking is low cost and is becoming a popular activity, particularly among women and older adults. Conducive physical environments that provide opportunities to put more walking into the routines of daily living might include visibly marked stairwells, well-lit parking lots built away from the building's entrance, and attractive walking and hiking trails.

James Sallis and colleagues in a study of physical environments in Southern California (1990b) hypothesized that a "facility-rich environment" encourages physical activity in at least two ways. First, exercise facilities can serve as visual reminders that prompt exercise behavior. Facilities close to one's home will be seen often and may repeatedly bring exercise to one's attention. Second, nearby facilities reduce some of the physical barriers associated with exercise, such as transportation issues and travel time.

Physical features of the local environment can also discourage participation in physical activity. Impoverished physical environments can dramatically affect participation in physical activity. In these instances they create obstacles by excluding opportunities for active leisure pursuits (e.g., lack of recreational spaces, accessible school facilities, health clubs) or by reinforcing opportunities to remain sedentary in carrying out daily routines (e.g., lack of sidewalks, poorly lit streets). In one community study, the authors found that although walking and cycling paths were available, the paths were under-utilized because they were poorly maintained, were inappropriate for joint use by walkers and cyclists, and did not provide routes that permitted continuous travel around town (Hahn & Craythorn, 1994).

Increasingly, social scientists have focused their attention on the characteristics of geographical areas. They have looked at the relation between living in an area with a certain set of socioeconomic characteristics and outcome measures such as increased mortality risk and unhealthy behaviors. These studies, sometimes called mixed-level studies referring to the hierarchical nature of the data (e.g., individuals clustered within areas), allow investigators to separate the environmental effects from the effects of individual characteristics. Social epidemiologists Irene Yen and George Kaplan (1998) examined whether the effects of living in federally designated poverty areas were related to changes in leisure-time physical activity over a nine-year period. Using data collected as part of the Alameda County Study, the researchers constructed a measure of residential poverty and reported that changes in scores for physical activity were .67 units lower for people living in poverty areas than for people living in areas with adequate levels of income. The authors found that the effect of residency is associated with a decline in physical activity even after taking into consideration individual characteristics of residence members such as age, education, smoking status, and alcohol consumption. African Americans and individuals with inadequate income living in the nonpoverty areas experienced declines in physical activity levels. Not surprisingly, the amount of decline in leisure-time physical activity was the largest among people residing in the poverty areas. These study results reinforce the view that the abilities of people to participate in physical activity depend on changing the features of their physical environment that give them more healthy options.

Role of Social Environments

Social environments consist of the nonphysical products of human interaction, which include the ideas shared by members of a particular group as well as the ways they come together to participate. The latter suggests that the environment includes a social context. What this means is that the groups to which people belong and their particular experiences within these groups underlie what people feel and what they do. *Social connectedness* is important in matters of good health. For example, social epidemiologists Lisa Berkman and S. Leonard Syme (1979) following a sample of 6,928 adults living in Alameda County, California, reported people with fewer meaningful social relationships were two to three times more likely to die than their better socially connected counterparts. Building on the work of Berkman and Syme, a number of studies have suggested that social relationships also enhance the positive health behaviors known to affect increased risk for cardiovascular disease (House, Landis, & Umberson, 1988). In these studies, social connection has been associated with improvement in behavioral health factors, such as smoking cessation, compliance to medical regimens, control of diet, and physical activity (Kawachi, et al., 1996).

An accompanying understanding of the importance of social connectedness considers ways in which people interacting with each other can influence the quality of living in a certain area. Individuals can restructure their personal environments to support increased levels of physical activity but, when united, individuals can create a synergy that can do much to effect change in their social surroundings. *Sense of community* is a phrase that has commonly been used to characterize the relationship between groups of individuals and their social structure (Chavis & Wandersman, 1990). It places importance on the feelings of belonging and on a shared commitment to one another and to the group. A strong sense of community has the ability to mobilize people for community action by affecting people's perceptions of their physical environments and their ability to change them.

The physical and social environments do not exist independently of each other. Their relationship connects individuals through the roles, statuses, and relationships that govern their social interactions as well as through the physical surroundings that give them access to healthy options. The synergistic roles of physical and social environments are important to the understanding of how environments affect participation in physical activity. Epidemiologists have incorporated both the physical and social environments into the concept of *behavioral settings* (Sallis, Bauman, & Pratt, 1998). Behavioral settings can promote physical activity when they provide the physical space (e.g., sports fields, health clubs, and bicycle trails) along with the social resources that we draw upon to interact with others. Changes to the physical environment in order to increase physical activity require place-based interventions (Yen & Syme, 1999). A place-based approach might include such activities as developing zoning laws to include public recreation areas near residential areas, creating safe bike lanes, and establishing community-policing programs to promote neighborhood walking. It might also include local tax incentives to businesses willing to promote goods and services conducive to physically active lifestyles, such as health clubs or retailers of sporting goods. Of course, certain behavioral settings can also derail people's best efforts to be physically active.

Although developing the appropriate physical and social environments is important to whether large numbers of people engage in health-promoting physical activity, trends suggest that features of active living environments are rapidly disappearing. Parks and other green spaces are being replaced by high-rise buildings, community recreational centers are being closed, and urban sprawl has created suburban communities where the automobile has replaced the needs for bike paths and sidewalks. Far fewer children now walk or bike to school for fear of the traffic, and people of all ages are discouraged from going out at night for fear of their personal safety. Two major surveys place security as a key factor in decisions discouraging participation in physical activity. Sociologist Catherine Ross (1993) found "fear of crime" to be the single most crucial deterrent regarding decisions to walk among the 2,000 respondents in her "Work, Family and Well-being Project." A similar concern for safety was found in study results recently released by the Centers for Disease Control (CDC, 1999). Among survey respondents in five states (Maryland, Montana, Ohio, Pennsylvania and Virginia) almost two thirds of men (63 percent) and nearly one half of the women (47.2 percent) living in unsafe neighborhoods reported low or no levels of physical activity.

Socioeconomic Status and Healthy Lifestyles

From a discussion of proximal social factors, we can proceed to discuss the relationship between healthy behaviors, such as active lifestyles and distal social forces. One approach to understanding the social determinants of health behaviors is to focus on the ways that people's specific positions in the social structure determine their experiences and behaviors. The relationship between socioeconomic position and health has been well documented. People in the lowest socioeconomic groups have the highest rates of morbidity and mortality (Minkler, 1997). The research conducted by Marmot, Rose, Shipley, and Hamilton (1978) first brought to attention the powerful connection between socioeconomic status and health. In their study of British civil servants, they found that individuals at the highest grade (administrators) had the lowest rate of coronary heart disease, whereas those at the lowest grade (mainly unskilled manual workers) had rates four times as high.

The concept of a healthy lifestyle has played a major role in sociological theory. In the Marxian view, lifestyle is largely determined by one's position on the social class ladder, signified by money and material possessions (Marx, 1986). Other social scientists have emphasized that the esteem, or *social status*, that people are accorded by those around them is key to understanding lifestyle behaviors. It was Max Weber's position that although social class is an objective dimension of social life signified by amounts of money or property, *social status* plays an important role in determining one's lifestyle (Cockerham & Abel, 1993). The consumption of goods and services conveys a social meaning that displays the status and social identity of the consumer.

The primary significance of social class is that it determines life choices. Unhealthy behaviors, including sedentary lifestyles, are acquired within social groups and are often influenced by powerful social forces in the general society. Those who have the means may choose to be physically active; those lacking the resources cannot easily choose and likely find their lifestyles determined by external circumstances (Crawford, 1981). Decisions about whether to adopt a healthy lifestyle reflect personal attitudes and preferences and thereby include an aspect of personal choice. But poor people are without the resources to access the full range of choices available to more privileged people.

Most people engage in some type of health-advancing behavior regardless of their socioeconomic position, but different social classes

Workers construct a neighborhood playground.

are likely to pursue different avenues toward health (Cockerham, Rutten, & Abel, 1997). Healthy lifestyles are patterns of voluntary behaviors based on choices from options that are available to people according to their life situations (Cockerham, Rutten, & Abel, 1997). People have a certain amount of control over their choices but not over the range of choices available to them.

For members of the upper and middle class, a person's physically active lifestyle serves as a measure of one's self-identity. According to sociologists Alphonse d'Houtaud and Mark Field (1984), good health is seen as a personal value to be sought and cultivated for one's own benefit, such as experiencing increased vitality and enjoyment of life. The lower class, in contrast, expresses a more utilitarian perspective in which health is seen as a means to an end, instead of an end in itself. Lower-class individuals may be less optimistic that their efforts to avoid poor health or other negative outcomes will succeed and thus be less apt to participate in health-promoting activity.

Apart from the evidence linking socioeconomic position with health matters there is growing evidence that the relative distribution of income in a society matters in its own right for health. Economic growth and prosperity are typically distributed unevenly within societies. *Income inequality* in the United States has reached unprecedented levels, with just 20 percent of the population now controlling 85 percent of the wealth and almost 67 percent of the earning gains of males in the last decade going to the top 1 percent (Minkler, 1997). The concept of relative income or *income inequality* is identified with the work of Richard Wilkinson (1996), who observed the negative relationship between life expectancies of people in industrial societies and the unequal distributions of income. Wilkinson hypothesized that the feelings of relative deprivation among those in the lower half of the income distribution contribute to increases in illness and death. In his well-known essay on the dysfunctional aspects of social stratification, sociologist Melvin Tumin (1953) surmised that inequalities in social stratification systems function to encourage hostility, suspicion, and distrust among the various segments of society. Nearly 30 years later his words ring true as the disparity between the rich and poor continues to grow. Members of social groups found in lower socioeconomic position experience poorer health and higher disease rates when compared with more privileged social groups, and the gap in mortality rates and income disparities continues to widen.

Health Consequences of Discrimination

Although socioeconomic status accounts for much of the observed disparities in health, explaining such differences in economic terms may be incomplete. As pointed out by sociologist David Williams (1999) in his study of the relationship between race and health, health differences persist even at equivalent levels of socioeconomic status. To understand more fully why some social groups participate less in physical activity, it is necessary to pay attention to *institutional discrimination*, the dimensions of bias and oppression that have become structured in American society (Feagin & Sikes, 1994). Discrimination is a socially structured phenomenon justified by an ideology that maintains privileges for members of dominant groups at the cost of deprivation for others. Institutional discrimination refers to discriminatory policies carried out in groups and organizations, and interpersonal discrimination refers to directly perceived discriminatory interactions among individuals operating in their private roles as citizens. Race- and gender-based barriers to education, employment, and housing are examples of institutional discrimination that affects health and health-related behaviors. Many groups experience discrimination in the United States today, but most notable among them are the discriminatory patterns based on race and ethnicity, gender, and sexual orientation. The impact on health and health behaviors can be worsened by the additional "psychological effects" of discrimination and prejudice (Hughes & Dodge, 1997). For example, a number of studies have confirmed deleterious health consequences to those who perceive they have been discriminated against. In one study, perceived racial prejudice as measured by a scale of collective disrespect toward blacks was associated with higher mortality rates (Kennedy, Kawachi, Lochner, Jones, & Prothrow-Stith, 1997). Similarly, in a study of the consequences of racial discrimination on blood pressure, young black men and women who reported experiences of racial discrimination had higher blood pressure (Krieger & Sidney, 1996).

Although discrimination has been clearly linked to negative health consequences, the ways in which it influences health behaviors, particularly physical activity, remains poorly understood. One of the more common approaches to studying health consequences of discrimination is indirect. Investigators, recognizing that discrimination is a difficult concept to measure, have instead compared health outcomes between a "subordinate" and "dominant" group (Krieger, 1999). If distributions of these outcomes differ, then researchers determine whether observed disparities can be explained by known risk factors. If so, investigators interpret their finding in the light of how discrimination may shape distribution of the relevant risk factors. If, however, a residual difference persists even after controlling for the risk factors, then additional aspects of discrimination (e.g., racial prejudice) may be implied as a possible explanation for the remaining differences. In a recent study examining the relationship between race and physical inactivity among a large sample of American adults, epidemiologist Carlos Crespo and colleagues (Crespo, Smit, Anderson, et al. 2000) reported levels of physical activity were much lower among Mexican Americans and African Americans compared with their white counterparts. The race differences persisted even after taking into consideration factors such as education, family income, occupation, poverty status, employment status, and marital status. The authors concluded that the racial burden of a sedentary lifestyle is not entirely explained by individual differences and that more research is needed to examine other social constructs; the deleterious impact of discrimination may be one of them.

There are likely parallels between racism, sexism, and heterosexism and the ways in which the effects of discrimination constrain efforts to put more physical activity into daily routines. An understanding of the ways in which race, gender, and sexual orientation shape physical activity experiences is critical to the understanding of who is likely to adopt a physically active lifestyle and who is not.

Conclusion

Despite increasing attention to health behaviors such as participation in physical activity, there has been an imbalance in the research concerning individual factors and distal and proximal social factors. We know a great deal more about the difficulties of individuals who remain involved in physical activity programs than we do about why many communities lack physical activity facilities, such as bike paths or public parks, or why certain social groups are marred in impoverished conditions. We know even less about how to change these health-damaging social conditions. Unfortunately, the bulk of health promotion programs are targeted at individuals, and the focus is on the "individual risk factors that we think we can do something about" (Blackburn, 1993).

The interest in changing the behaviors of individuals stems from the belief among many health professionals that changing individual risk factors is easier than tackling the many social problems plaguing society today. Individuals and their sedentary habits cannot be understood simply by directing programs of change only at them. Changing the sedentary behaviors of most Americans requires serious attention to developing interventions aimed at society's social structure. Despite the recent calls for the promotion of physical activity, the United States remains stubbornly entrenched in the idea of changing individuals rather than changing the social structure. The majority of health promotion programs in one way or another remained focused on the individual (Blackburn, 1993).

Health promotion efforts must combine with efforts directed at changing social conditions. To understand how individual behaviors are developed and to identify the most effective ways to change them, it is necessary to pay attention not only to the characteristics of individuals but also to the social conditions that affect their behaviors. Social epidemiologists call such interest *upstream analysis.* The underlying idea is that the social structure is a legitimate unit of analysis and that structural characteristics are distinct from characteristics of individuals. This perspective, which is also termed ecological thinking, moves us away from the almost exclusive focus on individualization of risk and emphasizes the importance of the social structures and processes within which risky health behaviors develop. The term "upstream" suggests that a better understanding of the role of the social structure will help us fend off some of the health problems that develop among individuals downstream (Yen & Syme, 1999).

Breaking Down the Book

Resistance to Exercise: A Social Analysis of Inactivity takes an in-depth look at the factors present in today's rapidly changing world that have imposed significant barriers to the formation of a more physically active society, including sedentary behavior. This inquiry is guided by four broad sociological themes. The first theme connects the failure of many people to be more physically active with the strong American ethos of individual responsibility, a cultural value that reaffirms that participation in physical activity is largely the responsibility of individuals. In so doing, individuals and their own behaviors, rather than society and its social structure, are seen as the primary solution for dealing with changing health-compromising behaviors such as sedentary lifestyles.

Social institutions are also viewed as structures that provide a sense of unity and stability necessary for the survival of society. The second theme focuses on the inability of our core institutions to keep pace with swift technological and inevitable social changes. Institutional changes such as the erosion of the traditional family structure and the inability of medicine to solve many of today's health problems are testaments to their inability to keep up. The values associated with our social institutions such as the traditional nuclear family, achievement standards in schools and a disease-centered health care system are tied to traditional middle class values that have created serious gaps in the health status and physical activity patterns among many Americans.

The third theme explores ways in which our social institutions have remained largely unresponsive to the changing demographics that have emerged in contemporary America. Trends such as the aging of the American population, the growing number of single parents, and the increasing presence of racial and ethnic minorities have brought to the forefront the need to address the social and economic inequities these social groups face and their disproportionately high levels of physical inactivity.

For the United States to achieve a more physically active society, it will require a new set of institutional norms. The fourth and final theme argues that central to the transformation to a physically active society must be the recognition that physical activity lifestyles are important and should be accessible to every American. Achieving a more physically active society must also include reinventing social norms associated with individuals working together for collective change.

This book consists of nine chapters. Chapter 1 looks at contemporary society and why sedentary living has become the norm. Chapter 2 deals with social institutions and trust. Chapter 3 provides a historical grounding that underscores the point that physical activity was included in the health promotion movement only after a century-long struggle to find its place among other lifestyle factors linked to health and disease. The health promotion efforts at the beginning of the 20th century also share several common themes with today's health promotion activities. They both respond to a society undergoing dramatic social change, and both began to raise questions about the effectiveness of promoting individual health behaviors such as physical activity without regard to changing social conditions.

The next four chapters shift the focus of the book in order to take a closer look at each of the four major social institutions prominent in American life. Chapter 4 examines the impact of changing family structures and what that means for helping people to adopt ongoing patterns of physical activity. Motives for participation in physical activity vary across the life span, ranging from instilling lifelong commitments in children and teenagers to balancing work and family obligations during mid-life to counteracting declines in physical capabilities in older adulthood. Changing institutional conditions that have jeopardized the place of physical activity in our schools is the subject of chapter 5. Particularly close attention is given to the failures of our educational system in doing a better job in helping youngsters develop skills and habits to participate in physical activity throughout their lifetimes. Chapter 6 considers how the changing way we work leads to obstacles to participation in physical activity. It also addresses how currently emphasized work-sponsored fitness programs are not enough, not only because they fail to reach the majority of today's workforce but also because they focus on changing individuals without sufficient attention to changing work environments. The all-too-narrow use of the curative medical model in today's health care industry is the focus in chapter 7. The failure to emphasize preventive approaches to health has caused health professionals to miss a great opportunity to help individuals establish commitments to physically active lifestyles.

Perhaps the larger task of this project is presented in the last two chapters, where the focus shifts from problems to possible solutions. Chapter 8 addresses the importance of social connectedness and its potential role in mobilizing individuals for participating in positive social change. It examines recent public health models associated with community building and the "new public health movement," with particular interest in individuals' roles in working together for collective change. Finally, chapter 9 outlines a broad-based framework that offers a multidimensional approach to both individual and institutional change. Change must involve not just asking individuals to change themselves; it must be part of a larger transformation that includes our social institutions.

2

Social Institutions and Trust

A **strong and stable family structure** *and durable social institu-*
tions cannot be legislated into existence the way a government can
create a central bank or an army. A thriving civil society depends on a people's
habits, customs, and ethics—attributes that can be shaped only indirectly
through conscious political action and must otherwise be nourished through
an increased awareness and respect for culture (Fukuyama, 1995:5).

We "create" social institutions, from the simplest to the most complex, while conducting all aspects of social life. Societies rely on social institutions, such as family and school, to pass on to succeeding
generations a set of values, expectations, and solutions from which
individuals can draw making their way through life. Some institutions rely on legal or external authority to promote individuals obe-
dience to rules and procedures. Other institutions (e.g., intimate social relationships) rely on social conventions that are self-enforcing
in the sense that no external authority is available to make sure that
people respect them. Most social institutions (e.g., education and
work) fall somewhere between the formal and informal structures.

Social institutions are more than the simple sum or average of individual characteristics. Unlike individual patterns of behaviors,
institutions are collectively shared and enacted modes of acting,

thinking, and feeling that are passed on through education and socialization. The major responsibility of social institutions is to aggregate individual actions into collective outcomes (Jackson, 1990). When two people work together, their synergy achieves something more than they would have achieved separately. As individuals, we have limited capacities, but as we come together and act in a coordinated fashion, our capacities increase. This process, known as *aggregation*, helps to give meaning to what is important in our lives (values) and to organize the rules that help people to frame and guide their actions (norms of behavior).

Aggregating individuals, social institutions provide "institutional rules" that help structure social interactions. *Institutionalization* is a term that refers to how behaviors of individuals become organized in a way that is standardized over time and similar from one situation to another. The concept of institution typically refers to adherence to a set of relatively enduring values and norms that are important because they help us reduce the overwhelming complexity of behavior alternatives. Institutional rules accomplish this by providing two types of information: the nature of sanctions for not obeying the rules and the probable future actions of others. Rules are understood by all parties and guide not only one's own future actions but also the expectations about future actions by others with whom one interacts. The culturally prescribed standards established by the major institutions in our society play a central role in constructing and expressing moral positions and values. The term *culturally prescribed* is important because it indicates that people are taught the criteria needed to make decisions that govern their lives. Thus, when we participate in social institutions such as the family, workplace, or school, we should have a relatively clear understanding of what such participation involves and the roles we should perform.

Unfortunately, many of our key social institutions fail to relay the importance of physically active lifestyles. For working-class families, participation in physical activity often becomes one of many competing sets of priorities. In a study of middle-class families, Kathryn Backett (1992) found "trade-offs" were frequently used to cope with tensions arising from busy lives and the difficulties in adhering to health-promoting behaviors. She found people in their daily lives were generally fatalistic about whether health-promoting behaviors such as physical activity could really do much to prevent disease. Health promotion specialist Collins Airhihenbuwa and colleagues (1995) have described a cultural "rest ethic" value among African Americans, in which during nonwork-ing hours a rest ethic is valued over engaging in more active pur-suits (Airhihenbuwa, Kumanyika, Agurs, & Lowe, 1995). This per-ception included an image of African Americans as involved in physical labor, both job and family related, and needing to rest to compensate for this labor. In yet another example, as people near retirement age and plan for an increase in their leisure-time pur-suits as a result of more free time, many of them do not include physical activity. They view active lifestyles as something reserved for the young, a type of thinking that is often reinforced by school systems that have failed to provide the basic skills for a lifetime com-mitment to physical activity or by a health care system that is more attuned to curing diseases than advising people on ways to prevent them. The logical extension of the failure of our institutions to pro-mote norms of physical activity suggests that the focus on changing individual health behaviors, such as increasing levels of physical activity, must be combined with efforts directed at changing value systems associated with our social institutions as well.

Institutional Trust

Survival in today's world requires trust in systems, or *institutional trust*. Trust, as conceptualized within the psychological literature, depends on feelings, emotions, and individual values and includes a kind of general expectancy that individuals will do as they say. Examples of such personal trust relationships are found in families, love relationships, intimate friendships, and other primary group associations. Initially, *personal trust* is built on evidence that the other behaves in a trustworthy manner, but as trust is gradually estab-lished and deepened, the behavioral indicators for trust are no longer needed.

Sociologist Anthony Giddens (1990) distinguishes between trust in people, or personal trust, and trust in abstract systems. System or institutional trust, in contrast to personal trust, is more cognitive and abstract, and typically is based on inferences about shared in-terests and common norms and values. From a sociological perspec-tive, institutional trust is conceived as a property of collective units, not of isolated individuals (Lewis & Weigert, 1985). By its very na-ture, system trust cannot supply the intimacy that personal trust offers. In contrast, system trust generally lacks intense emotional involvement but provides the security of day-to-day reliability. The complexity of social life is such that commanding all its specialized knowledge is impossible for an individual. The size and structural complexity of today's world prohibit most individuals from engaging in the incremental and repeated exchanges that contribute to the development of trust in more intimate settings.

Institutional trust thus is based on the concept of *agency*, in which individuals or organizations act on behalf of others known as *principals*. Responsibility for meeting basic human needs in differentiated societies is increasingly delegated to others, often to those we do not know. For example, people turn their assets or possessions over to experts—stockbrokers, mechanics, dry cleaners—to provide services they are unable to do themselves. Similarly, the weakening of the extended family has meant that the state and other formal organizations often substitute for kinship in providing for the needs of the young, the elderly, and the sick.

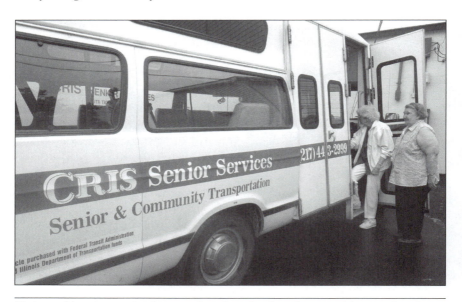

State and local organizations, rather than family, often provide care for the elderly.

A central theme of sociologist and philosopher Niklas Luhmann's (1970) theory of trust is the increasing importance of trust in a society constantly moving toward more technologically and organizationally complex forms of social structure. Luhmann argues that trust serves the same general function at the institutional level as at the personal level. But in addition, institutional trust provides a basis for dealing with uncertain, complex, and often threatening images of the future. By trusting "strangers" we reduce the complexity of the world because we do not have to consider every possibility.

Trust involves expectations of how the proprietors of our institutions will act in the future and thus, inherent in one's willingness to trust, is a certain measure of risk. Trust is "risky" because we are unable really to know what underlies other people's motivations. Trust requires "a leap beyond the expectations that reason and experience alone would warrant." Luhmann describes this process of acceptance as "overdrawing" on the informational base. Life is impossible without trust, and even the most cynical must extend some amount of trust. Trust reduces complexity and the need to plan for innumerable contingencies. Contracts, laws, and other regulatory devices substitute for trust, but even highly formalized systems cannot plan for every contingency and must depend to an important degree on trust. To trust, we believe that individuals and institutions will act appropriately, competently, responsibly, and in a manner considerate of our interests. A major reason we trust is that usually we cannot spell out everything a trusted person is supposed to do and not do (Govier, 1997).

Today such an assignment of trust is undergoing intense reassessment. Georg Simmel (1964) recognized that institutional trust creates its own power and under certain circumstances can lead to abuses of that power. According to Simmel, those who hold trust hold power. Whether power is based on control of money, property, information, or other sources, there is one common denominator: Those who have power are inevitably tempted to exercise it. Secrecy, and the physical, temporal, and social distance inherent in many agency relations, precludes the ability of most people to monitor the behavior of their agents.

Decentered Social Institutions

Today we are living through social changes that have radically transformed all aspects of work, family, and leisure time. An increasingly popular theme for those who write about the contemporary United States is a society in a rapid state of social and moral decline. Conservative critics point to the high incidence of street crime, the erosion of civility, and the loss of respect for authority; liberal critics turn to insensitivity for the poor and the disappearance of a concern for the common good (Farley, 1996). Political leaders, more attuned to re-election strategies than political accomplishment, the breakdown in family and community life, and the failures in public education, have cultivated a culture of resignation to the way things have become and a growing absence of trust.

Public confidence in the leadership of every major institution in the United States has fallen dramatically over the past 25 years (Putnam, 2000). Some observers suggest that the traditional values of home, work, family, and community no longer apply. Many of our major social institutions have become outmoded and unresponsive to today's changing world, as can be seen by the disintegration of family structures, the failure of schools to prepare youngsters, and an outdated governmental and political system that has abandoned whole categories of Americans and that is no longer able to solve many of the nation's social problems.

Americans today feel that the world around them is not moving in one clear direction and, in the words of sociologist Alan Wolfe, has lost its center. Wolfe's (1991) concept of *decentering* implies that social institutions no longer work by the models that people had been given to believe were, at some point in the past, "normal." In these decentered conditions, the traditional forms of social institutions no longer seem satisfactory. Decentering also implies that changes in any one area are rarely internally coherent; they occur at different paces and move in different directions. The complexities of change mean that old structures of social life and old expectations about how one should and will live one's life are replaced not by new ones but by incoherence and uncertainty. Society has undergone other significant times of transformation, such as the shift from an agricultural to industrial society, but as pointed out by scholars such as James Davison Hunter (1991), Anthony Giddens (1991), and Michael Goldfarb (1991), the current transformation is different from any other that modern society has known.

During periods of institutional upheaval significant tensions emerge among groups with competing interests. The central tension is a conflict, between what Hunter terms the impulse toward orthodoxy and impulse toward progressivism (Hunter, 1991). According to Hunter, *impulse toward orthodoxy* is an endorsement of stability through an external definable and transcendent authority, one that is a consistent, unchangeable measure of value, purpose, goodness, and identity, both personal and collective. *Impulse toward cultural progressivism* by contrast is defined by the "spirit of the modern age, a spirit of rationalism and subjectivism." Some people yearn for the return to traditional values of home, family, and work, and want to go back to what they believe to have been a golden age, even though they increasingly recognize that they cannot. Others support new and dynamic sources of social reform, although the absence of rules to guide them may prove disconcerting to many. They look forward to changes in the future while expressing some worries about where these changes may lead us.

Giddens (1991) also argues that the current social state of flux, which he calls *high modernity*, differs from the previous disruptions of social order in society. As the disappearance of clear structures undercuts traditional customs and habits, Giddens contends more people are on their own in making sense of an increasingly changing and complex world. In these decentered conditions characterized by a fragmentation of traditional centers of authority, people are confronted with an ever-increasing body of health knowledge. Uncertain to the core, people are occupied by worries about where these changes might lead and turn inward for answers. Lifestyle choices can promote a sense of stability and belonging for an individual by providing an anchor for the person in a particular social constellation of style and activity. In times of rapid and dislocating social and political change, people turn inward and can become preoccupied with their own self-interests.

Adopting a healthy lifestyle gives some individuals a coping strategy in a confusing environment. Within our individualistic culture, "self-control" is a commonplace strategy for the reduction of social complexity. Many individuals focus more intently on an immediate environment where they can reaffirm their own boundaries and exercise control. This type of reasoning might help explain why going on a diet, redoing one's hair, or getting in shape often follows the breakup of a personal relationship or other loss. Extending this logic to physical activity, the appeal of exercise clubs may be in its attractiveness as a means of coping behavior that reduces feelings of powerlessness.

For other individuals, when the workings of contemporary society get to be too much, lifestyles turn to unhealthy responses such as overindulgence in food or alcohol. Postmodern critic David Forbes (1994) warns that institutional upheavals induce people to become addicted to *false fixes*, or poor substitutes for genuine, mutually satisfying relations. A false fix can represent anything through which people lose flexibility to "maintain connectedness within shifting contexts and become fixed or dependent on one form of expression." These addictions may take the form of traditional "self-medication" techniques, such as the use of drugs, alcohol, and tobacco, or they can easily extend to overindulge in food or a couch potato existence.

However, in both extremes, individuals and their lifestyles, rather than society and its social and economic conditions, possess the primary solutions for dealing with the challenges to health confronting individuals. When lifestyle approaches are built around change only at the individual level, they fail to recognize the responsibility of society to develop and execute policies to lessen societal and environmental conditions that help generate the unhealthful behaviors people adopt.

Dealing with change is not easy; people are finding difficulty in coping with a world that daily becomes more complex and uncertain (Merry, 1995). The state of institutional flux and the absence of well-defined patterns of expected behaviors mean people have to decide for themselves the rules by which they structure their lives. Not surprisingly, a growing level of frustration has permeated the outlook of many Americans. Having little hope of improving their lives in any of the ways that matter and being filled with distrust, people have convinced themselves that nothing matters. Sociologist Michael Goldfarb (1991) contends that modern Americans are ruled by the *norms of cynicism.* In describing cynicism, Goldfarb views the current attitudes of many Americans as an unacceptable substitution for critical reasoning and a barrier to social change. Decentered social institutions have cultivated a culture of resignation to the way things have become.

Declining Social Connectedness

A number of social scientists have noted the disappearance of a "civically engaged" society and the loss of many people's connections with the life of their communities (Putnam, 2000). More than half of the people interviewed in one recent survey reported that their parents' generation did a better job in involving them in helping others and being a concerned citizen (Paxton, 1999). Two thirds of the people indicated that American civic life had dramatically declined as social and moral values had weakened. As people have been detached from their traditional ties to spouses, families, neighborhoods, workplaces, and churches, they find it more difficult to retain social connectedness. Robert Putnam in his recent book *Bowling Alone: The*

Collapse and Revival of American Community (2000), uses the decline of organized bowling leagues as a metaphor for the disappearance of active engagement in community activities. He documented the steady decline in people's participation in organized groups, ranging from the decline in church attendance to reduced support for labor unions and decreased interest in school service groups and fraternal and veterans' organizations. Putnam claims that Americans' propensity to participate in fewer organizations and groups in favor of isolating activities represents one of the most desocializing forces in the United States today.

As pointed out by Putnam, socially connected communities depend on the production of *social capital,* a term now commonly used to convey the ability of people to cooperate for common purposes. Social capital owes its origins mainly to the work of two sociologists, Pierre Bourdieu and James Coleman. Bourdieu first used the term in the 1970s to refer to the advantages and opportunities accruing to people through membership in certain community settings (Bourdieu, 1990). Coleman argued that besides skills and knowledge, a distinct portion of human capital concerns people's ability to associate with each other (Coleman, 1990). Whereas physical capital refers to physical objects and human capital refers to properties of individuals, social capital refers to connections among individuals' social networks and the norms of reciprocity and trustworthiness that arise from people cooperating with each other to overcome the dilemmas of collective action. Social capital is a feature of the social structure, not of the individual actors within the social structure. In this way social capital is different from the concepts of social networks and support, which are attributes of individuals. Social capital is about the ability of individuals to come together in a group to accomplish things they could not accomplish on their own.

Although Putnam uses bowling as a metaphor for participation in a variety of organizational activities, his analysis has far-reaching implications for participation in physical activity. George Kaplan and colleagues, using data collected as part of the Alameda County Project, reported that declines in physical activity were associated with the lack of membership in organized neighborhood groups (Kaplan, Lazarus, Cohen, & Leu, 1991). Similarly, in a study of nearly 20,000 adults, participation in a number of individual social relationships and neighborhood organizations also was related positively to increases in levels of physical activity (Ford, Ahluwalia, & Galuska, 2000).

Communities rich in social capital play an important role in influencing opportunities for participation in physical activity. As suggested by social kinesiologist Janet Harris, particularly in the United States a large number of community members immerse themselves in the process of developing social capital through sports and games. Her examples include the willingness of many adults to volunteer their time as youth sport coaches and officials, the increase in community fun runs to raise money for civic groups, and the presence of locally supported exercise classes and sport-centered civic clubs which offer opportunities for new friendships (Harris, 1998).

In today's world, however, people form different kinds of social networks and are perhaps connected only through work or family, often at the expense of social interactions with friends and neighbors. At a time when the need to increase opportunities for physical activity in the communities where people live is at its highest, the trend seems to suggest that the availability of such opportunities may be heading in the opposite direction.

The New Institutionalism

An alternative and more optimistic way to look at the chaos associated with today's social institutions is to consider a person's capacity to adjust rather than to disintegrate in the face of rapid social changes (Zijderveld, 2000). Sociologists have pointed to a number of positive features associated with post-industrial America. According to Francis Fukuyama (1999), today's society produces more of the two things that people value most in a modern democracy: freedom and equality. The extensive, rigid bureaucracies, which sought to control everything in their domain through strict rules, have been supplanted by the move toward a knowledge-based economy. The end result of these changes serves to empower individuals by giving them access to information and a more important role in taking social action (Drucker, 1992). The emphasis is no longer on rigid institutions but on networks that are flexible and alterable to suit the needs and desires of participating individuals. Such a post-industrial society will be characterized by less and less conflict as members come to recognize that by working together they will be able to solve the principal problems of society (Toffler & Toffler, 1995).

This perspective highlights the transactions between individuals and the contexts in which they occur and emphasizes the notions of reciprocity, interdependency, and mutual benefits. These processes form the basis of what is called the *new institutionalism*, an approach that emphasizes purposeful action on the part of individuals (Nee, 1998).

In her book *Trust in Modern Societies*, Barbara Misztal (1996) maintains that the conditions of modern society demand new bases of cooperation, one based on *collaborative trust*. People who do not trust one another will end up "cooperating" only under a system of formal rules and regulations that have to be negotiated, agreed to, litigated, and enforced, sometimes by coercive means (Fukuyama, 1995). Within the changing structure of our social institutions the goal is to connect obligations with responsibilities and reconcile the demand of choice, freedom and rights with the requirement of solidarity and reciprocity (Mistzal, 1996). She views trust as a valuable asset, one that develops out of the interplay of individuals and their private lives and the large institutions of public life.

Success in solving long-standing collective problems enables individuals to capture gains from cooperation. This perspective highlights the transactions between individuals and the contexts in which they occur and emphasizes the notions of reciprocity, interdependency, and mutual benefits. When people chart their own courses to reconcile individual and collective needs, our recentered institutions become instruments for resolving dilemmas at the societal level (Chmielewski, 1994).

For the United States to achieve a more physically active society, it will require a new set of institutional norms. Chief among them must be social norms associated with individuals working together for social change. If we are to achieve substantial increases in physical activity, an adequate understanding of the relationship between features of the social structure and health-promoting behaviors such as physical activity must include the role played by individuals. Thus, it must include aspects of both personal and collective responsibility. Because individual health behaviors such as active lifestyles are affected by the social structure, they represent the pathways through which the effects of social structure are mediated to individuals (Williams, 1990). In the end "individual behavioral change is the goal, but the point of attack must shift from within the individual to their social surroundings" (Yen & Syme, 1999).

As we will explore throughout the rest of this book, even though goals of cooperation and collaboration are fundamental to the achievement of a more physically active society, these goals in such an individualistic society may not be so easily achieved.

3

Physical Activity and Health in 20th-Century Perspective

In the 1970s and the 1980s evidence of a preoccupation with strenu-ous living was widespread. . . . With the success of the antibiotic revolution in reducing or eliminating many dreaded killers, the main health concern trans-ferred to the degeneration of the body rather than control of contagious dis-eases. . . The result was that growing numbers of Americans tried to alter their lifestyles. They watched what they ate, tried to control their diet, exer-cised more, stopped smoking, and tried to reduce stress in their lives. All of these behavioral changes could be accomplished by the self. With little or no reliance upon society, the individual seemed to be able to forestall the arrival of the Grim Reaper. Such thinking dovetailed nicely with American traditions of individualism (Rader, 1991:255, 258).

▼   ▼   ▼   ▼   ▼

One of the world's prominent cardiac experts, William Osler, in de-livering a series of lectures to the Royal College of Physicians of London, sounded a loud warning concerning the escalation of deaths due to heart disease. Osler, who spent most of his career at Johns Hopkins University before moving to Oxford University, depicted how the disease often cut down the lives of many a "well-set man from 45 to 55 years of age, who were overrun by the high pressure of modern life" (Osler, 1910). At the same time, Dr. Elliot Joslin, one of America's foremost experts in diabetic care, also delivered foreboding news. In an article published in the *Journal of the American Medical Association,* he confirmed the high death rate from diabetes (28 percent), and his patients diagnosed with the most serious conditions could hope to live no more than several years (Presley, 1991).

Although these warnings should not be particularly startling, what may be surprising is that they were not topics presented at recent meetings of the American Heart Association or the American Diabetes Association. They were concerns raised nearly 100 years ago by a small but well-respected number of physicians tuned to the diseases making an impact on American society. A 1903 editorial published in one of the country's most prestigious medical journals reported that the death toll due to heart disease was on the rise and rapidly becoming the number one killer of Americans ("Increase in deaths from heart disease," 1903). In 1900, one fifth of all deaths occurring in the United States were attributable to cardiovascular disease; by 1925, this number grew to more than one third of all deaths (Feinleib, 1995). Diabetes was also emerging as a matter of public concern. Before the discovery of insulin, doctors poorly understood the disease, and patients with diabetes were helpless as the disease pursued its deadly course; half the newly diagnosed diabetics were dead in two years, and fewer than 5 percent were still living 10 years later (Feudtner, 1995).

During the early years of the 20th century, medical conditions such as cardiovascular disease and diabetes would begin to rival infectious diseases such as tuberculosis and pneumonia as the primary cause of death among the U.S. population. The scientific discoveries and medical interventions that would take root, particularly in the beginning of the 20th century, corresponded with a decrease in disease-related deaths (table 3.1).

As we will explore in this chapter, three important developments would help shape the place of physical activity in the health movement of the 20th century. First, emerging explanations of the causes of sedentary living and disease played a crucial role in the development of current attitudes toward physical activity. It became increasingly evident that disease and mortality were tied to new ways of thinking about physical and social environments, as well as the responsibility of the individual for his or her own health.

Table 3.1   Leading Causes of Death in the United States

1900		1997	
Disease	**Percentage of all deaths**	**Disease**	**Percentage of all deaths**
Pneumonia	11.8	Heart disease	31.4
Tuberculosis	11.3	Cancer	23.3
Diarrhea and enteritis	8.3	Stroke	6.9
Heart disease	6.2	Chronic obstructive pulmonary disease	4.7
Liver disease	5.2		
Injuries	4.2	Unintentional injuries	4.1
Cancer	3.7	Pneumonia/influenza	3.7
Senility	2.9	Diabetes	2.7
Diphtheria	2.3	Suicide	1.3
		Kidney disease	1.1
		Chronic liver disease and cirrhosis	1.1

Adapted from USDHHS, 2000.

A second important trend would be the emergence of medical and scientific knowledge about diseases, particularly cardiovascular disease and diabetes. The increased sophistication of medical research and practice emerging in the early years of the 20th century would play an important role in the formation of attitudes toward physical activity. The acceptance of the germ theory of disease provided a sound scientific basis for laboratory research. The identification of the causes and specific strategies for battling infections allowed the medical and scientific communities to turn their attention to new health challenges, particularly those related to chronic diseases. As a better understanding of chronic diseases was developed, attention would then turn to the responsibility of the individual for his or her own health.

The third critical trend in the development of the current attitudes toward physical activity was the emerging understanding of the concept of behavioral health risk factors. Crucial to the acceptance of physical activity was the identification of certain personal characteristics associated with the incidence of diseases. The doctrine of individual responsibility to maintain physical activity would gain a foothold as the government used it as a centerpiece of its national health objectives. Each of these trends would play a crucial role in the formation of public attitudes toward adopting physically active lifestyles and by century's end situated the promotion of physical activity into a legitimate field in its own right.

The Sanitation Idea
and the First Public Health Movement

The first public health movement was a campaign to clean city streets and supply pure water and efficient drainage to city houses. The movement found its origins in England when Edwin Chadwick, a London lawyer and secretary of the Poor Law Commission, conducted studies of the life and health of the London working class in 1838 and of the entire country in 1842. The report of these studies, *General Report on the Sanitary Conditions of the Labouring Population of Great Britain*, provided clear evidence of the appalling conditions in which masses of the working people were forced to live. Chadwick's solution was based on the assumption that diseases are caused by foul air from the decomposition of waste. To remove disease, therefore, building a drainage network to remove sewage and waste was necessary. Chadwick further recommended a National Board of Health, local boards in each district, and medical officers in each district. Chadwick's report became known as the *sanitation idea,* and many of his suggestions were incorporated in Britain's Public Health Act of 1848.

Chadwick's ideas for sanitary and social reform gained widespread acceptance in other large urban centers of England and soon would spread to the United States. Local sanitary surveys were conducted in several American cities; the most famous of these was a survey conducted by Lemuel Shattuck, a Massachusetts bookseller and statistician. His *Report of the Massachusetts Sanitary Commission,* published in 1850, included vital statistics on the Massachusetts population, substantiating differences in morbidity and mortality rates in different geographic locations. Shattuck also maintained that people vulnerable to diseases were also those who either through ignorance or lack of concern failed to take personal responsibility for cleanliness and sanitation of their areas. Consequently, he argued that the city or the state had to take responsibility for the environment. The recommendations included improvement in the quality of drinking water and food, the establishment of state and local boards of health, and the collection and analysis of vital statistics. The report promoted sanitation as a critical means of preventing disease and laid the foundation for how we view the role of public health today.

The early public health movement was primarily concerned with the connection between the human body and the physical environment, but by the beginning of the 20th century, new hygienic approaches focused on the relationship between people and their social contacts. Tuberculosis, once viewed solely as a disease of the physical environment (e.g., poor housing and sanitation), became a disease connected with social contact as well (e.g., breathing, spitting, proximity). This change would have significant implications on how diseases would be viewed. Health promotion was transformed from a scrutiny of the space between bodies (the physical environment) to also include a scrutiny of personal hygiene. Disease control took on two dimensions: measures aimed at cleaning the physical environment and measures aimed at the individual. As knowledge about the sources and means for controlling disease was emerging, the United States witnessed the growth of public acceptance of disease control as both a private and public responsibility (Remington, 1988).

New ideas about causes of disease and about social responsibility stimulated the development of public health agencies and institutions (Hanlon & Pickett, 1984). As environmental and social causes of disease were identified, social action appeared to be an effective way to control diseases. When health was no longer simply an individual responsibility, it became necessary to form public boards, agencies, and institutions to protect the health of citizens. Sanitary and social reform provided the basis for the formation of public health organizations.

Federal activities in public health expanded during the late 19th century and early 20th century. In 1906, Congress passed the Food and Drug Act, which initiated controls on the manufacture, labeling, and sale of food. Federal activities also grew to include programs for promoting individual health and providing assistance to states for campaigns against specific health problems. Health reform played a significant role in this new social consciousness. The American Public Health Association devoted its attention to social reform, particularly in the cities. By the beginning of the 20th century, a new philosophy of social and political reform directly influenced health.

Investing in a healthy population would cost less than paying the price for premature and unnecessary mortality among the general population. Although physical activity was not an integral part of this movement, it would not be long before it would find its rightful place (Fee, 1987).

Sedentary Living and the New Urban Dilemma

Sedentary living was a frequent topic of discussion associated with the new social environment developing in the turn-of-the-century American cities. The urban population increased from about 200,000 people living in 6 major cities in 1800 to more than 18 million people living in 448 cities in 1890. The technological improvements in transportation, communication, manufacturing, and urbanization, with an immense increase in population, changed towns to cities and created a climate that both promoted physical activity and discouraged it. Sports and physical activity, as pointed out by sports historian Stephen Hardy (1981), were both a consequence of the negative features of city life and a positive outgrowth of the cities' technological improvements in communication and marketing. The transition from a rural-agricultural to an urban-industrial nation meant increases in crowded living conditions and also an increase in sedentary routines associated with work and leisure. Some physicians who were concerned with the increasing sedentariness of the new urban environment viewed physical exercise as the solution to passive living (Whorton, 1982b). Physical activity provided a response to "nervous exhaustion," a retreat from urban disorder, if only temporarily, to restore the mental and physical powers (Whorton, 1982b). The urban dilemma highlighted that the lack of participation in health-promoting behaviors could be partially explained by the lack of a conducive physical environment and the lack of individual initiative. As a higher standard of living, more free time, and greater discretionary income improved opportunities for physical activity among widening segments of the urban population, an increasing number of health reformers regarded physical activity as something to be marketed.

Early Health Promoters

During the last half of the 19th century, health reformers such as John Kellogg and Sylvester Graham stressed the capacity of individuals to avoid illness and were more interested in preventing diseases than curing them. Reformers were concerned with increased cleanliness, nutrition, and reform of dress, tobacco, alcohol, and morals, but many of them focused on fitness.

Among the first fitness promoters were the "strength seekers" (Paul, 1983). George Barker Windship, a practicing physician, was instrumental in connecting physical strength to good health. A Harvard degree and a solid medical practice helped Windship attract large crowds to his lectures on the benefits of strength building. The highlight of Windship's presentation was his demonstration of physical feats that he did at the conclusion of each lecture. An alternative to Windship's focus on strengthening activities was a milder system of calisthenics and games employing music and small pieces of equipment, such as wooden dumbbells and beanbags. The "new gymnastics," developed by Dr. Dioclesian Lewis, gained widespread popularity in the later decades of the 19th century. Because his method required only a minimum of equipment and expense and could be performed almost anywhere, they were appealing to women and children.

Arguably, the most visible of the fitness promoters success was Bernarr Macfadden, who developed a wide following in his highly publicized campaigns for natural healing of illnesses, which emphasized proper diet and exercise. Spectacular exhibitions were his specialty. He opened a chain of "Healthatoriums" in major cities that he promoted by putting on physical culture shows, and his magazine, *Physical Culture,* grew to a circulation of 100,000 in its first two years of publication (Ernst, 1991). He dedicated a long career, which included the publication of more than 150 books, to promoting physical well-being. Macfadden's advocacy of exercise and dietary reform had some popular appeal and some substantial medical support.

Macfadden, however, also had his fair share of critics. Health reformers such as Bernarr Macfadden were clearly outside the established medical societies. They were often considered quacks and, not surprisingly, became targets of the medical profession, most notably the American Medical Association (Mrozek, 1987).

The American Medical Association (AMA), first organized in 1847, played an important role in quality control of physician training through state licensing programs. Before the start of the 20th century, the practice of medicine in the United States was largely unregulated; licensure laws were almost nonexistent. By 1906, the AMA would emerge, largely under the leadership of Dr. Joseph McCormack, as a powerful national lobby with some 2,000 local representatives. The AMA began to reflect the views of its constituents, becoming more of an organization committed to "improving, and protecting, the economic position of its members" (Duffy, 1979). The reorganization of medical education helped to establish the cultural authority of medicine. The AMA took on political issues: It provided the specialized knowledge for intelligent legislation on highly technical problems and acted as a special interest group dedicated to raising the social status of doctors.

Not surprisingly, the powerful American Medical Association would flex its political muscles against the health reform movement. Throughout much of the 20th century, the AMA fought to redefine the practice of medicine in terms of scientific procedures for combating disease and illness. It was particularly concerned with discrediting popular therapeutic systems that were based on herbs, skeletal realignment, and other remedies that they believed to be unscientific. Physical activity was certainly among them.

Macfadden, like so many other health reformers, was not formally trained in medicine, and that did not sit well with the AMA. In 1924, the AMA published two articles condemning Macfadden and his magazine. The first article addressed the advertising that made *Physical Culture* commercially profitable, and the second described the "false literature" on which physical culturists such as Macfadden based their exercise principles (Ernst, 1991).

Macfadden in return openly criticized the medical community. He railed against the medical trust and opposed the use of drugs. Not surprisingly, Macfadden would be engaged in a lifelong battle against conventional medicine and the organization that promoted it. He criticized the AMA as an entrenched and intimidating monopoly (Ernst, 1991). His struggle with the AMA went on for years and ended only when he died in 1955. Bernarr Macfadden was among the first to promote views about the body and its proper care that today we generally acknowledge as an integral part of healthy living.

The Century's First Aerobic Fitness Fad

By the end of the 19th century, many urban dwellers became enamored with the bicycle, and many would soon take up the sport of "wheeling." Initially, only the well-to-do could afford bicycles, but when bicycles became less expensive, they also became a middle-class status symbol (Whorton, 1978). Because cycling was fun, unlike the ritualized drudgery of calisthenics, many otherwise inactive people were encouraged to take up the exercise. Between the period of 1870 and 1900, cycling would take on new heights of popularity. Cycling was adaptable as a new means of transportation around the city, and an industry emerged extolling its health benefits. Since the potential market would double if it attracted women, manufacturers made and promoted bikes especially for them.

Although many physicians encouraged cycling, the activity was not without its medical critics. Some medical specialists warned that such activity would cause curvature of the spine, biker's throat from inhaling dust, and reproductive problems in female bikers. Emphysema and other lung ailments were also associated with the sport. Criticism of bicycling and other forms of aerobic activity often focused on the perceived medical problems associated with overexertion. An increased risk of heart attacks during exercise had been noted by some observers, and individuals in strenuous exertion often appeared to resemble heart attack victims in their breathlessness and exhaustion (Park, 1997).

Physicians discovering hypertrophy of the cardiac muscle in devotees of the wheel were quick to diagnose "athletic heart" (Whorton, 1982a). Benjamin Ward Richardson, a leading English sanitary reformer who feared excess exercise, was among the first to warn of the new condition. Undue muscular development of the heart, he maintained, increased the pressure of the blood on vessel walls and caused a steady degeneration of the vascular system (Richardson, 1895).

Heart size was a matter of much concern and debate. Hypertrophy might explain enlargement (increase in thickness of the walls) or dilation (enlargement of the cavities and thinning of the walls). Cardiologists first associated the condition with soldiers. The noted physician J. M. Da Costa argued that the physical demands of long military campaigns eventually led to cardiac hypertrophy. Medical opposition to aerobic activities remained strong into the 1910s, as indicated in a report by Charles Stokes, Surgeon General of the U.S. Navy, on the long-term effects of athleticism on midshipmen at the Naval Academy. The report, published in 1911, announced that nearly a third of the Naval Academy athletes showed signs of disabilities or abnormal conditions. Fully one quarter of the disabled were afflicted with heart ailments, ranging from murmurs to dilatation (Whorton, 1982a).

The belief that excessive physical activity produced hypertrophy became securely seeded in many physicians' minds, and "sudden death" in athletics would also be a concern throughout the century to come. The concern about "athletic heart" dramatizes the uneasiness many physicians felt about the eventual effects of physical exertion: "Dull activities like gymnastics did not excite people to take sufficient exercise but enjoyable ones like cycling seduced them into too much" (Whorton, 1982a).

For many years, doctors and researchers thought that vigorous exercise was bad for adults. Faced with a growing number of participants in physical activity and armed with only the most rudimentary knowledge of the long-term effects of repeated stress to the heart, lungs, and nervous system, physicians approached physical activity with a great deal of caution (Whorton, 1982a). Most physicians felt insecure about their knowledge of physical activity, and the measures they suggested to their patients seemed ill defined and problematic. Only decades later would the pendulum shift from viewing physical activity as a precursor to impending structural injury to viewing it as an aid in developing stronger hearts and bodies. The role of physical activity would change as science and medicine learned more about the causes of diseases.

© Angela Costa

Physical activity is now viewed as healthy for adults.

Early Medical Views of Disease Associated With Sedentary Living

During the early years of the 20th century, little was known about the causes of diseases such as cardiovascular disease and diabetes. The early study of the heart focused on sudden death associated with *cardiac arrhythmia*. Deaths that occur within seconds or minutes, so-called sudden deaths, are usually caused by irregularities of heart rhythm, or arrhythmia, that are so severe that the heart cannot effectively pump blood around the body. Early Chinese physicians may have diagnosed cardiac arrhythmia and its association with sudden death when they spoke of a shortened life span correlated with irregularities of the pulse. Pulse theory, advanced in the 5th century B.C. by Chinese physician Pien ts'Io, laid the foundation for the study of arrhythmia. Centuries later, Galen connected the pulse with the workings of the heart. He thought that the pulse originated from the expansion of cardiac volume caused by inflation of the heart, which in turn showed that blood and air in the heart's cavities had warmed. Galen's pulse theory described many types of pulses and borrowed from the widely held belief of his day that every organ of the body and every disease was associated with its own unique type of pulse. Galen's theory endured virtually unchanged for the next few centuries into the Middle Ages. Not until 1578 and the work of William Harvey did health professionals begin to understand the role of the circulatory system. William Harvey was able to describe sudden death due to ventricular rupture. However, physicians still did not have a good grasp of the pathological processes of heart disease (Leibowitz, 1970).

The syndrome of anginal pain became recognized in the second half of the 18th century. *Angina pectoris* is a disease condition marked by brief onset of chest pain due to the deficient oxygenation of the heart muscle. Angina pectoris takes an extremely variable course, from mild, short attacks occurring at long intervals over many years, with death frequently the result of noncardiac causes, to severe, long, and frequent attacks ending in sudden death.

The development of electrocardiography (ECG) in the early years of the 20th century signaled the beginning of the modern study of cardiovascular disease. William Einthoven, a Dutch physiologist, developed the electrocardiograph in the Netherlands as an improvement over earlier, less-satisfactory tools for recording the electrical action of the heart. His revolutionary tool could distinguish patients suffering from heart disease from healthy patients (Einthoven, 1900). When Thomas Lewis successfully showed the electrocardiogram's medical utility in London, it became an invaluable tool in measuring heart disease. It earned Einthoven the Nobel Prize for Medicine in 1924. In 1912, James Herrick described the clinical syndrome of *myocardial infarction,* the death of some part of the heart muscle, or myocardium, due to obstruction of a coronary artery (Herrick, 1912). By 1918, with the help of the newly developed ECG, James Herrick was one of the first to measure the phenomenon (Howell, 1984).

By the early 1930s, physicians could present a complete electrocardiographic picture of coronary artery disease and forged the acceptance of a clinical distinction between angina pectoris and coronary thrombosis. Angina pectoris came to denote temporary but recurring episodes of pain stemming most often from a reduction of the blood supply to the heart (known as myocardial ischemia), and coronary thrombosis signified the longer-lasting, more intense, and more lethal pain resulting from a deprivation of blood flow so acute as to kill part of the heart muscle.

The new tools and knowledge available to medicine provided the understanding that a person could have heart disease yet continue to live. Large branches of the coronary arteries could be occluded without resulting in death (White, 1947). Such was the beginning of a true recognition of heart disease as an ongoing or chronic condition, something that individuals could develop over a lifetime and live with for many years.

Doctors poorly understood the condition of diabetes prior to the discovery of insulin. They prescribed a variety of ineffective treatments such as warm baths, alcohol, opium, and whatever other pharmacological treatments were fashionable at the time (Presley, 1991). Laboratory studies demonstrated that diabetic animals, when fed a diet reduced in calories, reverted back to normal metabolisms (Feudtner, 1995). Thus, a rigorous starvation diet, which did not work and in some cases worsened the condition, became the most popular treatment prescribed by most physicians during the pre-insulin era.

Among the great medical breakthroughs of the 20th century stands the work of Frederick Banting, a practicing physician in London, Ontario. During the summer of 1921, Banting and his colleagues John J. Macleod and Charles Best were able to isolate insulin, introducing the first effective long-term treatment for diabetes. After 1922, insulin freed patients with the disease from its former swift course toward death. In the decades after insulin was discovered, the development of antibiotics for infections and a variety of drugs to treat other ailments such as high blood pressure further improved the health of diabetics and added years to people's lives. Although insulin and other remedies prolong life, they do so without curing the disease.

Although physicians did not fully comprehend the mechanisms of diabetes, some recommended physical activity for their patients. For example, Apollinaire Bouchardat recommended a strategy of eating as little as possible and exercising to his patients. The biggest breakthrough concerning the beneficial role of physical activity on diabetes occurred in 1915, when Frederick M. Allen (1915) of the Rockefeller Institute systematically examined physical activity and carbohydrate tolerance in laboratory dogs. He found that exercise could double the dogs' carbohydrate tolerance from 100 grams to 200 grams. He soon used exercise with patients, including severely afflicted ones for whom exercise was generally discouraged. His findings led him to recommend that his patients become more physically active by running up and down stairs, jumping rope, throwing a heavy medicine ball, and turning somersaults.

Despite these positive results, physical activity remained a conservative protocol for the treatment of diabetes (Feudtner, 1995). Allen found exercise a useful companion to diet for diabetic patients, but he considered its value limited and felt that overweight diabetic patients should instead use fasting and a low-calorie diet for weight reduction. The general rule seemed to be that physical activity should be restricted to patients suffering only mild or moderate diabetes and that severely ill people were better off resting, as vigorous exercise might complicate their condition (Presley, 1991). It was not until the late 1980s that a consensus emerged among the medical community concerning the beneficial role of physical activity in the treatment of the potentially deadly disease.

Although medical breakthroughs increased the understanding of the physical consequences of disease, it became increasing evident that there would be no easy answers in finding cures. By the 1930s, there was a better understanding of the role of physical and social environments in disease formation. A growing but much less understood concept would be the belief that individual lifestyle had a great deal to do with promoting good health and preventing disease. Most physicians still felt uncertain about their knowledge of physical activity and their advice to patients remained ill defined and inconsistent. It would not be until decades later that the pendulum would swing from viewing physical activity in its most cautious terms to its role in developing stronger hearts and bodies. The benefits of physical activity would emerge as scientists and medical researchers learned more about the causes of disease, particularly chronic diseases.

New Deal Opportunities for Physical Activity

The economic crisis of the 1930s overshadowed all aspects of American life. Between 1929 and 1932, more than 25 percent of the labor force faced unemployment. Previously, Americans clinging to ideas of rugged individualism had been convinced that they alone were responsible for whether they worked or not. This was no longer the case, as millions of people wanted to work but no work was available. People began to see that having a job or being employed was the result not simply of individual traits such as initiative and hard work but also of social and political realities. People lost faith in the business community, so they looked to local and federal government for answers.

In 1933, newly elected President Franklin D. Roosevelt introduced his New Deal plan to tackle the problem of mass unemployment. New Deal policies on sport and physical recreation reflected the government's interest in addressing the major problems that many people were facing. Massive unemployment gave people lots of free time for recreational activities, and building new facilities meant the creation of new jobs (Wong, 1998). Embedded in the New Deal plan was the encouragement of sport and physical activity through programs such as the Civilian Conservation Corps, the National Youth Administration, the National Forest Service, and the Works Projects Administration (WPA). Between July 1935 and June 1941, the WPA spent $941 million on recreational facilities and $229 million on recreational services. Among the new facilities were 5,898 athletic fields and playgrounds, 770 swimming pools, 1,667 parks and fairgrounds, and 8,333 recreational buildings (Howard, 1943). The WPA construction and service projects afforded more recreational opportunities to the public.

Federal involvement in health activities was nothing new (Hanlon & Pickett, 1984). Federal activities included promoting programs for individual health and providing assistance to states for campaigns against specific health problems. But the crisis presented by the Great Depression brought action by the federal government in areas that had previously been left to state and local control. From banking regulation to support for small businesses, from public employment to old-age security, there was growing support for the federal government to do what state governments had failed to accomplish. As the federal bureaucracy in health grew, health programs requiring federal–state partnerships were developed. The need for expertise and leaders in public health increased at both the federal and state levels. The Sheppart-Towner Act of 1922 provided administrative funds to states to establish programs in maternal and children's health. The act instituted the federal practice of setting guidelines for public health programs and providing funding to states to carry out programs to meet these guidelines.

Federal government interest in health and social issues is clearly seen in its passage of the Social Security Act in 1935. Title VI of the act established federal aid to the states for public health assistance. Despite abundant data showing the need for some national health insurance plan, efforts failed (Mulcahy, 1994). The American Medical Association strongly opposed national health insurance and because President Franklin Roosevelt was more concerned with issues of unemployment and economics, the proposal failed. The thwarted national medical system would instigate the development of private health insurance.

As programs requiring federal–state partnerships for health grew, so did the importance of preventive medicine. However, it was not the medical profession that led the change to promote the importance of identifying the early signs of disease. Many places of employment began to require some form of physical examination to help evaluate a prospective employee's health (Buck, 1939). Life insurance companies found profit in assessing one's health before issuing a policy (Reiser, 1978).

Through life insurance medical examinations, individuals who sought life insurance believing that they were in good health sometimes learned that they suffered from such diseases as diabetes, high or low blood pressure, and a host of incipient chronic diseases that were discovered after the methods for detecting these ailments became more precise. Detecting diseases in their early forms through a periodic medical examination became common. But the annual checkup was devoted to more than the discovery of undetected disease. A major aim was finding and correcting harmful habits and poor hygiene (Reiser, 1978). The early diagnosis of diseases and ways of avoiding them through healthy habits were emerging, along with the movement for preventive medicine.

Large-scale epidemiological studies would soon help document more systematically how much disease existed in the population. Armed with emerging social survey methods developed in social science and epidemiology, the Public Health Service revealed a surprisingly high prevalence of chronic illness and disability among the U.S. population (Britten, 1939). In 1935 and 1936, the Public Health Service conducted the first national health surveys. These large-scale studies served to confirm the growing realization that many more Americans were facing chronic diseases. With the increasing success of antibiotics in combating infectious diseases by the middle of the century, diseases related to the slow "degeneration of the body" would become a greater health concern (Rader, 1991).

The Emerging Concept of Risk Factor

By the early 1950s most Americans still knew very little about the causes of chronic diseases, although for years many were well aware of the devastation caused by such disease, particularly heart disease. They had witnessed heart disease cutting life short for many of their friends and family members. An estimate by the American Heart Association, based on data from the U.S. National Health Survey, placed the number of individuals in the country with some form of cardiovascular disease at more than 10 million (U.S. National Health Survey, 1957-58).

In the middle of the decade, the National Health Education Committee along with Harvard doctors issued a statement that presented the public with the first mention of factors predisposing an individual to arteriosclerosis, heart attacks, and strokes (Lasby, 1997). The report, authored by eight physicians, five of whom were former presidents of the American Heart Association, cited heredity, overweight, elevated blood cholesterol, elevated blood pressure, and excessive smoking as risk factors to cardiovascular disease. James Watt, director of the National Health Institute, pointed to the growing segment of the medical profession who believed that exercise has a highly beneficial effect on the cardiovascular system and that it can help to prevent heart disease and prolong life (Watt, 1959). Moreover, in a report published in the *Journal of American Medicine*, these physicians noted, "Hard work itself is often wrongly blamed for this disease," and went as far as to suggest that moderate physical activity "appears to lessen the hazards of arteriosclerosis" (Lasby, 1997). The conservative American Medical Association was not ready to take a stand on any of the risk factors, including physical inactivity. The association was torn between those who wanted to wait for absolute scientific proof, a position usually favored by the leadership, and those who felt a responsibility to inform the public of the most up-to-date evidence, a position usually inspired by the affiliate associations and the medical community.

Of most significance to our present-day understanding of the relationship between exercise and heart disease was the creation of the National Heart Institute in 1949 and the initiation of several community-based studies. But it was a president afflicted with heart disease who provided the public with the first "detailed educational seminar on coronary heart disease" (Lasby, 1997).

President Dwight D. Eisenhower's heart attack in 1955 created an unparalleled interest in heart disease. The president's illness made the whole country heart conscious in a way that neither the American Heart Association nor the medical associations could have achieved by themselves (Lasby, 1997). The major news outlets published numerous reports about the possible causes and the drugs and surgical techniques available to treat the disease. The increased knowledge, however, did not bring about an immediate change in people's lifestyles because the medical experts could not agree on the causes of heart disease. Medical experts recognized that the disease affected those over 40 years of age and struck men more often than women. They also acknowledged the powerful role of family history, and they recognized a relationship between hypertension and heart disease but could not explain it. Although they remained puzzled about the effect of environmental stress, most cardiologists believed that coronary disease occurred more often among certain types of individuals, especially overworked businessmen at the prime of their lives and the top of their careers (Lasby, 1997).

Eisenhower's heart attack brought to the public's attention some of the assumptions about the relationship between heart disease and exercise. In the 1950s, cardiologists were generally opposed to such vigorous exercise as running upstairs and suspected such activities as precipitating events for a second heart attack. One such cardiologist, Paul Dudley White, a prolific author with more than 400 articles in medical journals and senior medical consultant to the president, expressed his views on the benefits of exercise not only to the president but to the public. Although an exercise enthusiast who favored an hour of exercise a day, Dr. White was cautious when it came to his heart patients. In his well-known text *Heart Disease,* he recommended the following:

> **A**cute coronary thrombosis must be regarded more seriously than most cardiac conditions, and rest in bed for weeks or months should be prescribed in order to assure as sound a healing of the myocardial infarct as possible. . . As the result of experience during the last twenty years I have found that a very satisfactory plan of treatment for the average case of acute myocardial infarction is one month of bed rest. . . . One month of gradually getting up and around (the first week in a chair a little more each day, the second week walking on the level increasing distances, the third week going slowly over the stairs once a day, and the fourth week going out for short daily rides, weather permitting), and a third month to consolidate the recovery nervously as well as otherwise. (White, 1947:501-502)

Not surprisingly, when the doctor learned that someone had sent Eisenhower a bicycle, he advised the president against using it. Dr. White prescribed a cautious program of exercise to the president, who returned to an active life. Eisenhower played golf regularly and was able to win a term of reelection as president. In 1956, President Eisenhower created by executive order the President's Council on Youth Fitness, which later would be changed to the President's Council on Physical Fitness and Sports.

Epidemiological Evidence

Jeremy Morris and colleagues are generally credited with the first modern epidemiological study of exercise (Morris, Heady, Raffle, Roberts, & Parks, 1953). Their 1953 analysis of records on 25,000 London drivers and conductors of double-decker buses revealed that the more sedentary bus drivers experienced greater frequency and severity of disease than the conductors. Angina pectoris was more common among the conductors, while the more fatal coronary thrombosis appeared more often among the bus drivers. Immediate deaths accounted for 31 percent in the drivers as opposed to 19 percent in the conductors.

In a follow-up comparison of postmen to sedentary civil servants, Morris found similar cardiovascular disease patterns. The more active group (postmen) had less incidence of coronary heart disease, and the disease they did have appeared in less severe forms. The authors concluded that psychological stress from work likely caused some of the heart disease but that the lack of physical activity at work was the greatest cause for the development of coronary heart disease (Morris et al., 1953).

Framingham Study

Another study that would radically alter how we would view heart disease and other conditions of sedentary living took place in a small town 12 miles outside Boston by the name of Framingham. The Framingham Study, started in the 1960s, was intended to help in the development and testing of methods for the early detection of heart disease. Before Framingham, epidemiologists relied on medical records and death certificates. Now it was time to learn more from the people themselves. Researchers recruited 2,336 men and 2,873 women from the town of 28,000 (Dawber, 1980). The general plan included the identification of a group that varied in the characteristics believed to be related to coronary heart disease. Subjects were then followed for a period of 20 years. During the study period, an effort was made to characterize each of the subjects by a number of bodily traits, life habits, or other factors that were believed to be related in some way to the eventual development of this disease.

The research got off the ground when Congress rushed through a bill giving $500,000 to study the causes of heart disease. Congress did not include physical activity in the original list of potential research, but a debate broke out among members of the advisory committee. The conflicting opinions reflected the medical debate of the times over the relationship of physical activity and heart disease. On one side, members of the advisory committee voiced the opinion that doing hard physical work or habitually engaging in vigorous physical exercise would produce higher rates of coronary heart disease due to increases in blood pressure. On the other side were those who felt that exercise benefited the cardiovascular system by increasing the total metabolism (Dawber, 1980). Several decades later, when the first results were in, the Framingham data would prove the advocates of physical activity correct. The Framingham Study demonstrated that sedentary men had nearly three times the rate of coronary heart disease as the most active men. Among women, smaller differences were found, but physically active women were 2.5 times less likely to experience heart disease than less-active women (Kannel & Sorlie, 1979).

The Framingham Study also represented one of the first serious attempts to measure the physical activity of the American population. Physical activity was assessed by an interview procedure in which subjects reported the number of hours spent at rest, on the job, and in extracurricular activities. A composite score called the physical activity index was calculated as the sum of the products of the hours spent at each of five activity levels (basal, sedentary, slight, moderate, heavy) times a weight factor based on the oxygen requirements for the level of activity. These weights ranged from 1.0 for the basal level to 5.0 for heavy activity. Thus, subjects would have a minimum daily physical activity index of 24, and a person engaged in heavy on-the-job activity might have an index of 42 (Kannel & Sorlie, 1979).

With the inclusion of physical inactivity as a risk factor in the Framingham Study, other studies designed to identify the causes of chronic diseases began to look at physical inactivity as a factor of disease. Of particular importance to the recognition of the relationship of physical activity to health are three projects that were successful in connecting physical inactivity to premature death. In 1951, 4,000 San Francisco longshoremen were followed for a period of 22 years (Thomas et al., 1981). The researchers kept careful records of the factors known to be related to heart disease, including a measure of physical activity expressed in calories burned. The men who used 8,500 calories or more during a work week had significantly fewer deaths from heart attacks than those who were less active. The risk of death from heart attacks declined steadily as the amount of physical activity increased. Those who used 9,500 calories a week had half the risk of those who used half that amount. Even when other factors, such as smoking, hypertension, and cholesterol levels, were statistically controlled, the difference remained.

A second important study, known as the College Study, found similar protective effects of physical activity (Paffenbarger, Wing, & Hyde, 1978). The study evaluated information supplied by Harvard and the University of Pennsylvania alumni who entered college between 1916 and 1950. When comparing the life expectancies among the most active (those who used 2,000 calories or more per week) and least active (those using less than 2,000 calories per week), the authors concluded that the physically active alumni lived an average of 2.15 years longer than their sedentary counterparts. Individuals who changed to an active life in middle age added time to their lives, giving optimism to the aging baby-boom generation (Paffenbarger, Hyde, Wing, & Hsieh, 1986).

In a third important study, Leon and Connett (1991) followed 12,000 men enrolled in the Multiple Risk Factor Intervention Trial over a seven-year period. The measurement of physical activity was quantified as mean minutes of physical activity per day performed at light-, moderate-, and high-intensity levels. Total physical activity was calculated and individuals were divided into three groups (high, medium, and low). The men in the high physical activity group, when compared to the middle group, had 63 percent as many fatal CHD events and sudden death and 70 percent as many deaths as men in the lowest grouping of physical activity.

These studies of college students, longshoremen, and a large cohort of healthy men are only a few examples of the many studies that contributed to the scientific credibility of the importance of a physically active lifestyle as a means of prolonging life. They have provided scientific corroboration that, along with biological risk factors such as hypertension and elevated cholesterol levels, the habits of sedentary living play a significant role in disease and premature death.

By the second half of the 20th century, the study of the causes of disease would include biological factors as well as specific behaviors of individuals. The principal model of disease causation became known as the *web of causation,* in which a variety of biological and behavioral risk factors are presumed to interact in the causation of disease (Diez-Roux, 1998). Biological factors such as family history of coronary heart disease, levels of serum cholesterol and triglyceride, and systolic and diastolic blood pressure; and behavioral factors such as cigarette smoking, obesity, and physical inactivity became the focus of attention. Epidemiology emerged as a science that would help unravel the multitude of causes of disease for which prevention and control programs could be developed (Krieger, 1994). Physical inactivity would be one of these causes.

Social Movements and the Fitness-Boom Years

The 1960s brought a renewed focus on social conditions. Most pressing were the needs of inner cities and ghettos for housing, education, and employment. Adequate medical care was denied to many citizens; the growing number of elderly required attention. Emerging from a century-long debate about the need for a national health insurance program, the passage of the Medicare and Medicaid Acts of the mid-1960s provided much needed social assistance to the poor and aged.

In the 1960s, there was further expansion of the federal role in health policy. Through the Kennedy and Johnson administrations, the federal government became increasingly involved in improving health care, such as by developing new mental health and community centers along with a program of environmental health.

The civil rights movement was changing the face of economic issues. In 1963, Kennedy's successor, Lyndon Johnson, made "war on want" a central platform of his administration and set up the Office of Economic Opportunity as a first step toward building a Great Society (Porter, 1999). Federally assisted medical care for the elderly and poor became two central features of these reforms. At the same time, pressure for equality was growing. Social unrest demonstrated in the anti–Vietnam War movement, civil rights efforts, and the women's movement created a climate that would affect physical activity. The civil rights and women's movements questioned whether sport and other opportunities for physical activity were truly available to everyone. The threat of a boycott by black members of the 1968 U.S. Olympic team was one of the earliest incidents to publicize the problems of black athletes. The women's movement too began to demand equal opportunity on the playing fields for women and men.

The period roughly from the mid-1960s to the early 1990s was also marked by a growing distrust in social institutions and deteriorating social conditions. Crime and social disorder began to rise, making inner cities problem areas in which to live. The decline of family as a social institution accelerated sharply in the second half of the 20th century. Marriages and births declined, and divorce soared. One of every three children in the United States was born out of wedlock. Although a majority of people in the United States had confidence in their governments and fellow citizens during the 1950s, only a small minority did so by the early 1990s. In 1958, 73 percent of Americans surveyed said they trusted the federal government to do what was right. By the early 1990s, this figure had fallen to as low as 15 percent (Fukuyama, 1999).

The period was characterized also by a growing disillusionment with the limits of modern medicine. Many Americans who had believed in medicine as a solution to all health problems were losing faith. For an increasing number of illnesses, for example, there was no one best treatment, and a murkier and more complex decisional context evolved in which different treatments had different types of trade-offs between benefits and risks. Since the patient rather than the physician must live with the consequences of these trade-offs, the assumption that physicians are in the best position to evaluate and weigh them was increasingly challenged.

The 1960s also furthered the concept of medicalization of a wide range of social problems (Goldstein, 1991). Sociologists use the term *medicalization* to refer to the process of turning something that was not previously considered medical into a medical matter. Homosexuality, drug addiction, and child abuse are examples of human conditions that have been medicalized. The medicalization of nonmedical conditions is based on arbitrary definitions from the cultural view of life. While some social scientists view medicalization as an opportunity for the medical establishment to help individuals, others view the process of medicalizing human affairs as an indication of the growing desires for power and profit of some in the medical field. According to Goldstein, the medicalization of everyday activities has a significant impact on health promotion efforts such as the ones directed at increasing levels of participation in physical activity.

> . . .the phenomenon of medicalization has increasingly turned from behaviors and attitudes that had been seen as deviant to behaviors and attitudes that are seen as normal. Part of this process is the specification of attitudes and behaviors that are "better" than normal; ones that are believed to prevent the occurrence of deviance or illness and maximize health and "wellness." In this context, the most frequently cited definition of health is the one put forth by the World Health Organization. Health is a state of complete physical, mental, and social well-being, and not merely the absence of disease or infirmity. (Goldstein, 1991:45)

The 1960s also saw an increased interest in holistic approaches to diseases. Holistic practitioners place emphasis on the whole person, making their approach to medicine stand apart from dominant medical practices. Rather than seeing a patient as someone who has a disease and needs a pharmaceutical remedy, holistic practitioners view the patient in terms of the patient's physical and social environments as well as his or her lifestyle behaviors. The holistic health movement centered on preventing and promoting health and taking responsibility for one's own health, instead of seeing oneself as a passive recipient of illness and disease.

The social and political climate emphasized the individual's role in health matters. Uneasiness about the power and control exercised by a dominant medical profession further helped to develop greater interest in self-care in the United States. The ideology of individualism and self-help as expressed in Barry Glassner's (1989) concept of the postmodern self in part explains the role of physical activity. That is, the individual, by attaining physical fitness, can achieve a degree of independence from medicine and its technology.

People were expected to take personal responsibility for their health largely because many lifestyle variables that contribute to health were assumed to be under individual control. The ethos of *individualism*, which gained momentum throughout the next several decades in response to a growing disillusionment with the limits of medicine and pressures to contain health care costs, assumes that individuals can make choices in relative isolation from their broader social environments. Thus, the stage was set for millions of Americans to take up physical activity in a way never witnessed before.

The Fitness Movement and American Individualism

During the 1970s and 1980s, sports and fitness activities became an obsession among many Americans (Gillick, 1984). Gallup pollsters estimated that 47 percent of adults aged 18 and older participated in some form of exercise daily, nearly twice the 24 percent reported in 1961 (Rader, 1991). Activities such as tennis, biking, and racquetball became popular pastimes. The fitness boom funded an enormous growth industry. Fitness clubs skyrocketed from 350 in 1968 to more than 7,000 by 1986 to support Americans' interest in fitness. Between 1975 and 1987, sporting goods sales in the United States increased from $8.9 billion to $27.5 billion (Rader, 1991).

Nothing seemed to match the popularity of jogging, which emerged as the most visible symbol of a "national exercise movement." In a 1978 survey commissioned by the Pacific Mutual Insurance Company, the Harris Organization found that only half of the 37 percent of American adults who were currently involved in exercise had done so for five years or more (Pacific Mutual Life Insurance, 1978). Interest in running was spurred by a number of best-selling books. Dr. Kenneth Cooper, the scientific father of running and an Air Force physician, published *Aerobics* in 1968, and by 1972 the book had sold nearly 3 million copies. Cooper (1968) told all Americans that they should get their heart rates above 130 beats per minute for a sustained period to benefit from exercise. His books provided a sound medical basis for the importance of physical activity.

The fitness movement was not without its critics. Several high-profile cases of sudden death while exercising dominated the popular press. The death of Jim Fixx, author of the best-selling *Complete Book of Running* (1977), revived concerns about athlete's heart reminiscent of those voiced at the beginning of the century. A study by several Rhode Island doctors suggested that the annual coronary death rate from jogging was approximately seven times the coronary death rate during more sedentary activities (Thompson, Funk, & Carelton, 1982).

The fitness movement was also criticized for its narrow range of participants. Profiles of joggers in news magazines featured middle-aged and middle-class men. Data collected by the U.S. Department of Health, Education, and Welfare in 1975 (USDHEW, 1978) revealed that 4.8 percent of Americans over age 20 reported jogging regularly during the preceding year; jogging was twice as common among men as women and increased in frequency with rising income. Kirshenbaum and Sullivan (1983) postulated in *Sports Illustrated* that the fitness boom was in large part imaginary. They pointed to the homogeneity of participants, who were more likely to be rich than poor, executives than blue-collar workers, white than nonwhite, college graduates than high school graduates, adults than children.

Today, sport and exercise historians continue to question whether there was a fitness boom. Unfortunately, as pointed out by Canadian epidemiologist Thomas Stephens (1987), attempts to measure physical activity prior to the 1980s are better characterized by the quantity of physical activity studies rather than their quality. If there was such a phenomenon as the fitness boom, it likely ran its course by the mid-1980s. According to national figures compiled from the data collected by Simmons Market Research Bureau, for every physical activity except golf, participation rates during the decade of the 1980s declined (Howard, 1992). The extent to which adults reported playing tennis and racquetball dropped 28 percent and 21 percent, respectively. The most dramatic reductions, however, were observed in the more traditional fitness activities. The number of adults who indicated that they jogged or ran during the previous 12 months prior dropped by more than 40 percent, with 8.2 million fewer participants in 1989 than in 1980 (Howard, 1992). Women's participation also decreased significantly, by 15 percent, most particularly in activities such as weightlifting, racquetball, and jogging.

Health Professionals Join Forces

Up until the 1980s, scientific interest in physical activity followed two separate tracks: studies conducted by epidemiologists and studies conducted by exercise physiologists. Since the early work of Morris and colleagues on the role of physical inactivity in the development of coronary artery disease, population-based studies on physical activity and health have refined, tested, and extended the exercise hypothesis regarding the risk of disease. About the time Morris published his work on conductors and bus drivers, Karvonen and colleagues developed interest in studying the association of different intensities of exercise on heart rate at rest and at work (Karvonen, Kentala, & Mustala, 1957). The second approach to exercise research pursued the relationship of physical activity to changes in functional capacity, usually measured as maximal oxygen uptake ($\dot{V}O_2$max).

In the 1970s expert panels and committees began to recommend specific physical activity programs or exercise prescriptions for improving physical performance and health. These recommendations were based on substantial clinical experience and on scientific data available at that time. The American College of Sports Medicine's position statement released in 1978 recommended that adults should develop and maintain cardiorespiratory fitness and a healthy body composition. These guidelines recommended exercise training three to five days per week at 60 to 90 percent of maximal oxygen uptake or heart rate reserve for 15 to 60 minutes per training session (ACSM, 1978). Although in some circles it was still common for scientists and clinicians to consider two somewhat competing views of the effects of physical activity—one on the role of physical activity in promoting health and the other on physical activity to improve fitness—these two schools would join forces during the health movement emerging in the 1980s and 1990s.

These studies along with others reinforced new thinking among medical professionals concerning the contribution of aerobic conditioning to beneficial cardiovascular changes. With physical activity, the heart's action becomes more mechanically efficient. The resting pulse rate becomes slower, and pulse-rate increases after physical exercise are less than before physical conditioning. At the same time, more physicians generalized their experience with cardiac patients to the general population, concluding that aerobic exercise could prevent heart attacks and premature death. The first official organizational endorsement came in 1972 when the American Heart Association published a physician handbook on exercise that included guidelines for exercise prescription in healthy persons (AHA, 1972).

Federal Monitoring of the Nation's Health

By the middle 1970s, public policy makers, particularly in the federal government, were confronted with a series of recurring health care crises. Health expenditures, which were 4.1 percent of the gross national product in 1950, nearly doubled by 1976 (Crawford, 1981). These crises centered on the cost, effectiveness, quality, and accessibility of health care. With health costs climbing and well more than 90 percent of the nation's health expenditures devoted to financing direct health care services to individuals, questions began to be raised about the return on governmental investments in terms not only of meeting the needs of the sick but also of improving the health and well-being of the American population as a whole. The United States in the 1970s was entering a period of fiscal austerity. A federal government battling inflation and escalating health care costs was ready, willing, and able to promote the concept of individual responsibility for health on the grounds of fiscal responsibility. In response to accumulated research and the widespread recognition that physical inactivity is a major public health issue during the last two decades of the 20th century, efforts to persuade people to adopt physically active lifestyles were put into high gear. Of great significance to health promotion would be the establishment of two agencies to address health needs at the national level, the National Institutes of Health (NIH) and the Centers for Disease Control and Prevention (CDC).

The National Institutes of Health

During the past century, NIH grew from a one-room laboratory in the attic of the Marine Health Service Hospital in New York to one of the world's largest biomedical research institutions. Over the years, the responsibilities of NIH grew slowly. Full congressional recognition of the importance of a national laboratory for biomedical research came in 1930 with passage of the Ransdell Act that renamed the hygiene lab the National Institute of Health.

In 1944, Congress passed the Public Health Service Act and authorized the NIH to conduct and support research projects and fellowships. Legislation passed in 1946 established the Research Grant Office in NIH to administer the extramural grant and fellowship programs for biomedical and health-related sciences. In 1946, the

NIH funded 850 grants totaling $2.5 million. In the early 1960s, C.P. Chapman at the Southwestern Medical School of the University of Texas was funded by the Heart and Lung Institute to study human adaptation to environmental and exercise stress. It was not until the late 1950s and early 1960s, when an ad hoc "study section" of applied physiology was changed into a permanent one, that financial support for physical activity studies became more available. In the years between 1963 and 1976, federal funds for the programs of the NIH increased approximately 580 percent, to a total approaching $840 million. The NIH, encompassing 25 separate institutes and centers, today is one of the world's foremost medical research centers and the federal focal point for health (Fox, 1987). In President Clinton's budget plan for fiscal year 2001, he requested $18.8 billion for the NIH, an increase of $1 billion, or 5.6 percent more than the 2000 appropriation.

Centers for Disease Control and Prevention

The second significant organizational development occurred with the founding of the Communicable Disease Center in Atlanta, which later became the Centers for Disease Control and Prevention (CDC). Today, the CDC has grown to become not only one of the world's greatest epidemiological centers but also an outstanding training center for various types of health personnel and a leading center for communication and education (Etheridge, 1992). Dr. William Foege was appointed director of the CDC in the spring of 1977, at a time when most of the money allocated for health went to the programs of Medicare and Medicaid.

Congress enacted the National Consumer Health Information and Health Promotion Act. The law had two parts: The first dealt with traditional public health areas such as immunization of children and control of venereal and other infectious and communicable diseases. The second allocated funds for the creation of an Office of Health Information and Health Promotion in the Department of Health, Education, and Welfare. The initial allocation for health promotion was quite modest: $7 million in fiscal year 1977, $10 million in 1978, and $14 million in 1979. The total of $31 million represented a substantial decrease from the original House version of $70 million and the Senate version of $49 million. The figure was lowered to overcome objections by the Ford administration to the health information and promotion section of the bill. The administration argued that this effort represented a duplication of services already performed by existing federal agencies (Etheridge, 1992).

In December 1977, CDC Director Foege formed a "red-book committee" consisting of 16 health professionals and lay members to study CDC programs and policies. The committee's charge was to study morbidity and mortality statistics and point out what had to be done to prevent illness and premature death. After lively debate, the committee drew up a list of the 12 most important health problems in the United States. The final list included alcohol and its consequences, cancers, cardiovascular diseases, contamination of drinking water, dental diseases, hazardous health exposures in the workplace, infant mortality, motor vehicle accidents, newly recognized diseases and unexpected epidemics, nosocomial infections, smoking, and vaccine-preventable diseases in children. Three others were added for special consideration: mental illness, social disorders, and stress. Although physical inactivity was not included among these health issues, the report served as the basis of the health promotion movement that would soon follow. Lack of physical activity was one of that movement's focuses.

The committee agreed that primary prevention was the best way for reducing morbidity and mortality. The committee also pointed to the fact that there was no agency in the United States responsible for advocating primary prevention. The technical knowledge to prevent much unnecessary death and disease was available; what was needed was a national commitment to apply that knowledge in a rational, efficient manner. CDC's close relationship with the states, its long experience in epidemiological investigations and surveillance, and its excellent laboratories made it the ideal choice to lead the nation's health promotion movement.

The Healthy People Objectives

The NIH stepped up its research on prevention as health education became increasingly important. The first phase of the government's strategy to improve the health of Americans began in 1979 with the *Healthy People* report (USPHS, 1979). The document, according to Secretary of Health, Education, and Welfare Joseph Califano, represented an "emerging consensus among scientists and the health community that the nation's health strategy must be dramatically recast to emphasize the prevention of disease." Califano said in the introduction of the *Healthy People* report, "We are killing ourselves by our own careless habits." The report set the stage for publication a year later of *Promoting Health/Preventing Disease: Objectives for the Nation* (USPHS, 1980), which listed 226 measurable goals in 15 priority areas under the general heading of "Preventive Services." The report suggested steps that could be taken by both private and public sectors to reduce morbidity, disability, and premature mortality. In addition to suggesting traditional health promotion programs such as immunization, occupational safety, and pre- and postnatal care, it addressed environmental health hazards and various lifestyle-related areas.

The report included several objectives related to physical activity. Examples of the physical activity objectives that were to be accomplished by 1990 included: (1) increasing the proportion of children and adolescents who participate in regular physical activity, (2) increasing the proportion of children and adolescents who participate in daily school physical education programs, (3) increasing the proportion of adults who participate in regular physical activity, and (4) increasing the proportion of people over 65 years old who participate in physical activity, such as walking. Inclusion of physical activity in the nation's first major preventive health initiative represented one of the first formal recognitions of the problem of sedentary living as a public health issue.

Despite the widespread publicity associated with the 1990 health objectives, many of those related to physical activity were not reached. Of the 11 proposed physical activity objectives, only the four objectives that applied to improvements in monitoring physical activity were achieved. Objectives concerning improvements in actual participation rates in physical activity were not reached. In September 1990, the Secretary of the U.S. Department of Health and Human Services, Louis Sullivan, released *Healthy People 2000*, the national objectives for health promotion and disease for the year 2000. The year 2000 objectives were built upon the 1990 objectives, with an expansion of health outcomes to include a greater emphasis on prevention.

The *Healthy People 2000* initiative challenged the nation to achieve three broad goals: (1) increasing the healthy life span of Americans, (2) reducing health disparities among Americans, and (3) access to preventive health services for all Americans. To achieve these goals, 300 measurable objectives in 22 priority areas were identified. Thirteen of the *Healthy People 2000* measurable objectives addressed physical activity and fitness, and two additional objectives targeted improvements in health status related to chronic disease and conditions linked to physical inactivity.

In 1996, the Public Health Service issued a midcourse review on the nation's progress toward achieving the goals set by the original plan. The report predicted that 110 of 226 objectives would be met by 2000; coronary heart disease death rates had declined along with the use of alcohol and tobacco. However, the review was not as optimistic regarding other health behaviors. There was not a decline in the number of adults who were overweight or an increase in the number who participated in regular physical activity. Overall physical activity in adults and strengthening and stretching activities in children had increased, but the percentage of sedentary people had not declined. The proportion of the population adopting sound dietary practices combined with regular physical activity to attain appropriate body weight had also declined. Concern for the declining number of children participating in daily physical education was

The number of adults participating in regular physical activity did not increase by the mid-1990s.

also evident. Of the 13 physical activity and fitness objectives included in *Healthy People 2000,* only one, increasing the number of work-site exercise programs, had reached its target objective. We still had a long way to go to improve the physical activity habits of the nation. Physical inactivity was a major public health problem in the United States, and what we needed was a major call to action.

The Surgeon General's Report on Physical Activity and Health

In 1995 a group of experts from a variety of fields was brought together by the CDC and the American College of Sports Medicine to evaluate the scientific evidence and to produce a clear, concise public health message regarding physical activity (USDHHS, 1996a). After a day and a half of presentations and audience discussion, the panel of experts weighed the scientific evidence and drafted a statement, the NIH "Consensus Development Conference Statement":

> **A**ll Americans should engage in regular physical activity at a level appropriate to their capacity, needs, and interest. Children and adults alike should set a goal of accumulating at least 30 minutes of moderate-intensity physical activity on most, and preferably, all days of the week. Most Americans have little or no physical activity in their daily lives, and accumulating evidence indicates that physical inactivity is a major risk factor for cardiovascular disease. However, moderate levels of physical activity confer significant health benefits. Even those who currently meet these daily standards may derive additional health and fitness benefits by becoming more physically active or including more vigorous activity. For those with known cardiovascular disease, cardiac rehabilitation programs that combine physical activity with reduction in other risk factors should be more widely used. (NIH Consensus Development Panel on Physical Activity and Cardiovascular Health, USDHHS, 1996a)

In July 1994, the Office of the Surgeon General authorized the CDC to serve as lead agency for preparing the first Surgeon General's report on physical activity (USDHHS, 1996b). The report was developed collaboratively with representatives from the Office of the Surgeon General; the Office of Public Health and Safety; the Office of Disease Prevention; the National Heart, Lung, and Blood Institute of the NIH; the National Institute of Child Health and Human Development of the NIH; the American Alliance for Health, Physical Education, Recreation and Dance; the American College of Sports Medicine; the American Heart Association; and other professional associations.

The new recommendation used years of accumulated scientific evidence to present to the public a new message concerning physical activity. The message was designed to be short and concise: "To meet the minimum requirement all adults 18 years and older should accumulate 30 minutes or more of moderate-intensity physical activity on most, preferably all, days of the week" (USDHHS, 1996b).

The new physical activity message is important in several distinctive ways. First, for years physical educators and health promoters have confined the range of acceptable physical activities to organized events such as team and individual sports or to the structured exercise programs found at many health and fitness clubs. This structured form of physical activity requires planning and follow-through that does not fit the busy lives of many Americans. The new recommendation extends the traditional exercise fitness model to a paradigm that embraces the notion of *active living*, which emphasizes physical activity that can be integrated into everyday life (Burton, 1994). Active living broadens the definition of traditional physical activity to include nontraditional, unstructured, and unregulated activities, such as housework, recreational activities, taking the stairs instead of the elevator, parking farther from the entrance and walking the extra distance, or bicycling to work. The message is that being physically active is an achievable goal for all members of society. The new recommendations make it easier for sedentary people to become active.

Second, the new recommendations also provide the public with information concerning what specifically constitutes an appropriate level of minimal physical activity. To provide the public with clear examples, an agreement on standards for appropriate levels of physical activity was reached. The minimum amount of physical activity required for health benefits can be achieved through activities that are sufficient to burn approximately 150 kilocalories of energy per day or 1,000 kilocalories per week. The time needed to burn 150 kilocalories of energy depends primarily on the intensity of the activities chosen—the more vigorous the activity, the less time is needed. The recommended levels of physical activity allow people to participate in a variety of physical activities, including sports and physical conditioning, occupational activities, and chores around the home. People can now be persuaded to choose from activities that fit their interests as well as their daily schedules.

The recommendations were also framed as the "accumulation of physical activity" throughout the day. This allows people to participate in short bouts of physical activity that add up to 30 minutes of activity each day, thereby encouraging people who find it difficult to schedule long periods of time for physical activity. The new recommendation allows people to meet the requirements of regular physical activity while simultaneously satisfying other obligations during the day at work and at home. It also encourages people who have not been physically active for years to begin a physical activity program with greater expectations for success.

Promoting Physical Activity: Approaches for the New Millennium

During the last few years, a change in thinking has permeated the field of health promotion. Whereas earlier national health strategies emphasized the modification of individuals' behaviors, more recent conceptualizations stress the link between strategies to change individual health habits and efforts to strengthen the social and environmental supports within the local community.

A key event in the development of the new approaches to health promotion was the publication in 1974 of *A New Perspective on the Health of Canadians* (Lalonde, 1974). The Lalonde Report inspired a series of initiatives starting with the Alma Alta Declaration on Primary Health Care in 1978 (WHO, 1978) and the Healthy Cities Project in 1986 (WHO, 1986). In the 1980s the healthy cities movement emerged, with its primary goals to create substantial healthy environments through processes that allowed public and private organizations to work in partnership to change public policies (Ashton, 1991). The model of healthy cities is based on planned change to improve community life and seeks to make health promotion highly visible and supported by the entire community. As outlined in one such initiative, The Ottawa Charter for Health Promotion (WHO, 1986), health promotion was defined as the process of enabling people to increase control over and improve their own health. The critical task was to change the mechanisms of social control and empower communities to define health agendas for themselves. Today many communities have adopted healthy city initiatives, particularly in Europe and Canada. More recently, they have also begun to appear in the United States (Tsouros, 1990).

In January 2000, Donna Shalala, Secretary of the Department of Health and Human Services and U.S. Surgeon General David Satcher launched *Healthy People 2010,* the 10-year health goals for the first decade of the new millennium (USDHHS, 2000a). The third round of the nation's health objectives contains broad-reaching national health goals focusing on two major themes: increasing the quality and length of healthy life and the elimination of racial and ethnic disparities in health status. Many of the objectives are designed to reduce or eliminate illness, disability, and premature death. Others target broader issues, such as improving access to quality health care, strengthening public health services, and improving the availability and dissemination of health-related information.

A central theme of *Healthy People 2010* is that both public- and private-sector organizations must share responsibility for improving the nation's health (table 3.2). The most recent round of objectives has progressed from simply assessing health status to forecasting what is possible through preventive interventions directed at both individuals and the social and physical environments in which they live.

Table 3.2   Physical Activity Goals from *Healthy People 2010*

Goal	Baseline %	Goal %
Reduce the proportion of adults who engage in no leisure-time physical activity	40	20
Increase the proportion of adults who engage regularly, preferably daily, in moderate physical activity for at least 30 minutes per day	15	30
Increase the proportion of adults who engage in vigorous physical activity that promotes the development and maintenance of cardiorespiratory fitness three or more days per week for 20 minutes per occasion	23	30
Increase the proportion of adults who perform physical activities that enhance and maintain muscular strength and endurance	18	30
Increase the proportion of adults who perform physical activities that enhance and maintain flexibility	30	43
Increase the proportion of adolescents who engage in moderate physical activity for at least 30 minutes on five or more of the seven previous days	27	35
Increase the proportion of adolescents who engage in vigorous physical activity that promotes cardiorespiratory fitness three or more days per week for 20 or more minutes per session	65	85

(continued)

Table 3.2   *(continued)*

Goal	Baseline %	Goal %
Increase the proportion of the nation's public and private schools that require daily physical education for all students		
Middle school	17	25
Senior high school	2	5
Increase the proportion of adolescents who participate in daily school physical education	29	50
Increase the proportion of adolescents who spend at least 50% of school physical education class time being physically active	38	50
Increase the proportion of adolescents who view television 2 or fewer hours on a school day	57	75
Increase the proportion of the nation's public and private schools that provide access to their physical activity spaces and facilities for all persons outside normal school hours	Not available	75
Increase the proportion of work sites offering employer-sponsored physical activity and fitness programs	75	36
Increase the proportion of trips made by walking		
Adults	17	25
Children	31	50
Increase the proportion of trips made by bicycling		
Adults	0.6	2
Children	2.4	5

Adapted from USDHHS, 2000.

Conclusion

The physical activity habits of many Americans at the beginning of the 20th century were not very different from those seen in today's gymnasiums and health clubs (Whorton, 1982b). Then, as now, equipment such as rowing machines and a variety of stretching devices were readily available for workouts at the gymnasium or at home. Larger, more concentrated populations in the city meant a greater market for sport and exercise equipment. Health reformers interested in physical activity advanced the idea that the body could be altered and perfected, and by doing so, people could increase their energy and improve their lives (Green, 1986).

The decline in infectious disease and the rise in relative importance of noncommunicable, chronic diseases led to the development of a new health paradigm in the mid-20th century. This involved a recognition of the role of multiple causes of disease, and a focus on changing the health habits of individuals. In its origins, public health was essentially ecological, relating environmental and community characteristics to health and disease. Emphasis shifted from the earlier interest in environmental factors to individual-level factors, and research focused on behavioral and biological characteristics as risk factors for chronic diseases. In the 20th century, as the growing importance of chronic disease led to the search for new causal factors, physical activity became an important strategy for treating and preventing disease. Particularly during the second half of the century, the importance of physical activity was recognized. By the century's end, physical inactivity was recognized as a major risk factor for diseases of modern society, and physical activity was considered important for preventing disease and promoting good health. The latest round of national health objectives, *Healthy People 2010,* reflect the progression from simply assessing health status to proposing preventive interventions directed at both individuals and the social and physical environments in which they live.

By the close of the 20th century, the concepts associated with public health had come full circle. The "new public health movement," which emerged during the last few decades, is not new at all. Many of today's health-promotional strategies were first suggested by the early health reformers, such as Edwin Chadwick, Lemuel Shattuck, Dioclesian Lewis, and Bernarr Macfadden. What differs today, however, is a general acceptance of the role of physical activity in promoting good health and preventing disease. What also is different from years past is the presence of social conditions that have made us a sedentary society. Will the new century witness a return to a society of active living? The answer to this question lies in whether our key social institutions are positioned for change.

II

▼ ▼ ▼ ▼ ▼

Social Institutions

CHAPTER

4

The Changing American Family

As changes in family structure *have become apparent to intellectuals, politicians, and ordinary citizens, a national debate has arisen over their nature and significance. The most widely embraced interpretation of family change is one of alarm and condemnation. Analysts and social critics across the political spectrum routinely blame "the breakdown of the family" for a host of modern social ills, extending from the drug epidemic and increases in violent crime to teenage pregnancy, child abuse and neglect, the decline of educational standards, and even the birth dearth. But a competing and less pessimistic perspective emphasizes the resilience of families, which are adapting rather than disintegrating in the face of social change, and the resourcefulness of individuals, who are able to build meaningful interpersonal bonds amid the uncertainty and fragility of modern relationships. (Gerson, 1991:35)*

▼   ▼   ▼   ▼   ▼

One of the most visible and important social institutions in American society is the family. Terms such as *home* and *family ties* typically conjure up images of harmony, togetherness, and safe haven. The family represents a powerful influence on all its members. The family provides children with a set of values and norms that are important in the formation of attitudes and preferences. Adult partners rely on each other for emotional support and much-needed assistance in balancing work and family obligations. Particularly as the population ages, parents and grandparents often rely on their children to help them deal with the challenges they encounter during their senior years.

Starting in the 1960s, American society encountered new ways of thinking about the roles and functions of family members. Today, the traditional family form—working father, homemaker mother, and children living under the same roof—has been replaced by one in which both parents work, neither parent works, or, increasingly, there is a single parent. Likewise, large numbers of people will spend a good portion of their lives alone, apart from their families, as single young adults, as divorced singles, or as older adults who are living longer but without a spouse due to death or divorce. The changing family structure has also led to decreased reliance on the institutionalized codes of family behavior and places importance on individually negotiated arrangements between partners and among members of the family. The changing family structure has introduced ambiguities in the role expectations of family members. Some mothers feel pulled between pursuing full-time careers and devoting full-time attention to raising their children. Fathers feel stressed by job insecurity and fears about making enough money to support the family and helping their spouses take care of the children.

More than half the children born today will experience the divorce of their parents, with many of them also dealing with the changes associated with their custodial parents' remarriage (Hetherington, 1992). The number of broken families reflects the strains between the work and the family arenas and increasing ambiguity in parental roles. Trust has also long been viewed as the cornerstone of family affairs. The maxim pointed out by sociologist Bernard Barber (1983) nearly two decades ago, "If you cannot trust your family, then whom can you trust?" still holds a large ideological appeal for many of us. The truth of the matter, as pointed out by Stephanie Coontz in her provocative book *The Way We Never Were* (1992), is that there was never a golden age of family life, a time when all families were capable of meeting the needs of their members. Although the idyllic image of the family is likely more illusionary than real, many people long for the return to a time when family appeared to provide protection from the outside world. The many changes, both internal and external, to the family today have made any return to "the golden age," whether imaginary or real, impossible.

Changes in the family structure undoubtedly have also affected participation in physical activity by family members. Decisions to adopt or not to adopt physical activity depend in large part on social relationships among family members. The *family systems approach* focuses on the reciprocal social interactions and relationships among family members, with particular interest in the supportive functions they may play. Factors such as the extent to which family members are interconnected, the extent to which resources are given and received, and the qualities of relationships among family members are all important. A supportive family is responsible for providing economic and emotional support, role models for the internalization of values, and opportunities for involvement in sports, games, and other forms of physical activity.

In this chapter we discuss ways in which changes in both roles and structure of families play a critical part in decisions to initiate and sustain participation in physical activity. We first focus on implications for children's involvement in physical activity, followed by a consideration of the challenges faced by adults in the middle stages of their lives. Finally, we give our attention to the ramifications for the growing number of Americans who are living well into their senior years.

Socializing Children Into Physical Activity

The family is fundamental to children's socialization into physical activity habits. Families teach skills and inculcate beliefs that can help to shape important attitudes and behaviors associated with participation in physical activity. Children typically remain within the family unit for 18 years or more, during the formative years. Families can help develop appropriate attitudes in children so they will remain physically active for a lifetime.

The family provides an initial frame of reference from which to view both the social world and the world of physical activity. Physical activity is a fundamental focus from birth, and parents are the first people to take an active role in a child's physical development. After an infant is born, parents usually can hardly wait for the child to crawl and walk. Early learning by infants is directly tied to movement experiences. The desire to walk, skip, run, and play is apparent in most youngsters. Most parents are eager for their children to be involved in physical activity, although during adolescence and early adulthood, young people often develop habits of inactivity that are permitted to become part of daily living.

Social scientists offer two approaches to explain the role that parents play in transferring to their children the necessary values and habits for a lifelong commitment to participation in physical activity. The first focuses on parents' role-modeling positive physically active habits; the second, the importance of instilling perceptions of competence in their children.

Parents As Physical Activity Role Models

One explanation of parental influence on children's physical activity habits is rooted in the theoretical concept of *role modeling*. Modeling begins with exposure to the behavior of individuals whose judgments, opinions, and actions are important to the child. These behaviors are observed, internalized, and exhibited later in appropriate situations as a reflection of basic role behavior. Not surprisingly, children share many of the health habits of their parents, including those that are health risking. Studies that examine relationships between the health behaviors of parents (e.g., smoking, diet, dental care, seat belt use) and the behaviors of their children—referred to as familial resemblance—generally find positive correlations (Doherty & Campbell, 1988). Children of parents who smoke are likely to take up smoking, children of parents who drink begin to consume alcohol at early ages, and children of parents who are obese tend to be overweight. A study of 1,300 mother-daughter pairs conducted by the National Heart, Lung, and Blood Institute confirmed overweight mothers are more likely to have overweight daughters (Morrison et al., 1996).

It follows that children of parents who engage in regular physical activity should also be more active than children with sedentary parents. The research on the modeling of parents' physical activity behaviors has produced mixed results. Freedson and Evenson's (1991) study of the physical activity patterns of children and parents first validated the idea that children exhibit physical activity patterns much like those of their parents. In their study, 30 children, ranging from five to nine years of age, and one of each child's parents were studied using a Caltrac activity monitor, a device to measure physical activity that is considered a significant improvement over the self-report techniques used in many previous studies (Balogun, Martin, & Ciendenin, 1989). Data on child and parent physical activity were collected for three consecutive days, including one weekend day. Similar parent–child patterns occurred in 67 percent (father and child) and 73 percent (mother and child) of the families. In a second study, Yang, Telama, and Laakso (1996) examined parental influences on children's participation in sport and physical activity, with data collected over a 12-year period. In a sample of 1,881 boys and girls, the authors found fathers' physical activity levels were related to children's habitual physical activity. A father's physical activity level was also a significant predictor of physical activity for boys and girls 12 years later. During the follow-up period, participation in physical activity was higher in families with two active parents than in families with inactive parents.

Similar patterns were reported in data collected as part of the Framingham Children's Study. Parents and their four- to seven-year-old children were categorized as active or inactive according to whether they were above or below the median activity level for their reference group. The effect of the parents' activity levels on their children was stronger for active fathers than for active mothers, but the strongest impact occurred in families in which both parents were physically active. In fact, children with two active parents were six times more likely to be physically active than children with two inactive parents (Moore et al., 1991).

Parents Instilling Values of Competence

Parents play an important role in encouraging children to be physically active as they help children interpret experience and influence their self-perceptions, expectancies, and value of specific activities. A second approach used to explain children's participation in physical activity focuses on whether the child develops a belief that he or she will be successful. According to the model of *value expectancy*, parents need to communicate a belief in their child's success in performing the activity (Eccles & Harold, 1991). A child's activity choices are contingent on his or her expectations of success and focal personal traits such as competence needs, achievement needs, motivational orientation, personal goals, and the value of participating in various activities. A study of 75 toddlers and their mothers revealed the important role that mothers play in instilling the values important for their children's future endeavors such as participation in physical activity (Kelley, Brownwell, & Campbell, 2000). For two years while mothers taught their young children challenging tasks, their controlling behavior and feedback to the children were observed and carefully recorded. A follow-up one year later assessed whether the mothers' involvement had any lasting impact on their children's ability to perform easy and difficult achievement tasks. The results showed that the maternal feedback and control predicted the children's persistence and avoidance of mastery experiences. When mothers' feedback was corrective and positive early on, children seemed to take on higher levels of persistence. These findings suggest that if parents provide supporting feedback on their children's physical activity early in life, the children might be better equipped to overcome obstacles to maintaining the healthy habits of active living as they go through life.

The child's perception of competence is critical to the development of a strong attraction to any physical activity. The importance of developing competence has been borne out in several studies. For example, in a study of 81 fourth-grade children and their parents, Robert Brustad (1993) reported that children were more likely to participate in physical activity if they perceived that they had the ability to compete. Children who had a lower opinion of their abilities, lower performance records, and fewer expectations for future achievement were less likely to participate. In another study, Craig, Goldberg, and Dietz (1996) found that increasing a child's belief that he or she can be good at an activity increases the child's physical activity levels.

Similar results were reached in a study of 160 mothers and 123 fathers and their respective children enrolled in a soccer program (Babkes & Weiss, 1999). The children were asked to complete a self-report on their soccer competence, enjoyment levels, intrinsic motivation, and parents' influence on their participation. Mothers and fathers reported their own attitudes and behaviors toward their child's participation. Children who reported higher perceived-competence levels described their mothers and fathers as positive exercise role models. Children who perceived their fathers as more involved in their soccer playing and as exerting less pressure to perform also had more positive responses.

The task for physical activity researchers is not only to better articulate the mechanisms that underlie how parents mold their children's values and behaviors regarding physical activity but also to develop effective strategies to increase the likelihood that these opportunities are used to their full advantage. Several intervention programs designed to increase shared physical activity among family members (e.g., parents and children) have been attempted; however, they have produced disappointing results. For example, Baranowski and his colleagues (1990) put together an ambitious family physical activity program for children (fifth through seventh grades) and their families. The 14-week program was conducted at a health facility conveniently located in the community. Families participated in a number of physical activities, including exercising to music together and attending educational sessions about why physical activity is important. The program was not successful in improving physical activity rates, primarily because attendance rates were quite low, reaching only 20 percent. Most families cited many work and school conflicts as the chief barriers against consistent participation. In a second example of a parent–child physical activity program, similar problems existed. Nader and his colleagues (1989) reported disappointing attendance rates (60 percent during weekly sessions and 40 percent in maintenance sessions) and no substantial improvement in a variety of health parameters.

These findings point to a larger question. How can parents be effective in communicating values and beliefs regarding habits of physical activity if they cannot find enough time to participate themselves? How can they be effective role models for physical activity when they cannot find the time to spend with their children? Balancing work and family responsibilities often leaves little time for parents' own participation in physical activity. Families have had to adapt in order to earn a living and care for their children. Time studies show that when a mother enters the labor force, 40 to 50 hours of combined paid and family work are added to the family system per week (Schor, 1991). Several studies have linked the total hours spent in paid employment to marital and family strain and to feelings of role overload. Commitment to family and work pull couples in multiple directions, resulting in time demands that often far exceed the total available hours in the day. When both husbands and wives spend too much more time at work, there is less time for taking care of the family and for leisure activity. In a study of 1,240 households, Searle and Jackson (1985) found work commitments to be the most important barrier to leisure-time activity.

The fact remains that most parents simply do not meet the minimal standards of regular physical activity in their own lives. The National Children and Youth Fitness Study II (NCYFS) analysis of students enrolled in 57 schools in 19 states also provides confirmation that parents are not apt to participate in physical activity.

According to the report, more than 42 percent of mothers and 48 percent of fathers of children in grades 1 through 4 did not participate in moderate or vigorous physical activity (Ross & Gilbert, 1985). Only 28 percent of mothers and 30 percent of fathers reported exercising three or more times per week. Even when parents are physically active, it is questionable whether they perform such activities in front of the children. The NCYFS reported that 58 percent of mothers and 61 percent of fathers did not exercise with their child in a typical week, and only 10.7 percent of mothers and 11.3 percent of fathers exercised on a regular basis with their children (Ross, Pate, Caspersen, Damberg, & Svilar, 1987). Fathers in particular are often absent at the times children are physically active, thereby minimizing the possibility that fathers are models for children's physical activity (Baranowski et al., 1978). Although many parents try supporting children's achievements by attending plays, ball games, and recitals, one study suggests that children have lost from 10 to 12 hours of parental time since the 1960s (Fuchs, 1988).

Sport sociologist Jay Coakley (1998) suggested that there has been significant change in what it means to be a good parent: Good parents are able to account for the whereabouts of their children 24 hours a day. One reason that we have more adult-organized recreational activities for children today is that such activities provide adult supervision and safety. Fifty years ago, it was possible to tell children to go out and play unsupervised, even in urban areas. Today, many urban and suburban communities are no longer safe for children. Over the past several decades, many parents have sought organized sport programs in which their children can be supervised by adults, often preferably not themselves.

Taken together, these studies point to the difficulty in staying connected through family participation in physical activity. Because so few parents are active—and even fewer of them participate with their children—the importance of parents in instilling positive habits of physical activity in their children may be overstated. Involvement in physical activities such as competitive sports are important for some children and their parents, but the teenage years in particular are often a time away from activities shared with parents.

Overinvolvement of Parents

Although some parents have difficulty in finding time to support their children's physical activity, others take interest in their children's physical activity to the other extreme. Only decades ago, children and adolescents were left alone to pursue their own forms of recreation. Today, adults have increasingly taken charge of young people's recreational activities, and children are often under considerable pressure to compete and to win. Parents often become so emotionally involved with their children's sports that they act in ways that damage relationships with children (Martens, 1996). While many parents think their actions are forms of encouragement, from the children's point of view, these actions are seen as forms of significant pressure. Family relationships may be damaged when children believe that their parents' attention to them depends too much on their playing sports and being good athletes. Fathers are likely to place greater demands on their sons than on their daughters to be successful in physical activity, especially organized sports. Sociologist Michael Messner's interviews with former athletes detail the dilemma between fathers and sons. Many men recalled the feeling that staying involved in sports was the only way to stay connected with their fathers. As boys, they yearned to receive attention from their fathers, but they found that the bonds they developed through sport did not carry over into nonsport settings (Messner, 1992).

The negative effects of parental pressures are likely reflected in the attrition rates from competitive youth sports. Although the participation in sports has doubled since 1975 for children up to 13 years of age, the number of participants beyond this age, especially in the adolescent years, steadily declines thereafter at an annual rate of 22 to 37 percent (Fernandez-Balboa, 1993). A large number of children participating in organized sport in any given year are likely to drop out. A survey of 10,000 boys and girls, sponsored by the Athletic Footwear Association (1990), reported steady declines in organized sport participation among adolescents. The most important reason for playing sport, according to the survey, was to have fun, but for many youngsters, it appears that they are a long way from having fun. Such declines in participation may be attributed in part to a part-time job or other after-school activities, but a large number of unsuccessful experiences and increased pressure from parents likely fit into the equation. Today, many youngsters find sport participation a very stressful, unhappy, and unrewarding experience. Because of the emphasis placed on winning by coaches and parents, a strong tendency exists to give playing time only to the most talented performers. Lost in the shuffle are the less-talented youngsters, who will be turned off to physical activity long before they ever find out the pleasures and health benefits of participation.

The worst problems of children's sports are caused by parental pressure, particularly when parents project onto the child the goals they wanted to achieve but failed to. Because competitive recreational activities more often reflect adults', rather than children's, needs, they add to children's stress and contribute to the "new family imbalance" (Elkind, 1994).

The new notion of childhood athletic competence has given some parents an opportunity for satisfying some of their own unmet needs through involvement in their children's sport activities. These parents immerse themselves in their children's youth sport program so that they don't have to deal with their own problems, such as their own bad marriages or work situations.

Disconnected Teenagers

For many young people, the adolescent years are associated with increased conflict with parents and with fewer family interactions than at earlier or later ages. Adolescence is a time when search for self-identity and independence are central issues, and conflicts between children and parents are commonplace. Adolescence represents the period of transition from childhood to adulthood, a time when lifestyles are being examined and adopted and when possibilities for the self are being accepted or rejected. Leisure activities among young people allow them to try out different kinds of personal identities, experiment with different kinds of relationships, and explore their emotional capacity. This period also is characterized by independence from the family and a great deal of exploration and experimentation with health-compromising behaviors, such as the use of alcohol, tobacco, and drugs. More than three quarters of American youth have tried at least a few puffs of a cigarette before age 18, and the prevalence of regular smoking among high school students increased from 27.5 percent in 1991 to 36.4 percent in 1997 (USDHHS, 1998).

The organization of adolescents' daily lives is different from that of their parents. Young adolescents have a great deal of free time to cultivate leisure involvements outside the family. School typically affords them a substantial amount of time for interaction with peers, and young adolescents have large amounts of time after school and on weekends for discretionary activities, many of which are carried out with their peers away from home and family. As youngsters progress from the late elementary grades through adolescence, peers (a group of individuals roughly the same ages who are linked by common interests) take on increasing prominence as a source of social support. Adolescents spend most of their waking hours with peers, either in school or during weekend and leisure activities. Attempting to carve out an identity distinct from both the younger world being left behind and the adult world still out of bounds, adolescents set their own standards in clothing, music, and physical activity habits.

Two basic reasons explain the influence of peer groups. First, peer groups are based on common interests that represent issues critical in the life of adolescents. Second, they provide guidelines for vital aspects of life. Peer groups are voluntary, and as such, they hold the threat of expulsion: If you don't do what the others want, they will make you an outsider. In a study of 418 adolescents aged 12 to 15, Smith (1999) systematically examined the importance of perceptions of peer relationship, physical self-worth, and physical activity motivation. The model he used was grounded in Harter's theoretical perspective, which proposed that perceptions of peer relationships would predict physical activity motivation (Harter, 1987). Smith's results illustrated the importance of peer relationships to adolescent motivation to participate in physical activity.

Shared physical activity with parents may be more difficult. Larson, Gillman, and Richards (1997) examined the shared "active recreation experiences" among fathers, mothers, and their young adolescents. Each was asked to carry a pager and a booklet of self-report forms for one week. When signaled, each family member recorded the nature of the activity in which he or she was engaged and answered the following questions: Do you wish you had been doing something else? How much choice did you have in this activity? How happy are you performing this activity? Adolescents reported the lowest levels of positive experiences in shared physical activities with their parents. The authors concluded that adolescents' leisure-time experiences are more accurately defined as with their peers and not with their parents. John Kelly (1983), a leisure study specialist, offered an interesting explanation for why children and parents drift apart. He contended that the role of physical activity in meeting the needs of parents and children differs too drastically for any attempts to participate together. Parents, unlike their teenaged children, are at a point in their lives when the desire for excitement and sensation seeking is low. Parents don't feel the compulsion to exert individuality through their leisure-time activities. In fact, they often resist and discourage adolescents who attempt to do so.

Although their interests may be different, it is still important for parents to stay connected with their teenage children. Brenda Robertson (1999), for example, examined the importance of family stability and lack of sense of attachment to parents on the propensity for youngsters to become involved in delinquent behavior as part of their leisure-time experiences. The author found that a lack of shared family leisure experiences and a perceived lack of parental interest in the teenagers increased the likelihood of male adolescents to engage in delinquent pursuits as part of their leisure-time activity. These findings highlight the importance of parents as facilitators for their adolescents' leisure. Strategies to bring parents back into the lives of their children are critical as families today are drifting apart instead of coming together.

Protective Effects of Marriage

Married people are typically considered to have a health advantage over the unmarried. Marital status has been shown to have important effects on health outcomes. Beginning with Emile Durkheim's (1897) evidence that unmarried men and women are more likely to commit suicide than those who are married, numerous cross-sectional, retrospective, and longitudinal or prospective studies have shown a lower incidence of many psychological and physical disorders among the married (Gove & Umberson, 1985). Mortality rates are generally lower for married than unmarried people and married people often engage in lower rates of health-damaging behaviors such as excessive drinking and poor eating habits (House, Robbins, & Metzner, 1982).

Married people are typically considered to have a two-pronged health advantage over their single counterparts. First, the supportive relationship, social ties, and intimacies that come with marriage influence health by promoting the psychological well-being of each spouse. Marital relationships can provide relatively stable, coherent, and regulated environments in which partners' support for one another influences the initiation and maintenance of health-promoting behaviors. Wickrama, Lorenz, and Conger (1997) tested this concept in a longitudinal study of marital quality and physical illness. More than 300 couples answered questions about three categories of marital quality (marital happiness, marital satisfaction, and marital stability), physical health (number of self-reported symptoms), and health-risk behaviors (eating a balanced diet, maintaining a healthy body weight, getting regular exercise, and using drugs and tobacco). Both the initial level of and the change in marital quality for husbands and wives correlated with the initial level of and change in physical health and health-risk behaviors. Of particular interest to our discussion, increases in physical activity were correlated with marriages judged to be happy, satisfying, and stable.

A second view of the protective effects of marriage focuses on the creation of social controls and regulation within the marriage relationship. Sociologist Debra Umberson (1992) suggested that marital relationships promote an external regulation of health behavior that deters activities that are detrimental to health. People who are concerned about the well-being of their spouses have a major stake in the other's good health. Her model of *external social control* is based on a concept of the consequences of commitment first advanced by psychologist Henry Becker (1960). According to Becker, an individual's decision to get married represents a new commitment to health behaviors; the future of the marriage may be at stake if the individual chooses to engage in behaviors that are contradictory to this commitment. Social interactions with one's spouse result in a sense of commitment and responsibility to one another and thereby increase positive health behaviors such as regular visits to the doctor or increased participation in physical activity.

Umberson (1992) tested her hypothesis in a study of 3,000 adults participating in the Americans' Changing Lives survey. She found that while there was a relationship between social control and health behaviors, it differed for wives and husbands. Married men were more likely than married women to report that their spouses attempted to control their health. When considering traditional gender role socialization, this should not be too surprising. Women assume nurturing roles within the marriage and are inclined to oversee their spouses' health behaviors. Although women may have exerted greater external social control over their husbands' health, interestingly enough, Umberson found it did not translate into increases in physical activity by men. In fact, among the couples who stayed married over the study's three-year period, it was the married women who experienced greater increases in physical activity.

Perhaps the differences can be understood relative to the previous socialization experiences or lack thereof in leisure-time physical activity. Married women may need a highly supportive husband who is an active sport participant and who encourages his wife in this form of recreation. That is, married women spend their leisure time with their husbands or, in some cases, with husbands and children. A majority of women in Umberson's study indicated that they were dependent on their husband's approval of their leisure-time activities. Spousal endorsement is critical to the leisure-time opportunities and choices of many women. The sharing of leisure may be different for married men, who are far more likely than their wives to have retained some regular leisure time spent away from home and family.

It is noteworthy that not all studies have found that the beneficial effects of marital status on physical activity apply only to women. For example, the data concerning sedentary lifestyles from the NHANES III study reported by Crespo and colleagues (2000) suggest that married men may have the advantage with regard to participation in leisure-time physical activity. They found that married men, especially non-Hispanic white and black men, reported the lowest incidence of sedentary living when compared with formerly married and never-married men. For women, however, marital status was not related to lower levels of physical inactivity. The authors suggested that many mothers' opportunities for leisure-time physical activity are often severely constrained by the social expectations incumbent in their roles as both wives and mothers.

Mixed Blessings of Parenthood

The transition to parenthood propels young adults into the expanded roles of spouse and parent. As sociologist Georg Simmel (1964) pointed out in his analysis of the differences between dyads and triads, such as when a pair of adults adds an infant to the family, roles and responsibilities change dramatically. Despite the complexity and importance of parenting, people typically received little or no formal instruction on becoming parents and they received inadequate support for carrying out the job. Parents must learn to manage multiple relationships within the family system and incorporate social systems outside the family including occasional recreation and medical services. Often this is accomplished by trial and error.

The time commitment involved in raising children presents additional obstacles to participation in physical activity, particularly for women. Positive attitudes and intentions toward physical activity may not be enough for many mothers. Verhoef and Love (1994) identified the major perceived barriers to exercise in an analysis of more than 1,000 women. Verhoef and Love compared mothers to women without children, and although the two groups did not differ in their desire to participate in physical activity, they differed on a number of perceived obstacles to participation, including lack of time because of family obligations, support from family or friends, and support from one's spouse (table 4.1).

Clearly, for the mothers, lack of time was a major barrier to exercising. The average number of hours per week that mothers spent on their daily activities was 87.5, compared with 54.4 for women without children. Mothers indicated an average of 8.3 hours per week in which they were entirely free to do whatever they wanted, compared with 18.7 for nonmothers. Major barriers to exercise, particularly for young mothers, were lack of support and lack of time, indicating that young mothers were more isolated than older mothers and women without children (figure 4.1). They also concluded that it was motherhood itself, rather than the number and ages of children, that created the obstacle to regular physical activity.

Juliet Schor (1991) emphasized the tremendous time pressures on mothers who work full-time, describing them as mothers constantly on the go who in reality have two jobs, one at the workplace and one at home. In her landmark study, sociologist Arlie Hochschild (1989) took us into the homes of contemporary two-career parents to observe how women take on "the second shift." She found that in only 20 percent of dual-career families do men share housework equally with their wives. Women in her study revealed that they accept this inequity in order to keep the peace and as a result often suffer chronic exhaustion and more frequent illnesses.

Women are more likely to invest more of themselves in their families than do their husbands. They are more likely to take greater responsibility for taking care of the children and spend considerably more time doing housework. Consequently, it is not surprising that women should find it more difficult to find time to be physically active. Women, upon marriage, generally assume the greater portion of domestic responsibility, decreasing their free time, while men's free time is essentially unchanged. Green and Hebron (1988)

Table 4.1   Barriers to Exercise Perceived by Mothers and Women Without Children

Perceived barrier	Mothers (%)	Women without children (%)
Lack of time because of work	46.4	44.3
Lack of time because of family obligations	63.3	11.7*
Lack of time because of other obligations	32.7	24.6
Lack of energy, too tired	48.4	45.8
Lack of athletic ability	19.0	18.2
Lack of self-discipline or willpower	43.9	46.7
Lack of self-confidence	13.5	13.1
Lack of interest in exercise	24.3	23.0
Dislike of physical discomfort of exercise	9.7	9.9
Self-consciousness, feeling ill at ease	10.6	11.2
Fear of injury	6.3	9.4
Long-term illness, disability, or injury	9.0	9.7
Lack of exercise programs, leaders, or accessible facilities	9.5	9.4
Cost	26.7	22.2
Lack of an exercise partner	30.1	27.3
Lack of support from family or friends	14.0	6.8*
Lack of baby-sitting services	24.7	0.0
Lack of support from spouse	10.5	5.6*
Enough physical activity in job	13.1	2.1
Enough physical activity in looking after children	19.2	0.7*
Enough physical activity in homemaking	19.8	4.7*

* $p < .05$.

From Verhoef & Love, 1994.

corroborated these findings in their study of marriage and leisure patterns among 700 women in England. Married men were regarded as having more free time than married women. Focus groups of Hispanic women recounted a great lack of cooperation from male companions (Mein & Winkleby, 1998). Many husbands and boyfriends were described as unsupportive of the women's interest in

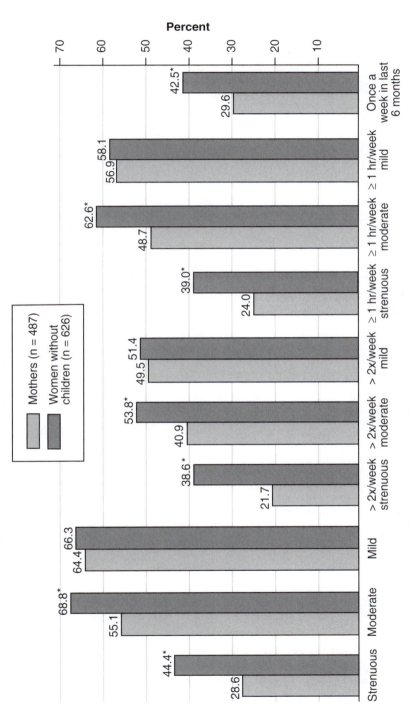

Figure 4.1 Exercise level among mothers and women without children.

*p < .01

From Verhoef & Love, 1994.

physical activity. The women felt that the multiple demands on their time and lack of partners' assistance in taking care of the children or household responsibilities were the chief obstacles to their participation in physical activity. The findings from these studies suggest that for women, life transitions associated with marriage, work, and children significantly reduce the available time for leisure pursuits (Deem, 1987).

The lack of change in physical activity patterns among fathers should not be too surprising. The organization of mothers' lives is more diverse than fathers'. In the majority of two-parent families, women are now employed either part-time or full-time. But irrespective of their employment status, most mothers are still viewed as holding primary responsibility for the day-to-day care of children and family. They spend much more of their time engaged in housework and care for family members. Even in shared leisure moments, mothers are more often called upon to put aside their own leisure interests and put the needs of others before their own. Many mothers stay home during the child-rearing years. Data from Statistics Canada (1990) indicated that 42.7 percent of mothers with children younger than three and 34.9 percent of mothers with children ages three to five are at home full-time. But even "stay-at-home moms" often find difficulty in participating in regular physical activity. In the *Well-Being of Canadians: Highlights of the 1988 Campbell Survey*, 53 percent of full-time homemakers were classified as inactive according to their daily energy expenditure on various leisure activities (Stephens & Craig, 1990).

Spending time with children at the expense of participation in one's own physical activity is particularly problematic in communities where opportunities for participation in physical activity along with child care options may be limited. Horne (1994), for example, in her study of more than 600 rural homemakers with preschool children, found that 25 percent of the women who were able to participate in physical activity once per week or less indicated that baby-sitting was a crucial barrier. For stay-at-home mothers, barriers to participation in physical activity included lack of support from spouse or partner, lack of support from other mothers in the community, and cost.

In all these cases, it appears that women face a dilemma in balancing family responsibilities with adequate attention to regular physical activity. The multiple commitments of marriage compete for time and energy, resulting in fatigue, strain, and irritability, which render many parents unable to fulfill marital and work roles and still have time for their children.

The physical activity experiences that were suspended during the raising of children resume for some parents when the children leave home. For example, Deborah Bialeschki's (1994) study of 53 mothers who were reaching the end of "active mothering" found that the women began pursuing external activities and that self and home took on equal weights as they began to review their lives. Mothers who made a transition from "active" to "inactive" motherhood appreciated the fact that their lives once again belonged to them. Emptynesters, as they are popularly labeled, experience a shift from leisure pursuits connected with family to activities outside the family, with friends, neighbors, and co-workers (Horne, 1994). The changing family context, as Horne described it, shows a predictable but curvilinear relationship with available leisure time (that is, greater amounts of leisure time before children arrive and after they leave home).

Marriage and the Search for Shared Leisure Time

Family counselors point to shared leisure activities as an important component of marital happiness. A less-understood pressure on married couples is associated with leisure-time physical activities pursued by one partner independent of the other. Consider, for example, the development by one partner of a serious commitment to running. It is common for a highly committed runner to run some 40 to 60 miles a week in training and even more when preparing for competitive events. Anecdotal accounts and case studies of runners depict a highly regulated training regimen of two to three hours a day and a meticulously planned schedule that includes aerobic workouts, speed work, attention to diet, and long weekend runs.

When work and family responsibilities curtailed the amount of running, serious runners developed feelings of unhappiness related to missing their workouts (Yair, 1990). The strong commitment to physical activity in some cases disrupts family events and is a source of significant family strain (Barrell, Chamberlain, Evans, Holt, & Mackean, 1989). Examples of family conflict emerge in cases where one spouse makes physical activity a priority and the other one does not. Sacks (1981) reported case studies in which individuals became obsessed with the idea of exercising; neglected social, work, or family responsibilities in order to engage in exercise; or grew despondent when deprived of exercise. The failure of leisure-time roles should be added to economic failure and failure in parenting responsibilities among the causes of divorce in contemporary America.

Family conflicts concerning nonshared physical activity can be stressful, perhaps more so for male partners of female exercisers. Rudy and Estok (1990) interviewed more than 300 female runners, and the women reported numerous problems with their spouses. The authors concluded that male spouses might assign a more negative meaning to the running activities of their wives and cited one spouse who said his wife's running meant she valued running more than saving her energy for family activities.

Conflicts over exercise may mask symptoms of another problem, that of a strained marital relationship. Fick, Goff, and Oppliger (1996) found that runners who reported high leisure–family conflict and low spousal support also scored lower on a measure of general family functioning; they concluded that leisure–family conflict may indicate more global family dysfunctions. Runners who are actively committed members of their families do not view the time and energy spent on running in themselves a significant source of conflict.

In a health promotion effort, Burke and colleagues (1999) devised a program aimed at reevaluating attitudes toward health and social support provided by partners in order to address the weight gain and physical inactivity found among many married couples. Thirty-four couples completed the 16-week program. Self-efficacy in diet and physical activity and the ability to identify barriers to healthy behaviors increased significantly in the program. Physical activity in the exercise group increased by 50 minutes of brisk walking per week, although this difference was not statistically significant. Although such programs prove that health promotion efforts can achieve short-term changes in exercise behaviors, they do little to abate the problems that confront many married couples—that of their relationships.

Dissolution of Marriage

No single event negatively impacts the American family more than divorce. Today it is estimated that 5 out of 10 first marriages will end in divorce. Each year 1.2 million children move from two-parent to one-parent families. More than one out of three children born in the United States experience the effects of divorce before reaching 18 years of age (Hetherington, 1992). Divorce typically results in disruption of daily family routines and the diminished economic situation of the mother, usually the custodial parent. The experience of divorce creates new responsibilities within the family. The role of the "new single parent" expands from daily management of the home and children to include being the major financial provider for the family. The first year after divorce is the most difficult in terms of financial and emotional crises. Despite the potential significance of transitions in marital status for health, few attempts have been made to study the role of divorce in disrupting family members' patterns of physical activity.

Divorce does not necessarily mean the end of a couple's relationship. In about half of divorced couples, ex-spouses maintain at least monthly contact. About four of every five divorced people remarry, with an average lapse between divorce and remarriage of only three years. The divorce rate of remarried people without children is the same as that of first marriages. Those who bring children into their new marriage, however, are more likely to divorce again. Does it make a difference which parent is absent from the home? In an attempt to answer this question, Furstenburg, Morgan, and Allison (1987) studied noncustodial parents and the nature of their contacts with their children. The authors concluded that noncustodial fathers tended to be more social and recreational with their children than custodial fathers or noncustodial mothers. Custodial mothers are left with the day-to-day work, such as parental discipline, homework assistance, and medical care. In a study that included single-parent status as a variable, participation in sports-club activity was higher for children from single-parent homes than for children with passive fathers (that is, fathers who did not engage in much physical activity). The authors concluded that in regard to a child's increased likelihood of participation in physical activity, having no father in the home is better than having a father who is not physically active (Yang, Telama, & Laasko, 1996).

It is possible that increases in stress that often accompany changes in marital status have a powerful effect on health behaviors including physical activity. Few studies have focused on the role marital transition plays in disrupting patterns of physical activity among family members. Two studies, though, attempted to describe the relationship between marital transition and participation in physical activity by spouses. In the first study, Umberson (1992), using a national two-wave panel survey (data collected at two different times), studied the consequences of a shift from a married to unmarried state on a variety of health behaviors. She found that the shift to being unmarried was associated with higher tobacco and alcohol consumption and greater reported weight loss in men and reduced hours of sleep per night and greater reported weight loss in women. However, her data revealed that the altered marital status had no impact on participation in physical activity.

In a second study, King and colleagues (King, Kiernan, Ahn, & Wilcox 1998) developed a more sophisticated design, which followed 302 women and 256 men over a 10-year period. Although most people reported a reduction in physical activity during the 10 years, changes in physical activity of men and women who went from married to single were not appreciably different from those who stayed married.

The conclusions of these studies should be taken with much caution. The authors in both studies acknowledged that their analyses did not allow the measurement of the acute effects of a marital transition, including changes occurring before and after the formal transition itself. Also, marital transition in both studies was defined as shifting from married to unmarried. This strategy did not separate individuals experiencing divorce from those whose spouses had died.

Although social relationships and their positive impact on health have been extensively studied and documented, the relationship between marital status and health-promoting behaviors such as physical activity remains unclear. Studies attempting to connect marital status with levels of participation in physical activity have had mixed results. Some have pointed to a positive impact; others, a negative impact; still others suggest that gender makes a difference. The problem with many of these studies has been the failure to go beyond the measurement of identification of married or not married and effectively measure the quality of social interaction experienced within and outside marriage. Clearly much more attention to the relationship between divorce and the physical activity habits of family members is needed.

Perils of Single-Parent Families

The dramatic increase in the number of single-parent households has created a two-tiered system of child rearing: two-parent households, in which domestic and economic roles are shared by two adults, and single-parent households, in which the entire economic and domestic burden is borne by one parent. The increase in divorce fueled the growth in one-parent families in the 1960s and 1970s, whereas today childbearing outside of marriage also contributes greatly to the growth in single-parent families (Bianchi, 1995).

Single-parent families are not new in our society. At the turn of the century, almost one out of every four children lived in single-parent homes, but this was largely due to the death of a parent, the result of a fatal illness or complications of childbirth. Today, single parenting is largely the result of divorce, separation, or bearing children out of wedlock. Birth rates to unmarried women increased dramatically from 25 per 1,000 women in 1975 to 45 per 1,000 in 1995 (CDC, 1998).

Parenting alone is more difficult and more stressful with fewer supports and fewer resources than parenting with a partner. Children from single-parent families are more likely to drop out of school, to become delinquent, to be poor as adults, to divorce, and to bear children outside of marriage themselves. Not all single-parent homes are headed by women, and even the term *single parent* may be a bit misleading. Contrary to popular perceptions, a substantial number of "single-parent" households include other relatives (e.g., a grandparent), nonrelatives, or a cohabiting partner who is not the child's parent. During the 1980s, father–child families increased faster than mother–child families. Almost one in five single-parent households is headed by a father, although only 3 percent of all children lived in this type of household: 218,000 children live with custodial fathers, and of these, 165,000 live with widowed fathers (Manning & Smock, 1997; U.S. Bureau of the Census, 1992c).

Poverty often creates challenges for single-parent families. Single parents are much more likely to be poor than otherwise similar married parents. Single-parent households are five times (53.4 percent) more likely to be classified below the poverty line as compared with two-parent households (10.4 percent) (U.S. Bureau of the Census, 1992a).

Economic disadvantage in conjunction with the absence of another adult in the household increases health risks for children. According to the National Center for Health Statistics (1991), problems in school performance (e.g., repeating grades, difficulties that require parent conferences, and school suspensions) were twice as common in single-parent families. Children in single-parent families also had a greater risk for asthma, and their overall health vulnerability score was elevated when compared with children from two-parent families (Dawson, 1991). Angel and Lowe-Worobey (1988), in their analysis of two national data sets, found that single mothers reported poorer overall physical health for their children than women in intact marriages.

There is some indication that physical activity may also be limited in single-parent families, but here too the research literature is very limited. In one example, McKenzie and colleagues (McKenzie, Sallis, Nader, Broyles, & Nelson, 1992) studied the physical activity patterns of a large bi-ethnic cohort of four-year-old children from low- to middle-socioeconomic-class families. Only 50 percent of the non-Hispanic white families and 60 percent of the Mexican-American families were headed by two married adults. Trained observers coded the behavior of 351 children (150 non-Hispanic and 201 Mexican-American boys and girls) during two 60-minute home visits and two unstructured recesses at 63 different preschools. The Mexican-American children were less active than non-Hispanic children at home and during recess, and both groups spent significant amounts of time in activities characterized by sitting and lying. More than 51 percent of time at home and nearly 26 percent at recess involved sedentary activities. In a second study of 120 healthy African-American and white children living in Birmingham, Alabama, youngsters from single-parent homes participated in more sedentary activities than youngsters from two-parent families. Lindquist, Reynolds, and Goran (1999) found that children from single-parent homes watched about 30 minutes more television per day than children residing with two parents. However, these same children reported more participation in physical activity than children residing with two parents by almost one day per week. The authors concluded that the increased amount of physical activity found among the children may reflect decreased amounts of parental supervision in both single-parent and two-parent homes, which is likely to lead to both increased hours of television watching and physical activity performed outside the home.

Same-Sex Parents

Gay and lesbian parents are often ignored by those who study family structure. Yang (1998) estimates that 31 percent of lesbians and 23 percent of gay men have children younger than 18 living at home;

Bozett (1989) estimates that 1 to 3 million gay fathers and 1.5 million lesbian mothers are rearing children in the United States. In some cases, children may have been from prior heterosexual relationships of one or both parents, adoption, heterosexual relations for the purpose of conception, or artificial insemination.

Gay men and lesbians, like their heterosexual counterparts, share the desire for stable, emotionally supportive, long-lasting family relationships. The sources of support, however, differ between same-sex and heterosexual family structures. For example, one study showed that for lesbian families, social support had a greater positive impact when it came from one of two sources: family members living within the household and supportive friends. The important role of friends in the lives of gay families was noted in a study of 50 same-sex male couples (Kurdek & Schmitt, 1987). Using a 16-item "perceived social support" scale, friends were scored significantly higher than family members on emotional support. These studies suggest that the social support from family in the home and friends are crucial to gay and lesbian families because the traditional social support mechanisms (e.g., parents) are often closed. Biological parents often have a difficult time in accepting the sexual orientation of their children and grow estranged from them, although the lack of relationship with biological family members may be overstated. Becker and Robison (1997) reported that when lesbian women were given a hypothetical situation in which they were no longer able to care for themselves and asked to identify who would take care of them, an equal number of respondents indicated their partner as indicated a biological family member.

Gay and lesbian households face many of the same struggles typical of heterosexual marriages, involving the usual concerns of housework, money, careers, and problems with family members (Badgett, 1998). In addition, gay and lesbian couples frequently encounter enormous political and social barriers in their pursuit of routine family relations. For example, there has been strong public opposition to permitting same-sex couples to legally adopt children. A study of national election trends from 1992 to 1994 showed that more than two thirds of the public disapproves of adoption rights for gay or lesbian partners (Yang, 1998).

The legal status of the homosexual family has been the subject of much legal debate. Lesbian and gay men have advocated for the inclusion of same-sex couples in the definition of the family. Some support for the concept came from the legal opinion from the New

York State Supreme Court in the *Braschi v. Stahl Associates* (1989) case. The presiding judge stated that the government's definition of family "should find its foundations in the reality of family life" and offered criteria for a definition of the family that did not require consideration of sex. These included: (1) the degree of emotional commitment and interdependence, (2) financial interdependence, (3) cohabitation, (4) longevity, and (5) exclusivity.

For the most part, politicians and judges have not been as supportive. The courts are often unwilling to recognize same-sex couples and unlikely to award custody of children to a homosexual parent in contested divorce proceedings. The passing of the Defense of Marriage Act by Congress in 1996 prohibits same-sex couples from marrying and claiming federal spousal benefits such as Social Security. While nearly half of Americans (48 percent) support equal rights for gays in terms of Social Security benefits, there is strong public opposition to same-sex parenting rights, particularly in the area of the legal adoption of children (Yang, 1998). A recent ruling by the Vermont Supreme Court gave the first real legal breakthrough for advocates of gay marriage. The court ruling that gay and lesbian couples are entitled to the same protections and benefits given to heterosexual married couples legitimatized civil unions. A host of conservative groups have condemned the decision as "immoral" and "dangerous" (Rosin, 1999). Gay and lesbian activists are likely to consider this long-awaited decision their most important legal victory to date. While they have won scattered decisions concerning specific partnership benefits, never before has a court affirmed that gay families are an essential part of a stable, mainstream family. A recent survey conducted by Princeton Survey Research Associates suggests a slow movement to supporting the idea, but currently the gay or lesbian family structure is far from being warmly received (Yang, 1998).

Lesbian and gay families also face significant obstacles in the area of health care that heterosexual families do not. A number of studies point to the nonacceptance of homosexuality among health care providers. In a survey of members of a California medical society, for example, more than 40 percent of the health care providers indicated a level of discomfort in treating homosexual patients (Mathews, Booth, & Turner, 1986). Similarly, a study of nurse educators revealed that one fourth of the respondents viewed lesbianism as wrong or immoral. More than half of the nurses indicated that a lesbian lifestyle was not a natural expression of human sexuality, and many suggested they should undergo some treatment for their lifestyle orientation (Randall, 1989). One third of the nurses felt that they would have difficulty conversing with a lesbian.

In a more recent survey of the membership of the American Association of Physicians for Human Rights, the majority of respondents reported instances of antigay bias affecting medical care (Schatz & O'Hanlan, 1994). Notably, 67 percent reported knowledge of lesbians and gays who had received substandard care or been denied care because of their sexual orientation. Fifty-two percent had observed colleagues providing reduced care or denying care to patients because of their sexual orientation, and 88 percent reported hearing colleagues make disparaging remarks about lesbian, gay, and bisexual parents.

Studies of health care trainees and professionals have demonstrated that their level of empathy and caring is negatively affected by the knowledge that the person being treated is homosexual, in part because of stigma associated with HIV infection and AIDS (O'Hare, Williams, & Ezoviski, 1996). Such prominent attitudes among some health professionals also make it difficult for gay men and lesbians to access appropriate medical care.

It would seem logical that negative attitudes in the delivery of health care to gay men and lesbians would have a negative impact on health habits such as participating in regular physical activity. Unfortunately, here we do not have good estimates. Gathering statistical information on gay and lesbian activities is a daunting task. It is difficult to survey individuals who often feel compelled to conceal their identities for fear of discrimination.

Stereotypes persist regarding the perceived importance of physical activity among the gay and lesbian community. One such example is the belief that lesbians, by rejecting the traditional female values, are less likely to be concerned with body image and choose not to participate in physical activity. For example, Herzog and colleagues (1992) reported lesbians to have higher weights and lower drive for thinness than heterosexual women. Likewise, in Gettleman and Thompson's (1993) comparison of gay men, lesbians, and heterosexual men and women, lesbians and heterosexual men were less concerned with their own physical activity and less dissatisfied with their bodies. It is likely that all women may be influenced by the cultural pressure to be thin, but the effect might be most pronounced in heterosexual women.

Understanding the physical activity habits of gay men and lesbians awaits the gathering and analyzing of good research data. One such effort is contained in *Lesbian Health Initiative,* a project under-taken by a Houston-based nonprofit organization created to pro-mote health and well-being in the lesbian community. With the as-sistance of more than 20 local lesbian organizations and businesses, Becker and Robison (1994) surveyed 612 lesbians. Using self-report measures of health, they found nearly half of the women reported being in excellent health and only 2 percent in poor health. More than 60 percent reported regular exercise with three fourths of those exercising at least three times per week. That this group was pre-dominantly white (81 percent) and highly educated (more than 87 percent had at least some college education) may in part explain the high rates of physical activity in their lives, which are well above the national levels.

What about the role of physical activity among gay men? Unlike lesbian women, the findings for gay men are more consistent. A num-ber of authors have proposed that while lesbian culture de-empha-sizes attractiveness, gay male culture places extreme importance on appearance (Pronger, 1990). For example, Siever (1994) reported that the gay men in his study placed a higher priority on physical activity in evaluating potential partners. A study by Beren and colleagues (Beren, Hayden, Wilfley, & Grilo, 1996) indicates that gay men, com-pared with heterosexual men, are more dissatisfied with their bod-ies. The authors speculated that gay men were perhaps more dis-tressed by general and weight-specific teasing as children.

Grossman and Wughalter (1983) investigated the leisure-time fit-ness beliefs and practices of gay men who voluntarily joined a local gym in Greenwich Village, New York, which was equipped with a full line of bodybuilding equipment. Exercisers reported spending nearly 9 hours per week at the gym, with an additional 5.5 hours outside the gym in largely aerobic activities. Subjects indicated their reasons for participation were for fitness (e.g., to maintain fitness, to build larger muscles) rather than social (e.g., to meet people for so-cial reasons, to meet other people for sexual activity).

As with heterosexual families, social support is important to the adoption of healthy lifestyles by members of same-sex families. Unfortunately, the data about the role of the same-sex family in sup-porting the physical activity habits of its members are very limited. Several studies indirectly suggest that same-sex families may pro-vide an environment that is more conducive to active lifestyles than their heterosexual counterparts. For example, in Lott-Whitehead and Tully's (1999) study of lesbian families, parents were found to be deeply committed to their families, placing their children's needs at the forefront. Despite the fact that a large segment of the lesbian community was not supportive of mothers with children and that they had been forced to curtail activity such as participation in lesbian social events, the mothers were still successful in creating family environments that balanced the needs of all members. Similar findings emerged from Bialeschki and Pearce's (1997) study of lesbian families. The lesbian parents, similar to heterosexual mothers, identified the importance of leisure time. But unlike their heterosexual counterparts, the lesbian women placed a great deal of importance on leisure time alone and with their partners. Green and colleagues (Green, Mandel, Hotvedt, Gray, & Smith, 1987), in a review of the literature, found that compared with heterosexual couples lesbian couples are more cohesive and more flexible and report greater satisfaction in their roles. These findings, although in much need of replication by other studies, indicate that perhaps same-sex female couples are able to overcome some of the obstacles for participation in physical activity that their heterosexual counterparts have not.

Growing Old and Family Ties

Since 1900, the number of Americans at least 65 years of age has expanded from about 3 million to more than 30 million, and the percentage of the graying U.S. population has increased from 4 percent to about 11 percent (Mancini & Blieszner, 1994). The ravages of inflation have seriously affected the economic security and vitality of many older Americans who live on fixed incomes. Today more than 3.4 million older adults live in poverty, and more than 1.2 million older adults live in nursing homes. However, beliefs about aging parents being neglected and abandoned are likely overstated. Approximately 6 percent of older men and 11 percent of older women actually live with one of their children. Studies of older people and their offspring suggest that contact is ongoing, whether it is face to face or over the phone. As Brody (1985) notes, families, not the formal health care system, provide 80 to 90 percent of medical and personal care. Activities such as household tasks, transportation, and shopping for elder adults become family responsibilities. Some recent evidence that the biological family's availability to its older members is greater than previously believed is found in Kolata's (1993) report on the family's willingness to assist elderly members. In a national sample of 12,000 Americans conducted for the National

Institute on Aging, between 30 and 40 percent helped aging parents financially in one or more ways. The study refutes the idea of scattered families and abandoned parents and grandparents.

But growing old in America is not without significant challenges. Conventional wisdom tells us that as we age, we become less active. Information from the Behavioral Risk Factor Surveillance System supports this contention. In the national telephone survey, when men and women aged 65 to 74 were asked, "How much physical activity did you engage in during the last month?" 33 percent of the men and 36 percent of the women reported no physical activity. These sedentary rates were even higher among the 75+ group: 38.2 percent of the men and half of the women reported no physical activity (USDHHS, 1994).

Although daily physical activity has been publicly advocated as a remedy for reducing many of the health risks affecting old people, many older men and women are not heeding the message. O'Brien Cousins (2000) asked 143 independent-living women aged 70 and older to respond to open-ended questions about their beliefs about six fitness activities: brisk walking, aquacizing, riding a bike or cycling, stretching slowly to touch the toes, modified push-ups from a kneeling position, and supine curl-ups. The women, while recognizing the health benefits of these activities, also expressed strong reservations about participating in them. The women felt physically vulnerable and unsure about their actual risks and benefits and, in the face of the uncertainty, were quick to identify health conditions as why they should be excused from fitness-promoting exercise.

But other reports suggested that when the type of physical activity is more clearly identified for study participants, the declining rates of physical activity among seniors are less observable. For example, Stephens and Craig (1990), in an extensive cross-sectional analysis of adult Canadians, found a significant decline in participation in more rigorous activities of swimming and cycling with age, but not in walking and gardening. In fact, with age, figures for walking increased for men (16 percent) and women (13 percent), as did figures for gardening, although just for women (20 percent).

O'Brien Cousins and Keating (1995) utilized focus-group interviews to study how senior women react to "life-stage changes," particularly as they affect participation in physical activity. The authors concluded that the previously physically active senior women adapted to life-stage changes in physically active ways, while previously sedentary women viewed similar life-stage

Photograph by Tom Roberts

Walking among older adults may be on the rise. This is a good indication that physical activity among older adults is increasing.

changes as creating barriers to their personal activity patterns. Thus, the key for staying involved in physical activity during the golden years is to come equipped with a lifelong commitment to physical activity.

Bereavement and Living Alone

Growing old also means dealing with the loss of loved ones. More than half (54 percent) of the women in this country who are 65 years or older are widowed, and more than one third live alone (Cavanaugh, 1993). Every year, 800,000 men and women experience the death of a spouse, which is a difficult life transition for all individuals but can be particularly traumatic when the partnership involved a sharp division between sex roles, leaving the survivor unprepared to assume the range of tasks required to maintain a household.

Widowhood seems to be associated with a higher mortality risk during the first months after the death of the spouse (Vinick, 1983). Several cohort studies report men at a higher risk than women during the first three months following the loss of a spouse (Fitzpatrick & Bosse, 2000). There may be other factors that increase the risk of mortality among the bereaved, such as decrease in network size and social support or changes in the social roles after bereavement. Men seem to be more affected by a decrease in network size and support than women, particularly if bereavement and retirement occur in the same period. They are reported to leave maintaining contacts outside work to their wives and are also more likely to rely exclusively on their wives. Widows and widowers live in a high-risk environment; a sense of hopelessness and helplessness may produce further stress and subsequent health problems or illness.

The process of bereavement is not always the same for men and women. Despite evidence suggesting that adaptation follows a similar course during the first two years after the loss of a spouse, Gass (1989) showed an increase of almost 40 percent in the death rate among widowers over the age of 54 during the first six months of bereavement. The death of a spouse for men may involve the loss of a sexual partner and companion, changes in decision making about household tasks and finances, relocation, and changes in social roles and lifestyles. Additionally, the supportive nature of the marital relationship is lost, and reminders or cues are absent for important daily activities. For the widower, changes in routine household chores can have adverse effects on health, especially if he has chronic health problems such as heart disease, diabetes, or hypertension, which may require a special diet and medications that his wife previously prepared. Meaningful relationships with friends and co-workers may be disrupted, which may contribute to an increased sense of social isolation and loneliness, which in turn has been associated with high rates of suicide, mental disorders, and mortality. However, widows may have less to lose in terms of roles than widowers because women generally carry the greater burden in the marriage as housewife, mother, employed worker, or volunteer outside the home. The tasks and responsibilities associated with these roles continue after the death of a spouse. On the other hand, men have a greater tendency to remarry than women and are thereby less prone to experience extreme role shifts.

Although we tend to focus our attention on the loss of a spouse, the elderly are also confronted with losses of children, siblings, parents, and even grandparents. The death of a parent, child, or sibling is as stressful as the death of a spouse and can also influence future emotional and physical health (DeVries, Della Lana, & Falck, 1994). The death of an adult child usually has a devastating and lasting impact on the physical and emotional health of aging parents. Furthermore, in addition to the emotional loss and the lessening support or assistance available for their health when an adult child dies, elderly grandparents may be forced to assume care or financial responsibilities for the surviving grandchildren. Few empirical studies have explored the death of a sibling and the relevance of such loss to elderly people. Past studies primarily focused on the death of siblings and the special meaning of the sibling relationship in childhood and have as yet failed to examine bereavement reactions among families during later life.

The period of grief and mourning after the death of a family member may be lengthy, although it is difficult to generalize as the duration varies by individual. Bereavement can result in negative consequences for physical health, including physical illnesses, aggravation of existing medical conditions, or new symptoms and complaints. The bereaved individual can potentially develop health problems precipitated by an increase in self-destructive behavior, such as smoking, drinking, or overeating. Individuals are likely to experience an escalation of existing health problems, which can lead to sudden death or suicide. Despite these problems, many bereaved family members adjust very well.

Loneliness is often the single greatest concern of people who lose a spouse and an important source of emotional support. Death of one's spouse causes changes in lifestyle and daily activities as well as in emotional and material resources. These changes increase the potential stress that families experience when coping with death. Depression and bereavement have been shown to reduce immune function, heighten susceptibility to disease, and contribute to declines in physical functioning and increases in chronic health problems. These results of the loss of a loved one are likely to have an impact on participation in physical activity, but unfortunately there is a dearth of systematic studies testing this claim. In one exception, Vinick (1983) found that newly bereaved widowers perceived their health as poor in the year following a wife's death and also reported less participation in physical activity. Bereaved men and women need to maintain social involvement with their family, friends, and community and possibly make new friends, which may serve to reduce stress and should positively affect their well-being and health. Tudiver, Hilditch, and Permaul (1992) examined the efficacy of a support group program for new widowers that focused on dealing with the grief process, nutrition, and exercise issues. The participants significantly improved their participation in physical activity during the first eight months. Social activities such as support groups for bereaved men and women make sense because they provide opportunities for older adults to be active, thus helping to minimize social isolation and the potential for health problems.

Caring for the Family Caregiver

More than one third of older adults develop health conditions that restrict their ability to perform activities of daily living (National Family Caregivers Association, 1997). As a result of the increase in these chronic health conditions, coupled with rising health care costs, many individuals are turning to at-home care for their ill older relatives. According to one source, 80 percent of those needing long-term care receive it from informal sources, such as families and friends, who function as *family caregivers*. Daughters and daughters-in-law tend to be the principal caregivers. Working daughters, not working sons, are assumed to adjust their work schedules for parent care. Some 28 percent of the caregiving women had quit their jobs to take care of an elderly parent. According to the National Family Caregivers Association (1997), more than 18 million people are family caregivers.

In the United States, fully one half of the children who are formally placed in the care of someone other than their parents are in kinship care or formal placements with relatives. The rapid growth in the number of children formally placed with relatives can be traced in part to federal and state laws and policies beginning in 1979, which promoted family caregiving for another family member's children. Although grandparents of all racial and ethnic groups provide primary care for grandchildren, this arrangement is particularly prevalent in African-American families. In the mid-1990s, 13.5 percent of African-American children were living with grandparents or other relatives, compared with 6.5 percent of Hispanic children and 4.1 percent of white children. Almost 30 percent of African-American grandmothers and about 14 percent of African-American grandfathers reported having had primary responsibility for raising a grandchild for at least six months at some point in their lives, compared with 10.9 percent of all grandparents (Roe & Minkler, 1998/1999).

Although caring for one's grandchildren brings many rewards, including keeping the family together, the arrangement has also been associated with potentially serious physical and mental health problems. Key among these is depression, which may develop because of difficulties in balancing multiple work, family, and social responsibilities at a time when many grandparents had hoped to have more time to themselves. The increased demand on the family caregivers' time and finances may be particularly disheartening when contrasted with noncaregiving grandparents' increasing freedom and leisure time. One study found that African-American caregivers were significantly more likely than their noncaregiving peers to have limitations in physical activities of daily living (Fuller-Thomson & Minkler, 2000). For example, nearly 29 percent of the family caregivers reported difficulties in climbing a flight of stairs or walking as little as six blocks.

Family commitments such as caregiving rank high among the constraints that prevent women from pursuing leisure-time activities, including physical activity (Searle & Jackson, 1985). A number of studies suggest that caregivers respond to the stress of providing care by engaging in negative health behaviors, including the reduction or elimination of regular physical activity (Connell, 1994). For example, King and Brassington (1997), in their analysis of 1,526 caregivers, reported that only 6.7 percent of women and 17.6 percent of men engaged in exercise three or more times a week at an intensity sufficient to increase their heart rate or breathing. When asked to rank six health areas about which they were most interested in learning more, putting more physical activity into their daily lives was a frequent response. The fact that physical activity was rated so highly underscores the utility of developing interventions aimed specifically at helping caregivers fit more physical activity into their daily routines. The authors concluded that supervised, home-based physical activity programs may provide a suitable avenue for regular physical activity among family caregivers, many of whom face serious time and emotional constraints to exercise.

Family caregivers as a group are vulnerable to health problems. In addition to the financial burden of medical bills or lost wages, the social and emotional costs can also be overwhelming. Family caregiving often interferes with the ability of the caregivers to meet their own needs because they put the needs of the loved one ahead of their own. Family caregiving has been associated with a variety of deleterious social and psychological states, including feelings of guilt and obligation. Henderson, Stalnaker, and Taylor (1988) studied 500 family caregivers and found that their sense of family obligations and expectations ranked high among the reasons they gave for their failure to fulfill their own leisure roles. Guilt is also a prominent theme in the lives of many family caregivers. Caregivers of older family members often must suppress feelings of resentment and anger, which contribute to feelings of guilt. Family caregivers attempt to allay feelings of guilt, but whatever they do is often never enough (Brody, 1985). Rogers (1997) found that family caregivers who were consumed by their caregiving role made personal sacrifices to avoid feeling guilty for not providing the best care possible. She noted that guilt prevented caregivers from feeling entitled to participate in leisure-time activities. Family caregivers tend to disregard the importance and benefits of leisure-time physical activities. The force of the caring ethic can be so strong that women, in particular, place the needs of others above their own to the point of denying their own needs, including those for physical activity.

The Family and Managing Chronic Disease

The family can have a significant impact on the health of its members, particularly when a family member is coping with life's stressful events, such as dealing with illness. Individuals who suffer from potentially debilitating chronic diseases go through a process of reflection as they attempt to make sense of what has happened to them. Making sense of their situation involves a period of adjustment in which a range of coping strategies may be adopted in order to maintain normality, control, and a sense of worth in the face of the long-term negative connotations that illness holds for them. They are encouraged to search for lifestyle explanations for their conditions by health professionals. Family members are positioned to shape the behaviors of the patient; they can monitor the patient's behavior and encourage direct adherence to the prescribed medical, dietary, or exercise regimens.

Physical activity plays a pivotal role in the management of chronic disease conditions. Cardiac rehabilitation programs, first developed in the United States during the early 1970s, pay close attention to the degree of physical exertion that can be undertaken safely. Physical activity is a central focus of cardiac rehabilitation programs, although many programs also address other factors, such as nutrition, smoking, stress reduction, and hypertension control.

Exercise programs for those suffering from chronic diseases have changed in recent years. Currently, less emphasis is being placed on office or hospital visits for electrocardiographic (ECG) monitoring or supervised group programs. Many patients are unable to participate in formal programs conducted in health care settings because of travel considerations, expense, or inconvenience. Consequently, more patients are being managed individually through home programs. Initially, individuals put very high levels of trust in health professionals such as their physicians. The high levels of trust in and dependence on these health professionals over time diminishes as people recover from the initial shock of discovering their illnesses. Members of the immediate family then become the primary source of support.

The diagnosis of serious chronic conditions can create major disruptions in family life. In the case of a heart attack, family conflicts, especially in the early stages of discharge from the hospital, often center around returning to activity, in the form of both exercise (e.g., walking, playing golf) and sexual activity. A heart attack is clearly a traumatic health event because of the threat of sudden death associated with it. Survival after the first few days radically improves the survival rate. Around three months following their heart attacks, many people are symptom free and are able to carry out many of the activities that they did prior to their heart attack (DeBusk, Kraemer, & Nash, 1983). Positive family relations, especially during the early stages of illness, are important to the long-term well-being of the sufferer. Adjustment to a heart attack follows one of two directions: Individuals may deny the condition by continuing with the lifestyle pursued before the diagnosis, or they may pursue a radical change in lifestyle to accommodate the new condition (Radley, 1989). Although coronary heart disease is the leading cause of death in women, heart disease has long been believed to be a male condition, and in many cases the consequences for women may be more serious. Returning to work after a heart attack or a coronary artery bypass is significantly lower in women than men (Brezinka & Kittel, 1995).

For some chronic disease sufferers, lifestyle changes are seen as futile. Their condition is not seen so much as chronic and manageable but rather as chronic and life threatening (Wiles, 1998). Rose and Robbins (1993) estimated that between 30 percent and 50 percent of cardiac patients experience anxiety, depression, or impairments in marital, family, and vocational functioning for up to three years. A diagnosis of coronary heart disease usually leaves a profound impact on an individual's self-image and sense of well-being. The diagnosis of disease is often not sufficient to trigger the necessary lifestyle changes for a better prognosis in the future. For others, the experience of a health trauma such as a heart attack allows them to make sense of why the event occurred and to make the appropriate lifestyle changes to see that it does not happen again.

Although participation in physical activity is critical in the long-term management of heart disease, many coronary patients experience difficulties in staying committed to their doctor-prescribed physical activity programs. Even the experience of life-threatening conditions such as a heart attack may not alter their long-term physical activity habits. Oldridge and Streiner (1990) reported that more than half of cardiac patients do not continue to be physically active beyond the first six months after their heart attack.

Compliance to physical activity prescriptions may be a greater challenge in disease rehabilitation programs that are complex, long, or inconvenient and that require major lifestyle alterations. Noncompliance to health management is a particular challenge among individuals dealing with type I or type II diabetes. The diabetic's medical regimen can include daily insulin injections and frequent monitoring of blood glucose levels in addition to maintaining an exercise program. In one study, subjects reported taking the vast majority (87 percent) of their diabetes medications on time but adhering much less to diet and exercise recommendations. Individuals with type II diabetes reported adhering to exercise prescriptions 53 percent of the time, while type I diabetics adhered only 31 percent of the time. Men (61.2 percent) reported adhering to exercise more than did women (48.6 percent). Subjects weighing more than 120 percent of ideal body weight adhered to their exercise regimen significantly less often than other subjects (49 percent vs. 69 percent). The family plays a critical role in helping loved ones deal with diabetes. Hanson and colleagues (1995) found that among 157 young adults with diabetes, positive family relations—high family cohesion and low family conflict—especially during the first years of illness, related to good metabolic control through positive adherence behaviors.

The Counterproductivity of Family Support

Spouses have identified the early days as the most difficult and frightening time in the recovery process (Bramwell, 1986). Marriage partners when confronted with a serious illness such as cardiovascular disease and diabetes must learn to manage their individual distress levels but must also figure out ways to deal with the new emotional needs of their partner. They feel responsible for their partner's welfare and are unsure whether they will know what to do if an emergency occurs. In fact, there is some evidence that when trying to help a partner in crisis, family members often become involved in ways that are counterproductive. Spouses in some circumstances overreact and actually discourage participation in physical activity. Spouses often overcompensate in a way that counteracts the positive results of the patient's striving to resume normal activity.

Conflicts over limitations on physical activity often characterize family interactions; patients want to test their capabilities, and other family members fear that such tests will have disastrous consequences. The fear of sudden death looms large in the minds of many individuals during the aftermath of a heart attack as well as in the minds of their spouses. They fear that they cannot handle the strains in their vocational and social life. In one study, husbands recovering from an uncomplicated myocardial infarction assessed themselves as moderately hardy, while their wives judged their husbands' cardiac capacity as severely debilitated and incapable of withstanding physical and emotional strain (Taylor, Bandura, & Ewart, 1985). It is common for the spouse to fear that exercise, even in a controlled environment, will precipitate a second heart attack. These fears are highly exaggerated, as William Haskell (1994) has shown in his analysis of medically supervised exercise regimens. Haskell calculated the risk of cardiac death due to participation in supervised exercise programs. The rate was only one in 60,000 participant exercise hours. At this rate, a typical rehabilitation program that has 95 patients exercising three times a week could expect a sudden cardiac event once every four years.

Another way that marriage can negatively affect health occurs when spouses undermine their own health or that of their partners through *protective buffering*, a strategy in which one partner denies worries and hides concerns from the other and yields to him or her to avoid disagreements (Coyne & Smith, 1994). John Finnegan and colleagues (2000) conducted 34 focus groups with 207 individuals who had experienced a heart attack. Approximately one third of the men and women who experienced a heart attack said in retrospect that they probably had been experiencing symptoms for days, weeks, or even months. The overwhelming majority of men and women reported that they had never planned what to do in the event of a heart attack, nor had they discussed symptoms and actions with their physicians or even their partners. Women were far more likely than men to report a delay in seeking treatment because they did not perceive a personal risk of heart attack. The majority of women said that they believed heart attacks were mainly a male problem. Of those women receiving a confirming diagnosis of heart disease, more than half of them described themselves as surprised.

Family members do a disservice when they contribute to the patient's denial of their symptoms. Behavior intended to be protective and supportive may actually have adverse consequences for the person one is trying to protect. Family members, for example, may allow, or even encourage, a family member whose health is at risk to deny the presence or meaning of symptoms. In a report by one medical doctor, nearly half the spouses (45 percent) initially discouraged their spouses from seeking medical care (Hackett & Cassem, 1983).

The protective buffering phenomenon may also be responsible for delays in seeking medical attention. Among cardiac arrest victims, immediate emergency medical services can often mean the difference between life and death. The longest delay occurs while the patient considers whether symptoms are significant and reaches a decision to seek medical care. Alonzo (1986) reported that the average time it takes a symptomatic individual to get to a hospital may be six times longer when the episode occurs at home (12 hours) than when it occurs at work or when out with friends (2 hours).

Coping With Fragile Families

It is a societal norm to expect that family members will provide support no matter what, but especially during hard times (Patterson, Garwick, Bennett, & Blum, 1997). When everyone else avoids a person in distress, comfort and unconditional love should be available from those at home. Unfortunately, this is not the case in many families. For individuals experiencing chronic or life-threatening illnesses, the lack of social support from close family members is frequently reported as a major source of additional stress (Pearlin, Mullan, Semple, & Skaff, 1990). Extended family members are often unable or unwilling to understand the sick person's situation and to offer adequate support; they often avoid contact with, involvement in, or conversation about the family situation and show nonacceptance of the condition (Patterson, Garwick, Bennett, & Blum, 1997). Relatives may respond by making insensitive comments, blaming other family members for causing the condition, or disagreeing about how the ill family member should be taken care of.

Although it is inevitable that chronic diseases increase family tensions, for individuals in marriages judged to be unhappy before the crisis, chronic disease is likely to stretch these existing tensions to the breaking point (Sotile, 1996). Problems that lingered below the surface during hospitalization become more noticeable when the spouse comes home. The return home and decisions about return to work, social commitments, and daily schedules increase family tensions. During the early crisis phase, many families pull together and rally around the afflicted individual, even when there have been major family conflicts, separation, or disengagement. However, a long history of struggle over trust, intimacy, or communication may create tension too great for the family to outlast. If a couple has a history of strained relationships, they may be unable to share feelings and reactions. Especially if the crisis lasts for months or years, the family support mechanisms may disintegrate, leaving the afflicted individual feeling left out and isolated (Sotile, 1996).

It is common for family members to pull together in times of crises; however, some families may be less effective in dealing with chronic conditions day to day. Patients who have suffered heart attacks or are dealing with daily management of diabetes have likely engaged in unhealthy behaviors for many years. Their unhealthy behaviors have also likely received social support for many years. Endeavors to change diet and physical activity habits while the family continues in the same patterns can be almost impossible. The successful management of chronic disease requires changes on two levels: changes directed at the individual and also total restructuring of unhealthy family ways. However, changing the health habits of the family is by no means an easy task. Families may not have established household routines that encourage careful attention to diet and exercise. Often family members do not or cannot provide social support to each other for health-enhancing diet or exercise patterns. In the face of problems and crises, some families are weakened, whereas others grow in solidarity and emotional strength. Some families grow and learn when confronted with traumatic experiences. But a poorly functioning

Families may not have adopted a household routine that encourages careful attention to diet and physical activity.

or underorganized family system might be too inflexible and tend to break apart (Sotile, 1996).

Conclusion

Many critics argue that a major problem with the American family is the emphasis on individual growth and fulfillment at the expense of commitment. Sociologist David Poponoe (1988), in his well-known critique of the changing institution of family, called for the return to the traditional nuclear family. People spend more and more time with other groups and activities, rather than investing their time, money, and energy in family life; this could spell the end of family life. Reducing the stability of the family undermines its ability to perform the most important task: taking care of each other, particularly children.

A competing approach to the American family focuses on the way in which families are adapting in the face of social change. According to postmodern critic Judith Stacey (1991), no longer is there a single culturally dominant family pattern to which the majority of Americans conform. In response to the loosening bonds of permanent marriage, the disappearing male family breadwinner and the growth of work opportunities for women have created a variety of new family and household arrangements.

The changing structures and responsibilities of the family have meant much less time for child rearing or caregiving to elderly parents and in some cases even the necessary emotional support necessary for a sustained marriage. These changes also have created challenges for increasing physical activity participation among family members. For many parents, attention to balancing work and family obligations often leave little time for their own leisure pursuits or to the physical activities involving their children. At the other end of the age continuum are the challenges associated with keeping people physically active as they face the declines in physical capabilities in older adulthood or have to deal with the loss of their social support network. Although the specific mechanisms of how family members influence the physical activity habits are still a subject in need of much clarification, those that study family interactions seem to agree that the family plays a vital role in cultivating the physical activity patterns among its members.

The long-term success in promoting physically active lifestyles will depend on finding genuine resolutions to the dilemmas and conflicts that confront families in contemporary society. As pointed out by Barnett and Rivers (1996), the portrait that emerges of the new family must be "one of men and women working together on both the work and home fronts to find personal challenge and satisfaction, to nurture each other, and, if they are parents, to raise children to be responsible citizens in a time of great change." Such an approach would also move the family to acceptance of and support for diversity in the forms families may take, it would reduce barriers to integrating such roles as work and family for employed parents, and it would promote gender equality in rights and responsibilities and options regarding parents and children.

The family is important for individuals, not just in childhood, but throughout the life course. People with close ties to their families report satisfaction with their life, their marriage, and their health and they are more likely to overcome personal and family crises. No doubt the family is changing, but at the same time we have no other institutionalized mechanisms comparable to the family for giving social support or for caring for children. Today's families cannot be the sole resource for cultivating the health habits of its members. Where children are concerned, the educational institution becomes a critical source of family assistance.

Photograph by Tom Roberts

CHAPTER

5

School
Physical Education
in Crisis

As *physical activity professionals* *our objective is to turn young people on to physical activity for a lifetime. We want our children and youths to be knowledgeable about physical activities, we want them to have the skills to engage in a wide variety of physical activities, and we want them to appreciate the lifetime benefits of being active. We want all these things because we hope that with knowledge, skill and appreciation they will be active and therefore healthy, both as children and adults. . . . [A]dult-organized physical activity programs should strive to teach children to become responsible for themselves, especially for their health through physical activity . . . Children need the opportunity to have some say about the activities in which they participate. Not every child will find all activities enjoyable, but every child should find some activities enjoyable if we give them the opportunity to experience a wide range of activities and to have some control over their participation. (Martens, 1996:303, 310)*

▼   ▼   ▼   ▼   ▼

Public concern about the quality of education is at an all-time high, while public confidence in the ability of our educational system to address these concerns is at an all-time low. So says educational reformist Phillip Schlechty (1997) in his highly publicized book *Inventing Better Schools: An Action Plan for Educational Reform*. According to Schlechty, something is fundamentally wrong with America's system of education as "too many children leave school without having developed the skills, attitudes, and habits of mind that will equip them to live in the twenty-first century."

Ever since the publication of *A Nation at Risk* (National Commission of Excellence in Education [NCEE], 1983), educational and political leaders, teachers, and parents have conceded that our system of education is badly in need of reform. The report made all too clear the low performance of American students. More than 15 years after the publication of this wake-up call to our educational system, there appears to be little improvement. For example, in the 1996 reading and mathematics "report card," which assesses achievement levels in over 20,000 fourth, eighth, and twelfth graders, fewer than 50 percent of the students performed at a minimal level of proficiency, with only 21 percent of fourth graders and 21 percent of eighth graders passing the reading and mathematics standards (Harms, 1998). U.S. educational spending over the last several decades has increased at triple the growth rate of the gross domestic product. Real per-student expenditures quintupled during the second half of the 20th century (Fuchs, 1996). Although funding for public schools has increased dramatically over the last several decades, the performance of the U.S. educational system as measured by a variety of standardized tests and international comparisons has not improved.

While there is a consensus among the many stakeholders in public school education regarding the need for school reform, there is little agreement concerning the sources or the solutions to the problems facing our educational system. Although the controversy concerning our schools is multifaceted, in simplistic terms, it can be understood from two contrasting positions. One side stresses the importance of developing an extensive knowledge base, one that is demanding, challenging, and academically rich in content. The public at large wants the educational system to teach students how to read and write, to calculate, and to develop strong work habits and self-discipline. On the other side of the debate are the advocates of strategies that stress social growth, value development, and behaviors that lead to creative, self-directed learning that focuses on problem-solving and critical-thinking skills. Critics of "raising standards" assert that school reform will not be successful until educators get students to participate in a schooling process to which they are willingly attracted and that they do not find confining and boring (Sarason, 1990). An emphasis on rote fact learning produces children who are unable to work in groups and fails to teach children how to think. Opponents of "process strategies" argue that they have been a dismal failure because you cannot think without the facts.

The public debate concerning the goals of education has placed school-based physical education programs under a microscope as well. The achievement debate has fostered a "back-to-basics" curriculum in many schools, leaving physical education programs to deal with serious skepticism about their relevance as part of the school curriculum. The *Nation at Risk*'s call for strengthening five basic areas—English, mathematics, science, social studies, and computer science—notably excluded physical health and fitness (NCEE, 1983). In fact, the report pointed to the inclusion of physical education in the curriculum as part of the problem. Declines in educational performance, according to the report, were in part attributable to the fact that nearly one fourth of the credits earned by general-track high school students are in such courses as physical and health education rather than in more "rigorous" courses.

As pressures to find room in the curriculum for math, science, and other core subjects escalate, time allotted to subjects such as physical education are continually being questioned. In many schools, physical education has become the "play course," the easy credit from the perspective of administrators, the filler course used to complete students' course schedules or to keep them occupied and out of trouble. School physical education programs have become targets for elimination as a number of states consider getting rid of physical education altogether. In light of recent efforts to cut back physical education programs and the lack of understanding by administrators and teachers, there is a growing concern for the future of physical education within the larger picture of education.

The academic achievement debate can be readily seen as an obstacle to developing educational objectives related to lifelong physical activity. One of the biggest obstacles to promoting activities with long-term benefits is the difficulty in measuring the long-term effects. But even if these measurements were available, the short-term thinking of many schools devalues what students will be or will not be doing 20 years from now. Most school boards, principals, and teachers are caught up in assessing immediate achievement levels.

They often are preoccupied with the pressing problems of today and can neither afford the time nor justify spending money on outcomes that will not be achieved until many years later.

Despite the precarious status of physical education in our formal education system, the school is still considered the ideal place for promoting health among adolescents (Pate, Small, Ross, Young, Flint, & Warren, 1995). Many experts have recommended that primary prevention of chronic disease be pursued through interventions directed at children. For families who do not have community resources for physical activity, the school physical education curriculum is the one place where all children have the opportunity to be physically active.

The focus on schools for addressing the physical activity needs of children and adolescents is based largely on the assumption that behavioral patterns such as physical activity are developed in childhood, a time when it is more likely to lower the risk of several chronic diseases and premature death, and carried into adulthood. One assumption is that children's attitudes and behaviors are more malleable than those of adults. A second assumption is that behavioral risk factors for chronic disease are stable over time. Although there is a dearth of evidence backing up these claims, common wisdom assumes that children who adopt healthy behaviors early in life tend to maintain these behaviors through childhood and into adulthood (Trudeau, Laurencelle, & Shepart, 1999). The educational system seems to be an ideal place for meeting these objectives.

Organizations such as the American Alliance of Health, Physical Education, Recreation and Dance (AAHPERD); the American Academy of Pediatrics Committee on Sports Medicine and School Health; and the American College of Sports Medicine have been particularly vocal regarding the need for school physical education programs to adopt health-related physical activity goals. The important role of physical activity is also recognized by its inclusion among the *Healthy People 2010* objectives (USDHHS, 2000b), which include recommendations that students in physical education classes spend more time being active, preferably engaged in lifetime activities (activities one can participate in over the course of a lifetime). Physical education specialist Daryl Siedentop (1998) laments, "One of the most intriguing, and disturbing, issues facing physical education is the apparent lack of interest in and support for physical education as a school subject at exactly the point in our history when fitness and sport seem to be more popular than ever before."

To meet the challenges issued by major organizations and national health objectives, school physical education programs will have to undergo a considerable reform of their current goals and practices. Four objectives guide our exploration. First, we examine why it is important to encourage health-promoting behaviors in children at an early age. Second, we examine the problems associated with developing new approaches to physical activity in a school value system that is entrenched in competition and individual accomplishments. Physical education programs use resources primarily to develop organized sports and teams at the expense of providing physical education experiences to all students and providing them with physical skills that will last a lifetime. Third, we look at some of the challenges facing the teaching profession today. Of particular interest is the failure to keep up with the current trends in health promotion. Finally, we examine how physical education programs have been less than effective in promoting physical activity among individuals at risk; they do so by concentrating on changing the individuals, with inadequate attention to the social environments of deprivation in which many of these children live.

Disturbing Trends Among Children and Youth

There is reason to be concerned about the activity habits of American children. Obesity is one of the most serious health problems facing the youth of the United States, and evidence suggests that the problem is only getting worse. For example, researchers comparing data from the National Health and Nutrition Examination Surveys found that 11 percent of young people from 6 to 17 years of age were overweight in 1988, compared with about 4 percent in 1963-65. In the 12 years between the second and third National Health and Nutrition Examination Survey, the prevalence of overweight has increased from 25 percent to 33 percent (Troiano & Flegal, 1998). Obesity results from an imbalance of energy intake (e.g., food consumption) and energy expenditure (e.g., calories burned through physical activity). Although the common belief is that children are consuming an increasing amount of calories, the energy output—the level of physical activity—is what has changed. Most children exceed the national recommendations for intake of total and saturated fat (Berenson et al., 1998).

Increasingly, children are electing sedentary leisure-time activities, such as television viewing, video games, and personal computing. In a recent national survey, Andersen, Crespo, and Bartlett (1998) studied the relationship between physical activity and television watching among over 4,000 children aged 8 through 16. Overall, 26 percent of the boys and 23 percent of the girls watched four or more hours of television per day. The percentage of children watching four or more hours increased dramatically among black and Hispanic boys and girls. For example, 43.1 percent of the black girls reported watching four or more hours of television per day. Boys and girls who watched four or more hours of television daily had greater body fat and a greater body mass index. Because physical activity effectively promotes long-term weight loss in obese children and adolescents, increasing the physical activity and decreasing the television watching of children and youths are critical to the solution of the growing obesity problem.

Television and computer activities are replacing physical activity among many children.

Although approximately 50 percent of severely obese children remain obese throughout adulthood, childhood obesity accounts for only about one third of the total cases of adult obesity (Hill & Trowbridge, 1998). In general, however, overweight adults who were obese as children tend to be more severely obese than those who became obese later on. Because an obese child is at risk for becoming an obese adult, primary prevention measures should begin early in life. Such measures include proper nutritional habits and appropriate physical activity to balance energy intake. Obese children are predictably more sedentary than their nonobese counterparts and, when given the choice, opt for sedentary activities over active ones (Epstein et al., 1995).

While many interested health professionals have focused their attention on the behavioral risk factors during childhood, attention is now being directed at the presence of biological risk factors in children and adolescents. A second concern for the health of children and adolescents is signaled by the increasing percentage of youths who have already begun to exhibit the biological risk factors associated with adulthood diseases. The *Shape of the Nation* survey reported that more than 40 percent of children aged five to eight exhibit coronary risk factors such as elevated blood pressure and high levels of cholesterol (National Association for Sport and Physical Education [NASPE], 1993). The children in the Bogalusa Heart Study (BHS) provide ample evidence about the early development of biological risk factors. The BHS is a long-term study of cardiovascular disease risk factors among more than 1,000 children and young adults. According to the study, by one year of age, infants are already consuming a diet comparable to that of adults with respect to high-fat, high-cholesterol, and high-sodium intake (Berenson et al., 1998). Further, the authors found that the total serum cholesterol levels developed by age two in many cases are comparable to levels found in young adults. Elevated cholesterol levels and blood pressure during childhood are associated with a higher-than-average risk for persistently elevated levels during adulthood (Clarke, Schrott, Leaverton, Connor, & Lauer 1978). Given the progressive nature of chronic diseases, their prevention should begin early in life. A recent report issued by the American Academy of Pediatrics Committee on Nutrition (1998) recommended screening children's cholesterol levels and encouraging a low-fat diet beginning in early childhood.

The Competitive School Environment

Despite the strong evidence linking physically active lifestyles to health benefits, most school programs remain highly sports centered (Wilcox, 1987). From organized after-school programs to the physical education class, the educational system socializes children by emphasizing experiences associated with individual achievement and competition. Beyond the inherently competitive nature of the sports and games that are part of interscholastic sport programs, individual achievement and competition are prominent within the traditional physical education curriculum as well (Robinson, 1990). For example, tangible rewards, such as grades, physical fitness certificates, and other honors, are determined by individual achievement ratings or a comparative ranking of individual student achievement.

Organized Interscholastic Sports Programs

Organized school sports represent an important source of social status for children and adolescents. Athletes, particularly males, but a growing number of females, are accorded recognition that guarantees them popularity in the student culture. Membership on a varsity sports team confers prestige among peers and recognition from teachers, administrators, and the local community. Pep rallies, homecomings, and other special activities associated with sporting events are major social occasions on most high school campuses. The National Federation of State High School Associations reported that 3,706,225 boys and 2,472,043 girls participated in more than 30 different high school sports in 1997 (Wuest & Bucher, 1999). About half of students nationwide, 42.3 percent of girls and 55.5 percent of boys, participate on sports team run by their schools (USDHHS, 1998).

The conventionally held wisdom is that sport is a good preparation for life. James Coleman (1961), in the classic *The Adolescent Society*, disclosed the extraordinary place sports hold in the status system of the American high school. However, Coleman also warned that athletics in some school climates could develop into its own subculture, a social system with distinct values that may be inconsistent with the goals of education. Nearly 40 years after Coleman's original study, sport sociologists are still questioning the connection between the school sport experience and positive long-term benefits. For example, social scientists Andrew Miracle and Roger Rees contend in their 1994 book, *Lessons of the Locker Room: The Myth of School Sports,* that there is no evidence to support the claim that sport builds character in high school or anywhere else.

In fact, a growing number of researchers even question the capability of the interscholastic sport experience to contribute meaningfully to the preparation for adulthood physical activity roles. For example, in a study of U.S. military personnel, former interscholastic and collegiate athletes did not differ from nonathletes in the intensity, duration, or frequency of adult physical activity (Morgan, 1986). Former school athletes are also no more likely than nonathletes to initiate an adult exercise program. Brill and associates' (1989) analysis of more than 400 former athletes and nonathletes revealed that nearly 60 percent of the former athletes were currently not exercising at all and that there were few differences between the two groups on a variety of health measures. Sallis and his colleagues (Sallis, Hovell, Hofstetter, Faucher, et al., 1989) provide perhaps the most revealing analysis of the failure of school sports to prepare children for a lifetime commitment to physical activity. In their study of adults, they found physical activity in adolescence to be one of the lowest of 25 correlates of adult vigorous activity. They also noted that among children involved in school sport programs earlier in life, watching sports on television was preferred over actual participation.

On the surface, these patterns may be surprising, but a closer look reveals marked differences between organized sports and the types of physical activity performed later in life. Because most adult physical activities are solitary and noncompetitive, we perhaps should not expect too much carryover from school programs that emphasize team sports. In adulthood, physical activities such as walking, cycling, and gardening may be easier to maintain than participation in sports, which tends to decrease rapidly with age. Those who get most of their exercise from sports will have to make lifestyle changes as they age and distance themselves from their school sport experiences. Since lifestyle factors, especially exercise, diet, and smoking habits, are critical to health, it is conceivable that formal athletic experiences simply do not provide the skills necessary to start and maintain regular exercise. As suggested in the Harvard Alumni Study, current physical activity and exercise levels are likely more significant predictors of current involvement than the participation in organized team sports earlier in life (Paffenbarger, Hyde, Wing, & Steinmetz, 1984).

However, we must be careful not rush to judgment concerning the role of interscholastic sport in establishing a lifelong commitment to physical activity. Powell and Dysinger (1987), after a review of six empirical studies of childhood participation in sports as antecedents to adult activity patterns, concluded that the existing evidence was mixed. As pointed out by Rod Dishman (1988), the results of past studies have been difficult to interpret because of the existence of a number of design and measurement problems. In particular, he points to the problem of "subject selection bias." Studies that are interested in assessing differences in present activity between former athletes and nonathletes, according to Dishman, do not always adjust for differences in age, physical fitness, and health status. Each of these factors has been related to adult physical activity and could complicate the interpretation of an observed association with a history of participation in sports. We need better studies in this area before any possible links can be made between childhood school sport experiences and continued participation later in life.

The Competitive Physical Education Class

The ethos of competition and individual achievement permeate the philosophy of many school physical education programs. Peer acceptance and status for athletes suggest that competence in the physical domain is highly valued among youths, particularly among boys (Duda, 1981). Youngsters high in perceived and actual physical competence perceived themselves to be more accepted by their peers and are rated higher in peer acceptance by their teachers (Weiss and Duncan, 1992). Evans and Roberts (1987), in their study of team selection among third- to sixth-grade boys, observed that order of selection was strongly tied to sport ability. The boys with the highest skills were typically chosen first to play, were afforded key playing positions, and when chosen as captains, perpetuated the importance of sport skill. These researchers further noted that less-skilled youngsters were relegated minor roles. Practices such as grouping by ability, using comparative information to determine grades, publicly charting student progress, and calling attention to those students who exhibit noteworthy performance force social comparison. Joan Duda's (1981) research on social comparison further supports the belief that sport skill is a domain in which children, particularly boys, use social comparison processes in order to determine their standing among their peers and thereby determine their self-worth.

Competitive physical activity programs may also serve to discourage some children and adolescents who are not good at sports or have not reached certain levels of physical fitness. Teachers treat students differently based on their sport skills and motor ability. Low-skilled students are often overlooked and as a result do not always receive enough practice trials to help improve their performance levels. It is not uncommon for these students to receive less skill-related feedback and more criticism from teachers. Portman (1995), in a study of 13 low-skilled elementary schoolchildren, found that the students held very definite negative attitudes toward physical activity. Their knowledge of being low skilled together with teacher's low expectations fostered an unwillingness to expend effort and to learn skills among the low-skilled students. Children are not inclined to stay involved in physical activity if they do not develop a minimum proficiency or if they feel that they are mismatched against their opponents. The theory of learned helplessness, borrowed from psychology, can give us insight into the long-term consequences for low-skilled students (Dweck & Wortman, 1982).

Youngsters who experience failure in competitive physical activity classes develop a belief that their failures are a result of personal inability, leading to a reduced incentive to participate because it is futile to do so. They tend to attribute failure to internal, uncontrollable factors such as low ability and have difficulty in accepting their own successes; such outcomes are typically attributed to external factors such as luck. Students have come to use a variety of strategies to protect themselves from failure, which might include chronic absenteeism from physical education class, inattention, and a desire to sit on the sidelines. Many low-skilled students quickly become discouraged, underperform, and look to get out of the physical education class as soon as possible.

Some teachers think it is important for pupils to learn to be competitive in sport because competition is a feature of life outside school and coming to terms with it is an important prerequisite to taking one's place in the adult world. Conversely, many other teachers have begun to question their practices; they have begun to examine why pupils show so much apathy and indifference toward physical activity both in and out of school. These teachers emphasize cooperation and downgrade competition as part of the process of preparing children for their futures.

Whether activities are structured cooperatively or competitively also affects children's judgments of their capabilities. A cooperative structure, in which members encourage and teach one another, promotes higher performance attainments than do competitive or individualistic structures. Less-talented members fare much better in successful cooperative systems than in competitive ones, they judge themselves more capable, they feel more deserving of recognition, and they are more satisfied. Skilled performers evaluate themselves just as positively as they do in competitive systems. Teachers need to promote a climate that recognizes effort and social support as well as competitive achievement. Too often, effort is overlooked in favor of individual achievement, and self-development comes at the expense of others in a win–lose environment.

Students need to be given more responsibility for planning, implementing, and evaluating their physical education classes. They need to help decide the activities they want to participate in, and they need to take more responsibility for the direction of their lives. With responsibility comes a sense of ownership and with it, a greater likelihood that more children will participate.

Physical Fitness Testing

A focus on individualistic tendencies in school physical education is prominently associated with the testing of each child's level of physical fitness. Physical fitness has long been a primary goal of physical education and is the component that is most frequently assessed in our public schools. The physical fitness status of American youth has been a matter of public concern for most of the latter half of the 20th century. Public clamor over youth fitness started in the mid-1950s, when data showed that the fitness levels of U.S. youths were far below their European peers (Kraus & Hirschland, 1953). Physical fitness for the next several decades emphasized motor performance, such as speed, strength, power, and agility. However, given the growing attention to physical activity as a preventive factor in cardiovascular and other chronic diseases, health-related fitness emerged as part of the school curriculum in the late 1970s.

The various components of physical fitness should be distinguished; they are classified as *motor skill fitness* or *health-related fitness*. Motor skill fitness is considered to be activity- or sport-specific and includes accuracy, agility, balance, coordination, power, reaction time, and speed. Health-related fitness is more general and encompasses components directly related to reduced risk of the diseases associated with sedentary living, including cardiovascular fitness, muscular strength, endurance, and body composition. A transition from motor performance testing to health-related fitness testing became apparent during the late 1980s with the adoption of new test batteries by AAHPERD and other national physical education organizations.

The information gathered from physical fitness tests is often misused. One such misapplication of physical fitness testing is its use in the assignment of student grades. The use of physical fitness testing for grading purposes can be very unfair. Heredity plays a role in the level of performance on fitness tests, and students may not reach either their own expectations or health-related standards no matter how hard they try or how long they practice. Bouchard and Perusse (1994) reported that biological inheritance accounts for substantial portions of physical performance and health-related fitness factors. Biological inheritance was reportedly associated with approximately 29 percent of habitual physical activity, 25 percent of cardiovascular fitness, 30 percent of muscular fitness, and 25 percent of relative body fat.

For youngsters who are overweight or in poor physical condition, the experience of physical fitness testing may also prove embarrassing. Both boys and girls often report an intense dislike for the humiliation and discomfort they experience in these testing situations. Measures of fat should be taken privately, and students should be told that their scores are personal and highly affected by heredity, practice, and effort. Unless administered carefully, fitness testing could dishearten youngsters and discourage them from future participation in physical activity. Such negative experiences lead to physical education avoidance and strong reinforcement of a sedentary lifestyle.

Physical fitness testing today remains a regular part of most physical education curricula. About one quarter (23.5 percent) of all states require administration of physical fitness testing in schools, and an additional 43.1 percent recommend their administration (Pate, Small, Ross, Young, Flint, & Warren, 1995). Among the school districts requiring or recommending fitness tests, 82.4 percent require or recommend them at the elementary school level, 94.1 percent require or recommend them at the middle or junior high school level, and 94.1 percent require or recommend them at the senior high school level.

Physical fitness has long been an important outcome of school physical education. Physical fitness is important in sport skill performance, and it is related to improved health. However, there has been a gradual conceptual shift away from physical fitness. Among many health experts, increasing physical activity is seen as more important than improving physical fitness or sport skills. Increasing physical fitness is not the health priority because the state of being physically fit does not carry over into adult life (Simons-Morton, O'Hara, & Parcel, 1987). In the past few years, physical educators have begun to evaluate the effects of various physical education programs on health, and the consensus seems to be that the most important public health goal for children is to increase their physical activity.

Trends in School Physical Education

More than a decade ago, supported by a number of professional organizations, Congress passed a resolution urging individual states to require daily physical education programs for all school-aged children. The resolution came on the heels of a report published by the American Alliance for Health, Physical Education, Recreation and Dance called *Shape of the Nation: A Survey of State Physical Education Requirements* (NASPE, 1993). The report revealed that as many as half of our young people are not engaged in sufficient physical activity to develop adequate cardiovascular fitness. One third of school-aged boys and girls were unable to complete a mile run in less than 10 minutes. The survey also found that only one state, Illinois, required all students from kindergarten to grade 12 to take physical education every day; eight states had no school physical education requirements.

The report did little to reverse the trends in school physical education. During the 1990s, enrollment in physical education had reached an all-time low. Recognizing the importance of adolescent health issues and the limited information in these areas, the CDC began the development of a comprehensive surveillance system in the 1980s titled Youth Risk Behavior Surveillance System (YRBSS). The system was designed to monitor adolescent health behaviors in the U.S. population and to track the progress toward achieving health objectives for the year 2000. According to the most recent data collected as part of the YRBSS, only 60.7 percent of high school boys and 51.5 percent of high school girls are enrolled in a physical education class (figures 5.1 and 5.2) (USDHHS, 1999d). More than half of high school students complete their graduation requirement in physical education during their last two years of high school. Just a little more than one third of high school seniors are enrolled in any physical education—girls, at 29.4 percent, are at a significantly lower rate than boys, at 43.8 percent. A more recent follow-up survey, *The Shape of The Nation 1997*, again warned of the dire consequences to our youth of the threat of discontinuing physical education programs (NASPE, 1997).

By race/ethnicity

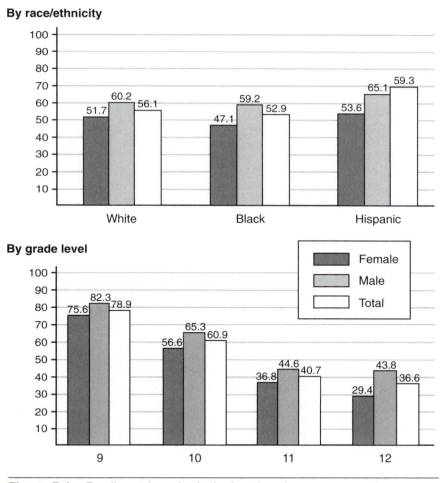

Figure 5.1   Enrollment in a physical education class.
From U.S. Department of Health and Human Services, 1999d.

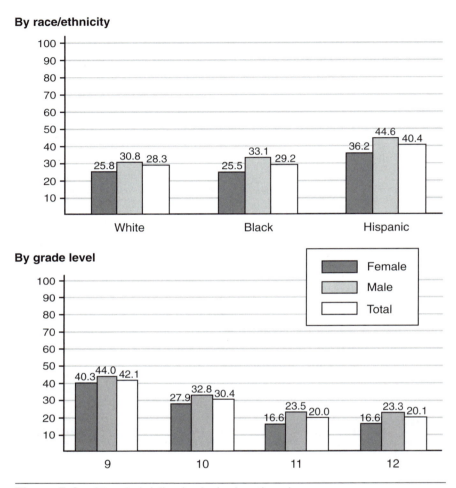

Figure 5.2 Attended daily physical education classes.
From U.S. Department of Health and Human Services, 1999d.

Declining Levels of Physical Activity at School

One would think that ample amounts of physical activity would be part of every physical education class. Actually, the opposite is often true. The results of several studies have pointed out that children often do not get much physical activity in their physical education classes. For instance, Parcel, Simons-Morton, and O'Hara (1987), in a study of elementary physical education classes, found that in a 30-minute class, the average child was vigorously active for only 2 minutes. Similar findings were reported by Faucette, McKenzie, and Patterson (1990) after observing 226 physical education classes. They reported that only 5 percent of class time was devoted to actual physical activity. A study of third-grade students in 95 schools showed children to be engaged in moderate to vigorous physical activity (MVPA) for only 36 percent of class time, far short of the 50 percent recommended by the national objectives. The physical education classes in that study provided the children with only 25 percent of the vigorous activity and 12 percent of the MVPA recommended per week for health purposes (McKenzie, Feldman, Woods, et al., 1995).

The limited amount of actual physical activity in physical education class has been documented in larger-scale studies using national samples as well (table 5.1). According to the most recent YRBSS (USDHHS, 1999d), only 76.3 percent of students in grades 9 to 12 who were taking physical education reported being physically active for at least 20 minutes a day.

More physical activity in the physical education curriculum is included in the national health objectives, which call for physical education programs to ensure that at least 50 percent of class time is

Table 5.1 Physical Activity During Physical Education Class

Exercised > 20 minutes during an average physical education class (%)			
Category	Female	Male	Total
Race/ethnicity			
White	72.4	83.8	78.7
Black	55.8	78.4	67.8
Hispanic	70.8	79.6	75.5
Grade			
9	72.5	84.4	78.7
10	70.2	79.4	75.1
11	68.0	82.0	75.7
12	60.1	82.3	73.4
Total	**69.6**	**82.1**	**76.3**

From U.S. Department of Health and Human Services, 1999d.

spent in physical activity. The American Academy of Physical Education, the American Academy of Pediatrics Committee on Sports Medicine and School Health, and the American College of Sports Medicine have been particularly vocal regarding the need for school physical education programs to adopt health-related rather than sport-related physical activity goals. This is recognized by the *Healthy People 2010* objective, which recommends that students in physical education classes spend more time being active, preferably engaged in lifetime activities (USDHHS, 2000a).

Even if all physical education class time were devoted to moderate to vigorous physical activity, there would not be enough time to promote optimal health benefits. One strategy would be to increase physical activity at other times throughout the school day. While physical education class is structured and children's participation is required, recess is typically unstructured and children's physical activity is voluntary. Recess, a staple of the elementary school environment, is a regularly scheduled time for unstructured physical activity. Recess represents one of the few times during the school day when children are free to move about and to interact with peers with minimal supervision.

Recess often promotes physical activity by getting children outdoors, but unfortunately, children are not always active throughout the recess period. Hovell, Bursick, Sharkey, and McClure (1978) observed children directly and concluded that they do not voluntarily engage in sufficient aerobic activity during recess to increase their cardiorespiratory fitness. More recently, an observational analysis of 287 boys and girls concluded that the students engaged in actual physical activity only 47.5 percent of the time, with the remaining time spent waiting for a turn to play, playing with toys while sitting down, and conversing with other students (McKenzie, Faucette, Sallis, Roby, & Kolody, 1997). They found that children were more active primarily during the first few minutes of the recess period and suggested that such strategies as installing more activity-promoting playground equipment and training of school personnel might well serve to increase the duration of physical activity.

The recess period remains one of the untapped sources of increased physical activity for youngsters. Some schools have eliminated recess periods for children, while others allow them to spend recess periods indoors, where school computers are available for homework and games (Dale, Corbin, & Dale, 2000). In 1999 the National

Association of Elementary School Principals (NAESP) endorsed recess as an important component in a child's physical and social development and encouraged principals to develop and maintain appropriately supervised, unstructured free play for children during the school day.

Besides recess, the school day provides other opportunities for physical activity. Before school and after lunch also are potential times for children to be physically active. McKenzie and his colleagues (2000) systematically observed and measured these opportunities in 26 public schools in southern California. They investigated the physical activity levels of boys and girls before school, at lunchtime, and after school. The data on physical activity were collected through a unique observation strategy known as System for Observing Play and Leisure Activity in Youth (SOPLAY). All potential areas for unstructured (not in physical education class) physical activity were identified in each participating school prior to the data collection. A total of 151 areas were targeted for observation, ranging from 2 to 8 per school. The areas included swimming pools, weight rooms, gymnasiums, outdoor marked courts, and grassy fields. Target areas were observed during three time periods (before and after school and during lunch period), and trained observers recorded one of three activity levels: active, very active, or sedentary. All the middle schools had areas that were available before and after school and at lunchtime. Although students were allowed to use these activity areas, the results indicated that very few students used them during leisure-time periods: Only 2 to 4 percent used them before and after school, and 20 percent during lunchtime. Students who took advantage of the play areas, however, were active. The researchers concluded that although physical settings were available for physical activity, school officials made little or no effort to promote physical activity. The authors also noted that some school policies were responsible for students' underutilization of physical facilities at school.

Recess and other opportunities for children and youths to participate in informal physical activities are important to their development. Many of these experiences require children to cooperate and teach them how to work together, how to take turns, and how to reciprocate. Such social skills are closely related to moral development. Children learn that by following rules that benefit the group, they gain the ability to continue to be physically active. The playing child is an active learner. If boredom sets in, new strategies are sought or old ones are used in a different way. Because children do not like to be bored and because play is self-motivated, a child continually selects activities to keep up interest. The child learns how to control the environment for his or her own use. In a world of passive television viewing, the lessons learned through play are essential. Yet schools continue to eliminate recess periods. Physical activities develop healthy bodies while teaching children to enjoy physical activity. Encouraging activities in which children engage eagerly and voluntarily is important. Longer recess times, not shorter ones, are in the best interest of children.

In some cases, administrators are likely just as happy if the students are not physically active outside of physical education class. For example, in one school district, administrators at three elementary schools initiated a Quiet Time Early Start program. The program was designed to cut down the amount of students' physical activity before school starts. Instead of engaging in impromptu physical activity after parents dropped them off on the way to work, students were instructed to sit calmly and quietly outside their classroom doors until the morning bell. The administrators felt the quiet time would settle students down before they headed to home-room class (White, 1999).

Developing a Lifetime Commitment to Physical Activity

Even if elementary and secondary school physical education programs were able to assist students in acquiring a desirable level of physical activity or fitness, this does not mean that children will be able to maintain these levels for a lifetime. Current school physical fitness objectives, as pointed out by physical education specialist Charles Corbin (1987), are only temporary. Helping people to maintain physical activity habits for a lifetime is what is important. Accordingly, to help children and adolescents develop a lifetime commitment to physical activity, school physical education programs must help children complete *higher-order objectives.* These include establishing personal exercise programs, learning to test their own fitness, interpreting their own results, and learning to solve their own fitness problems (Corbin, 1987). Unfortunately, the resources devoted to schools have been primarily used to develop organized sport- and team-oriented physical education programs instead.

Not all schools are entrenched in the throw-out-the-ball mentality. Some school-based physical education programs have implemented *conceptual physical education* (CPE) or personal fitness classes for high school students. The objective of CPE programs is to promote competence among all students and promote positive attitudes toward activity and exercise that will encourage them to adopt a physically active way of life. The CPE curriculum typically includes classroom lessons that teach concepts of health and fitness as well as laboratories or activity sessions that focus on personalized fitness programs, self-monitoring, and a noncompetitive environment for fitness assessment (Corbin, 1987).

Dale and Corbin (2000) examined whether students participating in CPE programs are more likely to remain physically active than those taking a more traditional physical education curriculum. As part of a longitudinal project called Project Active Teens, they tested this assumption. Part 1 of their findings indicated that two to three years after taking ninth-grade physical education, fewer CPE students reported sedentary behaviors than did the students who had taken a more traditional sports-based physical education program. Part 2 of the study examined students after graduating from college. Although differences were not observed, females who had taken the CPE curriculum met the *Healthy People 2000* objective that less than 15 percent of the population should be inactive. Females exposed to traditional physical education did not meet this goal. Men exposed to a CPE program reported significantly more participation in vigorous activity 12 months beyond graduation. Fewer CPE participants, both male and female, reported sedentary behavior than did participants in traditional physical education programs; although the differences were not statistically significant, they were in the right direction.

Teaching students how to maintain a physically active lifestyle must be considered a primary objective of school physical education. A program goal should be helping young people to make responsible decisions about participation in physical activity. Effective decision making involves knowing which activities to avoid as well as which ones to pursue. Throughout life, people are faced with many situations that may affect whether they remain involved in physical activity. Although schools attempt to help students learn how to make satisfying personal decisions, a major portion of teachers' time involves developing information or supplying it to students. Obtaining information, although important, is only one part of the decision-making process. Decision making also requires the individual to reason through problems.

Unlike many subjects taught in school, physical education often includes a substantial component of active play, which should hold a powerful allure for young people (Ennis, 1996). The intent of physical education programs is to develop positive attitudes toward physical activity that will substantially influence adult activity patterns. In the end, physical activity programs that prescribe activity for children can carry over into adulthood only if children become intrinsically motivated to perform the activities on their own.

In 1998, in response to the declining physical activity patterns among many of our children, the Council for Physical Activity for Children of the NASPE published recommendations concerning the amount of physical activity for children (NASPE, 1998). They proposed a Children's Lifetime Physical Activity model. That model provided the basis for the recent *Physical Activity Guidelines: Appropriate Physical Activity for Children* (Corbin & Pangrazi, 1998).

Prior to these guidelines, recommended amounts of physical activity for children and adolescents paralleled those suggested for adults. The new guidelines, however, acknowledge the need for more physical activity by youths as they go through their normal growth and development. The guidelines recommend that children accumulate at least 30 to 60 minutes of physical activity on all or most days of the week. The recommendations encourage elementary-school-aged children to accumulate more than 60 minutes, up to several hours, per day of age-appropriate and developmentally appropriate activity. The shorter attention span of children led the panel of experts to point to the merits of intermittent activity involving moderate to vigorous activity alternating with brief periods of rest and recovery.

It is highly unlikely that increasing time spent in physical activity in school classes or, for that matter, during the school day will come close to meeting the new guidelines for children's total physical activity. A strategy to connect schools with public and private community health and family agencies is the answer (Lawson, 1993). Unfortunately, the goals for many school physical education programs still cater to the individual achievements of highly skilled youngsters who are successful at sports.

The Teaching Profession

The educational reform movement has also directed its attention to the training of teachers. Several national reports on the status of education in the United States focus on the inadequate preparation of teachers and the failure of schools to attract better teachers. No doubt there is justification for some of these criticisms, but to blame the teachers for all the inadequacies of education ignores the many factors that affect the quality of instruction in schools but lie outside the control of the teaching professionals (Griffin, 1985).

The Competence Levels of Physical Education Teachers

The competence of public school teachers is constantly being questioned, and physical education teachers are certainly not exempted from the criticism. The problem of underpreparation of teachers is particularly acute at the elementary-school level. The elementary school is organized around the self-contained classroom in which one teacher provides instruction in all subjects. Many regular classroom teachers have little or no training in regular physical education (Karper, 1995). Most elementary classroom teachers have had only one course in physical education methods as part of their teacher preparation programs. States that have laws requiring physical education instruction in the elementary school seldom require the instruction to be done by a specialist teacher. Only eight states require those who teach physical education to have certificates in physical education (Pate, Small, Ross, Young, Flint, & Warren, 1995). A survey of elementary schools in California found that specialists taught only 7 percent of elementary school physical education (Sallis & McKenzie, 1991). Children would clearly benefit more from teaching by a physical education specialist than by the classroom teacher. A survey of 887 children in grades 4 to 6 found that student attitudes toward physical activities were significantly more positive in programs taught by a specialist with undergraduate physical education training than in programs taught by a nonspecialist teacher (Rahim & Marriner, 1997).

Each state has established minimum requirements that must be met by prospective physical education teachers before they become eligible to teach. Most state departments of education stipulate the number of college or university hours that must be completed before a person can teach physical education. This requirement includes specific courses in the theory and application of instructional methodologies and in educational psychology and also includes a period of supervised student teaching. The old assessment test for prospective teachers, National Teachers Examination (NTE), which was developed in the 1940s, has been replaced by a newer series of tests, known as the Professional Assessments Teacher Test (PRAXIS), developed by the Educational Testing Service. Prospective teachers take the preprofessional PRAXIS I test, which includes sections on mathematics, reading, and writing, when they apply to an educational institution in the second year of college. The PRAXIS II exam includes subject-area tests, and students usually take them as they are completing their teacher training program and seeking an initial license or certificate. Today, the majority of states require that students interested in teaching physical education take the PRAXIS exam (Pultorak, 1994).

One problem with the training of physical education teachers is that these certification standards have not kept pace with content knowledge related to promoting health and fitness (Goldfine & Nahas, 1993). Health and physical education teachers in grades K–12 who have expertise in the teaching of skills or the teaching of health often lack preparation critical to the teaching of health promotion. Eighty-two percent of the states issue separate health and physical education certificates, while 36 percent issue a combined certificate in health and physical education. Forty-eight percent permit certified physical education teachers to teach health education classes, although only 24 percent permit the reverse, health education teachers teaching physical education (Bennet & Peel, 1994). These figures suggest that these two fields are increasingly separated rather than brought together.

The school health education class is an important component of the overall effort to get children and adolescents involved in health-promoting activities such as physical activity. Many middle and junior high schools and senior high schools require health education to help provide students with knowledge and skills needed for a healthy lifestyle; however, a recent report, the School Health Education Profiles, acknowledges that many schools might not be covering all important topics areas or skills sufficiently (USDHHS, 2000c). For example, among the 36 states participating in the survey, the median percentage of schools reporting that they cover physical activity and fitness issues was only 73 percent. The report also points to the insufficient number of lead health education teachers who are academically prepared in health education and the low number of schools with school health advisory committees.

Colleges and universities have been slow to develop curricula and programs to prepare health promotion specialists (Pangrazi & Darst, 1991). It is important that teacher preparation programs be prepared to assess current needs and trends and make appropriate adjustments in order to better equip their students as teachers in the future (Bennet & Peel, 1994). However, much can be done in the way of in-service retraining of the current teaching staff. Several programs introduced in public schools have shown that it is possible to change the orientation of both the physical education and health education curricula by retraining teachers. One such program, the Sports, Play and Active Recreation for Kids (SPARK) program, for example, is aimed at training both classroom teachers and physical education specialists to implement a health-based physical education curriculum (Sallis et al., 1997). More programs like this one are desperately needed in our public schools. Unfortunately, while many districts recognize the need to link health objectives with education, retraining programs are often not the top priority of budget-conscious administrators.

Schools and Too Many Rules

Modern society places numerous demands on its teachers. The teacher is expected to take on multiple assignments as an instructor and a moral educator, and in many ways, teachers are expected to play the roles that other social institutions have neglected. Unlike the clients of most other professions, students are typically in class against their will (Sarason, 1990).

Discipline is a recurring problem for physical education teachers, taking much time away from the learning experience. The physical education environment perhaps lends itself to more discipline problems because some students who view it as a place to release energy may become too active and create discipline problems. The simple lack of classroom walls enables students to move freely and makes control of the group more difficult. Much of the school day is devoted to time away from learning. School days usually include about five hours of class time, but time actually engaged in real learning is much less than that. According to William Damon, in his book *Greater Expectations: Overcoming the*

Culture of Indulgence in America's Homes and Schools (1995), the teaching role has become a narrow, rule-bound endeavor that focuses more on satisfying the rules than on bringing out the best human potential in every student.

The teacher's attention is often on developing and maintaining order and avoiding confrontation with increasingly threatening and hostile youths. Physical education teachers, particularly in their first few years of teaching, often struggle with discipline concerns. O'Sullivan (1989) reported that school administrators expected first-year teachers to manage their classes effectively and that instructional goals were of secondary importance. They reported that teachers often gave in to the demands of their students in exchange for their cooperation. The teachers and students reported being happier after the curriculum was modified to have a recreational focus in exchange for student motivation and compliance.

In many school districts decisions concerning the physical education curriculum are determined by state requirements. Many states (82.4 percent) have a written curriculum for physical education; half of these states require compliance with the curriculum, while 33.3 percent only recommend compliance. Among the 83.3 percent of states that require or recommend compliance, 54.7 percent monitor district and school compliance. At the district level, most districts (93.1 percent) have a written curriculum and about two thirds of those districts (69.9 percent) monitor compliance.

Canned curricula are a way that administrators can be assured that the curricular objectives are being met. Although these curricula provide a common standard for what should be taught in physical education classes, principals and district administrators often think it unnecessary to involve the physical education teachers in the decisions about outcomes that should be achieved in their classrooms and gymnasiums. The increase in more structured, rule-bound curricula in the public schools that are imposed from above leads many teachers to perceive that they are losing control over what and how they teach. When teachers are not involved in the creation or modifications to the curriculum, chances of effective implementation are greatly reduced. Educators Lawrence Butler and Gerard Mergardt (1994) point out that what is most important in the teacher–administrator relationship is not what the administrators do for teachers, but what the administrators trust teachers to do for themselves.

Successful administrators encourage their teachers to make many of the educational decisions in their respective programs. Teachers who enjoy autonomy, selecting their own activities, and being involved in assessment procedures are the ones who will remain actively engaged with their programs and students. Reformers fail to consider that teachers perceive problems differently and that teachers who are not involved in curricular decisions resist new practices and continue established ones. If reforms and innovations are to succeed, teachers must be involved in the reform process (Fuchs, 1996).

Many current major educational reforms call for meaningful cooperation among teachers—collaboration that extends well beyond asking and offering advice to one another (Popewitz & Myrdal, 1991). Teacher collaboration breaks the isolation of the classroom and leads to increased feelings of effectiveness and satisfaction. For beginning teachers, this collegiality saves them from the usual sink-or-swim, trial-and-error ordeal. Teachers are encouraged to work together to alter the curriculum, such as by infusing a multicultural perspective or making connections between different subjects. In schools where collaboration is the norm, students can sense program coherence and consistency of expectations, and their achievement may well be a response to a better learning environment. Over time teachers who work closely together become more adaptable and self-reliant. Together they have the energy, organizational skills, and resources to attempt innovations that would exhaust an individual teacher alone. Teacher teamwork makes complex tasks more manageable, stimulates new ideas, and promotes coherence in school curricula and instruction.

Despite the advantages of teacher collaboration, there are substantial barriers to it. In most schools, teachers are colleagues in name only. As pointed out by John Little (1990), teacher working style is grounded in *norms of privacy* and noninterference. Most secondary schools, for example, are organized by subject matter, and most teachers view themselves as subject-matter specialists. The subject gives teachers a frame of reference and professional identity. Working within departments organized by subject, teachers affiliate with others in the same field in professional associations and informal networks. Inevitably, the insularity of the classroom sustains their stereotypes regarding the nature and importance of subjects other than their own. Thus, the capacity of teachers to pursue new curricular and organizational forms is limited not only by their relative isolation from one another during the school day but also by subject and departmental boundaries.

Teachers often spend the day in relative social isolation. This is particularly true for physical education teachers, who spend much of their time physically isolated as well in the gym or on the playing fields outside the school building. An obstacle to extensive collaboration by physical education teachers is found in the barriers between the academic teachers and those playing "secondary roles." These differences are sustained by the values attached to two different student bodies in two different curricular tracks. Preparation of college-bound students sets the standard, marginalizing the non-college-bound students along with their teachers and curricula. The case of physical education teachers is even more problematic because of the mental–manual dichotomy that prevails in Western societies. Kirk (1992) argues that the presumed superiority of mental and worklike activities in schools places physical education toward the bottom of the hierarchy of school subjects. Other teachers' marginalizing the physical education profession results in social isolation of the physical education teacher at school. Physical educators for the most part must be self-reliant. Day-to-day experience or trial-and-error learning rather than pedagogical exchange or peer evaluation becomes the means for professional development.

Many teachers face problems of role conflict, lack of autonomy, and social isolation resulting from their low status within the school's bureaucratic system. For decades, teachers have struggled with large class sizes. Although class sizes have been reduced in many classrooms, exceptions are often made for physical education. School administrators who believe that only play, not instruction, takes place in the gym are more than willing to saddle the physical education instructor with 50, 60, or even more students in one class. Even with a normal class size, a particular source of worry for physical education teachers is student safety, which demands constant alertness and attention to students' heterogeneous ability levels. Lack of resources, insufficient provisions for safety, and parental and public disinterest in schooling contribute to low teacher morale and even lower expectations for their students.

An increasing number of physical education teachers are becoming discouraged and abandoning the profession in great numbers.

Many talented teachers who remain have buckled under the pressure and resort to one of two coping mechanisms: a move to coaching as a primary emphasis or conducting physical education classes that are really recreation breaks, not educational experiences.

Physical Education and At-Risk Students

In one sense, living in today's complex world places all students at risk. As discussed in chapter 4, adolescence is one of life's most difficult periods. However, the teenage years create more problems for some individuals than for others. The label *at-risk* has been applied to youths who lack the skills and values necessary to thrive in our society. Their problems are viewed in terms of a developmental deficit; that is, they fail to learn certain skills or values that should be cultivated during the maturation period of adolescence. Being at risk creates a "common constellation of hazards" and consequences, which Brendtro, Brokenleg, and Van Bockern (1990) have summarized in these four categories: (1) a climate of futility that leads to feelings of inadequacy and fear of failure, (2) learned irresponsibility that leads to a health- and community-destructive lifestyle, (3) loss of purpose that leads to a self-centered, valueless lifestyle, and (4) destructive relationships that lead to a health-compromising lifestyle.

Risky behaviors, such as substance abuse, delinquency, and violence, and educational and vocational difficulties are not isolated behaviors but an integrated pattern. Unhealthy behaviors, such as poor food choices, cigarette smoking, and drug and alcohol use, seem to concentrate in some individuals, while in others, good nutrition habits, abstinence from alcohol and drugs, and physical activity tend to cluster together. This clustering of positive health behaviors serves as the underlying rationale for using physical activity programming to modify the behaviors of at-risk adolescents.

Many students who engage in behaviors that put them at risk for serious social or health problems are sent to *alternative schools*. The last several decades have seen a growing number of special or alternative schools designed to deal with youngsters who have been removed from regular high schools because of their risk for failing or dropping out and those who have engaged in drug use, violence, or other illegal activity or behavior problem. Today nearly 280,000 (2 percent) of all high school students attend alternative schools (Grunbaum et al., 1999). Although alternative schools are designed to address students' health and social-behavioral problems, these schools fall short in promoting physical activity experiences for students. Data from a Youth Risk Behavior Surveillance System survey (YRBSS) of nearly 1,400 students attending alternative schools revealed the following: Just slightly over one third (36.9 percent) were enrolled in a physical education class, only 19 percent attended daily physical education, and only 64 percent reported being active in physical education class for more than 20 minutes. The participation rates at alternative schools reflect consistently lower rates than those reported in traditional schools (Grunbaum et al., 1999).

Recently, the interest of educators and other health professionals in developing physical activity programs that focus on working with students who are deemed at risk has increased. Thomas Collingwood (1997) is among the most successful in using physical education programs to provide a healthier alternative for at-risk students. His approach is based on the application of a structured physical training program designed to develop positive values and life skills such as goal setting and planning. The form of physical activity is not recreational games or sports but activities designed to improve physical fitness levels, such as muscular strength training.

The potential benefits derive from the distinctive characteristics of the physical training process, which Collingwood (1997) argues are not possible in a traditional sit-down learning or counseling setting. A regimented physical training process is very quantifiable, easily monitored, and it is not easy to fake effort. It requires the participant to be active rather than inactive, and it can be demanding and uncomfortable. The specific goals of physical training require delayed feedback and expectations for long-term results. All these characteristics, says Collingwood, make the physical training domain so attractive for teaching lifestyle habits, life skills, and values.

Not all believe that such a demanding, structured physical fitness program will work. Although Collingwood's (1997) list of many successes provides some support, it is likely that many youngsters have been turned off to any structure as a result of the negative experiences associated with their schooling and their prior physical education classes.

Physical education specialist Don Hellison (1995), for example, takes a different approach to addressing the needs of at-risk youths. Hellison's program of sports and physical activity is geared toward helping youngsters take more responsibility for their own well-being and the well-being of others. Program participants are taught to take responsibility for their own effort and goals and social responsibility through respecting the rights of others (Martinek & Hellison, 1997). Physical activity provides the possibility of exploring and practicing values of teamwork, goal setting, and conflict resolution. The program includes many features that have the

Photograph by Tom Roberts

Children can learn important life skills such as working with others and setting and reaching goals from participating in a sport.

potential to help youths develop greater social competence, more autonomy, and heightened optimism in a social environment that places many obstacles in their path.

The approaches of Collingwood and Hellison both rely on the concept of *resilience.* Bonnie Benard (1991) defines a resilient child as one who has the ability to "bounce back" despite exposure to severe risks. Resilience allows youngsters to adapt and change, no matter what the risks. In schools, teachers can foster resilience by teaching to the students' strengths and showing them that they have innate resilience. Giving children and youths the know-how to bounce back could enhance their future possibilities despite adverse social conditions.

Although these approaches are certainly valuable for encouraging youngsters to deal with their own situations, they do not represent the complete answer. In fact, some criticism suggests that these programs may actually do a disservice because they address the children themselves and not the social and physical environments that poorly serve the children in the first place. This argument is summed up by sociologists Robert Pitter and David Andrews (1997:96):

*O*verall, current sport-based social problems initiatives face an insurmountable challenge when one considers the complexity of the problems they are trying to address with what amounts to a simple solution. . . . Although sport may provide a means of motivating youth and providing them with a more positive outlook on life, it cannot by itself reverse the chronic unemployment, poverty, violent crime, and housing decay impacting their life changes. To be successful, policies and programs must pay attention to broader problems of societal organization and special problems of the inner city.

The term *underserved* first emerged in the 1970s to describe poor people as victims of the lack of support services and opportunities in their neighborhoods. William Julius Wilson's (1987) *The Truly Disadvantaged: The Inner City, the Underclass, and Public Policy* outlined the problems of inner-city neighborhoods with unusually high concentrations of poverty. Wilson coined a new term, *underclass,* to describe the residents whose lives are adversely affected by structural characteristics and economic changes in inner cities. According to Wilson, inner-city poverty of the 1980s and 1990s was quite different from inner-city poverty in previous generations because employment opportunities had moved out of these neighborhoods.

That situation in turn leads to high rates of unemployment, demor-alization, drug use, and deterioration of schools. Many of the prob-lems confronting city schools are deeply rooted in the poverty, un-employment, and human despair that pervade many urban neighborhoods.

Schools in urban districts tend to be larger, have higher truancy rates, and less involvement from parents than other schools. Urban teachers are twice as likely as other teachers to report that violence is a problem in their schools. Today, one out of every four American children, 11 million young people, attend an urban school. In urban schools where most of the students are poor, two thirds or more of the children fail to reach even the basic level on national tests, and in many of our cities, more than 60 percent of the students do not con-tinue with schooling beyond middle school (Quality Counts, 1998).

The sources of risk are not just in the students' own behavior; they are found in the schools and in societal and family conditions out-side the school. All sources of environmental risk need to be ad-dressed. How children perform in school depends heavily on fac-tors beyond the control of the school, such as parental time and involvement, decent meals, whether the child arrives in kindergar-ten or first grade ready to learn, whether parents are in the labor market, and whether the neighborhood is safe. Improving both stu-dents' current levels of physical activity and their prospects for con-tinuing to be physically active throughout their lifetimes requires efforts in many different domains.

Conclusion

Despite major advances in the body of knowledge about physical activity, school physical education continues to be plagued with con-fusion over goals and an increased questioning of its relevance. As we enter the new millennium, it is apparent that despite widespread public understanding of the need for increased physical activity, support in the form of resources for physical education in our schools is rapidly eroding. In one survey of districtwide school administra-tors, less than half of them believed that their physical education programs were teaching youngsters to learn movement skills or to learn physical activities for a lifetime, and less than one third of the administrators believed that physical education experiences led to fitness gains (Sallis, McKenzie, Kolody, & Curtis, 1996).

Parents are also seriously questioning the place of physical education in an already crowded curriculum. Many parents are unable to identify any positive contributions that the physical education curriculum made to their children's education (Tannehill et al., 1994). Parents, many of them unable to establish patterns of regular physical activity in their own lives, do not support physical education because their own school physical education experience followed a "throw-out-the-ball" model of essentially an extended recreation period.

Administrators and parents are not the only group to question the value of high school physical education programs. In one inquiry, students who did not take elective physical education after completing the requirement said that they felt additional college-preparation coursework was more important than more physical education classes (Scantling, 1995). Many students find physical education irrelevant and not enjoyable (Carlson, 1995). A comprehensive study found that the negative physical education experiences reported by youngsters are related to the content of the physical education curriculum. More specifically, the nature of the curriculum and attitudes toward their teachers were identified as the most crucial determinants of negative attitudes (Luke & Sinclair, 1991). In the end, physical activity programs can be effective only if children become intrinsically motivated to be active on their own.

The problems caused by the failure of schools to help children develop the skills to participate in physical activity are only exacerbated when young people complete their schooling. The difficulty in getting people to be more physically active only gets worse as young adults enter the workforce.

6

Modifying Workers, Not Work

Work site health programs have emphasized the reduction of physical and mental health problems, while paying less attention to opportunities for cultivating highly positive states of well-being . . . [and] have emphasized behavioral change and lifestyle modification programs aimed at individual employees, while giving less attention to interventions involving the restructuring and enhancement of work environments. *(Stokols, Pelletier, & Fielding, 1996:139, 141)*

▼   ▼   ▼   ▼   ▼

Work occupies a place of great significance in the lives of most Americans. A good job performs many valuable functions, especially access to the financial means and abilities to sustain a certain quality of living. Pay, however, provides only one context that rewards work. Jobs perform many other valuable functions. They give the day and week a structure, mold one's personal identity, and under the right circumstances, contribute to a sense of belonging and a feeling of purpose and accomplishment (Jahoda, 1982). The average working person spends more than one third of his or her waking hours on the job. Even with the stress and dissatisfaction that one's occupation often can bring, for many Americans, there is no satisfactory alternative. Many people may joke about winning the lottery and quitting their jobs early, but in reality most people would continue to work (Meaning of Work International Research Team, 1987). It is no wonder that sociologists Paul Blau and Otis Duncan (1967) proclaimed occupation as the single most important predictor of social status in American society.

The workplace has been viewed as an important site for addressing the nation's escalating health care costs. Nearly one third of the country's trillion-dollar medical costs are paid by employers through employment-linked health insurance, workers' compensation, and other payment mechanisms (Kizer, Pelletier, & Fielding, 1995). In 1980, health care benefits cost employers only $968 per employee; however, by 1990 this figure skyrocketed to $3,250 (Anspaugh, Hunter, & Mosley, 1995). Today, business-supported health care expenditures often exceed $4,000 per employee and account for more than 14 percent of the gross national product, twice what the country spends on education and national defense. Double-digit increases in the cost of medical benefits are one of the biggest financial challenges for businesses today. Such a heavy financial burden has compelled employers to consider ways to curb these escalating costs. For answers, many employers now offer health-promoting programs.

Among the most ardent supporters of work-supported health promotion programs are the insurance companies. In the 1980s, insurance companies started determining their premiums based on modifiable lifestyle behaviors, such as smoking and physical inactivity. More than half of commercial insurers use "healthy habits" as an important risk classification factor in issuing policies (Stone, 1986). Calculating an individual's portion of the premium based on lifestyle behaviors in effect shifted the responsibility for a variety of potential health problems from the workplace to the individual. Critics of *risk rating* warn that such practices are contradictory to the fundamental principle on which insurance is based, namely, distributing risk across a much larger group.

During the past decade, work-supported health promotion programs in the United States have grown dramatically. It is estimated that 85 percent of work sites with 50 or more employees offer at least one health promotion program (McGinnis, 1993). Many work-supported programs have increased their offerings from just a fitness program to include an array of different activities. Programs vary but may include fitness programs, recreation activities, and health promotion programs, such as cancer and hypertension screening. Some businesses provide elaborate facilities, such as gymnasi-ums, pools, and fully equipped weight rooms, while others have made more modest investments, relying on refurbished equipment housed in underutilized work spaces. The types of physical activity services offered are also quite varied, ranging from the distribution of exercise-related materials, brown-bag lectures, and employee-led exercise classes to more extensive programs that include health screening, individual behavioral counseling, and frequent monitor-ing of physical activity practices.

The motivation behind the expansion of work health promotion programs is the belief that paying better attention to employees' health will translate into financial dividends for the company, both in terms of worker productivity and lower health care costs. How-ever, as we will see in this chapter, work-supported fitness program-ming has not lived up to the high expectations for a variety of rea-sons. We focus on three of these. First, the traditional models of employee fitness programs concentrate on changing individual health behaviors, such as diet, smoking, and physical inactivity. Pro-grams that focus on changing the health of individuals overlook many of the health-compromising conditions that are present in the work environment. They ignore such work factors as the physical and emotional demands of work.

A second concern is the inability of work-sponsored fitness pro-grams to keep pace with the changing way Americans work. In the context of rapid societal change, work-sponsored fitness programs also ignore the changing structure of work, such as the increases in contingent, part-time and low-skilled jobs. People are also experi-encing displacement in the workforce. Some are out of work because their training is out of date with the needs of contemporary jobs and their knowledge and skills have become obsolete. These work trends raise troublesome issues concerning worker's health benefits and protections and present complex challenges to establishing healthy lifestyles.

Third, many workers consider the workplace an inappropriate place to offer health promotion activities. Workers may distrust the company medical department and fear that their health records will be used against them by management. Even when health programs do not directly affect employment decisions, they can be seen as a way of influencing the employees' private lives through intimida-tion or coercion.

Growth of Work-Sponsored Fitness Programs

Working out at the workplace is not new. Bell Telephone Company organized exercise breaks for its office employees during the 1920s. However, it was not until the late 1970s and 1980s, when corporations faced issues of escalating health care costs, that they considered providing programs on-site to promote the health and well-being of their employees.

The emphasis of the early work-supported fitness programs were the high-level managers and executives. *Executive fitness programs* offered high-level managers, mostly middle-aged and male, a range of options, including physicals, personalized fitness programs, and individual health counseling. Soon, businesses moved from viewing fitness programs as the perks of upper management to making these programs available to employees at all levels.

By the late 1970s, many work sites were interested in expanding health promotion programs to a larger number of employees. In 1979, the Washington Business Group for Health reported that more than 50 percent of Fortune 500 companies surveyed offered at least some form of health-promoting services to their employees (Kiefhaber, Weinberg, & Goldbeck, 1979). The next 20 years witnessed a steady increase in work-supported fitness programming. In 1985 and 1992, the Office of Disease Prevention and Health Promotion of the U.S. Public Health Service conducted the National Survey of Worksite Health Promotion Activities. The surveys from both years involved a stratified random sample of private-sector companies with 50 or more employees. The data from these two surveys provide strong evidence of the growing interest in health promotion programs in the United States and have been used to evaluate progress toward achieving the work health promotion objectives outlined in *Healthy People 2000.* In 1985, more than half of the largest work sites, those with 750 or more employees, offered some form of physical activity programming (Fielding & Piserchia, 1989). By 1992, the number had grown to more than 81 percent. Hewitt Associates, in a more recent survey of more than 1,000 employers, reported that 91 percent offered physical activity as part of their health promotion efforts (Moskowitz, 1999). While the smaller work sites were less likely to offer exercise programs, which often require the most resources, data from the National Health Interview Survey suggest that 34.6 percent of U.S. workplaces offer some form of physical activity programming on-site (Grosch, Alterman, Petersen, & Murphy, 1998).

Photograph by Tom Roberts

Work-site physical activity programming is on the rise.

Perhaps the best-known employee fitness program is the Live for Life program sponsored by Johnson & Johnson (Fielding, 1994). The program, which started in 1979, provided its employees with basic tests of health (e.g., blood pressure screening) along with an assessment of physical activity parameters such as exercise habits and body-fat measurements. If high-risk conditions were identified, the company offered individualized programs that included core lifestyle improvement activities, such as behaviorally oriented programs dealing with nutrition, exercise, weight control, smoking cessation, stress management, and blood pressure control. Companies such as Johnson & Johnson use health-promoting activities to strengthen their image in addition to controlling health costs. Improving the health and well-being of employees makes a great deal of sense for a company like Johnson & Johnson, one of the largest producers of health care products (Wilbur, 1983).

To convince employees to engage in health-promoting behaviors, a growing number of employers offer a variety of inducements, the most popular being *compensatory* or *incentive programs.* These programs assume that employees can be motivated to change their health-risking habits with external rewards. The most common inducements are reduced fees for participation in exercise or weight-loss classes, but in many cases, incentives are in the form of merchandise, such as fitness equipment or clothing. Some companies have extended the model to rewards such as paid travel or additional vacation days.

More recent approaches include tying employee incentives to overall employer health benefits. The national health objectives recommend that insurance companies offer preferential rates on life and health insurance to groups engaged in health promotion programs at work. Insurance copayments or deductibles may be reduced or waived for ongoing participation in a health promotion program. In one survey of more than 350 companies, more than 20 percent gave awards to workers who had met specified health criteria, and 15 percent gave workers who met the criteria credits that they could use for additional fringe benefits (Moskowitz, 1999). In another incentive program, employees are not charged for health insurance provided that they remain tobacco free and weigh no more than 1.2 times their ideal weight (Nordhaus-Bike, 1997). Employees who sign up but are later caught smoking must begin paying for coverage and cannot participate in the work-sponsored program until they complete a waiting period. Those who do not meet the weight requirements are allowed to participate if they agree to lose the excess weight.

Some incentive programs resort to peer pressure to get fellow employees to adopt healthy lifestyles. As market demand has increased, insurers have gradually integrated financial incentive programs into a wider range of benefits. But to qualify, in the case of one no-smoking effort, employers in larger organizations had to certify that 90 percent of their employees are nonsmokers, while groups with fewer than 11 employees had to certify that 100 percent of employees are nonsmokers (Caudron, 1992).

Some programs have even introduced disincentives, the assessment of penalties for engaging in unhealthy behaviors. In one company, employees were charged $43 per month for smoking, $40 for high blood pressure, $12 for high cholesterol, $16 for lack of exercise, and $36 for excess body weight. Employees who met all five healthy criteria received an extra $30 per month off their health care premiums, whereas those who had all five risk factors paid an extra $117 per month (Caudron, 1992).

Strategies that use incentives or disincentives, and that are grounded on principles of behaviorism and operant conditioning, have drawn criticisms from several fronts. Although research on operant conditioning strategies suggests that incentive approaches may enhance initial participation in health promotion, such external rewards are not likely to alter long-term behavior. Moreover, there is very little evidence to support the use of extrinsic incentives as motivational tools to promote participation in physical activity. For example, in a study of the effectiveness of awarding prizes based on attendance at an exercise program, the incentive had minimal impact on attendance (Martin et al., 1984). Similarly, Estabrooks and colleagues found that fitness club participants who are given complimentary key chains did not experience higher attendance rates compared to a group of control subjects who received no incentives (Estabrooks, Courneya, & Nigg, 1996). Even if these approaches were effective, they raise ethical questions.

Priester (1992) points to two fundamental ethical issues. He first questioned whether the consequences of health typically associated with good health behaviors are within the control of the individual. Genetic predisposition to high blood pressure or obesity places certain workers in a different category from those who were blessed with "better parents." Second, he warned that incentives are often construed by the participant as coercive or manipulative and actually serve to undermine motivation and decrease worker trust in the organization. The traditional model of work-sponsored health programs pays too little attention to the root causes of many of the health problems of workers and thus denies the possibility that work and social environments are producing harmful health outcomes.

Promoting the Health of the Corporation

The expansion of work-sponsored health promotion efforts is based on the premise that a healthy and happy workforce will give more of themselves to the company and will perceive the program as a gesture of management's concern for them. Promoters of work-sponsored exercise programs are interested in connecting involvement in these programs with increases in worker loyalty and worker productivity.

Worker Loyalty

One goal of work-sponsored fitness programs is developing *worker loyalty*. Worker loyalty is important to employers because it is assumed to be related to good work habits and increased work productivity. Loyal workers are viewed as committed to their employers and intending to remain at their jobs long term. Rudman (1988), in his analysis of the relationship between use of the company fitness center and attitudes toward work and the company, found a direct relationship between level of physical activity and perceived level of work productivity. Fitness center users were more likely to believe that regular exercise helps them to be more productive, think more clearly about work-related problems, concentrate better on work tasks, and relate better to co-workers. Rudman also concluded that fitness center users held a positive attitude toward the company. He reasoned that the introduction of a work-sponsored fitness program increased employee perception of organizational support for good health practices.

It might seem logical to conclude that companies that provide extensive fitness and health promotion programs are able to capitalize on such efforts by maintaining a highly productive labor force. An alternative view suggests that the organization's employees who have a strong work ethic may not participate in on-the-job fitness activities. Two consequences of a strong work ethic may be a total focus on work assignments and a de-emphasis of leisure pursuits, particularly those performed on "company time."

Peter Mudrack (1992), business professor at Kansas State University, studied the question of whether highly driven employees regarded the company fitness program as a wasteful activity that only diverts attention and energy from the important work at hand. In a study of more than 300 employees, Mudrack found the opposite to be true. Individuals who scored high on a four-item measure of work ethic regarded the fitness program as a logical extension of work activities. These achievement-driven workers viewed the role of exercise in terms of its potential to enhance work performance, not take away from it. Baun and his colleagues (1986) argued that companies with a strong commitment to their fitness programs are better able to selectively recruit and retain individuals interested in fitness and that such people tend to be high achievers. Their main evidence for this speculation was a cross-sectional comparison of performance and job turnover rates of participants and nonparticipants in a company fitness program.

The question of whether work-sponsored fitness programs are responsible for instilling values of success in all employees is still debatable. A closer look reveals that the relationship between health promotion efforts and worker loyalty affects only a small number of workers. The small percentage of workers found in workplace fitness centers represent a subgroup of American society, those who have likely already developed a strong attachment to the company and desire to succeed. These people are likely to be loyal workers without the presence of work-sponsored fitness facilities.

Worker Productivity

Positive attitudes toward the corporation are nice, but more tangible measures of worker productivity are what employers are after. Many employers have been content to report subjective measures of work productivity, such as self-report measures of performance or employee morale. A rare exception to this is a study conducted by Bernacki and Baun (1984) of the relationship of job performance and exercise adherence in a corporate fitness program. The authors collected information on participation in the company fitness program and formal supervisors' ratings of work productivity. The authors found a strong association between above-average work performance ratings and participation in the corporate fitness program. Likewise, an inverse relationship existed between poor work performance and participation in the program. Although the authors were quick to acknowledge that this was only one study and that the research design prohibited establishing causal connections between work productivity and program adherence, these findings are consistent with employers' readiness to associate fitness programs at their work sites with the workplace productivity.

Employees who are not at work cannot be productive (Baun, Bernacki, & Tsai, 1986). Workplace productivity is often assessed in an indirect fashion using rates of absenteeism. Absentee rates in the workplace have become a major problem for most employers; they have risen more than 30 percent during the past 25 years (Higgins, 1988). Occupational work loss is difficult to measure but likely ranges from 5 to 40 days per year and is estimated to cost from $60 to $540 billion per year in the United States alone (Shephard, 1994). Several studies have attempted to link reductions of absenteeism with participation in work-sponsored fitness programs. For example, a study of a Canadian workplace that had a fitness program found that absenteeism was reduced by 22 percent and turnover by 14 percent compared with a reference company without such a program (Cox, Shephard, & Corey, 1981). Studies have shown that individuals with higher fitness rates are absent less than individuals with lower fitness levels, with differences ranging from 0.28 days to 2 or more days per year (Baun, 1995). A more recent study that examined the relationship between participation in a fitness program and work absenteeism concluded that program participants had a history of fewer absences before beginning the program. Therefore, it may be the case that selection is occurring; that is, it may be that workplace fitness programs attract employees who are less likely to miss work in the first place.

Unfortunately, limitations in the methodologies of many studies of work-sponsored fitness programs have made it difficult to analyze their benefits. Unlike laboratory studies, work-sponsored fitness programs are studied without an experimental control. Fitness programs cannot be introduced into a company without both the employees and those responsible for assessment being aware of the intervention (Shephard, 1996). The use of poorly validated measures of physical activity participation and aerobic fitness and the inappropriate use of comparison groups or units and methods of statistical analysis contribute to the current confusion concerning the effectiveness of work-sponsored fitness programs (Dishman, Oldenburg, O'Neal, & Shephard, 1998).

Another problem is that few employees stay involved in the program long enough to reap the program benefits or for researchers to determine what those benefits may be. For those who join workplace fitness programs, dropout rates are estimated at between 30 and 70 percent during the first three to six months (Dishman, 1982). There is a progressive increase in the number of employees who drop out of a corporate program during the first three months of its operation. As suggested by Roy Shephard (1996), in almost all cases where studies are conducted over longer periods of time, the advantageous effects of exercise on absenteeism are decreased essentially because of the high dropout rate from the programs. Typically, of the small percentage of employees who are initially recruited to the fitness facility, perhaps as few as 10 to 20 percent continue to comply with program requirements beyond the first few months (Shephard, 1996). If worker improvement is figured across the entire workforce, the gains in health-related fitness would actually be very small.

Despite the weaknesses of many of the studies on work-sponsored fitness programming, the intuitive logic that connects these programs with an improved corporate bottom line continues to hold much appeal for many business managers, who are quick to promote individual fitness programs and their perceived cost savings. The presumption that employees as well as the corporation are "healthier" as a result of their participation in work-sponsored health promotion programs is attractive. Managers like to think that workers will be more productive, use fewer health services, and be absent from work less. Certainly, better designed studies will clarify the benefits, but it is the logic behind connecting individual health behaviors, such as physical activity, with work productivity that is likely to lead us down the wrong path.

Current interest in connecting fitness programs with curtailing absentee rates is a good example. Absenteeism is typically defined as absence from work due to sickness, injury, or for some other personal reason. A wide range of factors influence absenteeism, and a good case in point involves many female employees. Absenteeism rates for women in most work environments are predictably higher than those for men. Women, as discussed earlier, often assume the role of caregiver within the family; they are the ones who stay home with sick children, take family members to health appointments, or attend to problems with aging parents and grandparents. Despite the fact that the majority of mothers are presently employed or looking for work, many jobs are designed as if workers were husbands with homemakers to provide domestic support (Hochschild, 1989).

Most employers do not consider the fact that a large number of their workers are either parents in dual-earner families or single parents. Workplace fitness programs will not promote the health of sick children, drive relatives to health appointments, or allow needy parents to take care of themselves. Viewed this way, it is not the health promotion program that will improve the problem of absenteeism—more flexible sick and family leave policies will. Unfortunately, employers are less willing to invest time and resources in making changes where they are likely to have the greatest impact on the health of both the corporation and all its employees: the environments both inside and outside the workplace.

Lack of Comprehensive Health Programs

Despite the wide variation among work-sponsored fitness programs, many share a general lack of comprehensiveness in their approach. A framework developed by O'Donnell and Ainsworth (1984) offers a clearer picture of what is meant by a comprehensive health program. A comprehensive health promotion program includes health-promoting activities in three categories: awareness, health management, and supportive environment. Activities in category 1, awareness activities, increase the participants' knowledge about and interest in specific health problems or issues and are designed to either persuade individual employees to engage in healthy behaviors or dissuade them from engaging in risky behaviors. Awareness activities might include newsletters, special events, flyers, posters, or educational seminars. Category 2, health management, focuses on various strategies to help individual employees make specific lifestyle changes. These approaches usually involve a personal health assessment followed by specific strategies such as goal setting to help individuals make the behavioral change. Category 3, supportive environment, focuses on providing health-promoting work conditions. Supportive workplace environments reinforce and sustain healthy lifestyles through efforts to encourage employees to engage in healthy behaviors, such as employer policies that ban smoking and employer-supported flextime to use fitness facilities.

Despite the growth of workplace health activities for employees, relatively few companies offer multiple and coordinated activities that give serious attention to organizational and environmental supports for modifying unhealthy behaviors. Bellingham and Isham's (1990) in-depth analysis of company case studies provides some interesting information about the philosophy behind many workplace health-promoting efforts. According to their analysis, businesses provide individual risk-reduction programs (categories 1 and 2) but do a very poor job in integrating disease prevention within their organizational policies (category 3). For example, they found only one company that included a supportive, positive health environment as a meaningful criterion in the performance appraisal process for management personnel. In fact, only four companies mentioned that the top managers in their organization even believed it was their responsibility to reduce excessive stress.

The businesses in Bellingham and Isham's (1990) analysis are likely not representative of all businesses that sponsor health promotion efforts. Yet company health promotion efforts often steer clear of creating corporate policies and regulations that would promote healthy behaviors through more supportive work climates. A 1994 survey of work-sponsored health promotion programs revealed that health promotion programs remained focused on changing individual health behaviors (Reardon, 1998). Using the categories developed by Bellingham and Isham (1990), this study found that the overwhelming majority offered category 1 and category 2 activities: 80 percent of the businesses offered educational activities, 74 percent screened for health risks through physical assessment, and 44 percent offered facilities for fitness. While most businesses had policy statements supporting positive health behaviors, few adopted corporate policies that would allow greater use of the fitness facilities or reduce stressful work conditions. It is not surprising that so few employees become active participants at the workplace fitness facility.

Health promotion specialists Crump, Earp, Kozma, and Hertz-Picciotto (1996) developed a more general conceptual model to guide the development and implementation of an effective health promotion program. It emphasizes the interaction between the health program and the context within which the program is introduced. Their model emphasizes three components of organizational context. The first component, *management support,* emphasizes the importance of support from workplace decision makers. The percentage of employees who believe their managers support their participation in a health promotion program and receive frequent confirmation from above is important to the long-term success of the program. The second component, *social environment,* is co-workers' support. The third component, *organizational resources,* is the presence of supportive policies and instrumental support that the company contributes, including facilities, salary, permanent budget, and release time for participation in the program.

Carolyn Crump and colleagues (1996) applied the organizational context model to 10 health promotion programs in federal agencies. Their data were collected from a variety of sources, including on-site surveys and interviews with program administrators and middle- and upper-level managers as well as focus group interviews of employees. The percentage of employees participating in agency-supported fitness activities ranged from 4.5 percent to 27 percent (table 6.1).

Table 6.1   Participation in Employer-Sponsored Fitness Activities at 10 Work Sites

Participation in fitness activities	Percentage of employees participating at each site									
Total	25	27	6.7	19	18	27	16	6.8	19	4.5
Men	16	22	5.6	18	18	29	11	12	11	7.3
Women	36	31	7.2	20	19	26	27	4.2	25	2.5
White	18	28	6.4	19	19	29	17	9.6	20	5.6
Other	36	23	7.5	19	20	19	17	4.7	18	0.0
High-level job	23	27	7.4	19	20	32	16	7.4	22	5.5
Low-level job	30	27	4.4	19	7.9	18	17	5.6	16	3.4

Adapted from Crump et al., 1996.

Although management support was important for encouraging employee participation, greater management support was related to a higher rate of participation by employees who were male, white, and in upper-level positions. Co-worker support was also important to participation for all employee subgroups, but time off for participation in fitness activities was particularly important among employees who were female, among ethnic minorities, and in lower-level jobs.

To promote greater participation in fitness activities by workers in lower-level positions, the workplace must minimally provide a certain level of organizational resources and a range of program hours in order to be responsive to all employees' needs and interests. Having time off to participate as well as having good on-site facilities is important for participation in fitness activities by employees in lower-level jobs (Crump et al., 1996). Without such organizational supports, equal participation across all employee subgroups is not likely to be achieved.

In addition to making the workplace environment more conducive to health-promoting behaviors, supportive environments must also change work conditions to allow all workers to feel comfortable. Individuals who feel different experience discomfort and stress if the differences are not understood and accepted by the majority group. An environment that fails to respect diversity may create tension and stress that may overburden minority workers. Diane

Hughes and Mark Dodge (1997) studied African-American women's exposure to a range of occupational stressors at the workplace, including two types of racial bias: institutional discrimination and interpersonal prejudice. Institutional discrimination included differences in salaries, benefits, job assignments, and opportunities for promotion. Interpersonal prejudice included interpersonal assumptions of incompetence and such issues as overhearing racial jokes. They found that institutional discrimination and interpersonal prejudice were more important predictors of job quality for these women than were other occupational stressors such as low task variety, decision authority, heavy workloads, and poor supervision.

Health promotion programs reflect the workplace culture that accommodates them. If a work environment is generally intolerant of differences, chances are that its health promotion programs are likewise intolerant. Conversely, a work environment that is demonstratively committed to diversity promotes inclusion of and sensitivity to those who are different. To be effective, workplace health promotion programs have to be "a natural outgrowth of a fundamental commitment to diversity" that is practiced throughout the organization (Aguirre-Molina & Molina, 1990).

Social environment is important in explaining employee participation in workplace exercise programs. Employees are more likely to participate in program activities if they believe it is the norm of the workplace to do so. Having a supportive social environment is particularly important for participation in activities that require greater time commitment, such as fitness programs.

It is critical for organizations to develop norms that promote both individual and organizational health. Without supportive norms in the organization as a whole, many health promotion efforts remain largely ineffective. Unhealthy organizational norms may actually pose the most dangerous risks to the health of the employees, particularly where the work conditions themselves present health risks to employees.

The Job As a Health Risk Factor

As far back as Jeremy Morris' original investigation of the health implications of driving a bus, sedentary occupations have been connected to health risks. Health hazards have long been part of the struggle of labor unions against profit-centered and uncaring management. Particularly before the implementation of worker safety laws, dangerous environmental conditions in factories, mines, and other workplaces led to thousands of deaths and countless debilitating work-related injuries. It was not until the early years of the 20th century that any serious legislation for worker safety appeared in the United States. Early in the 20th century, federal regulation that addressed safety and health issues focused primarily on very specific occupations that were considered to be dangerous. By the mid-1960s, the National Safety Council estimated that more than 14,000 deaths and two million injuries were occurring annually in American workplaces. At the same time, the general public was growing more and more concerned about the nation's responsibility to protect human health and the environment. By the 1970s, the concern for worker health and safety had reached such a level that Congress enacted the Occupational Safety and Health Act (OSH Act), which created three federal agencies, the Occupational Safety and Health Administration (OSHA), the National Institute for Occupational Safety and Health (NIOSH), and the Occupational Safety and Health Review Commission (OSHRC).

Physical Demands of Work

Although legislation and work policies have substantially reduced the number of workplace deaths and serious injuries, risks are still associated with many physically demanding jobs. For example, Mooney, Kenny, and Leggett (1996) studied the impact of the physical demands of shipyard work on the prevalence of injury. During the course of their two-year study, they found that 9 percent of the workers developed lower-back injuries, with the highest incidence found among those engaged in the two heaviest demand categories. Physical tasks such as repetitive heavy lifting, especially in twisted positions, and motor vehicle driving are well-established risk factors for back and neck pain.

Overall workplace injuries have decreased, but cumulative trauma disorders (CTDs) have risen steadily. CTDs are the result of tissue damage or pain produced when a worker is exposed to physically demanding work (Kerr, 2000). CTDs currently account for one third of all occupational injuries and illnesses reported to the Bureau of Labor Statistics by employers annually. In 1997, employers reported a total of 626,000 lost workdays. Employers pay more than $15 million in workers' compensation costs for these disorders every year. Back injuries are the most prevalent; approximately 75 percent of all

Americans will experience a back injury sometime during their working lives. CTDs, including carpal tunnel syndrome, account for a growing number of workers' compensation cases. Particularly prevalent among women because they operate the majority of computer workstations, CTDs account for more than 240,000 surgeries in the United States each year (Wrist Wrap, 1998).

Many employers look to the workplace fitness center to address the physical problems of the workforce. Many believe that attention to the individual risk factors among their employees is the answer to CTDs and other job-induced injuries among their workers. A number of individual risk factors have been studied in this regard, though very few have been clearly linked to CTDs. The strongest and most consistent associations have been reported for prior occurrence of a CTD, with somewhat weaker associations for age, obesity, smoking, and so on (Garg & Moore, 1992). Research in this area is difficult because musculoskeletal disorders do not occur exclusively in workers and because there is no simple, reliable, and reproducible test for most CTDs (Davis, 1999). Currently, there is very little evidence supporting an association between the occurrence of a CTD and general fitness, muscular strength levels, or the presence of psychological disorders such as depression and anxiety (Bigos, Battie, & Spengler, 1991). Employees look for answers in programs designed to rehabilitate the injured workers. However, holding individual workers responsible allows the employee to blame the individual, not the work environment.

Recently, OSHA proposed new rules requiring employers to protect employees in general industry workplaces who are at significant risk of incurring a work-related musculoskeletal disorder (WMSD). The proposed rules would require employers to develop a program to improve working conditions after at least one employee reports a work-related injury. For example, employers may be required to adjust workstations in that work area to make them less fatiguing on the body. OSHA estimates that the new rulings will cost employers a total of $4.2 billion, but they would save twice that amount in reduced health care costs and lost worker productivity. Some business leaders vow to oppose the new rules, saying that the costs would be significantly higher and that they would prefer to develop their own strategies for overcoming the physical and mental demands of many contemporary jobs. One consequence of the OSHA's proposed rules was an increase in awareness of the potentially health-compromising demands of the workplace environment on the worker.

Sedentary Work

At the other end of the spectrum from physically demanding jobs are jobs that require very little in the way of human physical effort. Technological advances in manufacturing, construction, transportation, farming, mining, and many other industries have substantially reduced the number of workers that are required to perform vigorous activity to make a living. The introduction of increased levels of automation and the presence of computers in the office have reduced the amount of physical movement on the job. According to William Haskell (1994), the peak energy requirement for most of these jobs does not exceed 3 METs (4 kilocalories per minute), which is less than 35 percent of the aerobic capacity of most healthy adults.

Musculoskeletal stress due to sedentary work is a problem in some workplaces. For many workers, the most vigorous job-related exercise is getting to work. In the office, for example, the administrative assistant can produce the documents needed, access files, and submit messages to other offices without ever leaving the keyboard. As a result, both the repetitive stress from increased use of the keyboard and the long periods of sitting create health risks.

There are numerous reports of a positive relationship between back pain and sedentary occupations that require sitting while working, such as bus and truck driving. Magnusson, Pope, Wilder, and Areskoug (1996) found that long-term vibration exposure while sitting was the highest risk factor for lower-back pain, more so than heavy or frequent lifting. Although other studies do not support a unique effect of sitting on musculoskeletal tissues or back problems, the health risks of sedentary occupations often become evident only years after working in conditions that were presumed safe (Hartvigsen, Leboeuf-Yde, Lings, & Corder, 2000).

The beneficial effect of occupational physical activity on health, particularly cardiovascular disease, has been well documented among men (Steenland, Johnson, & Nowlin, 1997). For example, Berlin and Colditz (1990), in a statistical review of a number of studies relating occupational physical activity to cardiovascular disease, reported an inverse relationship between level of activity and cardiovascular disease. Men in sedentary jobs nearly doubled their risk for heart attack.

Fewer studies have examined the influence of occupational physical activity on cardiovascular disease in women, but for women physical activity associated with a job may have a protective effect.

For example, Lapidus and Bengtsson (1986) followed a cohort of 1,462 Swedish women over a 12-year period. After the subjects detailed as completely as possible their physical activity during their work hours, they were assigned to one of four physical activity groupings: Women with light office work were assigned to group 1; women with shop work or light industrial work were in group 2; women with hospital work were assigned to group 3; and group 4 included women who performed heavy work. Workers who reported low physical activity at work had a significant increase in the incidence of stroke and death. Their greater risk for stroke and death remained even after statistically controlling for potential confounding factors, which included socioeconomic status, smoking habits, blood pressure, and cholesterol levels.

In a second example, Wilbur and colleagues (1999) studied 171 women employed in one of four occupations: registered nurses, nurse's assistants, telephone operators, and academic faculty. These occupations were selected because they were expected to vary in physical activity from low (academic faculty and telephone operators) to high (registered nurses and nursing assistants). The authors concluded that the women in work positions that did not provide the flexibility to move about on the job would be the most vulnerable to cardiovascular disease. The authors thought that the telephone personnel who were deskbound and whose work often required long hours of sitting would be particularly susceptible. While the results of their study did point to the elevated risks for telephone operators, a more surprising finding pointed to the health risks among the academic faculty. Although one might expect academic faculty to participate in a greater amount of leisure-time physical activity due to greater flexibility in work schedules and high educational levels (relative to the other occupations in the study), this was not the case. Nurses and nursing assistants, on the other hand, experienced health benefits likely due to the walking and bending associated with their jobs. Another study showed that the amount of daily physical activity letter and newspaper carriers got on the job reached the minimal level to promote physical fitness (Uusi-Rasi, Nugard, Oja, Pasanen, Sievanen, & Vuori, 1994).

Mental and Emotional Demands of Work

The problems associated with jobs in today's workplace are not always related to too much or too little physical activity. In recent years, interest in the consequences of the mental and emotional demands of the job for the health of workers has become front and center. During the transformation to an industrial age, many jobs were taken over by machines, leaving only jobs that were reduced to extremely simple, highly repetitive, monotonous operations that required few, if any, skills or training. Many of today's jobs are suffering the same unfortunate *de–skilling* as during the industrial revolution; jobs are becoming boring, mindless, and mentally fatiguing. Some people argue that de–skilling during the technological age adversely affects all levels of occupations—not just the clerical occupations but managerial and even executive jobs (McInerney, 1989). Braverman (1974) contended that management deliberately fragmented jobs into smaller and smaller tasks, separating the "thinking" parts from the "doing" parts in order to increase control over the process of production. Although some evidence suggests that "mindless" work activity may have negative health consequences, researchers have developed models that indicate that the work stress–health relationship is more complicated than that.

For many years researchers had tried unsuccessfully to demonstrate the existence of a relationship between job stress and disease. It was studying the dimension of job control that showed the link. Psychological strain and its subsequent health effects are a consequence of the joint effects of the demands of a job and the range of control available to the worker (Eakin, 1997). The job demand–control model postulates that the primary sources of job stress depend on two basic characteristics of the job: job demands and job control. *Job demands,* or workload, as defined by Karasek and Theorell (1990), are the stressors present in the work environment (e.g., high pressure for time, fast working pace, difficult and mentally exacting work). *Job control,* sometimes referred to as *decision latitude,* focuses on the nature and amount of discretion workers have over their jobs.

According to this model, the strongest adverse strain occurs when job demands are high and the worker's control is low. Good jobs, at least in terms of job control and job demands, offer workers some choice in how, when, and where they work. They also permit the worker to identify with and to value the output of the work; they offer opportunities for learning, personal growth, and career development; they provide adequate or good remuneration and benefits.

A number of studies have focused on workplace control and work demands and their possible link to cardiovascular disease. Individuals working in jobs that are characterized by high psychological demands and low decision latitude are at increased risk for heart disease and are more likely to develop more serious conditions over time.

A third approach to the stress and strain of the workplace takes a different tack. According to the model developed by Siegrist (1996), the emphasis should be on the reward rather than the control structure of work. The model suggests that effort spent at work is part of a socially organized exchange process to which society at large contributes in terms of occupational rewards. Having a demanding but unstable job and achieving at a high level without being offered a promotion are examples of stressful imbalance. The lack of reciprocity between costs and gains may cause a state of emotional stress that can lead to health problems. For example, DeJonge, Bosma, Peter, and Siegrist (2000), in a study of 11,636 employees, found that those who reported high efforts and low reward experienced higher levels of emotional exhaustion and psychosomatic and physical health complaints.

The research on work and family roles suggests that rewards outside of the workplace are important as well. Work–family research has been dominated by two competing hypotheses. The first, which has come to be known as a *role strain perspective*, suggests that people, particularly women, with multiple roles experience role overload, resulting in harmful effects on health and on participation in healthy behaviors (Verbrugge, 1986). Lee, Duxbury, and Higgins (1994) found that more than 25 percent of female workers thought of quitting because balancing work and family was too stressful, more than 85 percent felt that there were not enough hours in the day to accomplish everything that had to be done, and more than half felt that they did not have enough spare time for themselves.

A competing perspective suggests that participation in multiple roles produces a greater number of opportunities and resources for the individual that contribute positively to other areas. The *role enhancement* perspective suggests that each role brings benefits (e.g., increased social contacts, satisfaction, and self-esteem) and contributes to better health and greater psychological well-being. An accumulating body of literature consistently has found, for example, that employed, married mothers have better physical and psychological well-being than their unemployed counterparts (Waldon & Jacobs, 1989).

Linking Work Conditions to Sedentary Lifestyles

There is increasing evidence that the potentially health-compromising qualities of work, whether its physical or mental demands or sedentariness, can affect the amount of physical activity performed outside the workplace. The "unwinding" process has been shown to be prolonged after excessive overtime and after a day of intense and repetitive data-entry work. In one study, 56 percent of retail trade workers reported that fatigue and practical difficulties with work were an obstacle to involvement in sport and physical activity. Fatigue and a need for long recovery times after work can affect behaviors at home. At the end of the day, many workers are tired and stressed and just want to go home (Alexy, 1990).

According to the "spillover" hypothesis, individuals with demanding jobs that also limit autonomy and social interaction at work take part in fewer organized and goal-oriented activities outside work. The possible influences of work organization and work-related stress on the levels of physical activity during leisure time received some confirmation in a longitudinal project known as the Swedish Level of Living Survey (Johansson, Johnson, & Hall, 1991). The survey was commissioned by the Swedish government to provide ongoing documentation of the distribution of health status, income, education, and aspects of the social and work environment. During the 1980s, the annual survey became biannual and has provided a rich source of information concerning work and health issues. Johansson and his colleagues (1991) examined a subsample of 7,201 employed people, equally split between males and females. They investigated two basic attributes of work environment: job demands and work resources. Job demands included such factors as perception of psychological demands (e.g., "Is your work hectic?"), physical load (e.g., "Do you think your work is safe from the point of view of accident risk?"), and monotony (e.g., "Does your work involve many repeated and one-sided movements?"). Work resources included measures of personal freedom (e.g., influence over how time is used in work), learning opportunities (e.g., the experience of personal fulfillment on the job), and work process control (e.g., influence over the planning and setting of work pace).

The survey produced some interesting findings. First of all, sedentary leisure pursuits were positively associated with hazardous exposure and monotonous work for both men and women. The researchers also found that work resources, particularly lack of job control, were linked to a range of health risk behaviors, including sedentary behaviors. Employees in positions with low decision latitude were found to participate in more passive leisure-time pursuits than workers with more discretion over their work. These findings are consistent with those from a longitudinal analysis of workers who had experienced job changes. Those whose work transition meant richer job content and more job control increased their leisure-time participation in voluntary associations, including sport teams and other physical activities (Karasek & Theorell, 1990).

Using concepts from Karasek and Theorell's model of job demands and job control (decision latitude) and a measure of physical activity on the job, Brisson and colleagues (2000) studied a large sample of male (3,531) and female (3,464) white-collar workers. Sedentary behavior in their study was defined as participation in leisure-time physical activity less than once a week during the prior six months. For analytical purposes, measures of job demands, job control, and job strain (low, active, passive) were divided into four quartiles. The statistic known as odds ratios were used to measure the degree of association between the three mental components of work and leisure-time physical sedentary behavior. Sedentary behavior was most prevalent among male workers with low job control and with high job demand. Men in passive-work jobs were also found to participate in lower levels of leisure-time physical activity (Brisson, Larocque, Moisan, Vezina, & Dagenais, 2000) (table 6.2). These findings are consistent with the previous work that has demonstrated that greater psychosocial demands of work encourage a passive lifestyle outside of work (Johansson, Johnson, & Hall, 1991).

The findings for women were only partially supported. For example, leisure-time physical inactivity was not associated with job control or passive work for women. Leisure-time sedentary behavior was highest in the third quartile of job demands. In their conclusion, the authors speculated that women experiencing highly demanding conditions at the workplace combined with family responsibilities at home had less energy and time to be physically active outside of work, consistent with popular belief (table 6.2).

A recent study compared these two perspectives in an attempt to determine whether "spillover" from family to work and from work to family was related to reported participation in physical activity (McElroy, 2001). Data were used from the National Survey of Midlife Development in the United States (MIDUS). The analysis of 918 men and 676 women who worked full-time during the previous year revealed that family issues that spill over into work were related to lower participation in physical activity for both men and women. However, there were no differences in physical activity for those who experienced negative work experiences that spill over into

Table 6.2 Odds Ratios of Sedentary Behavior for Quartiles of Job Control, Job Demands, and Job Strains for Men and Women

Job control and job demands		Job strain	
Men	**Odds ratio (95% CI)***	**Men**	**Odds ratio (95% CI)***
Job control			
Q1 Low	1.5 (1.2–1.8)*	Low strain	1.0
Q2	1.1 (0.9–1.4)	Active	1.2 (0.9–1.4)*
Q3	1.1 (0.9–1.3)	Passive	1.4 (1.1–1.7)*
Q4 High	1.0	High strain	1.3 (1.0–1.6)
Job demands			
Q1 Low	1.0		
Q2	0.9 (0.8–1.1)		
Q3	0.8 (0.9–1.3)		
Q4 High	1.0 (0.8–1.2)		
Women	**Odds ratio (95% CI)***	**Women**	**Odds ratio (95% CI)***
Job control			
Q1 Low	1.1 (0.9–1.4)	Low strain	1.0
Q2	1.1 (0.9–1.4)	Active	1.1 (0.8–1.4)
Q3	1.0 (0.8–1.2)	Passive	1.1 (0.9–1.4)
Q4 High	1.0	High strain	1.2 (0.9–1.5)*
Job demands			
Q1 Low	1.0		
Q2	0.9 (0.7–1.1)		
Q3	1.2 (1.0–1.4)*		
Q4 High	1.0 (0.8–1.2)		

* p < .05.

From Brisson et al., 2000.

family life. These findings need replication but suggest that family experiences that spill over into work experience is problematic for both men and women. The reality is that work and family roles each have both harmful and beneficial effects. Work can benefit family life, and family life can benefit work, yet demands external to the workplace, such as children and spouses, often impair the ability of many employees to perform at peak levels.

The complexity of the work–family interface means policies and programs at the workplace must be different for different contexts. As pointed out by Grzywacz and Marks (2000) in their study of work–family conflicts, workplace programs such as flextime and family leave may be important for some working parents, but for others, policies that redesign jobs to reduce pressure at work and build supportive work environments may prove more beneficial in reducing work–family conflict.

Unfortunately, many employers remain intent in changing the health behaviors of their workers. In an era of employer-based responsibility for health care, efforts are increasingly directed at lifestyle behavior programs rather than at redesigning work environments to be safe, less stressful, and more rewarding (DeJoy & Southern, 1993). High-strain jobs need to be identified and redesigned to allow a better balance between workers' psychological needs for control, the day-to-day demands of their work, and the performance criteria of their employers. Paying more attention to the amount of personal control or discretion that workers exercise over the increasing expectations of them is critical to workplace reform. The implication is clear: Focusing on worker discretion, job control (decision latitude), and involvement instead of the individual's characteristics means focusing on the work environment and the characteristics of the job rather than on the individual in the job.

Employers also often fail to recognize the pressures that family problems place on individuals. By failing to anticipate the needs of their staff effectively, employers assume that job conditions at work or social responsibilities outside of work are the individuals' problems and should be resolved by the individual. Holding individual workers responsible for their work and social environments is an example of blaming the victim. It assumes that workers engage in risky behaviors both in the workplace and in their own personal lives because they choose to do so.

The Changing Way We Work

In the traditional construct of work, people were educated for a lifetime. Once hired, employees could expect to work at the same job and firm for the rest of their working lives. In return, employers would expect people to be loyal to the company and to stick with the company through good and bad times. The economic recession of the 1980s and 1990s prompted major changes in the security of work. The technological and information age contributed to the workers' heightened sense of job insecurity. Some people were displaced from work because their education had not kept pace with the demands for new knowledge and skills. For others, deregulation and the downsizing of companies created the specter of long-term job insecurity. The health-damaging consequences of job insecurity were well documented in the famous Whitehall study, a longitudinal analysis of British Civil Service workers (Ferrie et al., 1998). The Property Services Agency, a division within British government, was slated for privatization. The researchers systematically documented how the anticipation and the experience of restructuring during the organizational crisis had a significant negative impact on the health of many of the workers. Employees today face rapidly changing patterns of work, trends such as corporate downsizing, and a move to part-time and temporary work. Today, even though the economy has improved, more and more people in the workforce are experiencing displacement.

Changing Demographics of the Workforce

During the past 50 years, the composition of the U.S. workforce has changed substantially. For example, in 1960, 33 percent of the labor force was made up of women. By the year 2004, the U.S. Department of Labor projects that well over half of the labor force will be female (U.S. Department of Labor, 1993). Ethnic and racial minority groups have undergone patterns and rates of growth that have not been seen previously in the United States. The number of African-American women in the civilian labor force increased by almost 26 percent between 1985 and 1995. The latest projections indicate that nine million African American women will be in the labor force by the year 2005 (U.S. Department of Labor, 1993).

A report titled Workforce 2020 produced by the Hudson Institute (Judy & D'Amico, 1997) predicts that by the second decade of this century, race and ethnic minorities will constitute slightly more than half of the entrants to the U.S. workforce. Whites constitute 76 percent of the total labor force and will account for 68 percent in 2020. They estimated that the share of African Americans in the labor force will remain constant over the next 20 years at 11 percent and the Asian and Hispanic share will grow to 6 and 14 percent, respectively.

Growth of Part-Time and Contingent Work

Concomitant with increasing participation of women and minorities in the labor force, a growing proportion of the labor force is found in part-time and contingent employment arrangements. It is estimated that as much as 40 percent of the salaried female labor force is employed part-time (O'Reilly & Fagan, 1998). New work forms also rely on *contingent arrangements* such as on-call workers, day laborers, independent contractors, and temporary workers. The growth of contingent employees reflects organizations' attempts to reduce the costs of maintaining permanent staff and to increase staffing and scheduling flexibility. Contingent workers are concentrated in low-wage industries or occupations. Women constitute two thirds of all part-time workers and nearly three fifths of all temporary workers. These types of employment arrangements typically provide lower wages, few or no benefits, and no protection from employers and labor laws. These jobs are insecure; they may last only a short time and often end with little or no notice. Compared with regular workers, workers in contingent jobs are far less likely to receive work benefits, particularly health benefits. For example, one survey found that only 12 percent of contingent workers are covered by employer-provided health care, compared with over two thirds of regular full-time workers (National Commission on Working Women, 1990).

Reaching Hard-to-Reach Workers

Health promotion professionals grapple with how to organize health promotion activities that accommodate the growing number of contingent and low-skilled workers. Workplace exercise programs cannot be regarded as successful if they are underutilized and discourage certain segments of the workforce. The growing numbers of women and minorities entering the workforce demand new thinking regarding physical activity promotion efforts. For one, the growth in the labor force has been in the subgroup in American society for whom there exists a greater risk for a variety of illnesses and for whom large-scale disease prevention programs have been shown to be less effective than for higher socioeconomic and nonminority populations. Ethnic and racial minority populations are among the most conspicuously absent from health promotion programs (Aguirre-Molina & Molina, 1990). African-American men and women and white women are less likely than white men to participate in the health promotion programs available through the workplace. African Americans typically show the lowest recruitment rates (Brill et al., 1991). Latino and African-American men and women are more likely than white men and women to be employed in semiskilled, nonprofessional occupations.

Reaching blue-collar workers, who make up one third of the working population, also presents challenges. Blue-collar employees are less likely than white-collar employees to participate in exercise programs offered at the workplace. Moreover, blue-collar workers are also less apt to adhere to an exercise program once started (King, Carl, Birkel, & Haskell, 1988). Because of these differences, we would expect to find that white-collar and blue-collar workers view work-sponsored health promotion programs differently. Morris and colleagues (1999), in their study of differences between blue-collar and white-collar workers at a heavy-machinery manufacturing company, found this to be the case. Compared with white-collar workers, blue-collar workers reported more negative perceptions of the work-sponsored exercise program. White-collar workers reported more flexibility in their day to exercise, while blue-collar workers reported the least amount of scheduling flexibility. Traditional fitness programs did not work well because production workers were often tied to a production line and did not have the flexibility to walk away from their jobs to attend a seminar.

Many studies that address low participation in workplace health promotion programs focus on the characteristics of program participants, such as age, sex, or social class. When these factors differ from those of nonparticipants or from the general pool of employees, the inference is that the programs are not reaching certain employees. The next step is to examine why intrinsic characteristics of participants and nonparticipants matter. Employees might not participate in health promotion efforts because of elements of the program's design, not exclusively because of intrinsic characteristics (Wilson, 1990). Program designers must ask themselves several questions: Is the program offered at convenient times? Do the health programs consider the interests of most employees? Are programs offered at a convenient location for most employees?

The health care industry deserves part of the blame for the absence of many women, minorities, and low-skilled workers from company health promotion programs. One of the major reasons for the low participation of African Americans and Latinos in work-sponsored health promotion programs is the absence of cultural relevance due to the *monocultural* approach of these programs (Aguirre-Molina & Molina, 1990). Many health promotion programs tend to be generic in nature. When relevant cultural symbols are excluded from the fitness facility, it sends a message of the program's little regard for ethnic, racial, or economic variations among workers.

Attitudes of fitness professionals are also to blame. Many fitness directors would simply rather work with well-educated, motivated, healthy, white-collar workers than with employees who are likely to be slow to change their dietary or exercise habits (Pechter, 1986). Work-site health promotion programs need to hire health promotion specialists who are sensitive to the concerns of the entire workforce, not just the upper-level employees. Health promotion specialists need to recognize cultural differences among employees.

Employees' attitudes about the work-sponsored fitness program may depend on the level of support from management and co-workers. For some workers in lower-level positions, supervisors or managers serve as gatekeepers by controlling workers' access to health promotion activities. For instance, to keep production lines moving at one company, some supervisors refused to allow workers to attend health programs on company time. In one study, not only did white-collar workers feel more support from their supervisors, but they also reported more support from their co-workers and a stronger employer health orientation than did blue-collar workers (King, Carl, Birkel, & Haskell, 1988). This finding warrants some investigation because if blue-collar workers have more skepticism about the commitment of their employer to improving employee health, they will be less likely to participate in work-site health promotion programs.

Workplace fitness facilities themselves may not be enough. Many jobs today are no longer confined to a central location, a circumstance that certainly has significance for work-based fitness programs. Modern telecommunications has also significantly reduced the need for workers to be physically present in the same location as the company that employs them. An increasing amount of subcontracted work is today accomplished in a virtual workplace, a work environment in which employees are electronically rather than physically connected. Employees who work from their homes need to find an alternative to work-site exercise facilities.

King and colleagues' (1990) study of the employee preferences and needs of blue-collar and minority workers indicated the difficulty of keeping employees interested in exercise programs located at the workplace. Six hundred employees of a major aerospace company completed a questionnaire regarding exercise attitudes and behaviors. The respondents were categorized into three groups: current exercisers, former exercisers, and non-exercisers. Respondents from all three categories reported preferences for physical activity that could be performed on their own time rather than in a group or class. The employees showed little interest in physical activity programming available to them at the workplace. Health professionals need to pay more attention to alternative strategies for physical activity outside the workplace. One solution to encourage lower-class workers to be physically active is for employers to develop arrangements with facilities closer to where the employees live, perhaps at schools or in private fitness centers.

Unemployment and Too Much Free Time

For millions of Americans who are unemployed, the work and time squeeze is not a problem. All too often, unemployment leads to myriad health problems. In a study of more than 4,000 adults, Roberts and colleagues (Roberts, Lamb, Dench, & Brodie, 1989) observed that the unemployed had a lower health status than people holding jobs. Brenner (1980) estimated that a 1 percent increase in the U.S. unemployment rate results in approximately 37,000 additional deaths, with more than half of the deaths caused by increased incidence of heart attack and other cardiovascular diseases. Roberts and colleagues (1989) found that individuals experiencing unemployment and who participated in limited leisure-time physical activity were particularly vulnerable to health problems. Unemployment is also likely to impact participation in physical activity. In a study of unemployed youth in Britain, Francis (1984) found that employed youth were 13 percent more interested in sport participation than were unemployed youth, although the limited research should caution us not to overgeneralize their findings.

Unemployment can be viewed as imposing large blocks of unobligated time; however, this "free time" is not the same as leisure time. Unemployment for many people is so demoralizing that they find difficulty in including what they perceive as leisure-time activities. For example, in Francis Lobo's (1996) case analysis of 10 unemployed adults, unemployment was viewed as enforced free time and disengagement from physical activity was the norm. Several withdrew from physical activity because of the desire not to interact with other individuals. Sue Glyptis (1994) reported people without work reduce time spent on active, out-of-home, and social activities and increase their passive, solitary pursuits and lead largely home-centered lives. Warr and colleagues (1988) use the term "resigned adaptation," which involves reduced aspirations and lower emotional investment in the social environment which likely includes other people.

The major activity soon after a job loss is a new job search; however, after a month or two, job hunting lessens. After a while, individuals withdraw from job seeking and protect themselves from threatening events by avoiding social situations. Prolonged unemployment has been associated with a raised risk of smoking, problem drinking, and symptoms of anxiety and depression (Wadsworth, Montgomery, & Barley, 1999). The effect of prolonged unemployment on physical activity was demonstrated in a long-term study conducted by sociologist Lois Grayson (1993). Using data collected as part of the Canadian General Social Survey of Health, initially no differences in physical activity were observed between the employed and unemployed. But after the 25th week of unemployment, physical activity significantly declined.

Corporate Paternalism and the Rejection of Work-Sponsored Health Promotion

The nation's workforce has grown to distrust the motives of corporations. The rise of cynicism of those in less-stable and less-secure jobs and a more fractious and competitive workplace have been amply documented in national surveys of the U.S. workforce (Fukuyama, 1995). Constant corporate restructuring and downsizing, the movement of American jobs to foreign countries, heightened job demands, and reductions in health and pension benefits have all taken their toll on workers in the past decade and a half. More than half of the American public believes that the leaders of big businesses are more interested in their own power and status than the needs of their company or their workforce. All of this has a bearing on the loss of corporate loyalty among the workforce and the pessimism about the future that permeates the nation's workforce (Kanter & Mirvis, 1989).

Despite the presumably good intentions of workplace health promotion efforts, many of these efforts are also viewed with suspicion and distrust. The relationship between management and workers is fundamentally different from those involving other providers of health promotion services, such as between a local health department and community members. Employers stand to gain from a healthier, more productive workforce; therefore, workers may well question management's motives in providing health promotion programs. Workers may also view employer-sponsored programs as a form of *corporate paternalism,* the notion that the employer needs to protect its employees from what is seen as self-inflicted harm. The employer acts like a caring parent, protecting the employee and dispensing advice and policies concerning individual health behaviors. Many employees want little to do with employer's caring.

Abuse of Health Screening

Many current screening tests conducted as part of work-sponsored health promotion programs often are presented by management as benefiting and protecting both employee and employer. Employers often use health information to exhort employees to change. Health promotion often ignores other, more serious health threats, and health status data collected as part of risk-factor screening may influence promotions or dismissals.

Some employers use health screening as an insidious way of controlling their costs. By eliminating high-risk workers from their workforce, they hope to reduce absenteeism, health and disability insurance costs, and workers' compensation payments. Screening for existing health conditions has always been part of the process to eliminate workers who are susceptible to subsequent injuries and claims for compensation. In more recent times, the goal is to identify people who are at risk for a condition that they do not yet have (Stone, 1986). In times and places of high unemployment, employers have every incentive to use medical screening to select the healthiest and, in their minds, most productive workforce possible (Stone, 1986).There is very little information on how many companies actually use medical screening for purposes of employee selection and cost saving, yet it is apparent that medical screening is widespread. According to one survey, preplacement physical exams are required of 19.2 percent of employees in small firms (8-24 workers), 48.9 percent of employees in medium-sized firms (250-500 workers), and 83.3 percent of employees in large firms (more than 500 workers) (Stone, 1986).

One consequence of work-sponsored health promotion programs is the violation of individual rights and, in some cases, legal problems involving violation of confidentiality and privacy issues. Benefits managers say they have a legal right to obtain medical information to defend themselves against lawsuits and that plaintiffs give up their confidentiality rights when they initiate legal action. A case in point involves the Coors Brewing Company. The beer producer is one of many workplaces that ask all new hires to complete a health appraisal questionnaire as part of a wellness incentive program. Employees who complete the voluntary survey can have their health care benefit reimbursement levels raised form 85 percent to 90 percent. Those with high-risk factors get the boost only if they agree to participate in risk-reduction programs, many of which are administered at Coors's own wellness center. One of Coors's subsidiaries, Coors Ceramics, which also uses the wellness center, had convinced an administrative law judge to deny a widow's claim for survivor's benefits, using information from Coors's wellness center (Wise, 1995). The woman's husband had died of a heart attack, which she claimed was job-related, entitling his family to death benefits. Coors argued that the man's death was due to his smoking one and a half packs of cigarettes a day since he was 14 and a low level of physical activity. These health-compromising behaviors were documented as part of the man's health-screening exam and were turned over by the company as evidence in the trial. The judge deemed the medical records as sufficient evidence to deny the widow's claim to survivor's benefits.

Coercion to Participate

Employees may also perceive that they are being coerced by policies that require them to participate in exercise and weight-control programs. Changing individual behavior through coercion is never ethically justified in workplace health promotion programs. Employees should have the right to decide for themselves whether they will participate, and they should not be ostracized, penalized, or made to feel embarrassed for failing to do so. Voluntary participation and expanding rather than limiting employees' choices determine how ethical the practice of health promotion is (DeJoy & Wilson, 1995).

Work-sponsored health promotion and employee assistance programs may represent involvement in areas over which employers lack legitimate control. This is especially a problem when employees are not consulted during the planning process. For example, since 1991, Hershey Foods has had a program in which employees are screened for smoking, cholesterol, blood pressure, weight, and exercise habits. Employees then receive health insurance premium credits or penalties, depending on how they managed their health. In 1996, the company conducted employee focus group research and discovered two important facts. First, when employees were asked to whom they listened about health matters—the company or their personal physicians—the workers picked their doctors. Second, workers felt the workplace had no business intruding into their personal affairs. Hershey Foods has maintained a fitness center on corporate grounds since 1979. Although participation is not required of any employees, said Renee Karstetter, health promotion specialist at Hershey, she did concede that "some people think we're trying to push it down their throats" (Ziegler, 1997).

Community health educator Kathryn Green (1988) suggests that employers and workers have different responsibilities for health at work, related to the degree to which they control a given circumstance. Workers' responsibilities include their health-related behaviors on and off the job. According to Green, the primary responsibility of the employer should be to provide a safe and healthful work environment, and participation in any work-sponsored fitness program should be strictly voluntary. Even then, it may be impossible to promote good health behaviors among employees without crossing into corporate paternalism and creating employee resentment.

Her position may be a bit extreme, given that we know that employers can implement a variety of programs to promote physical activity among healthy workers and boost compliance with treatment among many who are dealing with chronic health issues. The key likely rests in the ability of the company to adopt an organizational culture that embraces healthy living from a comprehensive perspective. It also hinges on bringing workers and managers together to jointly determine a plan that meets the health needs of both individual workers and the company.

Conclusion

The workplace potentially offers a unique setting in which to promote physical activity. Employees will have to assume greater responsibility for their own health if businesses are to contain costs associated with the chronic conditions of sedentary living. A commitment to a healthful working environment should be satisfying to the worker as well. Work-site health promotion programs have the potential to become "win-win" partnerships between employees and the organization (Pelletier, 1993). For employers, the perceived benefits of exercise programs might include reduced health care costs and sick leave, better morale, and better-quality work. The ability to attract and retain key personnel, to enhance worker productivity, and to improve public image are certainly important goals of any business. But health promotion should also mean that workers enjoy less stressful jobs, flexible working hours, and work environments that are physically safe.

The target of change in many work-sponsored programs is typically the employees, and not the organization itself. The long-term success of a work-site exercise program can be enhanced by modification of the total work environment to support a more active lifestyle for all employees.

Health promotion efforts need to be part of a larger corporate strategy that shows equal concern for individual lifestyle modification and the provision of safe and healthful working conditions. Work-sponsored fitness programs should not exist independently of the health care industry, but this requires a health care system that embraces *preventive services* that intervene before more serious medical conditions develop.

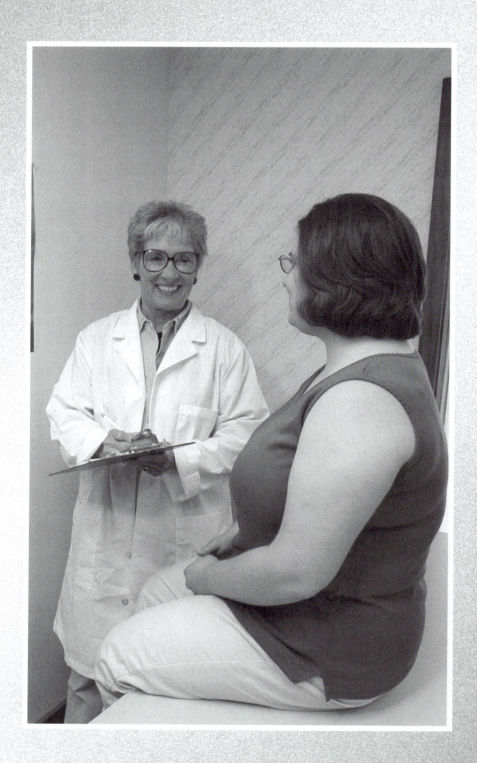

Prevention
and the
Health Care System

Twentieth-century medical education has not emphasized maintenance of health and prevention of illness as major duties of physicians. Physicians see their principal task as identifying and treating disease in a patient complaining of symptoms. This task, overwhelming as it is, can drain doctors' energy and time and leave little room in their schedules for apparently healthy persons. Part of the solution is developing forms of practice that spread out the burdens of treating disease. But reorganization of practice and delegation of tasks are not enough. The educational institutions of modern medicine must examine the view of illness they teach to medical students and residents, and recall the one described in the second century A.D. by Galen (1951, p. 5): "But since, both in importance and in time, health precedes disease. So we ought to consider first how health may be preserved, and then how one may best cure disease." (Reiser, 1978:421)

▼   ▼   ▼   ▼   ▼

During the last several decades, the United States has made considerable progress in addressing the major diseases associated with sedentary living. Since the 1960s, the United States has experienced a major downtrend in the number of deaths due to chronic illnesses, such as heart disease and stroke. These declines are largely a result of the increased understanding of the physiological mechanisms associated with chronic diseases. The successes in the early detection and treatment of biological risk factors, particularly hypertension and blood cholesterol levels, have also helped. Although mortality rates for many chronic conditions have declined in recent years, the death rate in the United States remains higher than in most other developed countries (USDHHS, 2000). One reason for the high incidence of chronic diseases is the failure of the United States to control the levels of behavioral risk factors, such as poor diets and lack of physical activity.

As a result, in recent years, public health officials have called on the health care system to pay greater attention to prevention. For example, in 1996, the U.S. Preventive Services Task Force (USPSTF) and the American Heart Association (AHA) recommended that all primary-care physicians advise their patients about a healthy diet and regular physical activity as part of the preventive health examination (USPSTF, 1996). Physicians are in an ideal position to advise their patients to improve their physical activity levels. Nearly 80 percent of Americans call on a primary-care physician at least once a year. Physicians' status makes them credible sources for conveying preventive health messages. In fact, in one national survey, the family physician was identified as the leading source for health-promoting information, preferred over the family, school, media, and employers (Feldman, 1993). Primary-care physicians are in a unique position to offer ongoing reminders to their patients to become more physically active and to consume a more appropriate diet (USDHHS, 1996b).

Despite their distinctive position, most physicians do an inadequate job in counseling their patients to be physically active. In one study, only 15 percent of sedentary adults who had visited a physician for a routine checkup in the past year received advice concerning physical activity (Friedman, Brownson, & Peterson, 1994). An audit of charts from physical examination visits also revealed low rates (7 percent) of physical activity counseling (Madlon-Kay, Harper, & Reif, 1994). Physicians also widely fail to provide adequate physical activity counseling to patients who are typically considered at risk for chronic diseases. For these reasons, one of the national health objectives includes increasing to at least 50 percent the number of primary-care physicians who appropriately assess and counsel their patients about physical activity (USDHHS, 1990).

For most of the 20th century, the medical model has dominated approaches to health care. The principal characteristic of the medical model is its focus on repairing disease-induced damage to the body. Preventive services that lend themselves to objective confirmation (for example, pap smears and blood pressure and cholesterol readings) are prescribed more frequently than cognitive or behavioral services, such as stress and physical activity counseling. Clinical services cause doctors less concern than counseling services. We have not trained doctors to be interested in prevention, and in fact, many physicians practicing prevention have traditionally been relegated to a second-class status in the medical profession (Scutchfield, 1989). Implicit in this biological orientation is a conviction that social and cultural factors only marginally influence disease. Sociologist Robert Crawford (1980: 373) summed up this point as follows:

Medical practice is an individualized treatment mode, a mode which defines the client as deficient and which reconstructs the individual's understanding of the problem for which help is being sought. That reconstruction individualizes and compartmentalizes the problem, transforming it into its most immediate property: the biological and physical manifestations of the individual, diseased, human body. The answer to the problem is then logically held to be found in the same professional individual treatment, not in the reordering of the social, political and environmental circumstances in which the individual exists.

In this chapter we explore how today's health care system has been slow to respond to the need for prevention and management of the health conditions associated with America's sedentary society. The emphasis on the "curative system of health" has resulted in many missed opportunities for health professionals to intervene before the onset of more serious health conditions. The rewards of preventive medicine are much less striking and less immediate than the rewards associated with curative medicine. Even when health professionals are concerned with issues of prevention, they often frame the problems in biological or physiological terms. The philosophy behind the *medical model* that has limited preventive medical efforts has also prevented physicians and other health professionals from promoting regular physical activity.

The first sections of the chapter focus on the role of physicians. We first look at the inadequacy of the concept of *sick role* that underlies much of the thinking about health and disease. Second, we examine the reasons why physicians do such an ineffective job of counseling their patients to include more physical activity in their daily lives. Then we look at the challenges facing medicine, particularly the large-scale efforts to cut medical costs that have affected preventive services.

The remainder of the chapter focuses on other health professionals, including the growing number of exercise specialists. Here too we explore how the predominance of the medical model has contributed to the difficulty in getting people to adopt regular patterns of physical activity. In particular, we examine the problems associated with the failure of many allied health professionals to work together as a team and to effectively deliver important health messages, especially those about increasing physical activity.

The Medical Model and the Sick Role

Although people seek health advice from friends and family members, they do not formally enter the health care system until they meet with a licensed physician. Physicians enjoy considerable autonomy in executing their professional skills and occupy a position of authority over their patients. This hierarchy is based on the cultural norm that insists that those who are ill must cooperate with their physicians. Talcott Parsons (1951) was one of the earliest sociologists to recognize that society must have an established means for dealing with those who seek help from the medical profession. Parsons defined the *sick role* in the relationship between doctors and patients. He argued that having authority over their patients is necessary for physicians because they have the knowledge and necessary experiences that the patients do not. He viewed the sick role as a temporary social role designed to return sick people to a state of health as quickly as possible.

The sick role includes certain expectations for both the physician and patient (table 7.1). The sick person is placed in the role of patient, whose primary obligation is cooperating with the medical expert to cure, or at least to control, the disease. The doctor expects full cooperation from the patient, whereas the patient expects the doctor to apply her specialist knowledge and skills for the benefit of the patient. Doctors are expected to be objective and emotionally detached and to be guided by rules of professional practice. There are three key elements of the sick role. First, no one holds the individual responsible for being sick. Second, the individual is exempt from normal responsibilities so that he can concentrate on returning to good health. Third, the individual agrees that the role is undesirable, that he will seek competent help for the illness, and that he will cooperate in getting well. While the sick role excuses people from performing their usual responsibilities, it also obligates them to seek medical treatment and to follow the prescribed remedy for recovery. Not following a physician's orders or failing to seek medical care violates this role. In such instances, the responsibilities for illness and the accompanying failure to return to good health are assigned completely to the individual.

Table 7.1   Distinguishing Characteristics of the Sick Role and the At-Risk Role

Sick role	At-risk role
Doctor centered	Patient centered
Biomedical solutions	Lifestyle solutions (e.g., diet, physical activity)
One-way information flow	Two-way information flow
Emphasis on individual change	Emphasis on changing social environment (e.g., work, family situations)

Chronic Conditions and the Sick Role

In the classical medical model, illness is characterized by reliance on a qualified physician with goals of complete recovery. The goal of restoration of health is not possible in an age when many people are dealing with chronic conditions with poor or limited recovery prospects. Today, it is estimated that one in three Americans suffers from a condition that develops slowly over many years. Although people can live with these conditions for many years, they are largely incurable (Iezzoni, 1996). Chronic illnesses by definition are long term and usually permanent events in an individual's life. Having a serious chronic disease means living a life of ill health and dealing with the discomforts and frightening experiences of the disease. It also requires dealing with the constant disruptions in one's social environment, such as disruptions at home and at work.

Because it applies to temporary, acute physical illnesses, the sick-role framework does a poor job in addressing the lifestyle changes necessary to manage chronic illnesses or prevent them in the first place. Leo Baric (1969) was one of the first to consider the limitations of the sick-role model. In describing these inadequacies, Baric developed the concept of the *at-risk role* for the individual who is conscious of being susceptible to a specific disease and wants to do something to reduce the possibility of acquiring the disease. Baric noted that individuals who participate in the health care system do so in varying states of health. He offers four categories that capture the essence of these different levels: healthy, at risk, ill, and convalescent.

Healthy people are free of disease and have not yet acquired certain dangerous health habits nor have they reached an age at which they run a higher risk of developing a health threat. Examples include adolescents before taking up tobacco, women before having children, or middle-aged men before experiencing symptoms of heart disease. The second category includes people *at risk*, individuals who are engaged in certain activities or experience certain circumstances that increase their vulnerability to disease over that of the rest of the population. Individuals who are obese, smoke, or lead sedentary lives fit into this at-risk category. So do individuals who experience physiological changes (e.g., high blood pressure, high blood cholesterol levels) that increase the likelihood of developing chronic disease. This category also includes men who are more than 40 years of age and women entering menopause. The third category, the state of *illness,* applies to individuals who have acquired a health disorder and are under supervision of a medical professional. If the illness is prolonged over time, the individual is classified as *convalescent.* This category includes individuals engaged in ongoing treatment or rehabilitation before they regain their full normal capacity.

Physicians should sensitize their at-risk patients to the health risks they incur when they engage in unhealthy behaviors believed to be related to the chronic diseases for which they are at risk. Putting patients' lifestyle issues into a disease framework offers potential efficiency; any disease theory brings together a body of knowledge about symptoms, etiology, and treatments and provides the direction in which to proceed once a diagnosis is made. The disadvantage is that it focuses on only part of the problem and often neglects a range of possibilities, particularly the "points of leverage" associated with changing lifestyle behaviors (Mechanic, 1995). The sick role simply does not address the goal of patients' taking charge of their lifestyles and thus is an inadequate framework for the millions of Americans who engage in behaviors that are likely to compromise health or who are already living with the consequences of chronic diseases.

Doctor–Patient Relationships

The exchange of information between doctor and patient can be either doctor-centered or patient-centered. In the paternalistic, doctor-centered model, the exchange is largely in one direction, from physician to patient. At a minimum, the physician should give the patient legally required information on treatment options and obtain informed consent to the treatment recommended. Beyond this, however, the patient is a passive recipient of whatever amount and type of information the physician chooses to reveal.

The sick role considers the doctor–patient relationship in paternalistic terms. Physicians assess patients' medical conditions and identify appropriate plans of action, encouraging patients to consent to the interventions suggested. Patients trust physicians, who act as parent figures, to decide what is in the patients' best interests (Beisecker & Beisecker, 1993). This approach is based on high physician control and low patient control and characterizes the typical medical consultation. This doctor–patient model has been characterized as *doctor-centered* since it situates the physician at the heart of the health care system. Doctors who adopt a doctor-centered approach focus on the physical aspects of the patient's disease and apply tightly controlled interviewing methods aimed at reaching a diagnosis as quickly as possible. Patients put themselves in the hands of members of the medical profession believing that their medical training and expertise make them competent at diagnosing health problems and prescribing suitable remedies. For some illnesses, patients derive considerable reassurance from being able to rely on the doctor and thus being relieved of burdens of worry and decision making.

Being at risk for or living with a chronic health condition gives the patient special responsibilities, which start right in the doctor's office during the information exchange process. Types of information that the physician might communicate to the patient include the natural history of the disease, the benefits and risks of various treatments, and a description of the treatment procedures. This information is primarily technical knowledge that most patients will not have. Information that patients might reveal to the physician includes their health history, aspects of their lifestyles, their concerns about the disease, and their knowledge of various treatment options. The physician typically has no way of knowing about this information that the patient brings to the encounter except through direct communication with the patient in this or prior consultations.

At the other end of the continuum are physicians who adopt a less authoritarian style and make the doctor–patient relationship more of a partnership in which the doctor and patient share responsibility. In this model, the information exchange is two-way. The physician typically informs the patient of all relevant information about available treatment options, the benefits and risks of each, and potential effects on the patients' psychological and social as well as physical well-being. The first type of information exchange ensures that all relevant treatment options are on the table, and the second ensures that both the physician and patient evaluate these within the context of the patient's specific situation and needs rather than as a standard menu of options whose impact and outcomes are assumed to be similar for clinically similar patients.

Patient participation in decision making makes good sense for several reasons. First, individuals at risk for or living with chronic health conditions are expected to adhere to a medical regimen, which may include frequent appointments with physicians and other health care professionals, taking prescribed medications, and maintaining a therapeutic regimen (e.g., an exercise program). The individual must also come to terms with an altered view of the future and develop strategies that ease the problems associated with participating in everyday activities, such as employment and family responsibilities. Behavioral prescriptions have to fit meaningfully into the realities of the patient's daily living. In the conduct of preventive medicine, the patient is as much an "expert" as the doctor. Inadequate patient involvement may interfere with the patient's acceptance of treatment and may explain in part the high rates of noncompliance to many medical regimens. When the health problem has both physical and behavioral components, as is the case with many chronic diseases, the doctor-centered communication style is likely to be less effective.

Doctors who apply a disease-centered model emphasize reaching a clinical diagnosis as quickly as possible. In contrast, doctors taking a more patient-oriented approach recognize the importance of people's subjective experience and their own meanings of health and illness. Recognizing patients' beliefs and experiences as essential to the adoption of healthy behaviors makes the patient-centered relationship valuable in dealing with diseases of sedentary living.

Fully involving patients in clinical decisions presents a daunting challenge for many physicians. Patient-centered approaches require doctors to spend more time listening to patient problems and to use open-ended questions that encourage expression of feelings and clarify concerns. Doctors develop a particular consulting style, doctor-centered or patient-centered, which they use consistently and do not vary in relation to the patient's problems. Byrne and Long (1976), in one of the first comprehensive studies of doctor–patient consulting styles, found that 75 percent of the physicians used the doctor-centered relationship. A recent follow-up suggests that doctor–patient consultation styles have not changed much. In an analysis of more than 3,500 clinical decisions, Braddock, Edwards, and Hasenberg (1999) reported that surgeons (21.8 percent) and primary-care physicians (18.9 percent) infrequently involved their patients in complete discussions of clinical decisions.

Because chronic disease problems are likely to increase with the aging of the population, the medical profession's continued reliance on a diagnostic disease model will become less efficient in addressing the burden of illness seen in primary medical care. The irony, as pointed out by a medical sociologist, David Mechanic (1995), is that "while so much of the challenge in health care is social to enhance the capacity of individuals to perform desired roles and activities the thrust of the health enterprise is technologic and reductionist, treating complex social medical problems as if they are amenable to simple technical fixes."

Physicians and Physical Activity Counseling

The vast majority of physicians believe it is their responsibility to educate patients about changing the risk factors associated with chronic disease, such as advising their patients to be physically active. The problem is that many doctors have not trained to do so. In one of the most comprehensive studies of physician attitudes toward and competence in health promotion, Weschler and his colleagues (1996) examined the extent to which 400 primary-care physicians agreed with the health promotion and disease prevention recommendations put forth in the *Healthy People 2000* objectives. They asked physicians to indicate, on a four-point scale, the importance of each of 14 types of health-related behavior in promoting the health of the average person. Most of the physicians reported that eliminating cigarette smoking, avoiding the use of illicit drugs, using seat belts, and abstaining from alcohol were very important for promoting health (figure 7.1). The doctors assigned less importance to matters of diet and exercise, though they were still rated as important. Only 49 percent of the respondents rated avoiding saturated fats and excess calories and engaging in moderate daily physical activity as very important for health. Fewer physicians (37 percent) considered other health promotion goals—including a balanced diet, engaging in aerobic exercise at least three times a week, avoiding stress, decreasing salt in the diet, and minimizing sugar intake—as very important for the average person.

The researchers also asked the physicians in the study to indicate the extent to which they felt prepared to counsel patients, the extent to which they believed they were successful in helping patients achieve changes in behavior, and given appropriate support, how successful they felt they would be in changing the physical activity habits of their patients (figure 7.2). Despite the high numbers of physicians who felt prepared to give advice about exercise, only a small minority (4 percent to 13 percent) described themselves as currently successful in helping patients change their exercise habits. Only a handful of physicians were optimistic about their potential to help their patients rid themselves of their sedentary ways, even given appropriate support systems.

Physicians do a better job in physical activity counseling when responding to biomedical factors. For example, physicians are more generous with their exercise advice to those who have already suffered a heart attack or who display biological risk factors. In an analysis of data collected from seven states and Puerto Rico, the CDC (USHDDS, 1999c) reported that 70.3 percent of individuals with a history of heart disease received physician advice to exercise, while only 40 percent without heart disease received similar admonitions to exercise. Kreuter, Scharff, and Brennan (1997) reported a similar inclination to provide advice in their study of the nature of exercise counseling among two large patient groups: individuals with biological risk factors (i.e., high cholesterol levels or high body mass index [BMI]) and individuals with behavioral risk factors (i.e., a diet high in fat or who engaged in insufficient exercise). Patients with a high BMI were roughly 1.6 times more likely to be told to get more physical activity. Patients with high cholesterol were 1.4 times more

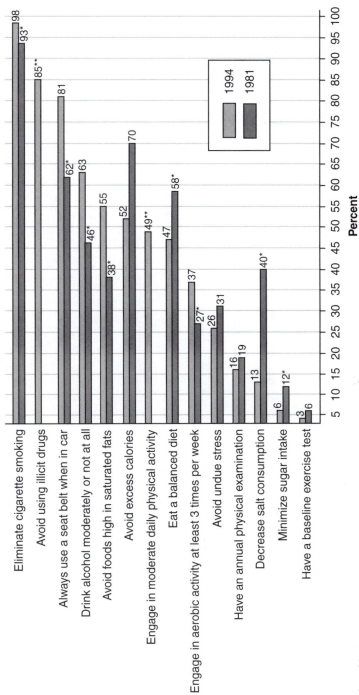

Health behavior

Eliminate cigarette smoking — 98, 93*
Avoid using illicit drugs — 85**
Always use a seat belt when in car — 81, 62*
Drink alcohol moderately or not at all — 63, 46*
Avoid foods high in saturated fats — 55, 38*
Avoid excess calories — 52, 70
Engage in moderate daily physical activity — 49**
Eat a balanced diet — 47, 58*
Engage in aerobic activity at least 3 times per week — 37, 27*
Avoid undue stress — 26, 31
Have an annual physical examination — 16, 19
Decrease salt consumption — 13, 40*
Minimize sugar intake — 6, 12*
Have a baseline exercise test — 3, 6

Legend: 1994, 1981

Percent (5 10 15 20 25 30 35 40 45 50 55 60 65 70 75 80 85 90 95 100)

* p < .01
** Question not asked in 1981

Figure 7.1 Percentage of physicians who perceived various forms of health-promotion behavior as "very important" for the average person.

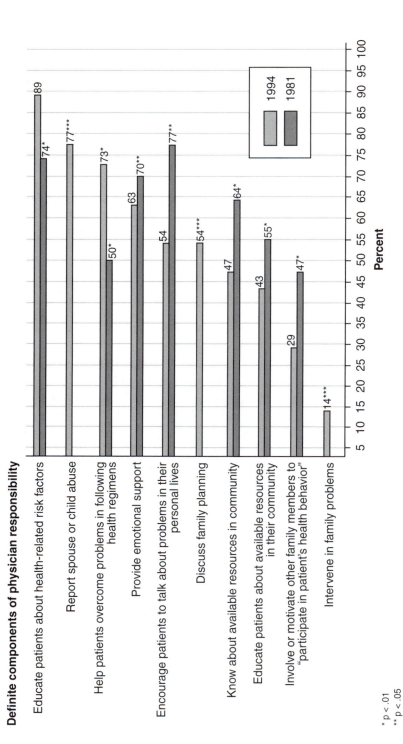

Definite components of physician responsibility

Percent

* p < .01
** p < .05
*** Question not asked in 1981

Figure 7.2 Percentage of physicians who considered certain responsibilities related to health promotion as "definitely" part of their role.

likely to be counseled to increase physical activity and almost twice as likely to be counseled to eat less fat. However, only 22 percent of patients with a behavioral risk profile (lack of exercise and poor eating habits) received physician advice to make lifestyle changes.

Physicians' decisions to offer physical activity advice may also depend on their beliefs that patients will be successful. Such decisions are often based on stereotypical beliefs about social class or race (van Ryan & Burke, 2000). Taira and colleagues (1997) found that physicians were much more likely to discuss exercise with high-income patients than with low-income patients. In another study, Poduri and Grisso (1998) conducted in-depth interviews with more than 200 African-American women living in public housing projects in Philadelphia. The authors found that physicians gave prevention topics a low priority during medical consultations with these women. Only 34 percent of the women reported having a discussion with their health care provider regarding the prevention of heart disease. The women were given an opportunity to state how, if at all, their health care providers had broached the topic of physical activity. Physicians advised none of the sedentary women to become more physically active. The authors suggested that physicians may not discuss lifestyle changes with these low-income patients due to their beliefs that their patients will not comply with suggested lifestyle changes and the doctor's inability to deliver such messages in an effective way.

Part of physicians' failure to provide physical activity advice to their patients rests in the disconcerting fact that many physicians fail to include regular physical activity into their own daily routines. Kenneth Wells and his colleagues (1984) examined the personal health habits of 149 physicians who were members of a county medical society in California. They found that 59 percent of the physicians believed they weighed too much, and 73 percent reported one hour or less each week of exercise. In a more recent survey of health habits among 298 primary-care physicians, Abramson, Stein, Schaufele, Frates, and Rogan (2000) found that 27 percent of the physicians admitted to not participating in aerobic activity, and 61 percent participated in no strength training. Physicians who exercised were more likely to counsel their patients to exercise. These findings suggest that an effective strategy to increase physical activity counseling by physicians might be promoting more physical activity among the physicians themselves.

Skills in changing behaviors are necessary for incorporating effective physical activity counseling into clinical practices. Lawrence

Weed (1997) argued that traditional medical training continues to reward memorization to the exclusion of other skills, leading to outdated and inefficient application of medical knowledge in medical practices. Many physicians-in-training complete their residencies poorly equipped to deal with many chronic health problems and understand little about the behavioral aspects of disease. Although medical schools are increasing the behavioral science curriculum, they have yet to include sufficient training in learning theory and behavior-modification procedures for routine use in preventive medicine (O'Neil, 1995). Few schools teach all medical students techniques in behavior modification. Physicians require a greater understanding of learning theory to employ behavior modification techniques correctly and completely.

The key to acceptance of prevention and health promotion among physicians lies with the gatekeepers to the practice of medicine, the medical schools. Yet medical schools often pay only lip service to prevention while remaining entrenched in models of curative care. Students are shaped by a curriculum that emphasizes basic biology, solving biological questions, and surgical manipulations. Training in prevention is not an integral part of most physicians' education, either in medical school or residency training. Unfortunately, most medical school staffs are experts in biological sciences rather than in behavioral sciences. The intense attention to biological technology in medical and social education is appropriate because many acute illnesses require both sophisticated machinery and technical knowledge of pathophysiology. However, biological technology is insufficient in light of changing disease patterns.

Preventive Messages in Cost-Cutting Times

Doctors frequently identify a shortage of time as the principal obstacle to performing more preventive services. Many physicians feel they need to limit the scope of their obligations to each individual patient if they are to meet the demands of all their patients. Physicians are taught to focus quickly on the chief complaint presented to them and perform a focused physical examination to confirm their impressions. General practice consultations average about six minutes, and doctors who include discussion of preventive services typically add two minutes to the office visit (Kottke, Brekke, & Solberg, 1993). In today's busy medical practices, pressures of time demand more tightly controlled, doctor-centered consultations, leaving little time for encouraging patients to pursue healthy lifestyles.

Many doctors believe that the best way to stay on schedule and retain an image as caring professionals is to limit their services to the problems that patients bring to the clinic. Patients also expect the physician to focus attention on the problems for which they seek help and commonly are not interested in physician-initiated recommendations for preventive services. Patients visit clinics and physicians' offices primarily in response to pain or dysfunction. The public has learned to expect quick cures and is often not receptive to lifestyle solutions. A single drug without disturbing side effects is the type of treatment appealing to many.

These factors work against provision of preventive services in favor of popular cures presumed to be quick fixes. Many physicians oblige patients' wishes and often prescribe pharmaceutical solutions. This is particularly true for the problem of obesity. The medical approach to obesity is fixated on the physical condition. Yet is it really obesity that poses the health risk? An alternative hypothesis is that obesity is merely a symptom of other lifestyle behaviors that are the

© Terry Wild Studio

Someone who is overweight is more likely to receive diet advice than physical activity counseling from his or her physician.

true link to chronic disease. Many medical strategies for controlling body weight (e.g., liquid diets, over-the-counter and prescription diet pills, liposuction) do not address changing the patients' lifestyle behaviors in a meaningful way. Someone who is active but overweight may be at less risk for health problems than a sedentary person of average body weight (Gaesser, 1996). Physical inactivity and poor diet are the true risk factors, and body size becomes less relevant when these two factors are considered together. If lifestyle behaviors are primary causal factors for obesity, then an emphasis on the medical management of obesity misdirects attention from the specific underlying lifestyle behaviors.

The discussion topics of lifestyle counseling, such as high-risk sexual behavior, inappropriate eating patterns, alcohol abuse, and sedentary living often prove embarrassing to the patient and, consequently, are awkward for the physician to bring up. Many patients will not change their behavior, or will not change it for long, based on the physician's advice. Patients resist changing lifestyle choices that often bring them great pleasure and that are difficult to change, even though these choices contribute to disease. The physician's advising changes in diet and exercise requires patients to discontinue highly positive reinforcing behaviors (eating) and to start less reinforcing behaviors (exercise).

Many physicians favor pharmacological methods of risk-factor reduction over behavioral remedies such as modified diet and physical activity programs. Physical tests can be documented through traditional measures of scientific verification, and physicians are comfortable with them because they are quick and simple to administer and more likely to be reimbursable. Exercise remedies are not available in a bottle, so many patients opt for other fat-reduction methods available in pill and bottle form. But if reduction in body size occurs without meaningful, long-term changes in activity and diet, then the long-term health value is questionable and may even be negative. Preoccupation with weight loss prevents the individual from devoting mental and physical energy to behavioral changes that might be far more successful in leading to happiness, self-esteem, and higher levels of holistic health and well-being (Hawks & Gast, 1998).

Physical activity in combination with dieting has been acknowledged as a complete weight-loss strategy, and therefore one might expect people attempting to lose weight to be more willing to embrace a strategy that includes regular exercise. Gordon, Heath,

Holmes, and Christy (2000) found that this is not necessarily the case. From data collected from 2,769 men and 4,490 women, the authors reported that 45.6 percent of individuals trying to lose weight did not engage in any physical activity, and only 15 percent reported participating in physical activity on a regular basis. The authors further suggested that what is missing is a specific weight-control message that could be easily communicated to physicians and the public. The message needs to communicate two clear points. First, the message needs a clear recommendation for the amount of exercise necessary for weight loss and weight maintenance. Second, individuals trying to lose weight need to be instructed on how to better manage their caloric intake, including how to monitor food portion sizes.

Presenting preventive messages also costs money. Whether primary-care doctors are in a fee-for-service solo practice or a uniform-fee managed care plan, their incomes often depend on the volume of patients served. This can create a disincentive for prevention that takes more time than absolutely necessary during the office visit. David Hahn, a practicing physician, and his colleague demonstrated the potential success of a single clinician with an organized protocol and a commitment to dispense brief prevention messages to patients (Hahn & Berger, 1990). Hahn's protocol took an average of only 2.1 minutes to provide very brief advice on health habits and to schedule follow-up visits for services requiring more time. Following the protocol resulted in no decline in the number of patients seen per month, presumably because less time was spent on less-efficient methods of delivering preventive messages. Despite the success of Hahn's protocol, in most clinical practice settings, many physicians do not include many preventive activities.

Several programs have been developed to help physicians provide physical activity counseling to their patients. The INSURE program, for example, includes medical education seminars designed to train physicians in specific counseling techniques that they can accomplish in two to five minutes. Emphasis is placed on encouraging moderate-intensity exercise, especially walking. During a one-year period, 34 percent of patients receiving the specific exercise-counseling messages initiated exercise, compared to only 24 percent of a designated control group (Logsdon, Lazaro, & Meier, 1989). While some intervention programs of this type have yielded promising results, the problem is that many physical activity counseling interventions lack a theoretical basis. The exception is an intervention program known as Patient-Centered Assessment and Counseling for Exercise (PACE). The program is based on the stages-of-change behavioral model, which emphasizes the importance of identifying the strength of a person's intention to maintain or change patterns of behavior (Prochaska & DiClemente, 1983). In an intervention study using the PACE program, physicians were trained to provide three to five minutes of physical activity counseling based on the patient's current style of readiness. The validity of the physical activity counseling was assessed among 255 patients. The authors reported that the brief activity counseling from a health care provider led to important increases in physical activity, at least in the short term (Calfas, Sallis, & Oldenburg, 1997).

Recent efforts also have focused attention on the environment in the doctor's office. Advocates of preventive care are becoming more aware that the practice environment accounts for much of the inability to deliver efficient preventive services. Most efforts designed to encourage physicians to include more active-lifestyle counseling have used strategies such as reminders to physicians, physician training, and counseling incentives. These approaches fall into the same trap as programs designed to promote individual physical activity; that is, they focus on changing the individual physician and often fail to take into account the environment in which the physician practices. Instead, as suggested by Schwartz and Cohen (1990), what is needed are strategies that concentrate on giving physicians more effective tools to change office environments through planned organizational change.

The Direct Observation of Primary Care Study (Schwartz & Cohen, 1990) was designed to identify the office dynamics of a family medical practice. A network of 138 community-based family physicians from 84 practices agreed to participate in the study, which included direct observation of clinical encounters, chart audits, and questionnaires for patients and physicians. Several factors contributed to difficulties in running a smooth office operation. Among them were the degree to which role expectations were clear and shared among the staff, the degree to which there was clear and shared communication among the staff, and the efficiency of the office in moving patients through the system. Physicians and staff described being sometimes overworked and burned out and admitted to constant tension within the practice. Among the medical practices, a sense that some physicians were not effective in working as a team was frequently mentioned. This study gives insight into the problems and complexity of many primary-care practices today. Practices need to be viewed as dynamic systems in which different combinations of features may facilitate or hinder a willingness to make available more effective prevention services for their patients.

The Agency for Health Care Policy and Research has launched the Put Prevention Into Practice (PPIP) program, which provides resources and educational materials to encourage physicians to practice preventive medicine (McGinnis & Griffith, 1996). The PPIP program integrates many different interventions into an organized, comprehensive program designed to address patient, clinician, and environmental barriers. Besides physical activity, the program advocates increased participation of the medical community in screening mammography, condom use, weight control, and smoking cessation. Even if physicians can overcome personal and environmental barriers to physical activity counseling, most health insurance programs specifically exclude reimbursement for preventive services. Third-party payers often view preventive medicine as something everybody should pursue and therefore a service that they should not cover. An insurance system is viewed as a risk-sharing pool to protect people from rare events, not to pay for services used by everyone (Schauffler, 1993). In 1995, the CDC formed the agencywide Managed Care Working Group to guide its efforts to foster partnerships between national and local public health agencies and the rapidly growing managed care industry to promote prevention and to improve the public's health.

Emergence of Managed Care

Changes in health care financing have had a tremendous impact on the traditional ways of delivering health care. American physicians for many years relied on a fee-for-service approach. Patients would pay the physician directly for health care services rendered. Today, cost containment strategies or managed care plans have largely replaced the old fee-for-service health system. The two most popular forms are the preferred provider organization (PPO) and the health maintenance organization (HMO). A PPO plan includes specific, independent health care providers who charge the organization for services used by members. In an HMO setup, a member typically pays a predetermined fixed fee, in exchange for which a group of health care providers provide all necessary health care for members. In this arrangement, the member knows the annual medical bill in advance, and the health care providers share with the HMO part of the financial risk for the cost of care provided to the members.

The fastest growing of the two basic managed care approaches are HMOs, which grew from covering 6 million people in 1976 to covering more than 51 million by the mid-1990s (Sleeper, Wholey, Hamer, Schwartz, & Inoferio, 1998). On the surface, it would seem that capitation (uniform fees for all health care users) would shift the focus of care from treatment to maintaining wellness and thereby support the inclusion of preventive services. However, this has not happened; in fact, the opposite has occurred. Since the health care providers are paid a set fee, to make a profit they must be efficient and avoid unnecessary procedures. As discussed earlier, most primary-care doctors' incomes depend on the volume of patients served, and thus doctors look for ways to reduce the volume and costs of services to each patient. This creates barriers to doctors' providing preventive services (Hovell, Kaplan, & Howell, 1990). A report released by the nonprofit Partnership for Prevention (Maddox, 1999) found that although HMOs generally did a better job than other plans in providing preventive services, coverage for preventive services remains largely inadequate overall. Financial reimbursement for preventive services is only a fraction of today's health care costs. Only 3 percent of health care expenditures go toward prevention (Schauffler & Chapman, 1998), and only about 25 percent of large corporate plans cover preventive services at all (Dauer, 1994).

Services related to encouraging physical activity are seldom compensated. Managed health care organizations are reluctant to pay physicians to talk to patients and rarely compensate for the cost of preventive services that emphasize lifestyle choices. Even if the provision of service is verifiable, the effectiveness of many preventive interventions is not yet accepted by third-party payers. Who is to say whether a patient's improved health was a result of the physician's counseling? The difficulty in attributing improved health to a specific service such as physical activity counseling makes both individual patients and third-party payers reluctant to reimburse physicians for preventive services (Hovell, Kaplan, & Howell, 1990).

Preventive services that include counseling for physical activity and other health-promoting behaviors have not received a groundswell of support from the federal government either. For example, Medicare's ban on reimbursement for preventive services focuses its policies squarely on acute illnesses and acute exacerbations of chronic diseases (Schauffler, 1993). If the largest third-party provider of health care services does not show a strong commitment to prevention, it is difficult for other providers, or the public, to be committed to prevention of rather than reaction to the causes of disease. Third-party payers often view preventive medicine as something everybody should pursue and, therefore, a service that they should not cover. An insurance system is viewed as a risk-sharing pool to protect people from rare events, not pay for services used by everyone (Schauffler, 1993).

Allied Health Professions

Modern health care involves the work of many different health care professionals. Nearly nine million people work at all levels in the field of health care today (Pew Health Professions Commission, 1998). At the heart of successful preventive health activities are the *allied health professionals.* These health professionals include specialists such as physical therapists, health educators, public health workers, and social workers. During the past several decades, the exercise specialist has emerged as a new field among the allied health professions. Exercise professionals offer their services in a variety of settings, including hospitals, clinics, private physicians' practices, health clubs, and other commercial health and fitness facilities.

The professionalization of medicine led directly to medicine becoming a monopoly. Laws restrict medical licenses to only graduates of approved schools, and only graduates are eligible to become the faculty members who train the next generation of physicians. As health care became institutionalized, its occupational structure has come to reflect the stratification of the larger American society. Traditionally, physicians have been responsible for directing health care decisions, with allied health professionals acting in supplemental roles. The rigid stratification in medical practice has promoted an increasingly large gap between physicians and nonphysician health care providers. The common notion that physicians are the only providers of primary health care has created barriers between physicians and other professionals who help meet the health-related needs of their patients.

Following the lead of medicine, many allied health professionals are pushing for exclusive licensing and tighter control over accreditation and training programs. Since the 1960s, increased specialization in the preparation of allied health professionals has become the dominant trend. As pointed out by physical education specialist Hal

Lawson (1992), current methods for addressing people's health needs are based on the concepts of the machine and the assembly line from the early industrial age. We compartmentalize each health service into physical, spiritual, emotional, social, or intellectual dimensions, and then those who "possess a specialized separate responsibility" can claim and market their own unique product (Lawson, 1992). We have become a credentialed society in which employers use diplomas and degrees to determine who is eligible for jobs. One major reason that we require credentials is the sheer size and anonymity of American society. Because employers have little personal knowledge of potential workers, they rely on outside organizations to help them choose the most qualified. Because of accelerated rates of change in technology and knowledge, these organizations take on even greater importance. Specialized roles have resulted in equally specialized programs of study founded on self-proclaimed, named, and protected knowledge bases. The outcome of this trend is the narrowing focus of each specialization and the diminished interest in collaboration.

Competence and the Exercise Specialist

For the most part, exercise specialists have had difficulty in finding their niche in the health care system. One explanation for the reluctance to recognize the role of exercise professionals involves their perceived competence. Previously, physical education teachers, coaches, and former athletes were the only pool from which clubs could hire qualified trainers. Many in this pool made the switch to the booming fitness field but were not adequately prepared for their new responsibilities. Today, although conditions have improved, many exercise specialists have limited or sometimes no training.

Consider, for example, the new growth occupation of personal fitness trainer. Once reserved only for movie stars and other clients with the resources to pay large hourly fees, today personal trainers are available to a variety of clients (Jones, 1996). Personal trainers meet with clients individually in their homes, over the telephone, or at clubs on a regular basis, sometimes five or six times a week. The personal trainer conducts a fitness assessment, develops specific goals for each client, and coaches the client through the workout.

Exercise trainers are responsible for providing correct information to people who are trying to develop and maintain health and fitness, but the physical fitness profession is largely unregulated. Most states allow people who have not completed a certified program to advertise their services as counselors or specialists. This combination of loosely regulated services and consumers who are anxious to improve fitness but not always well informed about services has resulted in a certain amount of quackery, particularly in the personal fitness industry. During the past several years, concerted efforts have been made to improve the preparation and practice of exercise specialists. The development of a credentialing system is one such effort (Henderson, 1987).

Credentialing systems fall into distinct categories: state licensing systems and certification systems. The highest form of credentialing is licensure. State licensing legislation restricts the use of certain titles and functions to a certain professional group. This legislation delegates to an outside agency the responsibility of ascertaining the credentials of candidates for a license, developing and implementing licensing standards, investigating complaints, and disciplining practitioners who are substandard. Allied health fields that currently have licensing systems include occupational therapy, physical therapy, dietetics, environmental health, speech and hearing, physician's assistants, and medical records. Professional groups in these fields encourage other health occupations to take on the challenge of developing a system for state licensing. So far the exercise profession has not been successful in establishing licensing.

The most common approach to improving the standards of the exercise profession is certification. Certification restricts the use of a title, rather than both title and function as in licensure. The title that is certified should represent information important to consumers and employers. Those served by a certified exercise specialist should expect services of at least acceptable quality. Certification practices typically rely on more than one measure of proficiency. These include education, testing, supervised field experiences, and disciplinary practices. Today, several hundred different methods of acquiring certification are available in the fitness industry, ranging from comprehensive training to weekend workshops and even mail-order competence tests.

Several national organizations have developed certification tracks for professionals interested in promoting physical activity. In 1983 the American Council on Exercise (ACE) began certification programs and examinations for aerobic instructors and personal trainers. ACE offers four types of certification for fitness professionals. The personal trainer certification is for individuals who provide one-on-one fitness training. The group fitness instructor certification is

© Cleo Photography

Currently, many physical activity professionals are certified, but none are licensed.

for fitness instructors who lead group exercise programs. The lifestyle and weight-management consultant certification is for individuals who offer comprehensive weight-management consulting that addresses nutrition, behavior modification, and fitness. The clinical exercise specialist certification is for individuals working with diseased populations. Since 1985, more than 88,000 people have taken ACE exams and more than 40,000 ACE-certified professionals are active in the United States and 77 other countries (ACE, 2001).

The American College of Sports Medicine (ACSM) has developed a two-track certification program; each track has three levels. The health and fitness track includes certification as a health/fitness director, health/fitness instructor, or group exercise leader. The clinical track includes certification as a program director and exercise specialist. ACSM also recently introduced a certificate of enhanced qualification (CEQ). This is available to those who already have certification as a health/fitness instructor, exercise specialist, program director, or health/fitness director. CEQs are available in advanced personal training, and topics such as exercise and the older adult, nutrition and exercise, and diabetes and exercise.

An advantage of a certification system is its potential for enhancing status. Also, employers, policy makers, consumers, and other professionals would have access to explicit standards of professional conduct, thus facilitating decisions about using the health services of exercise professionals. Perhaps more important, third-party payers would have standards by which to determine how or whether to reimburse for exercise services. These certification programs are headed in the right direction, but they are likely to fall short of the mark in the competitive marketplace for health services. What we need is a licensing process that is similar to the other practicing health professions. Licensure would give exercise specialists legitimacy in delivering exercise services.

Obtaining licensing for health professionals will not be an easy task. Federal laws restrict reimbursement for services to licensed professionals. Each of the 50 states must be approached and effectively lobbied. Resistance from other professions and health care industry groups must be overcome. Other professions have an interest in protecting their territories from erosion. Industry groups tend to resist new licensing because licensed professionals raise costs, and these costs are passed on to consumers and their insurance companies.

Some are optimistic that someday exercise specialists will become licensed allied health professionals if efforts under way in California are successful. In February 1997 a new state law, the Physiotechnol-ogy Practice Act, was proposed in the California legislature by State Senator Watson. Senate Bill 891 proposed the creation of a California Panel on Health and Fitness Instruction to undertake a study and make recommendations regarding the standardization of the qualifications and practices of health, fitness, and wellness instructors. The bill, noting that no uniformly accepted standards or parameters exist for exercise and fitness professionals, proposed the establishment of a field known as physiotechnology, which would include those interested in the application of the art and science of physical conditioning and the use of passive, active, and resistive exercise to maintain and improve human function. The bill identified two levels of practice, *the health fitness consultant* and the *physiotechnologist*. In the first case, the licensing process would allow the health/fitness consultant to perform nondiagnostic fitness assessments on healthy individuals without prior medical clearance.

At the second level, the physiotechnologist would be licensed to practice clinical exercise physiology and aspects of public health promotion related to the maintenance or improvement of physical function. The physiotechnologist would perform routine screening, including the documentation of prior medical history before exercise testing, explaining procedures and protocol for the exercise testing, and identifying the contraindications to an exercise test. The physiotechnologist might also perform fitness assessments to high-risk or diseased individuals in physician-supervised settings. Although the bill has not yet passed through the California State Senate, if it does pass, it would represent the first licensure of exercise specialists and would go a long way to giving credibility to the services rendered by the exercise profession.

Ultimately, a credentialing system, whether through certification or licensure, is judged by the degree to which it is accepted by consumers, other professions, employers, policy makers, and the public. An issue here is that the pressure of the marketplace is insufficient to provide the quality control necessary to protect consumers (Schenk & Lewis, 1999). Unfortunately, the benefactors of the health and fitness industry seem satisfied with the current system.

Establishing the legitimacy of physical activity promotion as a component of the health care system will likely depend on the role played by the exercise profession. All professionals involved in physical activity promotion, including group exercise leaders and personal fitness trainers, must earn the right to promote their services. This can only be done once the exercise profession is regulated by a series of credentialing ethics. Competence is necessary for exercise professionals, just as it is for doctors and other health professionals. As the body of knowledge about fitness continues to grow, it will be even more important that the people providing exercise assistance are qualified to do so, and strict certification mechanisms will have to be put into place.

If exercise specialists are to become recognized as respectable members of the health care system, they must become more politically active. This will not be easily achieved, as exercise specialists will have to compete with other more-established professionals for territory and confront increasing resistance by policy makers and third-party payers to professionalization and its accompanying rising costs. Until the public takes a stand, it is highly unlikely that the push to license all exercise professionals will come to fruition. To date, the public has not seemed to take much interest in who is coordinating their exercise programs.

Turf Wars Among Health Professionals

Given the large number of professions that work within the health care industry, a considerable potential for interprofessional conflict exists among the various health professions. Not surprisingly, a lack of mutual understanding and respect sometimes strains relations between health professionals. Although the quality of patient care depends on the ability of health professionals to work together, health professionals sometimes undermine one another's efforts.

In some instances exercise physiologists have teamed up with orthopedic specialists and physical therapists in sports medicine clinics, but for the most part exercise professionals have not been well integrated into the managed care system. For example, in Abramson and colleagues' (2000) study of exercise counseling among physicians, only 34 percent of physicians who advised aerobic exercise referred their patients to a physical therapist, and less than 6 percent referred patients to an exercise physiologist. In a study of 107 general physicians and 58 practice nurses from 19 group practices, practice nurses were seen to have the main responsibility for cardiovascular health promotion among the patients. Health professionals, with their training in interpersonal relationships, group work, and interdisciplinary team skills play a vital role in the development and functioning of the interdisciplinary team unit and in all major phases of its work, including assessment goal setting and care planning and monitoring evaluation.

One group of exercise professionals that have made some inroads into medical practice is the athletic trainer. Athletic training was first established to provide quality health care for injured athletes in the school setting. As certified health care providers, athletic trainers provide services such as evaluation and management of athletic injuries and exercise and fitness programs to injured and healthy athletes at a fraction of the cost of such services delivered in the doctor's office. Many people with sport injuries who are treated by athletic trainers may not need referral to more expensive health care providers. Since the 1970s, athletic trainers have worked in sports medicine clinics as health care professionals, and in some states, they have begun receiving third-party payments. Athletic trainers are making their way into rehabilitation clinics, assisting physicians in the office, or providing outreach services to schools and other sport organizations. Today, athletic trainers may find work in hospitals and may be added to the physician-hospital organization or other HMO program. The athletic training program is a selling point for many HMOs that want to position themselves as complete health care packages (Forbis, 1996). Some athletic trainers are even evaluating the plausibility of setting up sport and physical activity HMOs and PPOs for school districts, sport organizations, and managed care programs, with services organized much the same way as in traditional managed care programs (Forbis, 1996).

The complexity of health care needs in the emerging system will require the health professional to be able to work effectively as a team member. A test of the effectiveness of a team-delivered approach to physical activity counseling is presently under way. The largest clinical trial yet to test the effectiveness of primary-care-based physical activity counseling is the Activity Counseling Trial, a multicenter, randomized, five-year clinical trial involving 874 men and women from four medical practices in three different states (King, Kiernan, Ahn, & Wilcox, 1998). The specific goal of the trial is to evaluate the effectiveness of three different approaches to primary-care physical activity counseling. The three approaches are hierarchical, meaning that each intervention builds on the services provided in the previous one. Level A, standard care control, involves messages from the primary-care physician to include more physical activity in daily living. The physicians' recommendations are the current national recommendations for physical activity. In level B, staff-assistance intervention, the physician's advice is given additional reinforcement through staff assistance that does not require great expenditures of time or resources, such as individually tailored advice via newsletters and mail-back cards. Level C, staff-counseling intervention, is the most staff-intensive intervention. Besides the physician's advice and mail interaction, patients receive ongoing telephone counseling, additional in-person counseling, and behavior-changing classes. The trial is still going on but should provide significant insight into the team approach among health professionals in promoting physical activity.

In a team environment, it is common for some knowledge areas to be shared with others. Patients suffer as the result of other effects, such as poor teamwork and poor communication among health care professionals. A common educational base that might allow a health care team to work more effectively as a cohesive group is lacking between physicians and allied health professionals. As pointed out by Ilona Kickbusch (1989), the health professions need to lift themselves above petty professional squabbles over specialized fields of intervention. Physicians' teaming up with other health professionals and support staff members will likely magnify their ability to deliver effective messages about physical activity.

Health Professionals as Advocates for Social Change

Many health professionals have a strong professional ethos of one-to-one intervention that values and respects the individuality of each client. Health professionals give much attention to screening, immunization, lifestyle changes, and risk-factor modification but rarely discuss the need to involve themselves in changing the social system to promote better health.

The focus on changing individual behavior is quite evident among most exercise specialists, most particularly personal fitness trainers. These exercise specialists typically provide clients with instruction, advice, and support for exercise but ignore the obstacles that might contribute to low compliance in certain occupations, including physicians. An increasing number of personal fitness trainers now offer client sessions on lifestyle management. The new *lifestyle coaches* who address areas from eating habits to stress reduction have simply expanded the range of individual behaviors that they address (Cantwell & Rothenberg, 2000).

Health professionals must pay attention to changing oppressive situations instead of just focusing on the people trapped in them. The job of health professionals should not stop at advocating for individual behavioral change by their patients or clients. Health care professionals should act as liaisons between the individual and the family, school, or other parts of the health care system. Sociologist Charles Blackburn (1993) points out the inadequate advocacy training given to many health professionals. Their training, according to Blackburn, predisposes them to underestimate the extent and impact of social conditions, such as poverty, on health. Health professionals, Blackburn argues, view social factors as posing additional burdens on the adoption of health-promoting behaviors instead of seeing them as the fundamental cause of much ill health and many premature deaths.

Many organizational constraints restrict direct-service workers from engaging in advocacy activities and limit workers' discretion, thus narrowing the influence that they are able to have. Health professionals have been subject to real and perceived restrictions through federal and state laws governing their political activity. The result has been their passivity and failure to participate in issues of advocacy and social reform (Thompson, 1994).

Health professionals who do not normally advocate as a part of their job may find it uncomfortable to advocate as aggressively or consistently as may be necessary to succeed. Typically, undergraduate and graduate curricula in most health professionals typically offer few opportunities to gain practical experience in community organizations, policy advocacy, and social problem solving (Raber & Richter, 1999). Health professionals also find themselves in a structural and ideological contradiction. Many health professionals avoid the confrontation implied by changing the system because their profession is part of the system that needs to be changed (Rose, 1990). Recognizing their fears of retribution or an uncomfortable future relationship with certain agencies is an important first step. There are legal protections against retribution, and getting past these fears to be an effective advocate is essential.

Prevention implies both an individual and a group responsibility. Absent a national health care system, which has not received much support among the population, the alternative is stepping up efforts in preventive services. For the preventive approach to succeed, its advocates must first win over the medical establishment and the private insurance industry. Money spent on current medical services would have to be diverted to educating the public about nutrition and physical activity. Increased efforts in these preventive services will encounter intense opposition if vested institutional interests are jeopardized. For example, physicians will feel threatened if they do not see it as their role to prevent illness and disease.

During the 1990s, the Pew Health Professions Commission, a program of the Pew Charitable Trust, was established and charged with assisting health professionals, workforce policy makers, and educational institutions in responding to the new challenges of the changing health care system. In its first several reports, the Pew Health Professions Commission affirmed that the education and training of health professionals were out of step with the health needs of the American people. They criticized many programs charged with promoting health that did not show enough interest in the obstacles in the social environments where people live. In its third report, the commission identified a list of 21 competencies necessary for meeting the changing needs of the health care system in the 21st century (table 7.2). According to the commission, the major way to improve health and to control costs is to make the health care system more efficient and more responsive to the population's health needs and to improve the way we deliver health care to the population as a whole.

Table 7.2   Twenty-One Competencies for the 21st Century

1	Embrace a personal ethic of social responsibility and service.
2	Exhibit ethical behavior in all professional activities.
3	Provide evidence-based, clinically competent care.
4	Incorporate the multiple determinants of health in clinical care.
5	Apply knowledge of the new sciences.
6	Demonstrate critical thinking, reflection, and problem-solving skills.
7	Understand the role of primary care.
8	Rigorously practice preventive health care.
9	Integrate population-based care and services into practice.
10	Improve access to health care for those with unmet health needs.
11	Practice relationship-centered care with individuals and families.
12	Provide culturally sensitive care to a diverse society.
13	Partner with communities in health care decisions.
14	Use communication and information technology effectively and appropriately.
15	Work in interdisciplinary teams.
16	Ensure care that balances individual, professional, system, and societal needs.
17	Practice leadership.
18	Take responsibility for quality of care and health outcomes at all levels.
19	Contribute to continuous improvement of the health care system.
20	Advocate for public policy that promotes and protects the health of the public.
21	Continue to learn, and help others learn.

From O'Neil, 1995.

Conclusion

The focus of the American health care system has centered on the treatment of acute health problems instead of emphasizing strategies that prevent chronic illnesses in the first place. Preventive services have been and will continue to be inadequate under the current medical paradigm. The current system is out of touch with the population's chronic health problems. The medical model remains entrenched in our health care system, jeopardizing the health and well-being of Americans. In particular, the outdated health care system has created numerous barriers to the adoption of physical activity lifestyles.

The health care providers have generally failed to address the deteriorating health status of their surrounding communities, whether affluent or underserved. This reluctance to become involved in community health reflects the long-standing split between preventive and curative medicine in the United States. There is little question that if we are serious about reorienting our approach to health from cure to prevention of illness, medicine must become more of a social science. This is not to say that we should disregard traditional biomedical approaches, but rather that we need to view the production of disease in terms of an interaction of social environments with human physiology. Consideration of the community is important because, as Meredith Minkler (1997) reminds us, the community reflects the most fundamental principle in health promotion, "starting where the people are."

PART

Communities and Transformations

8

Building
Active Communities

We hold that the most effective and proper center of gravity for health promotion is the community. State and national governments can formulate policies, provide leadership, allocate funding, and generate data for health promotion. At the other extreme, individuals can govern their own behavior and control the determinants of their own health up to a point, and should be allowed to do so. But the decisions on priorities and strategies for social change affecting the more complicated lifestyle issues can best be made collectively as close to the homes and workplaces of those affected as possible. This principle assures greater relevance and appropriateness of the programs to the people affected, and it offers greater opportunity for people to be actively engaged in the planning process themselves. (Green & Kreuter, 1990: 322)

▼   ▼   ▼   ▼   ▼

Most Americans understand that they put their health at risk if they give in to the many health-compromising temptations of modern living. People who eat too much or exercise too little recognize that they are likely to face health problems, especially as they age. However, a much less-understood influence on health is social connectedness, which, broadly defined, includes such qualities as social ties, social integration, and social support. Social connection, as discussed in chapter 4, is important in explaining how families help family members. Family connectedness is very important in times of crisis (e.g., adherence to a cardiac exercise rehabilitation program) or just in establishing daily routines of physical activity. An attentive understanding of the impact of social connectedness includes the ways that social interactions tie individuals to organizations and to groups that extend beyond the family, to the places where they work and attend school and the neighborhoods that they call home. For this understanding, we need to focus our attention on the issues associated with *socially cohesive communities.*

Communities come in many different forms, from rural towns to sprawling suburbs to large commercial and industrial cities. Communities are more than geographic locations, and social scientists have moved away from defining a community as only a physical setting. The community includes a culture with values, norms, and attachments to the community as a whole as well as among its parts. It is a place where many people work, make purchases from local businesses, and participate in religious and educational activities. It is more than a grouping of people who have different common goals; rather, it is better viewed as a living organism, with interactive "webs of relationships between people and their organizational structures" (Wallack, Dorfman, & Jernigan, 1994).

A community approach to health promotion is based on the assumption that behavior is greatly influenced by the environment in which people live and particularly by the local values and standards of acceptable behavior. Social connectedness is important in making the community a healthier place to live. For example, researchers in community health have have examined the concept *sense of community.* A sense of community, as outlined in chapter 1, is a complex concept that emphasizes how individuals and community development respond to each other. Health promotion specialists McMillan and Chavis's (1986) definition of a sense of community highlights four key characteristics: *membership,* the feeling of belonging and personal relatedness; *influence,* the feeling that one can make a contribution to a group; *integration and fulfillment of needs,* the expectation that one's needs will be met through membership in the group; and *shared emotional connection,* the belief that members share mutual concerns. The importance of a sense of community stems from its effect on people's behavior, perceptions about their physical and social environments, and willingness to participate in activities to change them. The most productive community health promotion strategy is one that raises awareness and concern for unhealthy behaviors such as physical inactivity and simultaneously enables community residents to devise their own strategies to change the behaviors.

Interest in developing community-based health promotion strategies comes at a time when social interaction within communities is in a steep decline. Many social scientists have noted the loss of many people's connections with the life of their communities. Although several theories have been advanced to explain the disconnectedness that so many people feel in today's communities, most social scientists trace its origins to the changing patterns of industrialization and urbanization. Not only did the industrial revolution change the structure of society by concentrating many people in cities, but it also altered the quality of the relationships on which a sense of cohesion rests. The growth of urban industrialism has steadily eroded the structure of local community and has led to a decline in the importance of locally based social relationships and an increase in the importance of individuals' being able to take care of themselves.

This chapter has four objectives. First, we look at several sociological explanations for the challenges facing today's communities. We pay particular attention to why communities have become less cohesive. Next, we examine some new thinking in the health promotion field. The latest push for healthy communities emphasizes the efforts of individuals to take an active role in reshaping both their own individual behaviors and their risk-producing social and physical environments (Stokols, 1996). Whereas earlier health promotion strategies emphasized the modification of individuals' health habits, more recent approaches link behavioral change with efforts to strengthen the social and environmental supports within the local community. Third, we look at some promising community interventions that have been used to promote physical activity. Finally, we look at some challenges that these new approaches face within today's community structures, many of which are still tied to the more traditional health promotion efforts, focused on changing individuals one at a time (Minkler, 1997).

Searching for Community in a Changing Society

Recognition of the importance of social connectedness to communities dates back over 100 years to Emile Durkheim's (1897) demonstration that suicide rates were highest among populations with weak social ties and lowest among those with strong social ties. Durkheim (1933) felt the key to "community social cohesion" is the degree to which members of a society feel united by shared values. He used the term *anomie* to refer to feelings of detachments or rootlessness. Establishing intimate relationships and offering a sense of meaning and purpose to life, small groups serve as a buffer between individuals and the forces and rapid changes of society that they often do not understand.

Changes in community cohesiveness can be understood with the help of the concepts of *gemeinschaft* (community) and *gesellschaft* (society), first developed by German sociologist Ferdinand Tonnies (1957). *Gemeinschaft* characterizes a premodern society consisting of a close network of personal relationships based heavily on kinship and on the direct, face-to-face contact that occurs in a small, closed village. Individuals were bound to one another in a web of mutual interdependence that touched all aspects of life, from family to work to leisure activities. People conducted all aspects of their lives—social, business, and religious—with the same people. There was little geographic or social mobility, so people tended to live out their lives in the position to which they were born, their position being determined by family and individual characteristics.

A system of social exchange and reciprocity evolved into a new type of relationship, *gesellschaft*, developed to meet the demands of the new marketplace. Social relationships became formalized and impersonal; individuals did not depend on one another for mutual support to nearly the same extent as before. Since a person's role was largely influenced by his or her functions, people who had the same functional role were largely interchangeable. It mattered little where or with whom business was transacted as long as the job got done.

Wirth (1938) proposed that the growth of cities was largely responsible for the disappearance of community and provided a theory of urbanism to explain the phenomenon. He defined a city as a relatively large, dense, and permanent settlement of socially heterogeneous individuals. The massive migration of people into cities and then to the surrounding suburbs caused profound changes in interpersonal relationships. His theory of urbanism predicted that the size, density, and heterogeneity of cities would lead to new social arrangements that were very different from those in small towns and rural areas. Nonurban communities are characterized by primary group relationships that involve face-to-face contacts between persons who meet and interact with one another in nearly all phases of life, including work, family, and worship. The larger population found in the city precludes familiarity with every other person, often leading to anonymous lives, transitory relationships, role segmentation, and isolation (Wirth, 1938). Sociologist Herbert Gans (1962) viewed the isolation and impersonalization of *gesellschaft* as extending beyond urban areas. The framework of laws and other formal regulations that characterizes large, urban, industrial societies has penetrated down to the small, rural communities as well. He concluded that suburban life is as detached as urban life. This produces a sense of dislocation in many people, which Gans believed to be the cause of many social ills, from a rise in crime to the isolation and loneliness of older people. The modern community has also left its mark on health issues.

The impersonality of suburban life can make it more difficult to establish a large network of acquaintances.

The Roseto Effect

The effect of changing social forces on health was the subject of a 30-year study of Roseto, a small Italian-American community in eastern Pennsylvania (Wolf & Bruhn, 1993). In 1955, the town was chosen for study because of its remarkably low mortality rates from heart disease. To learn the reasons for Roseto's unusually low incidence of heart disease, researchers from the University of Oklahoma compared medical histories of a large sample of Rosetans and four neighboring communities. They found that cardiovascular disease was much lower in Roseto than in several neighboring towns, despite similar prevalence of conventional risk factors such as high cholesterol, high-fat diets, and smoking. Roseto did stand out from the other communities in one significant regard: the strong social support reflected in unusually close family ties and community cohesion.

During the early years of the study, the investigators marveled at the town's stability, family cohesion, and social supportiveness and identified these community characteristics as major factors in the low incidence of heart disease. As described by the team of researchers, the community included warm and neighborly people. They were found to be mutually trusting and mutually supporting. The hospitality of local residents served to counteract stress, and their way of life emphasized cooperation and sharing rather than competition.

Over the years, as problems of modern living began to infiltrate the life of this small community, the researchers could document a dramatic increase in health problems. The social changes that Roseto had resisted for years would finally catch up to them in the 1960s. As the community experienced a decline in cohesiveness, measured by the loosening of family ties and increased unemployment, cardiovascular disease rose dramatically (Wolf & Bruhn, 1993). Although there were criticisms of the methodology of the earliest Roseto research, more recent longitudinal investigations have also suggested that as the sociocultural buffers dissipated, the risk of heart disease and mortality increased in the next generation of Roseto residents (Egolf, Lasker, Wolf, & Potvin, 1992).

These findings, commonly termed the "Roseto effect," have been widely cited as the first evidence for both the positive health effects attributed to community social cohesion and the health-impairing agents that have emerged in modern society. Today, "poor health of the community" has come to represent not only a social peril (that is, alienation and lack of sense of connection to others) but also an environment that promotes unhealthful behaviors, such as poor nutrition, high smoking rates, alcohol abuse, and sedentary living. The changing postindustrial society, in which individuals often lack secure connections to family, work, and neighborhood, has generated a range of new disease-producing agents related to social isolation.

Growing Social Isolation

Social scientists have turned to the observations of Alexis de Tocqueville for an understanding of the causes of the social isolation many Americans have experienced. Tocqueville, a Frenchman who traveled widely in 19th-century America, compared democracy in the United States with democracy in Europe (Tocqueville, 1835). Tocqueville marveled at our ability to form and participate in voluntary associations and civic groups. He believed that the connections within groups counteracted the isolating tendencies of the American character and allowed American citizens to participate in a democracy. He also warned, however, that the individualistic values so important to the American character could eventually lead to isolation of individuals and threaten American democracy.

A number of writers today have suggested that Tocqueville's assumptions were right and have pointed to how segmented American society has become. Francis Fukuyama (1995) suggests that disinterest in voluntary associations is in large part responsible for the decline in America's social connectedness, leaving communities with members who are suspicious of one another. The disappearance of a well-connected community has been perhaps articulated best in the work of Robert Putnam, a Harvard political scientist. According to Putnam, Americans' tendency to participate in fewer organizations and groups is responsible for the decline in many American communities.

Robert Bellah and colleagues, in their book *Habits of the Heart* (1985), explore the struggle in America between individualism and commitment to others. In pointing to how "unfettered individualism" has led to a culture of isolation, these sociologists have reasoned that a good balance between public and private aspects of life is key to the survival of the modern community. One of the strangest voices on modern community is that of Amitai Etzioni (1993) who describes the community as a place where people are too concerned with individual rights at the expense of social responsibilities. Each of these approaches frames the disappearance of the community in similar terms. We have become too concerned with the well-being of the individual at the expense of the interest of the community. What is needed is an emphasis on connecting individuals so that they can collectively address their own community problems.

The New Public Health Movement

The new push for physically active communities requires individuals to take an active role in changing both their own behaviors and their social and physical environments and is based on two fundamental principles. The first principle is recognition that most public health challenges, including encouraging people to be more physically active, require more comprehensive approaches that go beyond individual lifestyle changes to the creation of supportive environments within which healthy living can take place. The second principle acknowledges that for social changes to be long-lasting, they must be rooted in the social and political base of organization and leadership within the community itself (Brown, 1991). In the next two sections we take a closer look at each of these principles.

Social Ecological Approaches

The first major theme of the new public health movement is a shift from a person-focused to an environmentally based approach to community health promotion (Stokols, 1996). This perspective is rooted in the interrelations among environmental conditions and human actions. This focus actually is not a new one, as we saw in chapter 3. The 19th-century development of public sanitation recognized that overcrowding was the major cause of epidemics and illness. Whereas the 19th-century public health movement focused on disease prevention through modifying the physical environment, the new public health movement emphasizes change to physical and social environments.

Strategies that combine individual and environmental perspectives are emphasized in the *social ecological paradigm*. The term *ecology* refers to the study of the relationships between organisms and their environments. Early ecological analyses were concerned with plant and animal populations and their natural habitats but were later extended to the study of people and their social environments. "It takes a village to raise a child," a proverb and more recently the title of a book written by Hillary Clinton (1996), captures the essence of an ecological approach; that is, the individual is inseparable from the environment and is supported or neglected by many social systems and groups. The social ecological perspective assumes that the effectiveness of health promotion programs can be enhanced significantly through the coordination of individuals and groups acting at different levels (Stokols, 1992).

Child development specialist Uri Bronfenbrenner (1979) gave us one of the first descriptions of how environment shapes human development. He described the environment as a series of interrelated social systems, each with the capacity to influence, directly or indirectly, the course of the individual's growth. Specifically, Bronfenbrenner divided social environmental influences on behavior into four levels: microsystem, mesosystem, exosystem, and macrosystem. The microsystem refers to face-to-face influences in specific settings, such as interactions with family and informal social networks. The mesosystem means the social settings in which the individual is involved, such as the family, school, and church. The exosystem refers to the forces within the larger social system, such as unemployment rates that affect economic stability. The macrosystem refers to cultural beliefs and values that affect both the microsystem and the macrosystem.

Bronfenbrenner (1979) understood that an individual's development is profoundly affected by events that occur in settings where the person is not even present. For example, Bronfenbrenner's model acknowledges the important role that parents play in directly influencing values for physical activity among their children through face-to-face contact but also recognizes that the way a parent is treated on the job by management and colleagues also affects the messages that parents pass along to children.

McLeroy, Bibeau, Steckler, and Glanz (1988), building on the work of Bronfenbrenner, applied ecological thinking to the field of health promotion. Their ecological model for health promotion consists of five levels: intrapersonal factors, interpersonal or small-group factors, institutional factors, community factors, and public policy. These levels are shown in table 8.1.

Efforts at all levels help ensure the success of health promotion programs. For example, a program to increase physical activity is likely to be more effective if it is accompanied by safer and better-lit places to walk (community level) or flextime policies at the workplace that allow time to use the work-site fitness facilities (institutional level). Similarly, individuals must take full advantage of health promotion programs available at work, school, or other places in the community (intrapersonal level). They must also invest time and effort to formally regulate access to physical activity, such as by

Table 8.1   An Ecological Model for Health Promotion

	Factors	Description
1	Intrapersonal factors	Characteristics of the individual, such as knowledge, attitudes, behavior, self-concept, skills, developmental history, etc.
2	Interpersonal processes and primary groups	Formal and informal social network and social support systems, including the family, work group, and friendship networks
3	Institutional factors	Social institutions with organizational characteristics and formal (and informal) rules and regulations for operation
4	Community factors	Relationships among organizations, institutions, and informal networks within defined boundaries
5	Public policy	Local, state, and national laws and policies

Adapted from McLeroy et al., 1988.

lobbying for inclusion of physical activity counseling in the preventive services covered by Medicare or reinstitution of a daily physical education requirement in the state standards for graduation from public schools (public policy level).

Empowering Communities to Change

The second component of the new public health movement involves allowing people to define their own needs, goals, and priorities and to be involved in directing their own solutions. *Empowerment* refers to the process of gaining influence over events and outcomes important to the large social organization (Shor, 1992). In its broadest definition, empowerment involves people's assuming control over their lives both at the individual level and at the level of their social and political environment. The link between the individual and community-level change is an important concept in the work of Brazilian educator, Paulo Freire. His concept of *critical consciousness* is an example of a method that engages people in a problem-posing and problem-solving exchange. The central theme of Freire's methodology is that rather than simply receiving information, the learner is an equal partner with the teacher in the learning process (Freire,

1973). Freire questioned the frequency with which education reinforces powerlessness by treating people as objects who receive knowledge rather than providing opportunities to engage in active dialogue and to challenge the conditions that keep them powerless. Through a structured dialogue, group participants listen for issues that relate to their own experiences, discuss common problems, and devise strategies to help transform their situations (Wallerstein & Bernstein, 1988).

Freire's ideas are easily adaptable to community health conditions and community members' role in changing them. For change to occur, the individual and community must directly experience a need for change. One method for catalyzing this perceived need for change is through popular education methods in which the learner becomes transformed from passively accepting the environment to critically observing the effect of the environment on the self and becoming aware of his or her ability to change the environment. This approach to health promotion engages people to assess critically the social, historical, and cultural roots of their problems and to develop strategies to change their personal and social lives.

Unique components of Freire's model are critical thinking and analysis of the root causes of one's situation in society, which serve to link individual responsibility and collective responsibility for promoting good health. The integration of these two concepts has been missing from many past models of health promotion. Some argue that the social system and its underlying risk conditions, such as poverty, powerlessness, and unemployment, should be the target for interventions to reduce mortality and morbidity. Others argue that the target should be the individual and his particular risk factors. Community strategies offer a potential bridge to close the gap between risk environments and individual risk factors. Earlier models focused sometimes on the individual or sometimes on the community, but rarely both (Green & Kreuter, 1990).

Closely related to the concept of individual empowerment is community empowerment, or *community competence* (Zimmerman, 1990). A competent community is one that is involved in the development and utilization of resources by community members and one that has increased sophistication in coping with problems and issues. The health capabilities and potential for action of a community are important to the health status of its members. From his work in community psychology, Cottrell (1976) linked community competence to health outcomes, observing that increased community competence allows the individual greater participation in society. His explanation is that in any given social interaction, participants learn not only from perceptions and experiences of their own actions, but also from their perceptions and experiences of the actions of others. Individuals' responses become guided by the responses they expect from others and by perceptions of what others expect from them. The integration of individuals into trusting and functioning collective entities prepares them for taking action to change the community by stimulating and supporting neighborhood and community action projects.

Empowerment is not a commodity to be acquired but a transformation process requiring ongoing action. Through increased knowledge of their community, residents can claim a larger share of the power associated with the decision making for their community. Important health issues within the community can be identified and resolved, leading to an improved quality of life and to a sense of collective action.

Social scientists have long puzzled over why some communities are prosperous and cohesive, while other communities are not. One answer is *social capital,* defined as those features of social organization—such as the extent of interpersonal trust between citizens, norms of reciprocity, and density of civic associations—that facilitate cooperation for mutual benefit. The ability to associate depends on *norms of reciprocity,* or the degree to which individuals develop interpersonal trust and are able to subordinate individual interests for mutual benefit. Feelings of belonging and a shared commitment to one another and to the group are important for reciprocity. Mutually concerned people who trust one another enough to be able to exchange criticism constructively, establish codes of personal conduct, and enforce social sanctions against what is judged as undesirable behavior create and enforce communal norms.

The availability of social capital has also been linked to solving health issues in communities. Kawachi, Kennedy, and Glass (1999) studied the possible mechanisms that link social capital to health. They proposed that the link between social capital and good health may work in one of three fundamental ways. First, according to these epidemiologists, social capital may influence the health behaviors of people living in a community by promoting more rapid diffusion of health information. Messages concerning the importance of health-promoting behaviors such as physical activity or the availability of fitness facilities and health programs circulate more rapidly in communities that are socially connected. Second, they reasoned that social capital at the community level may work to promote healthy behaviors by exerting social control over health-risking behavior. The members of a community high in social capital are activated against forces both intentional and unintentional that are counterproductive to good health. Finally, they viewed socially connected individuals as critical in times of financial concerns. For example, socially connected networks are likely to be more successful at coming together to thwart off budget cuts that may undermine the availability of health promoting services and opportunities.

Community Health Coalitions

Intervention strategies aimed at strengthening communities by bringing together members of community agencies, institutions, and concerned citizens to combat chronic health conditions are gaining popularity. Cooperation among private, public, and voluntary sectors in community-wide intervention programs is necessary if broad-based community goals are to be realized. These alliances, or *coalitions,* offer a mechanism for individuals to change community conditions that affect health. The word *coalition* is derived from two Latin roots, *coalescere,* to grow together, and *coalitio,* a union (Feighery & Rogers, 1989). Coalitions differ from other community groups in that they are composed of individuals with diverse and sometimes conflicting interests. Coalitions provide an avenue for recruiting participants from diverse constituencies, such as political, business, human service, social, and religious groups as well as less-organized grassroots groups. These partnerships are alliances in which all share risks, responsibilities, resources, and rewards for common effort. Coalitions can maximize the power of individuals and groups through joint action, they can increase the critical mass behind a community effort, and they can help individuals achieve objectives beyond the scope of any single individual or organization (Brown, 1984).

Community health specialists Frances Butterfoss and colleagues (1993) point to a number of reasons why community coalitions are positively situated to achieve changes at the community level.

Community coalitions allow individuals and groups to become involved in new and broader issues without having the sole responsibility for managing the changes. An organization of diverse interests that can combine people and material resources promote objectives that go beyond any one individual or organization. Community coalitions can also mobilize more talent, resources, and approaches to influence an issue than any single organization could achieve alone (table 8.2). Coalitions are also positioned to improve trust and communication and to reduce contention and conflict among groups. By joining forces and working toward a collective goal, diverse groups are more likely to cooperate than compete with each other.

Table 8.2   Advantages of Community Health Coalitions

1	Coalitions enable organizations to become involved in new and broader issues without having the sole responsibility for managing the issues.
2	Coalitions can demonstrate and develop widespread support for issues.
3	Coalitions can maximize the power of individuals and groups through joint action by increasing the critical mass behind a community effort.
4	Coalitions can minimize the duplication of efforts and services.
5	Coalitions can help mobilize more talent resources than a single organization.
6	Coalitions can recruit participants from diverse constituencies.
7	Coalitions can develop trust and cooperation among groups that would normally compete with each other.
8	Coalitions may be more flexible to find new resources in changing situations.

Adapted from Butterfoss et al., 1993.

Although collaboration is a key principle of health reform, to expect it to happen automatically is unrealistic. Despite the overt collective purposes of an organization, most individuals and groups are also concerned about protecting their own interests. Groups and organizations will enter into collaborations if they can see that their needs will be met and that they will benefit in some way. Working with other agencies results in some loss of independence and control and requires the investment of scarce resources in building partnerships. If the purpose of coalitions is to pool scarce resources to address common problems, it is important that members perceive decisions as fair and see that the benefits of participation outweigh the costs of undertaking the task alone.

Community-based coalitions have been successful in influencing long-term health practices for their communities. For instance, the COMMIT (Community Tobacco-Control Programs), funded by the NIH, require coalitions of citizens to develop local strategies to decrease tobacco use (Thompson, Wallack, Lichenstein, & Pechacek, 1990-91). The 22 communities, eight-year, $45 million COMMIT project stressed community participation through the development of community boards and task forces. The Planned Approach to Community Health (PATCH) and other community-based chronic disease initiatives sponsored by the CDC encourage the formation of local coalitions for community health planning and implementation (Suen, Christenson, Cooper, & Taylor, 1995).

Community Coalitions to Promote Physical Activity

Although attempts to promote physical activity through coalition efforts are still in their infancy, they hold much promise. The formation of a community coalition to promote physical activity should be seen as an effective means for sharing resources, increasing the awareness of the public and decision makers, and building momentum for community-wide physical activity improvements. Examples of potential participants in such physical activity coalitions include parks and recreation departments, local public health departments, schools, community service clubs, local chapters of nonprofit agencies, professional organizations, hospital auxiliaries, and civic and business leaders. Two examples of successful community partnerships to promote physical activity—the Bootheel Heart Health Project and the Kansas LEAN School Health Project—illustrate the promise of future intervention efforts.

The Bootheel Heart Health Project

In 1989, in cooperation with the CDC, the Missouri Department of Health began a cardiovascular disease risk reduction project in the Bootheel area of southeastern Missouri (Brownson et al., 1996). The medically underserved rural area is characterized by high rates of poverty and low educational levels. High mortality rates from coronary heart disease were also prevalent among the five counties clustered in southeastern Missouri. The long-term goal of the Bootheel Heart Health Project was to reduce morbidity and mortality due to cardiovascular disease, and the shorter-term project objectives focused on reducing the major modifiable risk factors for cardiovascular disease, including physical inactivity. The development of coalitions was ensured by involving local leaders and community groups in the planning process. Local leaders were identified through established agencies and through word of mouth. Once a year, each coalition submitted a proposal to the Missouri Department of Health for local projects. Each of the county coalitions received about $5,000 per year to carry out community-based interventions.

Coalitions selected their own priorities from a list of possible cardiovascular disease-related interventions provided by project staff. Examples of specific projects included annual heart-healthy fitness festivals that involved exercise demonstration, registration for exercise classes, and walking clubs. The most frequently held activities were walking events. Significant improvement in five risk factors, including physical activity rates, was observed for communities with active coalitions. Over a five-year period, communities with active coalitions experienced a significant decline in rates of physical inactivity. The decline in physical inactivity observed in the Bootheel project suggests that a community-level reduction in cardiovascular disease risk may be achievable through relatively low-cost interventions. Over the project period, the annual cost of the Bootheel project was approximately $105,000.

Kansas LEAN School Health Project

A second example of the development of an effective community coalition to promote physical activity is the multiyear Kansas LEAN School Health Project, with a mission of promoting environmental change to increase physical activity and reduce fat intake among schoolchildren. This project was patterned after a national program called Project LEAN (Low-Fat Eating for America Now) sponsored by the Henry J. Kaiser Family Foundation of Menlo Park, California (Samuels, 1990). The Kansas Health Foundation provided a two-year grant to design, test, and evaluate a comprehensive chronic disease prevention program for youths in two communities, one a remote rural community and one a midsized city (Harris et al., 1997). In phase I, the Kansas LEAN (Leadership to Encourage Activity and Nutrition) model consisted of forming partnerships to make changes in schools and in the broader community. Each community partnership consisted of various community sectors, such as government

Community coalitions are more effective when participants are part of the planning stage.

and business, coming together to ensure that children and their families would have additional opportunities outside school to select lower-fat foods and participate in fitness activities.

Each coalition focused on creating individual and environmental-level changes. Activities such as fitness assessments and lessons in preparing low-fat snacks were designed to increase children's health knowledge and health-promoting behaviors. Harris and colleagues (1997) reported more than 250 community changes in the two communities, including programs such as parent–child aerobic classes in conjunction with the local YWCA. In both communities, the evaluation found statistically significant increases in students' knowledge of nutrition among students in the schools that participated in the project. Students' fitness levels also increased in the schools of the two communities that participated in the project.

In phase II, six community coalitions were formed around three specific objectives: the modification of school meals, integration of nutrition education in the classroom, and increased physical activity opportunities (Dzewaltowski, Estabrooks, Gyurcsik, in press).

Coalition members included members of the state, county, and city departments of health; a grocery store chain; a pizza business; the State Cooperative Extension Service; a local television station; and a variety of other organizations. Within schools, teachers, food service personnel, and coaches who have substantial influence over children's opportunities for healthy diet and more physical activity were also actively involved. Coalitions were given the mission to use their community resources and devise specific interventions to meet the objectives of the project.

Although schools were given materials to integrate into physical education and classroom curricula, each school was free to develop unique promotion efforts that met the particular diverse needs of its school and community. Participants were 3,454 students in grades K-8. Physical activity was assessed indirectly through pacer, push-up, and curl-up tests to measure changes in physical fitness, cardiovascular endurance, and muscular endurance. Results showed significant improvements in cardiovascular endurance and upper-body and abdominal strength. Many community changes were also made by each of the six coalitions. Examples included the formation of exercise classes at community centers and local churches, daily fitness breaks, and coalition-sponsored sport (basketball and volleyball) events.

Currently, the Kansas LEAN project is focusing on four new communities (Dzewaltowski et al, in press). Physical activity in phase III is being measured directly rather than indirectly through measures of improvement in physical fitness. The project is ongoing and should produce promising results in the near future.

Physical Activity Coalitions in At-Risk Communities

Developing effective community coalitions to promote physical activity in impoverished areas presents unique challenges. Many urban areas are besieged with numerous problems that endanger the health of people living there. Poverty and unemployment as well as low educational attainment are all greater in urban areas (Speers & Lancaster, 1998). Undesirable social conditions in urban areas have created environments of risk, which foster the emergence of numerous threats to health (Panel on High Risk Youth, 1993). In low-income communities, individuals confront numerous barriers to the maintenance of healthy behaviors because of few personal resources and adverse social influences (National Heart, Lung and Blood Institute, 1995). Underfunding of public services, violence, tensions among ethnic or racial groups, unhealthy behavior patterns, and urban stress increase disease, disability, and premature death.

The absence of social cohesion within many U.S. urban communities impedes attempts to improve those communities from within (Freudenberg, 1998). Although these community residents are often labeled as "hard to reach," they are hard to reach because their individual situations are so threatening they feel they have little time, energy, or resources to participate in larger community structures and activities. Those with the most severe health problems, the poor, the undereducated, and the unemployed are typically those with the least access to sources of community power (Wallack, 1994). As a result, they are rarely politically organized and are cut off from community political processes and community power structures. These groups are often left out of the process of defining problems and developing programmatic solutions. Because of their social and political isolation, they become the objects of services and programs, which, while often well intended, fail to solve problems. Participation in community health coalitions is critical for community members who lack access to healthy environments, including safe and inexpensive places to exercise (Freudenberg & Manoncourt, 1998).

The Physical Activity for Risk Reduction Project

Several projects give us hope for changing physical activity levels among members of at-risk communities. The Physical Activity for Risk Reduction project (PARR) evolved from a model in which community members play a central role in defining their own needs, identifying their own strategies for change, and participating in carrying out the actual programs. Seven large, predominantly African-American housing projects in Birmingham, Alabama, were included in the project, five with 450 or more apartment units and one smaller contiguous housing complex (Lewis et al., 1993). The community residents were generally poorly educated and unemployed or working in service occupations. Almost one third of the participants in one survey reported no participation in physical activity. The major goal of PARR was to develop community coalitions with the express purpose to improve the physical activity levels among the residents. The basic intervention involved a community-based exercise program devised by a coalition staff and conducted by one part-time physical activity leader. Physical activity programming included activities such as walking, aerobic dance, and low-impact aerobics.

An intervention program was developed to measure the role of community involvement in delivering a successful physical activity program. Residents were actively engaged in the development of their physical activity programs. They were asked to participate in resi-dent-based focus groups that provided feedback concerning program preferences, suggested types of physical activity, times that would be most convenient for group sessions, and perceived barriers to physical activity. Periodic meetings of project staff and resident coun-cils were designed to help keep the community actively involved.

The project results were mixed, and the project organizers noted that some community coalitions were more organized than others. Increases in physical activity were observed in communities with strong coalitions. Organized communities had regularly scheduled and well-attended resident council meetings, and community leaders and residents were actively involved in the programs. Less-organized communities did not have well-attended council meet-ings and fewer physical activity programs were being conducted in these communities. In communities with poor organization, recruit-ment of physical activity leaders was difficult. The absence of well-organized community coalitions resulted in little or no improvement in physical activity.

The Families in Good Health Program

Improving physical activity participation in impoverished commu-nities often requires changing public policies. Health-promoting policies are decided by some legislative or executive authority and are intended to support health-promoting environments for constitu-ents of a given territory. The Families in Good Health program (FGH) found out that changing city ordinances was key to improving physi-cal activity among that city's citizens.

Beginning in the 1980s, large influxes of Southeast Asian refugees settled in the city of Long Beach, California, including many from Vietnam, Cambodia, and Laos. Lack of physical activity is prevalent among Vietnamese immigrants: 40 percent of Vietnamese men and 50 percent of Vietnamese women do not engage in enough physical activity. One of the FGH program's goals was promotion of physi-cal activity and healthy eating (Foo et al., 1999).

The program staff wanted to start some community gardens as a way to increase community members' level of physical activity. For nearly a year, the staff worked with community leaders to identify and obtain land for the community gardens. A local group agreed to donate a vacant commercial lot to the program. In May 1996, the staff successfully recruited 50 Southeast Asian families to participate in the community garden project. During the summer of 1996, the staff approached the city council to discuss a policy for reducing the water costs for the community gardens but soon learned that zoning laws made it illegal for the land to be used for community gardening. To continue, they had to apply for a zoning variance to allow community gardens as a conditional use in the commercial zone. While the group was discussing with the city about a conditional-use permit for the community garden, a city commissioner released some negative statements to the press about the purported lack of upkeep of the gardens. The city commissioner said that "huts were being built" and that "people were relieving themselves" in the gardens (Foo et al., 1999).

In response, a prominent physician enlisted the *Long Beach Press Telegram* to report on the positive aspects of the gardens and the benefits to the community of supporting such efforts. The combined effects of positive publicity and enthusiastic efforts by community gardeners to meet city requirements overcame objections to the gardens. In January 1997, FGH received the city planners' recommendation for approval of the conditional-use permit for the community garden.

Challenges to Effective Health Coalitions

The ability of coalitions to function effectively to address local health issues relies on the ability of members to work together. They must overcome a number of obstacles to accomplish this. The first barrier to effective health coalitions is the time it takes to develop and carry out programs. A number of key individuals need to be included in planning, which increases the time the process requires. The time allocated for the community-analysis and intervention phases is determined by the slow pace at which the community considers problems and takes action. It is reasonable to plan on up to two years of preliminary work even before the start of a community-wide project (Mittelmark, Hunt, Heath, & Schmid, 1993).

Many community health promotions rely too much on professional expertise. A second barrier to effective coalitions is following a professional expert model, or what health educator Guy Steuart (1993) has termed a *social control model*. In this model, professional expertise is the dominant component of the community health agenda. Program priorities, design and implementation of activities, and evaluation of the program are dictated by outside professionals. Certainly, trained professionals have much to offer community health programs. Many are armed with the latest knowledge and techniques and typically have access to more information than the members of the local community. But Steuart contends that problem solving by outside experts, if not carefully exercised, "clientizes" community members, meaning that they develop a dependency on consuming the products and services determined by the professional experts. It is the membership of the community that has the expertise in specific community practices and culture to identify the community's real health needs. A coalition formed to address a health issue may have difficulty in mobilizing ordinary citizens. This is particularly true when community volunteers are used in relatively rudimentary roles and activities of the program are already identified.

Since coalitions primarily consist of individuals representing diverse community organizations, role conflict frequently occurs. Individuals and groups often question the appropriateness of developing physical activity programs when an array of more pressing health, social, and economic concerns are apparent, particularly in underserved communities. A third barrier to an effective health coalition is a lack of trust among coalition members; without trust, each member carefully protects its own resources and turf. Klitzner (1993) studied strife among members of community coalitions and reported that greater diversity in membership was related to more difficulties in sustaining coalition efforts. They found distrust and competition fell along social class lines as well as racial and ethnic lines.

Some community coalitions are characterized by rigid ideological orientations that offer less tolerance for diverse points of view within the organization. Chronic conflict among members or few resources to resolve such conflicts when they arise are likely to impair the operation of the group. The absence of trust causes organizational members to look upon change with suspicion. Some members equate change with manipulation; others fear that their positions of power and privilege will be challenged by innovation. To cope, some coalition members may form protective groups or alliances, and in extreme cases, they look for ways to sabotage the efforts of the coalition. These alliances are founded on a "survival mentality" that undermines the collective potential of the organization (Allen & Allen, 1987).

A fourth barrier is the tendency of one or more groups within the coalition to assume a disproportionate amount of power. For example, many coalitions have executive committees that are responsible for coordinating coalition activities and that have final decision-making authority, particularly about budgets and expenditures. Hierarchical organizations, however, can limit participation, particularly among community residents. Many community groups are not accustomed to working within a hierarchical organization.

Coalitions can use up important community resources. A fifth barrier to the effectiveness of health coalitions is competition for resources, including volunteer time or attention from formal agencies. Coalitions may misdefine problems and implement ineffective interventions that waste limited community resources. This may affect the ability of communities to mobilize to address other significant local problems.

The crucial challenge in many communities is not the introduction of health coalitions but the extent to which health initiatives survive the initial phase. The long-term maintenance of health programs are realized when communities integrate health-promoting activities into the routines of business, government, education, and family. The term *institutionalized* or *sustainability* refers to the long-term viability and integration of new programs and services within a community (Mittlemark, Hunt, Heath, & Schmid, 1993). In the absence of a community structure to assume ownership, innovative programs are unlikely to be continued (Steckler & Goodman, 1989).

The ability of coalitions to function effectively is contingent on the nature of the community, their members' abilities to work effectively together, skills and knowledge available for defining and addressing local problems, the availability of local or outside resources, and overcoming many obstacles. Coalitions can show the effectiveness of working together to solve local problems, but if coalitions fail, communities may learn that working together is not effective and may become skeptical about collaborative approaches. Unless coalitions are perceived by their members and the broader community as successful in addressing community problems, they may lead to the disempowerment of communities. On the other hand, successful health collaborations are synergistic and can achieve more significant and longer-term outcomes than would be achieved by groups or agencies working alone.

Conclusion

The new health promotion movement is at the forefront in the call for efforts to develop meaningful health improvements in communities. Avoiding the health-damaging consequences of sedentary living depends largely on the ability of local communities to restructure conventional activities in a way that offers greater opportunities for physical activity. These undertakings are based on the premise that real improvement in physical activity will not come so much from encouraging individuals to change, but rather from initiating large-scale efforts to change the social and physical environments of communities.

The prospect of a future physically active America hinges on the quality of decisions made by federal, state, and local governments, by business and industry, and by community organizations and health professionals, including meaningful changes to organizational and public policy. Unfortunately, increased public awareness of the health risks associated with physical inactivity has failed to ignite any measurable collective strategy that would have an extensive influence on physical inactivity. A critical missing aspect of legislative policy, as pointed out by Abbey King (1994), is an overarching long-term plan on which to build and direct local, state, and national policy initiatives concerning physical activity. The unveiling of the new *Healthy People 2010* objectives (USDHHS, 2000a) serves as a strong starting point for changing this.

The transformation to a physically active society also requires new thinking about social institutions. This and previous chapters emphasized the role of key social institutions in creating hurdles to achieving a physically active society. We have examined how social institutions reaffirm value structures that undermine goals of physical activity, and we have considered what the current state of institutional confusion means to the prospects of creating a physically active society. The logical conclusion from the failure of social institutions is that efforts to change the high rates of physical inactivity must combine strategies of changing individuals with those directed at changing the values and social norms present in our social institutions. Chapter 9 offers some suggestions.

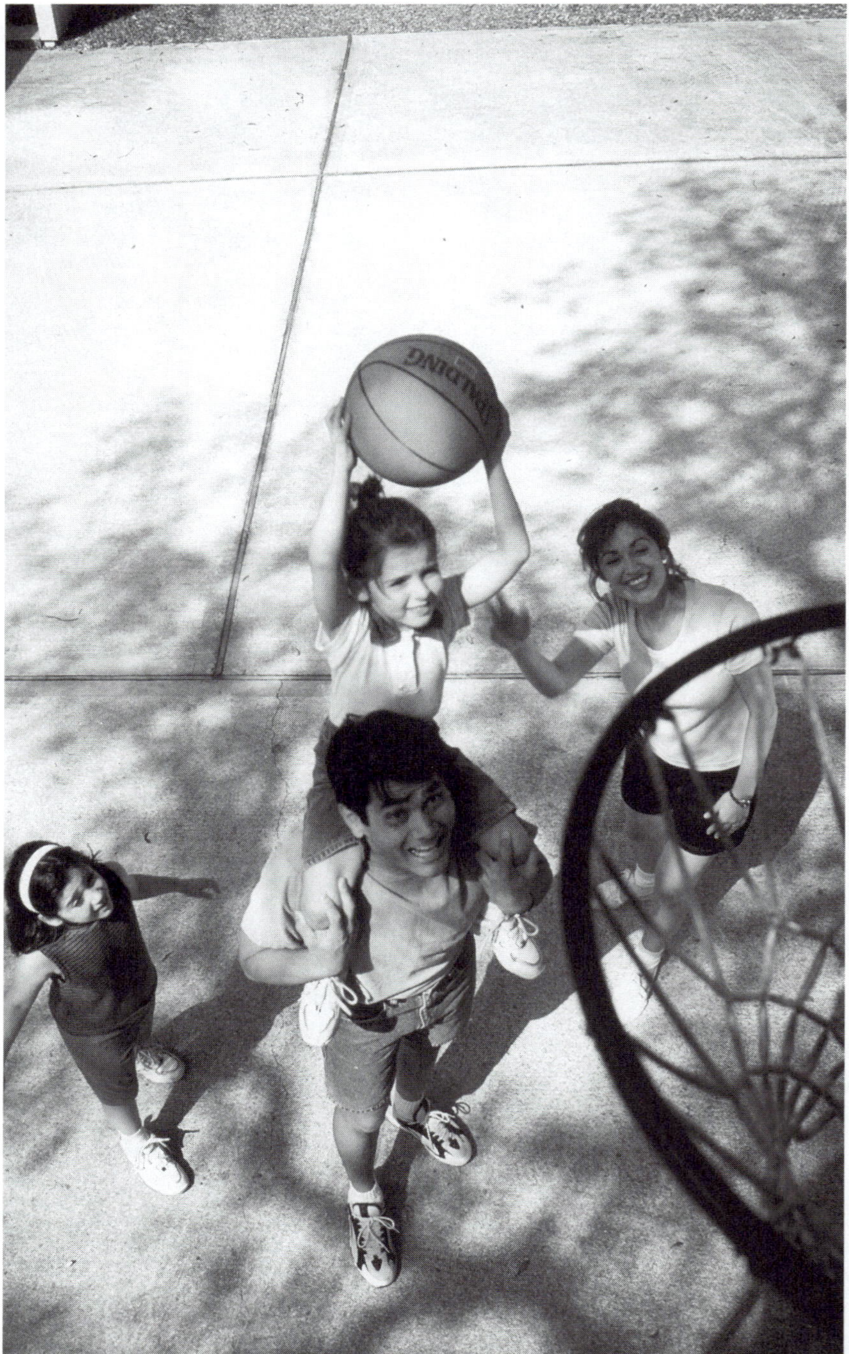
SPALDING

Recentering Social Institutions and the Transformation to a Physically Active Society

*T**he challenge of educating a committed citizenry** is to change the societal and university paradigm from a strategy of competitiveness to one of collaboration, from a perspective of scarcity to one of sufficiency and inclusion, and from a stance that looks for expedient solutions to one that engages and commits to a series of values and a way of life. This paradigm shift lies beyond simple curricular adjustment: It resides in epistemological questions about who we are and how we shall live our lives with others. That challenge, so well observed by de Tocqueville and eloquently elaborated in Bellah's Habits of the Heart, resides essentially in the tension between the individual and the larger global community. . . . When we think of skills necessary to engage as active, responsible citizens, we must think in both individual and institutional terms. (Gabelnick, 1997:30)*

▼   ▼   ▼   ▼   ▼

In his analysis of changing social institutions, sociologist Alan Wolfe (1991) captured the uneasiness many Americans feel about moving into the 21st century. Wolfe remarked that people who had visited the United States after World War II and came back at the dawn of the new century would observe a world that was hardly recognizable. He pointed to the tremendous upheaval that most Americans are experiencing in their personal lives. Family roles have changed so rapidly that people are finding it difficult to know how to relate to each other. Schools are constantly under fire for failing to provide the competencies necessary to compete in the adult world. People cannot keep up with new work demands and the new skills that they require. Changes have also taken place in the population's age composition. Although many Americans are living longer, many well into their 70s and 80s, they are spending their expanded years living with chronic degenerative diseases and a health care system ill prepared to deal with them. At a time of great uncertainty Wolfe concluded that by century's end, the only certainty was the presence of traditional models of social institutions that no longer worked and the absence of new ones that would help guide people's lives.

Although Wolfe did not consider the impact of a decentered society on participation in physical activity, the 21st century has also brought a great deal of apprehension and anxiety about the physically inactive lifestyles of so many Americans. Despite the compelling epidemiological and medical evidence connecting physical activity to good health, most Americans participate in limited amounts of physical activity.

Throughout this analysis, I have attempted to illustrate how the current state of our social institutions has a distinct bearing on how and even whether we participate in physical activity. I have tried to outline some debates and ambiguities presently affecting core social institutions that have contributed to considerable difficulties for many Americans to include physical activity into their daily routines. I also have attempted to advance the proposition that to achieve a healthy and physically active society, individuals and the organizational structures to which they belong need to change. This standpoint assumes that we will not accomplish any perceivable movement toward a physically active society without commitment to a new value orientation, one that recognizes our obligations to one another and to society as a whole.

Framework

In this chapter, I offer a framework to structure a meaningful change toward a society that is fully engaged in physical activity.

The framework is presented in figure 9.1 and consists of three key elements:

1. Developing individual responsibility
2. Changing intrainstitutional norms
3. Fostering interinstitutional collaboration

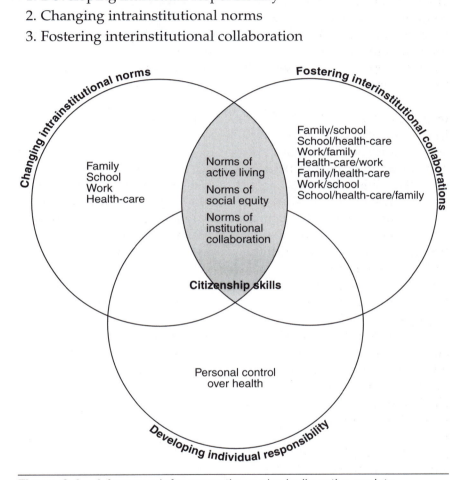

Figure 9.1   A framework for promoting a physically active society.

Transformation to a physically active society requires changes in all three circles. Stepping up efforts in only one of the areas will likely fall short of producing deeply embedded and long-lasting social changes.

The areas in the figure overlap format to convey that the change will require a consideration of goals that are sometimes independent of each other but in other instances are related. For example, cooperative strategies for institutions to work together are ineffective if individual social institutions promote values that continue to dissuade participation in physical activity. Likewise, social institutions' promoting values that are conducive to participation in physical activity will be unsuccessful if individuals fail to take an active role in changing their own health behaviors. Before we use the framework to consider specific changes within each of our four core social institutions, let us first take a closer look at each of the three circles.

Developing Individual Responsibility

Transformation to a physically active society will require significant actions by all individuals. All of the educational campaigns and improved access to opportunities for physical activity in the world will not increase physical activity if people do not actively participate in the change process. Changing to a physically active society will require people to accomplish two objectives: to take *personal control over their own health* and to develop *citizenship skills* that enhance their interaction with the people around them.

Personal Control Over Health

A growing body of health research literature emphasizes the importance of increased personal control over life events (Ziff, Conrad, & Lachman, 1995). A sense of personal control refers to the degree to which individuals perceive events in their lives as consequences of their own actions. Individuals are likely to be successful in changing their sedentary lifestyles under three conditions: if they believe that their current lifestyle poses a health threat to them, if particular behavior changes will reduce this threat, and if they can make specific changes (Bandura, 1997). Perceptions of control result in a number of specific behaviors important to good health, including regular physical activity, actively seeking information about health problems, and getting medical care.

While the importance of being in personal control seems obvious, social psychologists have used a variety of terms and concepts in their attempt to explain what personal control means. One of the most frequently identified psychosocial determinants of personal control is self-efficacy. Self-efficacy refers to beliefs in one's capabilities to organize and execute the course of action required to produce a given outcome. Such beliefs influence the activities that individuals choose to pursue, the degree of effort they are willing to put forth, and how long they will persist in the face of obstacles and failures. Because physical activity is composed of challenging tasks, requiring considerable expenditure of effort and continued persistence, developing high self-efficacy toward physical activity is considered one of the most important determinants of the successful adoption of a physically active lifestyle (McAuley & Blissmer, 1999).

Exercise psychologists have identified two specific forms of self-efficacy (DuCharme & Brawley, 1995). *Barrier self-efficacy* assesses individuals' perceptions of their abilities to exercise regularly in the face of competing distractions. These obstacles or barriers might include injury, illness, work and family commitments, and so on. A second related yet distinctive form of self-efficacy known as *scheduling self-efficacy* gauges individuals' perceptions of their abilities to organize, plan, and schedule physical activity into their daily lives. Both barrier and scheduling self-efficacy are important components of individual personal control over health and are essential to successful maintenance of regular physical activity.

Citizenship Skills

The process of creating a physically active society also requires individual responsibility in the form of citizenship skills, a commitment to collective action that is in the best interest of the society as a whole. People can change their physical activity levels not only through self-development but by acting collectively. People need to become more directly involved in building support for changes in public policy that are conducive to increasing levels of physical activity. To shape their social future, people must believe themselves capable of accomplishing significant social change, what health promotion specialists term *collective efficacy* (Bandura, 1997). Collective efficacy gives groups of individuals with a shared vision the capacity to organize and execute the courses of action required to effect changes.

Citizen action has made a difference to long-term changes in risky health behaviors. The most visible example is the successful citizens' campaign against drinking and driving. In 1990, Mothers Against Drunk Driving (MADD) announced an ambitious plan to reduce the proportion of alcohol-related traffic fatalities by 20 percent by the year 2000 (MADD, 2000). Central to MADD's plan was a comprehensive set of state legislative priorities, including administrative license revocation and lowering the blood alcohol content limit to 0.08. In 1980, an estimated 28,000 traffic deaths in the United States were alcohol related. By 1998, the organization's goal had been achieved: Traffic fatalities were reduced to fewer than 16,000, an all-time low.

More recently, an aggressive strategy that involved citizen participation has also been launched against the marketers of tobacco products ("California's anti-tobacco," 2000). Many of the anti-tobacco efforts have been directed at protecting nonsmokers from the advertising and promotional practices of the tobacco industry, protecting citizens from secondhand smoke (e.g., smoking bans in restaurants and workplaces), and eliminating targeted tobacco sales to minors. Legislative and regulatory action, boycotts, and lawsuits are some tactics citizens have employed to counter the enormous resources of the tobacco industry. Both of these forceful health campaigns against drunk driving and against the use of tobacco contain specific activities designed to generate political action against the powerful forces that promote unhealthy products and behaviors.

Citizens can also play a significant role in changing the nation's level of physical activity. Consider the issue of the declining number of physical education classes in the public schools. Collective citizen advocacy to stem the dwindling number of classes could be directed at local and state legislators. In recent years, state legislatures have become increasingly interested in holding public schools responsible for achieving outcomes related to their missions. A recent survey of more than 1,000 concerned parents revealed that parents' attitudes toward school physical education are starting to change. Parents perhaps are less willing to stand by and witness the reduction of their children's physical education classes (AAHPERD, 2000).

A second strategy might be to join forces with private enterprises that have a stake in the maintenance of physical education programs. According to American Sports Data (2000), sport and exercise equipment manufacturers, concerned about the declining physical activity habits of America's youth, have set aside $1 million for a lobbying drive to pass federal legislation that would encourage school districts to expand physical education. Through collective citizen action, concerned people can gain access to key opinion shapers (e.g., media) and decision makers who have the ability to advance physical activity initiatives further.

Changing Intrainstitutional Norms

The second category of the framework focuses on changing the values promoted through our social institutions and changing social and physical environments so that they promote norms of good health. Social norms change when people start to think and do things differently because they believe that other people are thinking and doing things differently. Supportive environments make physical activity a high priority rather than just an afterthought. Institutional norms of active living can support a physically active society by increasing formal and informal sport and exercise opportunities. Institutional norms of social equity can indirectly promote physical activity by altering social, political, and economic factors that impede access to healthy and active environments for everyone (table 9.1).

Norms of Active Living

Important to the achievement of a physically active society is the development of a social norm for physical activity. Cultural norms need to send positive messages concerning the importance of being physically active and to make the "healthier (and more active) choice the easier choice" (Allen & Allen, 1986). In the past few years, physical

Table 9.1   Suggested Institutional Changes Conducive to a Physically Active Society

Institution	Norms of active living	Norms of social equity	Norms of institutional collaboration
Family	• Increase emphasis on the family as the center for physical activity. • Develop independent leisure-time physical activities for all family members. • Increase the home base for physical activity. • Reclaim the physical spaces around the home for physical activity.	• Expand family and medical leave benefits. • Meet the needs of "nontraditional" family forms. • Provide access to affordable child and parent care.	• Increase family communication concerning healthy lifestyles. • Support physical activity for family members entering their senior years. • Increase active involvement between parents and adolescents.

(continued)

Table 9.1 *(continued)*

Institution	Norms of active living	Norms of social equity	Norms of institutional collaboration
Education	• Develop physical education curricula that promote physical activity for a lifetime. • Promote higher-order fitness objectives. • Train teachers in the latest physical activity promotion strategies. • Promote efforts to include physical activity throughout the school day.	• Promote increased levels of educational attainment. • Promote social advocacy among physical education teachers and coaches. • Expand after-school programs. • Provide increased opportunities for physical activity among racial and other under-served groups.	• Better integrate health and physical education curricula. • Collaborate with other components of the school curricula.
Work	• Increase participation in work-sponsored fitness programs. • Develop physical activity programming with women and minorities in mind. • Promote more physical activity throughout the workday.	• Increase access to quality health care for all workers. • Develop a commitment to diversity throughout the corporate culture. • Provide health insurance plans that include preventive services. • Create work conditions that are safe and rewarding. • Address the economic inequities of under- and unemployment.	• Develop collaborative efforts between employers and employees to promote physical activity.

Institution	Norms of active living	Norms of social equity	Norms of institutional collaboration
Health care	• Train all health professions in skills promoting physical activity. • Develop rigorous standards for exercise specialists.	• Step up efforts to recruit members of minority groups to the health professions. • Promote social advocacy among health professionals. • Develop a commitment to diversity throughout the health care profession.	• Better integrate the services of exercise specialists in team health care. • Develop a health care team approach to promoting physical activity. • Provide a more diverse set of skills in the training of health professionals.

activity specialists have endorsed the concept of *active living,* the integration of physical activity into everyday life (Burton, 1994). An outgrowth of the idea of active living is known as the "sports for all" movement (Curtis & Russell, 1997). The movement is an effort to counter the elitist notions associated with participation in physical activity. Advocates are particularly concerned with extending physical activity experiences to all people, particularly groups that were formerly excluded, such as the disabled, the elderly, and the poor.

Norms of Social Equity

Institutional norms of social equity can promote physical activity by altering the social, political, and economic arrangements that impede physical activity for certain groups of people. Social policies influence standards of living and basic social conditions (income and educational levels, dwelling places, and job opportunities that affect the availability of behavioral options). Institutional norms that promote equitable access to important economic resources, such as employment and education, are critical precursors to sustained participation in physical activity. Proper economic, living, and working conditions will not guarantee physically active lifestyles. However, a sound educational system, available medical services, and a good work situation unquestionably contribute more to healthier living than do poverty, poor education, and unavailable health services. Unequal access to life opportunities and resources contribute to the failure of many people to adopt healthy lifestyles.

Norms of Institutional Collaboration

Constructive change in the physical activity habits of Americans requires a system of social institutions that encourages cooperation. The ability to work together for change requires new thinking within each of our key social institutions. Norms that encourage working alone and individual assessment of problems must give way to strategies that bring groups of people together to solve their problems. Family members, teachers and other school personnel, management and workers, and health care professionals need to overcome their rigid self-protecting tendencies for appreciable social change to occur.

Norms of Interinstitutional Cooperation

Changes within our social institutions create dilemmas for people because change occurs at different rates. For example, an increasing percentage of families depend on the earnings of wives and mothers (a rapidly changing pattern of work), but many women still are in charge of home activities (a slowly changing pattern in family roles). As another example, in most communities, adolescents finish their school day by two or three o'clock in the afternoon (a slow pattern of change in education), yet parents typically work until early evening, leaving the adolescents largely unsupervised during most of the afternoon hours (a rapid pattern of family change). A closer

Table 9.2 Suggested Interinstitutional Changes for a Physically Active Society

Norms of interinstitutional collaboration

Establish stronger collaborations between parents and school personnel.

Develop policies to ensure universal health insurance.

Develop work policies that help balance family and work responsibilities.

Develop better integration between the workplace and the health care system.

Develop community-based health and physical activity coalitions.

Promote health and physical activity coalitions in underserved communities.

collaboration between communities and schools could help solve this dilemma. At the most basic level, school buildings could be used as activity centers after school hours. At a more cooperative level, community members could work with parents and businesses to find some common ground in school hours and work hours. At the interinstitutional level, local and federal policies could help parents balance family and work responsibilities with rules mandating greater flexibility in their work schedules. Other ideas are presented in table 9.2.

Transforming the Institution of Family

The ability of the family to play a more positive role in developing physically active lifestyles depends on the emergence of a new family value, one that David Elkind (1994) has labeled the *vital family*. A family is vital to the extent that it energizes and nurtures the abilities and talents of all its members. What distinguishes the vital family is its recognition that family members undergo continuous change and to survive must rely on each other for support. This includes decisions about healthy behaviors such as physical activity. Balancing the needs of children and adolescents with the physical activity needs of adults is key to making the family more amenable to physically active lifestyles.

• **Locate the family as the center for physical activity.** Adopting patterns of regular physical activity must become a significant family affair. It should be a goal for all families to plan physical activity as a family and for parents in particular to demonstrate to children that physical activity can be an enjoyable way to spend time together. We must impress upon families the importance of doing physical activities together, through family vacations or just spending time together walking or enjoying the outdoors together. By sharing physical activity, parents serve as positive, active role models for their children and for each other.

• **Develop independent leisure physical activities for all family members.** Although participating in shared family activities is important, equally important are opportunities for family members to participate in physical activity outside the family structure. Sometimes this might mean encouraging children to participate child-initiated and child-run activities, or it might include parents' finding time away from their children to participate in physical activity with other adults. This is particularly important for women, who

© Dusty Willison/International Stock

A goal for all families is to plan physical activities in which all members of the family can participate.

face greater challenges to finding leisure-time opportunities in their lives.

- **Increase physical activities available in the home.** Although many communities offer opportunities to participate in physical activity, many Americans prefer to spend their leisure time at or around their homes. The "home gym" should become a fixture in the American home. Among the reasons for the appeal of home-based physical activity is its capacity to allow flexibility in exercise time. Home-based programs allow people to squeeze exercise in, even in the face of unexpected conflicts. The daily schedule of the typical American family means that its available time for exercise varies from week to week and hour to hour. The changing demands on free time brought on by sick children or social and job-related expectations often contribute to low attendance in community-based exercise programs. Home-based physical activity programming is increasingly acknowledged as an effective substitute for hospital-based programming for people dealing with chronic illnesses such as cardiovascular disease (King, Haskell, Taylor, Kraemer, & DeBusk, 1991). Supervised home-based exercise programs are as effective and sometimes more effective than programs carried out in more structured settings such as fitness clubs and hospitals (DeBusk et al., 1994). Health care personnel and perhaps local fitness providers can recommend structured home-based rehabilitation programs as an appropriate alternative to a formal exercise facility.

• **Reclaim the physical spaces around the home for physical activity.** Children's activity levels have been associated with the number of play spaces near their homes and the time children spend in these play spaces (Sallis, 1997). Where neighborhoods are perceived as dangerous, children are less likely to engage in physical activities such as playing softball or basketball at the neighborhood park or simply playing with others in front of the house. Parents can work within neighborhood groups to promote active play in safe environments. Adults could volunteer to supervise the area to address safety concerns, while children can remain in charge of their physical activity. Group walking clubs can help instill a feeling of safety in numbers and help counteract the fears that otherwise discourage people from utilizing the neighborhood that surrounds their homes. Encouraging family members to view the spaces around their homes more creatively is also important. Taking care of lawns and gardens, completing household chores (e.g., painting, garage clean-up), and walking the dog should be given higher status as means for meeting physical activity needs.

• **Increase family communication about healthy lifestyles.** Healthy lifestyles are more likely to be adopted if family members support one another's good health habits. Teaching children good health habits must start early in their lives and be reinforced at home. When teachers send educational materials home with students, parents can use these opportunities to discuss strategies to promote physical activity and healthy eating. Adult family members need assistance in adopting good habits such as regular physical activity as well. Communication about good habits among family members is included as an objective in the *Healthy People 2010* goals (USDHHS, 2000a). The objective is to increase to at least 75 percent the proportion of people aged 10 years and older who have discussed issues related to good health with family members on at least one occasion during the preceding month. The goal should also apply to extended family members such as grandparents, particularly those who are living alone.

• **Support participation in physical activity for family members entering their senior years.** Many people entering their senior years grew up at a time when physical activity was not promoted. Not having developed habits of physical activity, many seniors do not view this phase of their lives as the time to start developing them. Regular physical activity can help people with chronic disabling conditions improve their stamina, muscle strength, psychological well-being, and quality of life by increasing their ability to perform the activities of daily life. We must develop even more aggressive strategies to help seniors appreciate the importance of including physical activity into their daily routines. Getting doctors and other health care professionals to send this message is certainly part of the solution, but family members (e.g., spouses and adult children) also need to take an active role in this regard. The current generation that grew up in a climate of knowledge about physical activity is likely to bring better habits of physical activity to the senior years, but for now, family members are an essential source of support.

• **Recognize the variety in family structures.** Today's families take on many different forms, from the traditional nuclear family to single-parent families, families with same-sex parents, blended families, extended families, and so on. The changes in the family should be viewed as the logical aftermath of our changing world. New family forms require new values of acceptance of these new social arrangements. The first step is to abandon the conservative attack on new family structures. The second step is to recognize the full range of health needs present in these new family forms. New health promotion strategies should eliminate barriers to integrating work and family for single and other custodial parents, promote equity in access to insurance and health care for same-sex couples, and recognize the rights of all children regardless of the marital status of their parents.

• **Expand family and medical leave benefits.** Perhaps the biggest norm change lies in the understanding that families cannot raise their children alone. Although we cannot mandate families to spend more time together, policy-level changes can furnish families with more time. More stringent policies and laws are required at a broader societal level to ensure parents much-needed time and flexibility in their daily schedules. For example, the United States has long fallen short in the provision of family-oriented support; it is one of the only industrialized countries without paid maternity leave or health benefits guaranteed by law. The Family and Medical Leave Act (FMLA), for example, provides only unpaid leave and only to individuals working in establishments employing at least 50 workers, disproportionately excluding low-wage workers. According to a report by the U.S. Department of Labor's Commission on Family and Medical Leave (1996), 64 percent of workers who said that they needed leave reported that they were unable to take it because they could not forgo income by taking unpaid leave.

• **Provide access to affordable child and parent care.** Affordable child care arrangements for working parents is another area in need of improvement. The supply and quality of affordable child care in the United States falls far short of the demand, particularly for infant and toddler care and after-school care. Recent federal, state, and local budget cuts have further reduced the supply of child care for the children of the working poor, who are now more likely to be left home alone or with a sibling. Many people, particularly women, now also have to look after elderly dependents. Only 9 percent of elderly dependents in need of assistance are able to use paid providers. The arrival of the baby-boom generation into the ranks of the elderly will compound the strain. A growing number of companies are offering assistance such as flexible work schedules and financial support for child care. But fewer than one third offer any backing for elder care (Taylor, 2000).

Transforming the Institution of School

Several recent reports, such as *Physical Activity and Health: A Report of the Surgeon General* (USDHHS, 1996) and *Guidelines for School and Community Programs to Promote Lifelong Physical Activity Among Young People* (USDHHS, 1997), call on schools to play a central role in addressing our nation's problems of adulthood physical inactivity. If the school health goals for the nation are to be achieved, action must be taken to make sure that health-fitness goals and developing physical activity skills for a lifetime are embraced in school curricula.

• **Advocate physical education curricula that promote physical activity for lifelong learning.** Physical education programs for young children should focus on attainment of proficiency in fundamental skills and movement concepts. In the upper elementary grades and middle school years, students should be exposed to a variety of activities in sports, dance, aquatics, and outdoor pursuits.

As students progress through the high school years, they should have the opportunity to develop competence in areas that are personally meaningful. These experiences allow students to identify activities that are enjoyable and satisfying to them.

• **Promote higher-order fitness objectives.** The need to teach students how to maintain physical activity throughout their lifetimes is apparent when we examine the high prevalence of diseases of sedentary living among the adult population and the escalating costs of treating them. Program goals should focus on helping young people learn how to make responsible decisions about their participation in physical activity. The ability to make responsible choices requires the individual to reason through life situations and to solve problems. In addition to teaching how to execute certain physical activity skills, teaching students to assess the pros and cons of various practices and teaching them the skills to overcome any barriers are also important. Helping students to develop, evaluate, and revise personal exercise programs should be the major focus of the physical education curriculum. Corbin (1987) recommends a hierarchy of fitness objectives, among them, the ability to evaluate a personal fitness program and to solve personal fitness problems. Teaching students problem-solving skills enables them to make meaningful decisions throughout life, when teachers and parents are no longer present to make the decisions for them.

• **Train teachers in the latest physical activity promotion strategies.** The nation's physical inactivity problem can improve only if qualified health promotion professionals are prepared to lead the movement in grades K-12. Colleges and universities must do a better job in preparing instructors to teach the latest health promotion strategies. Several school programs have shown that retraining teachers already on the job is also possible. One such program aimed at training both classroom teachers and physical education specialists to implement a health-based physical education curriculum resulted in increased amounts of physical activity during physical education classes (McKenzie, Faucette, Sallis, Roby, & Kolody, 1997). Efforts at in-service and continuing education need to be made available to teachers on the job.

• **Include more physical activity throughout the school day.** Increasing the amount of physical activity during all physical education classes is essential if schools are to play a substantial role in promoting physical activities among our youth. Increasing physical

Photograph by Tom Roberts

Teachers can be retrained to implement more physical activity during physical education classes.

activity outside physical education class would also help young people achieve recommended levels of physical activity. For children in preschool or elementary schools, recess can be better used to encourage more unstructured physical activity. For older youths, schools can incorporate more physical activity opportunities during free time and elective periods. Drop-in fitness facilities and semistructured intramural activities before, during, and after school would provide active alternatives to just hanging out with friends.

• **Establish stronger collaborations between parents and school personnel.** More interaction between parents and school personnel is critical to making more children physically active. Parents, teachers, and administrators need to break down traditional role barriers and to share authority in order to achieve common goals. The interactions between the family and school must be viewed as a two-way street by which parents can help the school and schools can recognize the needs of the family. There are several ways that schools can involve families in physical education. Family members can support developmentally appropriate physical education opportunities by learning about the school's physical education program and working with teachers to augment physical activities at home. Parents can get more involved in such school activities as special events and evening programs designed to encourage and reward children for participation in physical activity. Schools can also offer physical activity opportunities for parents and other family members.

• **Better integrate the health and physical education curricula.** Health-compromising lifestyles often include unhealthy habits in more than one domain. Although it is not always the case, sedentary lifestyles are often accompanied by poor nutritional habits, smoking, and alcohol abuse. Physical education teachers need to work more closely with health educators to design sound curricula that address a comprehensive healthy lifestyle.

• **Develop collaborations with other school departments.** School personnel from a variety of areas must work together to help students adopt healthy behaviors. Evidence for successful collaboration between different groups within the school has been demonstrated in several innovative school programs. One such program developed collaboration among school food service programs, physical education teachers, and classroom teachers (McKenzie, Nader, et al., 1996). Other possible partnerships within the school include the integration of physical education with traditional academic areas. Math lessons that involve calculating fitness scores or reading comprehension lessons that use sport-related stories are just two examples of the kind of curricular integration that can meet student learning objectives and also thwart efforts to cut back the physical education program.

• **Expand after-school programs.** Forty percent of adolescents' waking hours are discretionary and uncommitted (Carnegie Council on Adolescent Development, 1992). These hours represent an opportunity to help children grow and acquire important social, emotional, cognitive, and physical skills and to help them develop lifelong interests. *A Matter of Time* by the Carnegie Council on Adolescent Development (1992) put the spotlight on the role schools can play in developing a constructive use of nonschool time. Expanded after-school programs provide more opportunities for adolescents to learn skills that are either not usually available in the crowded school curriculum or introduced only superficially. Improvement in sport skills is one common example, but more opportunities for teens just to be physically active are equally important. These opportunities are particularly important in impoverished communities because the school often represents the single source of extracurricular opportunities.

• **Promote social advocacy by physical education teachers and coaches.** School-based physical educators can do much to enhance community programs and ensure that neighborhood activities complement those sponsored by the school. For example, coaches can become involved with the governing bodies of community youth sport and recreation programs, help recruit qualified coaches, and help secure adequate funding. Physical education teachers can help school and community youth sport and recreation programs become an extension of the school's physical education program and help ensure that they have sufficient resources and facilities to accommodate the needs and interests of all children. Physical education teachers and coaches can also play an active role in demanding higher standards for entrance into their professions.

• **Promote community health and physical activity coalitions.** To increase opportunities for participation in physical activity, schools need to take a greater role in working with other community groups. Health coalitions with the objective of increasing opportunities for participation in physical activity should include groups from nine different sectors: government (e.g., state or county department of health), health (e.g., private-practice physicians), education (e.g., local university), transportation and environment (e.g., national park service), business (e.g., local chamber of commerce), media (e.g., television stations), recreation (e.g., senior centers), religion (e.g., churches and synagogues), and volunteer groups (e.g., Girl Scouts and Boy Scouts; USDHHS, 1999a).

• **Promote health and physical activity coalitions in underserved communities.** Physical activity programs that are connected with schools often miss a large segment of the school-age population: the significant number of young people who drop out of school. More than 500,000 of the 9.5 million 15- through 24-year-olds who were enrolled the year before left school without completing a high school degree (McMillen, Kaufman, & Klein, 1997). Closer collaboration between communities, employers, and schools could help solve this dilemma. Cooperative partnerships among businesses, health and social services, schools, and recreation and leisure service agencies can expand physical activity facilities and opportunities, which are desperately needed in many of our communities.

Transforming the Institution of Work

Employers have a large portion of the responsibility to control medical costs. In an era of employer responsibility for health care, employers have directed effort at individual health promotion and exercise programs. Work-sponsored fitness programs are important; however, successful efforts to promote physically active lifestyles among employees most go beyond individual-change strategies and include changes to work conditions and other aspects of employees' lives.

• **Increase participation in work-sponsored fitness programs.** Work-sponsored fitness programs must extend beyond employees who are already committed to a physically active lifestyle. Programs need to be tailored to people who are less than optimally active. Offering employees a variety of simple, low-cost physical activities may be an effective and cost-efficient way to increase physical activity among all employees. For example, walking programs require almost no expense and can be performed in a variety of places in and around the work site.

• **Develop physical activity programming with women and minority groups in mind.** The increasing numbers of women and minorities in the workforce demand new thinking about work-sponsored fitness programs, particularly because women and minorities are conspicuously absent from most of these programs. One approach to increasing the participation of workers from all segments of the organization is to more aggressively market the program to all employees. Women and certain ethnic and racial groups are often found in positions that have limited access to work-sponsored health promotion services. Work-sponsored fitness programs that are responsive to the needs of ethnic and racial minority groups include exercise programs that can be performed at the workstation or at home. They should include culturally relevant symbols and materials that demonstrate a true sense of cultural understanding. A good first step is involving women and minority workers in the program planning. They can help identify specific needs and provide advice on the best way to reach others in situations like theirs.

• **Develop more opportunities for physical activity throughout the course of the workday.** Despite the widespread recognition of a positive association between regular physical activity and health,

American adults remain predominantly inactive, both on the job and off. Many individuals spend most of their working days sitting behind a desk or in front of a computer screen. Ways to put more physical activity into the sedentary work patterns found in many offices are needed. Because most jobs require minimal amounts of physical activity, the choices made during the workday represent important opportunities for participation in physical activity. Organizational policies and strategies should be developed to encourage more physical activity in the daily routines at work. Besides frequent stretching and walking breaks, incentives can be put into place to encourage walking throughout the workday (e.g., encouraging walking to a co-worker's desk instead of sending an e-mail). Signs that encourage physical activity strategically placed by the escalators or elevators have been shown to increase the use of stairs (Russell, Dzewaltowski, & Ryan, 1999). These "point-of-choice prompts" are a relatively inexpensive way to encourage physical activity.

• **Develop partnerships between workers and management.** Health promotion practices at the work site must guard against perceptions of inappropriate coercion to be involved in health promotion efforts. Employee participation should always be voluntary, and alternative forms of health services that match their unique work conditions and their level of trust should be made available to all employees. Given the likelihood that conflicts of interest may emerge, it is crucial that work-sponsored fitness programs develop and adhere to ethical standards and guidelines for ensuring the confidentiality of health information. Safeguards may include the use of third parties to gather, code, and analyze employee health data. The use of independent contractors rather than company employees to run the fitness program may decrease concerns that confidentiality will be breached (Stokols, Pelletier, & Fielding, 1995).

• **Develop a commitment to diversity throughout the corporate culture.** Work environments must guarantee pleasant and fair working conditions for all employees. Organizations need to develop policies that minimize discrimination and provide aggressive mechanisms to enforce the policies. In tolerant work environments, work-sponsored health promotion programs are more effective because they are a part of "a natural outgrowth of a fundamental commitment to diversity throughout the entire organization" (Aguirre-Molina & Molina, 1990).

• **Develop work policies that help balance family and work responsibilities.** Conflicts between an employee's work schedule and the schedule of community facilities frequently result in difficulties in accomplishing personal and family tasks. Schedule compatibility has two components: (1) how the worker's schedule matches the schedules of other family members and (2) how the worker's schedule matches the availability of community services. Workers, particularly those who are subject to strict time policies, have trouble getting to the doctor, dentist, dry cleaner, and athletic contest. More flextime policies will certainly help, but more innovative scheduling of school activities, such as Saturday teacher conferences and evening school performances and athletic competitions, are also in order. School athletic programs could involve parents and businesses in scheduling sport events and practices.

• **Better integrate the workplace and the health care system.** Work-site fitness programs can also play a greater role for the increasing number of workers who are returning to work after an extended bout with chronic diseases. Work-site health professionals in collaboration with medical personnel can develop a plan for monitoring the employees' physical status for work, improving their compliance with prescribed medical regimens, and encouraging the development and maintenance of improved health habits.

• **Increase access to quality health care for all workers.** Most work-sponsored health insurance plans address the medical needs of permanent employees and typically ignore workers in other arrangements, such as contract, seasonal, and temporary workers. Spouses and dependents of workers and retirees, who are likely to have less access to corporate health programs than employees, should also be included. An option might be to provide tax exemptions for health insurance companies that provide insurance to adults and their families who are unemployed, self-employed, or contract workers or who work for small companies that do not provide coverage.

• **Promote health insurance plans that include preventive services.** Most work-sponsored health insurance plans do not pay adequate attention to health promotion services for their employees. Particularly needed are health insurance programs that better integrate health promotion and disease-prevention strategies with the medical services covered by health maintenance programs and preferred-provider organizations. Businesses need to work with the insurance industry to take advantage of every possible way to cover more preventive services. One approach is to earmark up front a percentage of the premiums for preventive services. Private insurers might begin offering more affordable policies for children and allowing parents to carry children's coverage into adulthood. Federal policy changes are important also; Medicaid eligibility could be expanded and coverage extended beyond the present levels, and Medicare coverage could include better support for preventive health.

• **Create work conditions that are safe and rewarding.** In an era of employer-based responsibility for health, employers' efforts are increasingly directed at lifestyle behavior programs rather than at developing safe and rewarding working conditions. Jobs must be developed with employees' interests in mind. This includes giving employees more control and decision-making responsibilities over their jobs. Good jobs should offer opportunities for learning, personal growth, and career development. Both workers and management must take responsibility for improving work conditions. Throughout business and industry, too few managers are rewarded for supporting positive work conditions for their employees. Safer and healthier work environments must be built into the reward system for both managers and employees.

• **Address the economic inequities caused by under- and unemployment.** American society faces continuing challenges to provide adequate incomes, opportunities, and economic security for all its members. The inequality in the distribution of earned income since the 1970s has dramatically increased. The wealthiest 1 percent of the population now owns almost 39 percent of the total household wealth of the nation (Wallace, Green, & Jaros, 1999). Part of the solution for better health must be reducing income inequalities through better income distribution throughout society. Although a substantial across-the-board minimum-wage increase is generally met with great resistance, businesses and community officials could work together to identify an appropriate "living wage" for their area. Recent federal legislation that dramatically altered the welfare system has also contributed to the growing number of low-paid workers. According to the Personal Responsibility Work Opportunity Reconciliation Act signed into law in 1996, adults receiving government aid are required to begin work within two years of receiving aid (O'Campo & Rojas-Smith, 1998). Individuals coming off the welfare rolls are likely to be employed in low-skill and low-paying jobs. Programs and assistance must be available to allow them to become economically self-sufficient. To achieve this goal, providing all those employed with a living wage, postsecondary education, and job training must become priorities. But efforts cannot stop here. Coalitions need to be formed to help identify strategies to increase the number of good jobs available in the community.

Transforming the Institution of Health Care

For the large number of people experiencing health problems related to physical inactivity, a change in the organization and delivery of health care is necessary. A shift from a physician-dominated medical model for the treatment of disease to a community-based health care system emphasizing health promotion and disease prevention is key.

• **Train all health professionals in skills of promoting physical activity.** Significant change must also occur in the way we train our health professionals. Most health care providers lack essential knowledge and skills related to physical activity, including specific information about the health benefits of becoming physically active. More specifically, primary-care physicians need to be taught the knowledge and skills for delivering preventive messages. Allied health professionals should also become more knowledgeable about nutrition and physical activity counseling. This should include the development of a standard physical activity curriculum in the training of physicians, nurses, social workers, and other health professionals. Professional certification and licensing organizations should also require health care providers to demonstrate physical activity knowledge and counseling skills.

• **Develop rigorous standards for exercise specialists.** The physical fitness profession is largely unregulated, and most states allow people who have not completed a certified program to advertise their services as fitness counselors and exercise specialists. Competence is as necessary for exercise professionals as it is for doctors and other health professionals. All professionals in physical activity promotion, including group exercise leaders and personal fitness trainers, should be required to demonstrate high levels of competence before they can promote their services. This can be accomplished only through a serious regulation and credentialing process. Certification by a credible exercise organization should be the minimum, but ultimately licensing for all exercise professionals must be put into place.

• **Step up efforts to recruit members of minority groups to the health professions.** Members of minority groups are conspicuously absent in many of the health professions. Physicians, nurses, social workers, and exercise specialists can help remedy this situation by consciously looking for highly motivated minority students and encouraging them to enter the health field.

• **Develop stronger collaborations among health professionals.** Cooperative efforts by the physician's office and other health professionals in the community may be successful in developing the longitudinal programming necessary to encourage positive health behaviors, such as participation in physical activity. When health professionals collaborate, both time and expertise are used in the most efficient way; mistakes and duplication of services are minimized, and the expertise and experience of many trained health practitioners are brought together in an environment that values consultation and teamwork (O'Neil, 1995). In an example of one effort to reduce the costs of cardiac rehabilitation and increase the convenience of physical activity, multiple health care providers working as a team provided a successful structured, home-based exercise program (DeBusk et al., 1994). A team approach to the delivery of exercise rehabilitation must take full advantage of well-qualified exercise specialists.

• **Develop stronger medical collaborations with the community.** Because of the time constraints of a busy medical practice, patients would benefit from referrals to corporate or community exercise programs. These programs have the advantages of structure, convenience, built-in systems for reinforcement, and opportunities for socialization. Health professionals must embrace individuals, families, and communities as full and equal partners in health care decisions and give them the information they need to consider available alternatives and make informed choices for themselves.

• **Promote social advocacy among health professionals.** Health professionals must be cognizant of public policy affecting the health care system and, ideally, politically active in advancing it. Given their expert knowledge and direct involvement in providing and administering health care, health professionals have a special obligation to act on behalf of and in concert with the public as advocates for healthy public policy. Although the "individual client" will always remain the centerpiece for change, health professionals must learn to do a better job in advocating for structural changes (Walz & Gove, 1991). Advocacy by health professionals could include working in coalitions to increase opportunities for physical activity available in schools and in communities. Health professionals can also work together to change the often restrictive practices found in government programs such as Medicare and Medicaid. Social action could also take the form of providing free or low-cost preventive services, such as physical activity counseling for the poor or uninsured.

Conclusion

Although prospects for returning to a physically active society are greater now than in many decades, we cannot expect rapid changes. Modifying a long-standing resistance to exercise among many Americans and altering protracted social and economic inequities will not take place overnight. Strategies for change, whether programs to promote physical activity among targeted groups or policy initiatives designed to affect larger numbers of people, will be driven by the pace at which groups are mobilized into action.

A transformation to physical activity at the social level, like individual change, will also be filled with false starts and setbacks. Even when new policies and programs are firmly in place, changes in the overall prevalence of sedentary living are likely to be painfully slow. American society, with its tendency to place overwhelming importance on the present and the short term, must become patient when changes seem not to occur quickly enough.

A physically active society inevitably will face innumerable barriers. These barriers are likely to range from political and legislative opposition to a struggle for limited resources with other health concerns and media indifference to social explanations for our physical inactivity problem. Issues relating to public health and preventive medicine have had difficulty in getting the attention of the public policy makers. Often it takes a national crisis to get the needed attention, but even that does not always work, as we witnessed with the slow response to the AIDS epidemic. Health professionals must continue to emphasize the consequences of physically inactive lifestyles. It will be difficult to overcome the stereotypical notion that physical activity is something to be performed in one's "spare" time.

To be sure, a successful transition to a more physically active society will mean overcoming competition with special-interest groups that are actively promoting their own health interests and forming collaborative partnerships that benefit all parties. Problems of sedentary living often taken a back seat to many other health promotion areas when it comes to federal, state, or local attention. Until the promotion of physical activity develops a louder voice, there will be powerful groups that will do a more effective job in protecting their own interests. The time is now for advocates of active lifestyles, citizens, and policy makers alike to make their voices heard.

Final Thoughts

Most people agree that healthy lifestyles are a fundamental good for individuals and for society. Sedentary lifestyles, after all, impose many costs on people who are not themselves directly engaged in risky health behaviors. The burden of sedentary lifestyles, for example, may place family members at physical risk (e.g., from the emotional stresses associated with caring for an unhealthy spouse) or may cause individual financial hardships (e.g., loss of a job or overwhelming medical bills). Sedentary lifestyles that cost billions of health care dollars and lost wages place an economic drain on society as a whole.

To the extent that the repercussion of sedentary behaviors is "other-regarding," to use an expression introduced by sociologist John Stuart Mill (1939), society must deal with their collective costs or, as termed by economists, their *negative externalities* (Stone, 1982). We create a dilemma when we allow individuals the right to engage in behaviors that are ultimately detrimental to their health and sap the economic resources of society. Society certainly benefits from the improved health of its citizens but at the same time must balance personal freedom and individual choice with the common good. The health of a population is enhanced when individuals have some freedom and some collective responsibility, but not too much of either (Bunker, Stansfeld, & Porter, 1996). The lines between private and individual responsibility and public and collective responsibility are not easily drawn.

Throughout the 20th century (as discussed in chapter 3), government has played an increasingly important role in promoting the health of the nation. Promoting physical activity as part of a national, state, or local agenda can go a long way to ensure its distribution among wide segments of American society. Local governments, for example, can play a key role in building an infrastructure that supports physical activity, such as walking and biking for commuting, shopping, and other routine activities. Federal governments can also play a role by altering the economics of physical activity through reducing subsidies for industries that rely on sedentary behavior and increasing subsidies for industries that promote physical activity.

However, in the debates concerning changing health behaviors, policy makers repeatedly struggle over how far government can intrude into the choices of individuals. As played out in bipartisan American politics, solutions to issues concerning healthy lifestyles follow two very different paths. For conservatives, the answer has been to privatize problems and to give the individual as much margin as possible to make health choices. On the other side are social liberals who frame solutions to health issues in measures of reduced harmful social environments. People do not want to be told what to eat, what to drink, and how much to exercise. One of the most significant challenges to a physically active society is a compelling desire by many individuals to preserve their own autonomy and individuality and, in the words of Howard Leichter (1991), to "be free to be foolish." Seen from this perspective, promoting physical activity as part of a national agenda involved the question of how far the government of a democratic society can go in regulating personal behaviors.

A physically active society depends not only on balancing individual and collective needs but also on the ability of those involved in research to reappraise the philosophies and methodologies that guide their research. With few exceptions, the research on physical activity—including many of the studies discussed in this book—is based on *methodological individualism,* research procedures focused on the measurement of individual characteristics (Diez-Roux, 1998). Criticism of this approach has been levied, particularly against those who study sport and physical activity. As early as 1985, Alan Ingham called for the field of health and physical education to go beyond frameworks that analyze only personal characteristics. In a similar vein, Demers (1988) pointed out that the biophysical approaches found in most departments of physical education and kinesiology also emphasize the individual. Methods of natural science are largely ineffective for studying the social dynamics of physical activity because they fail to study people "in the round" (Maguire, 1991).

We will be able to understand the dynamics underlying sedentary behaviors only if we address appropriate research questions about individuals and their social systems. Researchers interested in studying physical activity need to embrace a new paradigm, one that equally involves the causal connections in social structures and those in individuals (Susser & Susser, 1996). The problems of sedentary living challenge health and physical activity researchers to develop theoretical models of physical activity that explain how group and individual variables interact in shaping behaviors. Contextual analysis or "mixed-level models" have emerged in several fields to help examine the effects of collective or group characteristics on individual outcomes and the effects of these outcomes on group variables (Snijders & Bosker, 1999).

We can achieve a physically active society only if we can overcome the challenges of truly making healthy lifestyles available to all members of society. One of these challenges is to more adequately consider diversity. More information is needed not only about patterns of physical activity among minority groups but also about the reasons that minority groups are underrepresented among people who participate in physical activity. Many physical activity researchers are content in describing demographic characteristics of individuals and their levels of participation in physical activity. Instead, we need to ask questions about how society shapes individuals' particular health status, and how the health status of minority groups reflects their positions within the larger society.

When Americans in the year 2099 look back to the first decades of the 21st century, what will they find? Will they find a nation that continued to rely on individual initiative to overcome obstacles to participation in regular physical activity? If America continues to depend on individuals in their private capacity as individual consumers, patients, and self-motivated persons to attempt to overcome the challenges to sedentary living, it is unlikely that it will become a physically active society.

But perhaps when our children and grandchildren look back to the early years of the new millennium, they will see something very different. Maybe they will see schoolyards filled with activity throughout the day and community centers holding parent–child exercise classes side by side with classes for senior citizens. They may find a corporate culture with norms that address safer and less stressful working conditions and physical activity programs that are appealing to all workers. Perhaps they will also find a health care system that takes the role of preventive medicine seriously and views physical activity as an integral component of good health. Although in many respects we can be optimistic that the future holds a return to a more physically active society, the question remains whether physical activity will play a major role in the health movement beginning to take shape in the new century.

The new national health objectives, *Healthy People 2010* (USDHHS, 2000a), certainly provide a real cause for optimism. In the latest round of objectives there are two particularly important themes. The first is the goal to eliminate health disparities between different segments of the population, including those relating to sex, race and ethnicity, education, and sexual orientation (Davis, 2000). In addition to recommendations targeting increases in physical activity and physical education, the health initiatives aim to attract more minorities to the health care professions. A critical part of improving health care is to increase the number of health professionals who are members of underserved minority groups, specifically African-American, Hispanic, and American Indian populations. Also, for the first time since the inception of national health goals in 1979, the recommendations includes sexual orientation.

The second theme is that both public- and private-sector organizations must share responsibility for improving the nation's health. The procedures used in the development of the latest rounds of objectives also involved a broad-based constituency. *Healthy People 2010* represents the collective work of 250 state and federal health agencies and 350 national organizations. A series of seven focus groups of members of the Healthy People Consortium, led by professional facilitators, provided input in the creation of the national objectives. Through public meetings and a Web site, people from across the country were encouraged to provide comments. The document was released at a conference held in Washington, DC, most appropriately titled "Partnerships for Health in the New Millennium."

Donna Shalala, former secretary of the Department of Health and Human Services, captured the possibility of reaching a healthier and more physically active society in the introduction of the *Healthy People 2010* objectives:

Achieving the vision [a healthy society] . . . requires individuals to make healthy lifestyle choices for themselves and their families, clinicians to put prevention into their practices. It requires communities and health-promoting policies in schools, worksites. . . . Above all, it demands that all of us work together. (USDHHS, 2000a)

Let's hope that we do.

References

A.C. Nielsen Company. (1992-93). *Nielsen report on television.* New York: Nielsen Media Research.

Abramson, S., Stein, J., Schaufele, M., Frates, E., & Rogan, S. (2000). Personal exercise habits and counseling practices of primary care physicians: A national survey. *Clinical Journal of Sports Medicine, 10,* 40-48.

Aguirre-Molina, M., & Molina, C. (1990). Ethnic/racial populations and workplace health promotion. *Occupational Medicine, 5,* 789-807.

Airhihenbuwa, C., Kumanyika, S., Agurs, T., & Lowe, A. (1995). Perceptions and beliefs about exercise, rest, and health among African-Americans. *American Journal of Public Health, 9,* 426-429.

Ajzen, I. (1985). From intentions to actions: A theory of planned behavior. In J. Kuhl & J. Beckman (Eds.) *Action control: From cognition to behavior* (pp. 11-39). New York: Springer-Verlag.

Alexy, B. (1990). Workplace health promotion and the blue collar worker. *American Association of Occupational Health Nurses Journal, 38,* 12-16.

Allen, F. (1915). Note concerning exercise in the treatment of severe diabetes. *Boston Medical and Surgical Journal, 123*(20), 743-744.

Allen, J., & Allen, R. (1986). Achieving health promotion objectives through cultural change systems. *American Journal of Health Promotion, 1,* 42-49.

Allen, R., & Allen, J. (1987). A sense of community, a shared vision and a positive culture: Core enabling factors in successful culture based health promotion. *American Journal of Health Promotion, 3,* 40-47.

Alonzo, A. (1986). The impact of the family and lay others on care-seeking during life-threatening episodes of suspected coronary artery disease. *Social Science and Medicine, 22,* 1297-1311.

Alonzo, A. (1993). Health behavior: Issues, contradictions and dilemmas. *Social Science and Medicine, 37,* 1019-1034.

American Academy of Pediatrics Committee on Nutrition. (1998). Cholesterol in childhood. *Pediatrics, 101,* 141-157.

American Alliance for Health, Physical Education, Recreation and Dance. (2000). Parents recognize the importance of physical education. *Update,* (November/December), 1.

American Association of Cardiovascular and Pulmonary Rehabilitation. (1995). *Guidelines for cardiac rehabilitation programs* (2nd ed.). Champaign, IL: Human Kinetics.

American College of Sports Medicine. (1978). The recommended quantity and quality of exercise for developing and maintaining fitness in healthy adults. *Medicine and Science in Sports and Exercise, 10,* vii-x.

American College of Sports Medicine. (1990). The recommended quantity and quality of exercise for developing and maintaining cardiorespiratory and muscular fitness in healthy adults. *Medicine and Science in Sports and Exercise, 22,* 265-274.

American Council on Exercise. (2001). About ACE. Retrieved from the World Wide Web: http://www.acefitness.org/aboutace/.

American Diabetes Association. (2000). Facts and figures. Retrieved from the World Wide Web: http://www.diabetes.org.

American Dietetic Association. (2000). Nutrition and you: 2000 trends. Retrieved from the World Wide Web: http://www.eatright.org.

American Heart Association. (1972). *Exercise testing and training of apparently healthy individuals: A physician's handbook.* Dallas, TX: American Heart Association.

American Heart Association. (1992). Statement on exercise: Benefits and recommendations for physical activity programs for all Americans: A statement for health professionals by the Committee on Exercise and Cardiac Rehabilitation of the Council on Clinical Cardiology. *Circulation, 86,* 340-344.

American Heart Association. (2000a). Cardiovascular disease statistics. Retrieved from the World Wide Web: http://www.americanheart.org.

American Heart Association. (2000b). *Heart attack and stroke facts, 2000.* Dallas, TX: American Heart Association. Retrieved from the World Wide Web: http://www.american heart.org/Heart and Stroke A-Z guide/cvds.html.

American Sports Data. (2000). The superstudy of sports participation. Retrieved from the World Wide Web: http://www.americansportsdata.com/ss_participation1.htm

Andersen, R., Crespo, C., Bartlett, S., Cheskin, & Pratt, M. (1998). Relationship of physical activity and television watching with body weight and level of fatness among children. *Journal of American Medical Association, 279,* 938-942.

Angel, R., & Lowe-Worobey, J. (1988). Single motherhood and children's health. *Journal of Health and Social Behavior, 29,* 38-52.

Anspaugh, D., Hunter, S., & Mosley, J. (1995). The economic impact of corporate wellness programs. *AAOHN Journal, 43,* 203-210.

Applebaum, R., & Chambliss, W. (1995). *Sociology.* New York: Harper Collins.

Armstrong, D. (1988). Historical origins of health behavior. In R. Anderson, J. Davis, I. Kickbusch, D. McQueen, & J. Turner (Eds.), Health behavior research and health promotion (pp. 8-21). Oxford: Oxford University Press.

Ary, D., Toobert, D., Wilson, W., & Glascow, R. (1986). Patient perspective on factors contributing to nonadherence to diabetes regimen. *Diabetes Care, 9,* 168-172.

Ashton, J. (1991). The Healthy Cities Project: A challenge for health education. *Health Education Quarterly, 18,* 39-48.

Athletic Footwear Association. (1990). *American youth and sports participation.* North Palm Beach, FL: Athletic Footwear Association.

Babkes, M., & Weiss, M. (1999). Parental influence on children's cognitive and affective responses to competitive soccer participation. *Pediatric Exercise Science, 11,* 44-62.

Backett, K. (1992). Taboos and excesses: Lay health moralities in middle class families. *Sociology of Health and Illness, 14,* 255-274.

Badgett, M. (1998). *Income inflation: The myth of affluence among gay, lesbian, and bisexual Americans.* New York: Policy Institute of the National Gay and Lesbian Task Force and The Institute for Gay and Lesbian Strategic Studies.

Balogun, J., Martin, D., & Ciendenin, M. (1989). Calorimetric validation of the Caltrac accelerometer during level walking. *Physical Therapy, 69,* 501-509.

Bandura, A. (1977). Self-efficacy: Toward a unifying theory of behavior change. *Psychological Review, 84,* 191-215.

Bandura, A. (1997). *Self-efficacy: The exercise of control.* New York: Freeman.

Baranowski, T. (1978). Perceptions of adolescents' attempted influence on parental behaviors. *Dissertation Abstracts International, 38,* (10-A), 6342.

Baranowski, T., Simons-Morton, D., Hooks, P., Henske, J., Tiernan, K., Dunn, J., Burkhalter, H., Harper, J., & Palmer, J. (1990). A center based program for exercise change among Black-American families. *Health Education Quarterly, 17,* 179-196.

Barber, B. (1983). *The logic and limits of trust.* New Brunswick, NJ: Rutgers University Press.

Baric, L. (1969). Recognition of the "at-risk" role: A means to influence health behavior. *International Journal of Health Education, 12,* 24-34.

Barnett, R., & Rivers, C. (1998). *He works, she works: How two-income families are happy, healthy, and thriving.* Cambridge, MA: Harvard University Press.

Barrell, G., Chamberlain, A., Evans, J., Holt, T., & Mackean, J. (1989). Ideology and commitment in family life: A case study of runners. *Leisure Studies, 8,* 249-262.

Baun, W. (1995). The impact of worksite health promotion programs on absenteeism. In R. Kaman (Ed.), *Worksite health promotion economics: Consensus and analysis* (pp. 131-146). Champaign, IL: Human Kinetics.

Baun, W., Bernacki, E., & Tsai, S. (1986). A preliminary investigation: Effect of a corporate fitness program on absenteeism and health care cost. *Journal of Occupational Medicine, 28,* 18-22.

Becker, B., & Robison, A. (1994). *Houston area health care needs assessment for lesbian, gay, bisexual, and transgender women.* Houston: Montrose Counseling Center.

Becker, H. (1960). Notes on the concept of commitment. *American Journal of Sociology, 66,* 32-40.

Becker, M. (1974). The health belief model and personal health behavior. *Health Education Monograph, 2,* 191-215.

Becker, M. (1993). A medical sociologist looks at health promotion. *Journal of Health and Social Behavior, 34,* 1-6.

Beisecker, A., & Beisecker, T. (1993). Using metaphors to characterize doctor–patient relationships: Paternalism versus consumerism. *Health Communication, 5,* 41-58.

Bellah, R., Madsen, R., Sullivan, W., William, M., Swidler, A., & Tipton, S. (1985). *Habits of the heart.* Berkeley: CA: University of California Press.

Bellingham, R., & Isham, D. (1990). Enhancing CVD related behavioral changes in the workplace: Corporate comparisons and cultural issues. *American Association of Occupational Health Nurses Journal, 38,* 433-438.

Bennet, J., & Peel, J. (1994). Health and physical education teacher certification practices in the United States. *Journal of Health Education, 25,* 239-243.

Benson, V., & Marano, M. (1992). *Current estimates from the National Health Interview Survey.* Hyattsville, MD: National Center for Health Statistics.

Beren, S., Hayden, H., Wilfley, D., & Grilo, C. (1996). The influence of sexual orientation on body dissatisfaction in adult men and women. *International Journal of Eating Disorders, 20,* 135-141.

Berenson, G., Srinivasan, S., & Nicklas, T. (1998). Atherosclerosis: A nutritional disease of childhood. *American Journal of Cardiology, 82,* 22t-29t.

Berkman, L., & Syme, S. (1979). Social networks, host resistance, and mortality. A nine-year follow-up study of Alameda County residents. *American Journal of Epidemiology, 109,* 186-204.

Berlin, J., & Colditz, G. (1990). A meta-analysis of physical activity in the prevention of coronary heart disease. *American Journal of Epidemiology, 132,* 612-628.

Bernacki, E., & Baun, W. (1984). The relationship of job performance to exercise adherence in a corporate fitness program. *Journal of Occupational Medicine, 26,* 529-531.

Benard, B. (1991). *Fostering resiliency in kids: Factors in the family, school, community.* Portland, OR: Western Center for Drug-Free Schools and Communities.

Berryman, J. (1992). Exercise and the medical tradition from Hippocrates through antebellum America: A review essay. In J. Berryman & R. Park (Eds.), *Sport and exercise science: Essays in the history of sports medicine* (pp. 1-56). Urbana, IL: University of Illinois Press.

Bialeschki, D. (1994). Re-entering leisure: Transition within the role of motherhood. *Journal of Leisure Research, 26,* 57-74.

Bialeschki, M., & Pearce, K. (1997). "I don't want a lifestyle—I want a life": The effect of role negotiations on the leisure of lesbian mothers. *Journal of Leisure Research, 29,* 113-131.

Bianchi, S. (1995). The changing demographic and socioeconomic characteristics of single parent families. *Marriage and Family Review, 20,* 71-97.

Bigos, S., Battie, M., & Spengler, L. (1991). A prospective study of work perceptions and psychosocial factors affecting the report of back injury. *Spine, 14,* 141-147.

Blackburn, C. (1993). Making poverty a practice issue. *Health and Social Care, 1,* 297-304.

Blair, S., Kohl, H., Barlow, C., Paffenbarger, R., Gibbons, L., & Macera, C. (1995). Changes in physical fitness and all-cause mortality: A prospective study of healthy and unhealthy men. *Journal of the American Medical Association, 273,* 1093-1098.

Blau, P., & Duncan, O. (1967). *The American occupational structure.* New York: Wiley.

Bleier, R., & O'Neil, T. (1975). *Fighting back.* New York: Stein and Day.

Booth, M., Bauman, A., Oldenburg, B., Owen, N., & Magnus, P. (1992). Effects of a national mass-media campaign on physical activity participation. *Health Promotion International, 7,* 241-247.

Bouchard, C., & Perusse, L. (1994). Heredity, activity level, fitness, and health. In C. Bouchard, R. Shephard, & T. Stephens (Eds.), *Physical activity, fitness, and health: International proceedings and consensus statement* (pp. 106-118). Champaign, IL: Human Kinetics.

Bourdieu, P. (1990). *The logic of practice* (R. Nice, Trans.). Stanford, CA: Stanford University Press.

Boyle, R., O'Connor, P., Pronk, N., & Tan, A. (1997). Stages of change for physical activity, diet, and smoking among HMO members with chronic conditions. *American Journal of Health Promotion, 12,* 170-175.

Bozett, F. (1989). Gay fathers: A review of the literature. *Journal of Homosexuality, 18,* 137-162.

Braddock, C., Edwards, K., & Hasenberg, N. (1999). Informed decision making in outpatient practice. *Journal of the American Medical Association, 282,* 2313-2320.

Bramwell, L. (1986). Wives' experiences in the support role after husbands' first myocardial infarction. *Heart and Lung, 15,* 578-584.

Braschi v. Stahl Associates. (1989). 74 NY 2nd 201, 543 N.E. 49, 544 N.Y.S. 2d 784.

Braverman, H. (1974). *Labor and monopoly capital.* New York: Monthly Review Press.

Brawley, L., Martin, K., & Gyurcsik, N. (1998). Problems in assessing perceived barriers to exercise: Confusing obstacles with attributions and excuses. In J. Duda (Ed.), *Advances in sport and exercise psychology measurement* (pp. 337-350). Morgantown, WV: Fitness Information Technology.

Brendtro, L., Brokenleg, M., & Van Bockern, S. (1990). *Reclaiming youth at risk.* Bloomington, IN: National Education Service.

Brenner, M. (1980). *Current developments.* Washington, DC: Bureau of National Affairs.

Brezinka, V., & Kittel, F. (1995). Psychosocial factors of coronary heart disease in women: A review. *Social Science and Medicine, 42,* 1351-1365.

Brill, P., Burkhalter, H., Kohl, H., Blair, S., & Goodyear, N. (1989). The impact of previous athleticism on exercise habits, physical fitness, and coronary heart disease risk factors in middle-aged men. *Research Quarterly for Exercise and Sport, 60,* 209-215.

Brill, P., Kohl, H., Rogers, T., Collingwood, T., Sterling, C., & Blair, S. (1991). The relationship between sociodemographic characteristics and recruitment, retention, and health improvements in a worksite health promotion program. *American Journal of Health Promotion, 5,* 215-221.

Brinkley, J., Eales, J., & Jekanowski, M. (2000). The relation between dietary change and rising U.S. obesity. *International Journal of Obesity Related Metabolic Disorders, 24,* 1032-1039.

Brisson, C., Larocque, B., Moisan, J., Vezina, M., & Dagenais, G. (2000). Psychosocial factors at work, smoking, sedentary behavior, and body mass index: A prevalence study among 6995 white collar workers. *Journal of Occupational and Environmental Medicine, 42,* 40-46.

Britten, R. (1939). Scope and method of the nationwide canvass of sickness in relation to its social and economic setting. *Public Health Reports, 54,* 1663-1687.

Brody, E. (1985). Parent care as a normative family stress. *Gerontologist, 25,* 19-29.

Bronfenbrenner, U. (1979). *The ecology of human development.* Cambridge, MA: Harvard University Press.

Brown, A. (1984). *The art of coalition building: A guide for community leaders.* New York: American Jewish Community.

Brown, R. (1991). Community action for health promotion: A strategy to empower individuals and communities. *International Journal of Health Services, 21,* 441-456.

Brownson, R., Smith, C., Pratt, M., Mack, N., Jackson-Thompson, J., Dean, C., Dabney, S., & Wilkerson, J. (1996). Preventing cardiovascular disease through community-based risk reduction: The Bootheel Heart Health Project. *American Journal of Public Health, 86,* 206-213.

Brustad, R. (1993). Who will go out and play? Parental and psychological influences on children's attraction to physical activity. *Pediatric Exercise Science, 5,* 210-223.

Bryant, J., & McElroy, M. (1997). *Sociological dynamics of sport and exercise.* Englewood, CO: Morton.

Buck, R. (1939). The physical examination of groups. *New England Journal of Medicine, 221,* 883-887.

Bunker, J., Stansfeld, S., & Porter, J. (1996). Freedom, responsibility, and health. *British Medical Journal, 313,* 1582-1585.

Burke, V., Giangiulio, N., Gilliam, H., Beilin, L., Houghton, S., & Milligan, R. (1999). Health promotion in couples adapting to a shared lifestyle. *Health Education Research, 14,* 269-288.

Burton, T. (1994). Issues in policy development for active living and sustainable living in Canada. In H. Quinney, L. Gauvin, & T. Wall (Eds.). *Toward active learning: Proceedings of the International Conference on Physical Activity, Fitness, and Health* (pp. 207-212). Champaign, IL: Human Kinetics.

Butler, L., & Mergardt, G. (1994). The many forms of administrative support. *Journal of Physical Education, Recreation and Dance, 65,* 43-47.

Butterfoss, F., Goodman, R., & Wandersman, A. (1993). Community coalitions for prevention and health promotion. *Health Education Research, 8,* 315-330.

Byrne, P., & Long, B. (1976). *Doctors talking to patients.* London: HMSO.

Calfas, K., Sallis, J., & Oldenburg, B. (1997). Mediators of change in physical activity following an intervention in primary care: PACE. *Preventive Medicine, 26,* 297-304.

California's anti-tobacco advertising, education campaigns reap success [Editorial]. (2000). *Alcoholism and Drug Abuse Weekly, 28,* 6.

Cambridge Systematics (1999). *Unclogging America's arteries: Prescription for healthier highways.* Washington DC: American Highway Users Alliance.

Cantwell, S., & Rothenberg, B. (2000). The benefits of lifestyle coaching. *IDEA Personal Trainer, 11,* 24-31.

Carlson, T. (1995). We hate gym: Student alienation from physical education. *Journal of Teaching in Physical Education, 14*, 467-477.

Carnegie Council on Adolescent Development. (1992). *A matter of time: Risk and opportunity in the nonschool hours. Report of the Task Force on Youth Development and Community Programs.* New York: Carnegie Corp.

Carrasquillo, O., Himmelstein, D., Woolhandler, S., & Bor, D. (1999). Going bare: Trends in health insurance coverage, 1989 through 1996. *American Journal of Public Health, 89*, 36-42.

Caudron, S. (1992). Are health incentives disincentives? *Personnel Journal, 71*, 35-40.

Cavanaugh, J. (1993). *Adult development and aging.* Grove, CA: Brooks Cole.

Centers for Disease Control and Prevention. (1992). *1992 BRFSS summary prevalence report.* Atlanta, GA: U.S. Department of Health and Human Services.

Centers for Disease Control and Prevention. (1998). *National vital statistics report.* Hyattsville, MD: National Center for Health Statistics.

Centers for Disease Control and Prevention. (1999). Neighborhood safety and the prevalence of physical inactivity—Selected States, 1996. *MMWR, 48*, 143-146.

Centers for Disease Control and Prevention. (2000). Prevalence of leisure-time and occupational physical activity among employed adults—US, 1990. *MMWR, 49*, 420-424.

Cervero, R., & Gorham, R. (1995). Commuting in transit versus automobile neighborhoods. *Journal of American Planning Association, 1466*, 44-52.

Chavis, D., & Wandersman, A. (1990). Sense of community in the urban environment: A catalyst for participation and community development. *American Journal of Community Psychology, 18*, 55-81.

Chmielewski, P. (1994). New institutional analysis: Its logic and basic principles. *Studia-Socjologiczne, 3-4*, 134-135, 217-253.

Clarke, W., Schrott, P., Leaverton, W., Connor, W., & Lauer, R. (1978). Tracking of blood lipids and blood pressures in school age children: The Muscatine study. *Circulation, 58*, 626-634.

Clinton, H. (1996). *It takes a village: And other lessons children teach us.* New York: Touchstone Books.

Coakley, J. (1998). *Sport in society: Issues and controversies.* Boston: McGraw Hill.

Cockerham, W., & Abel, T. (1993). Max Weber, formal rationality, and health lifestyles. *Sociological Quarterly, 34*, 413-425.

Cockerham, W., Rutten, A., & Abel, T. (1997). Conceptualizing contemporary health lifestyles: Moving beyond Weber. *Sociological Quarterly, 38*, 321-342.

Colditz, G. (1999). Economic costs of obesity and inactivity. *Medicine and Science in Sports and Exercise, 31*, S663-S667.

Coleman, J. (1961). *The adolescent society.* New York: Free Press.

Coleman, J. (1990). *The foundations of social theory.* Cambridge, MA: Harvard University Press.

Collingwood, T. (1997). *Helping at-risk youth through physical fitness programming.* Champaign, IL: Human Kinetics.

Connell, C. (1994). Impact of spouse care giving on health behaviors and physical and mental health status. *American Journal of Alzheimer's Care and Related Disorders and Research*, 26-36.

Conrad, P. (1987). Who comes to work-site wellness programs? A preliminary review. *Journal of Occupational Medicine, 29*, 317-320.

Conrad, P., & Kern, R. (1981). *The sociology of health and illness: Critical perspectives.* New York: St. Martin Press.

Coontz, S. (1992). *The way we never were: American families and the nostalgia trap.* New York: Basic Books.

Cooper, K. (1968). *Aerobics.* New York: M. Evans with Lippincott.

Corbin, C. (1987). Physical fitness in the K-12 curriculum: Some defensible solutions to perennial problems. *Journal of Physical Education, Recreation and Dance, 58*, 49-54.

Corbin, C., & Pangrazi, R. (1998). *Physical activity guidelines: Appropriate physical activity for children.* Reston, VA: National Association for Sport and Physical Education.

Coser, L. (1974). *Greedy institutions: Patterns of undivided commitment.* New York: Free Press.

Cottrell, L. (1976). The competent community. In B. Kaplan, R. Wilson, & A. Leighton (Eds.), *Further explorations in social psychiatry.* New York: Basic Books.

Cox, M., Shephard, R., & Corey, P. (1981). Influence of an employee fitness program upon fitness, productivity, and absenteeism. *Ergonomics, 24*, 795-806.

Coyne, J., & Smith, D. (1991). Couples coping with myocardial infarction: A contextual perspective on wives' distress. *Journal of Personality and Social Psychology, 61*, 404-412.

Coyne, J., & Smith, D. (1994). Couples coping with a myocardial infarction: Contextual perspective on patient self-efficacy. *Journal of Family Psychology, 8*, 43-54.

Craig, S., Goldberg, J., & Dietz, W. (1996). Psychological correlates of physical activity among fifth and eight graders. *Preventive Medicine, 25*, 505-513.

Crawford, R. (1980). Healthism and the medicalization of everyday life. *International Journal of Health Services, 10*, 365-388.

Crawford, R. (1981). Individual responsibility and health politics. In P. Conrad & R. Kern, *The sociology of health and illness* (pp. 468-481). New York: St. Martin's Press.

Crespo, C. (2000). Encouraging physical activity in minorities. *Physician and Sportsmedicine, 28*, 36-51.

Crespo, C., Keteyian, S., Heath, G., & Sempos, C. (1996). Leisure-time physical activity among U.S. adults. *Archives of Internal Medicine, 156*, 93-98.

Crespo, C., Smit, E., Andersen, R., Carter-Pokras, O., & Ainsworth, B. (2000). Race/ethnicity, social class and their relation to physical inactivity during leisure time: Results from the Third National Health and Nutrition Examination Survey, 1988-1994. *American Journal of Preventive Medicine, 18*, 46-53.

Crump, C., Earp, J., Kozma, C., & Hertz-Picciotto, I. (1996). Effect of organizational level variables on differential employee participation in 10 federal worksite health promotion programs. *Health Education Quarterly, 23*, 204-223.

Curtis, J., & Russell, S. (1997). *Physical activity in human experience: Interdisciplinary perspectives.* Champaign, IL: Human Kinetics.

d'Houtaud, A., & Field, M. (1984). The image of health: Variations in perception by social class in a French population. *Sociology of Health and Illness, 6,* 30-59.

Dale, D., & Corbin, C. (2000). Physical activity participation of high school graduates following exposure to conceptual or traditional physical education. *Research Quarterly for Exercise and Sport, 71,* 61-68.

Dale, D., Corbin, C., & Dale, K. (2000). Restricting opportunities to be active during school time: Do children compensate by increasing physical activity levels after school? *Research Quarterly for Exercise and Sport, 71,* 240-248.

Damon, W. (1995). *Greater expectations: Overcoming the culture of indulgence in America's homes and schools.* New York: Free Press.

Dauer, C. (1994). Benefits of prevention outweigh costs: Experts. *National Underwriter, 98,* 42-44.

Davis, R. (2000). Healthy people 2010: Objectives for the United States. *British Medical Journal, 320,* 818-819.

Davis, T. (1999). Do repetitive tasks give rise to musculoskeletal disorders? *Occupational Medicine, 49,* 257-258.

Dawber, T. (1980). *The Framingham Study: The epidemiology of atherosclerotic disease.* Cambridge, MA: Cambridge University Press.

Dawson, D.A. (1991). Family structure and children's health and well-being: Data from the 1988 National Health Interview Survey on child health. *Journal of Marriage and the Family, 53,* 573-584.

DeBusk, R., Kraemer, H., & Nash, E. (1983). Step-wise risk stratification soon after acute myocardial infarction. *American Journal of Cardiology, 12,* 1161-1166.

DeBusk, R., Miller, N., Superko, H., Dennis, C., Thomas, R., Lew, H., Berger, W., Heller, R., Rompf, J., Gee, D., Kraemer, H., Bandura, A., Ghandour, G., Clark, M., Fisher, L., & Taylor, C. (1994). A case management system for coronary risk factor modification following acute myocardial infarction. *Annals of Internal Medicine, 129,* 721-729.

Deem, R. (1987). Unleisured lives: Sport in the context of women's leisure. *Women's Studies International Forum, 10,* 423-432.

DeJonge, J., Bosma, H., Peter, R., & Siegrist, J. (2000). Job strain, effort-reward imbalance and employee well-being: A large scale cross-sectional study. *Social Science and Medicine, 50,* 1317-1327.

DeJoy, D., & Wilson, M. (1995). *Critical issues in workplace health promotion.* Boston: Allyn and Bacon.

DeJoy, M., & Southern, J. (1993). An integrative perspective on worksite health promotion. *Journal of Occupational Medicine, 35,* 1221-1229.

Demers, P. (1988). University training of physical educators. In J. Harvey & H. Cantelon (Eds.), *Not just a game: Essays in Canadian sport sociology* (pp. 159-172). Ottawa: University of Ottawa Press.

DeVries, B., Della Lana, R., & Falck, V. (1994). Parental bereavement over the life course: A theoretical intersection and empirical review. *Omega, 29,* 47-69.

Diez-Roux, A. (1998). Bring context back into epidemiology. Variables and fallacies in multi-level analysis. *American Journal of Public Health, 88,* 217-222.

Dishman, R. (1982). Compliance/adherence in health related exercise. *Health Psychology, 1,* 237-267.

Dishman, R. (1988). Supervised and free-living physical activity: No differences in former athletes and non-athletes. *American Journal of Preventive Medicine, 4,* 153-160.

Dishman, R., Oldenburg, B., O'Neal, H., Shephard, R. (1998). Worksite physical activity interventions. *American Journal of Preventive Medicine, 15,* 344-361.

Doherty, W., & Campbell, W. (1988). *Families and health.* Beverly Hills, CA: Sage.

Drucker, P. (1992). *Managing for the future: The 1990s and beyond.* New York: Dutton.

Dryfoos, J. (1994). *Full service schools: A revolution in health and social services for children, youth, and families.* San Francisco: Jossey-Bass.

DuCharme, K., & Brawley, L. (1995). Predicting the intentions and behavior of exercise initiates using two forms of self-efficacy. *Journal of Behavioral Medicine, 18,* 479-497.

Duda, J. (1981). *A cross-cultural analysis of achievement motivation in sport and the classroom.* Unpublished doctoral dissertation, University of Illinois, Champaign.

Duffy, J. (1979). The American medical profession and public health: From support to ambivalence. *Bulletin of the History of Medicine, 53,* 1-22.

Durkheim, E. (1897). *Suicide* (J. Spaulding & G. Simpson, Trans.). New York: Free Press. (Reprinted in 1951).

Durkheim, E. (1933). *The division of labor* (G. Simpson, Trans.). New York: Free Press.

Dweck, C., & Wortman, C. (1982). Learned helplessness, anxiety, and achievement motivation: Neglected parallels in cognitive, affective, and coping responses. In H. Krohne & L. Laux (Eds.), *Achievement, stress, and anxiety* (pp. 93-126). New York: Hemisphere.

Dzewaltowski, D., Estabrooks, P., & Gyurcsik, N. (in press). Promoting physical activity through community development. In J.L. Van Raalte & B. Brewer (Eds.), *Exploring sport and exercise psychology.* Washington, DC: American Psychological Association.

Eakin, J. (1997). Work-related determinants of health behavior. In D. Gochman (Ed.), *Handbook of health behavior research: I. Personal and social determinants.* New York: Plenum Press.

Eccles, J., & Harold, R. (1991). Gender differences in sport involvement: Applying the Eccles expectancy-value model. *Journal of Applied Sport Psychology, 3,* 7-35.

Edmondson, B. (1996). Work slowdown: Work demographics from 1994 to 2005. *American Demographics, 18,* 4-7.

Egolf, B., Lasker, L., Wolf, S., & Potvin, L. (1992). The Roseto effect: A 50-year comparison of mortality rates. *American Journal of Public Health, 82,* 1089-1092.

Einthoven, W. (1900). On the normal human electrocardiogram and on the capillar-electrometric examination of some heart patients. *Pflugers Archiv fur die Gesamte Physiologie, 80,* 139-160.

Elkind, D. (1994). *Ties that stress: The new family imbalance.* Cambridge, MA: Harvard University Press.

Ennis, C. (1996). Students' experiences in sport-based physical education: (More than) apologies are necessary. *Quest, 48,* 453-456.

Epstein, L., Valoski, A., Vara, L., McCurley, J., Wisniewski, L., Kalarchian, M., Klein, K., & Shrager, L. (1995). Effects of decreasing sedentary behavior and increasing activity on weight change in obese children. *Health Psychology, 14,* 109-115.

Ernst, R. (1991). *Weakness is a crime.* Syracuse, NY: Syracuse University Press.

Estabrooks, P., Courneya, K., & Nigg, C. (1996). Effect of a stimulus control intervention on attendance at a university fitness center. *Behavior Modification, 20,* 202-215.

Etheridge, E. (1992). *Sentinel for health: A history of the Centers for Disease Control.* Berkeley: University of California Press.

Etzioni, A. (1993). *The spirit of community.* New York: Touchstone.

Evans, J., & Roberts, G. (1987). Physical competence and the development of children's peer relations. *Quest, 39,* 23-35.

Fagard, R., & Tipton, C. (1994). Physical activity, fitness and hypertension. In C. Bouchard, R. Shephard, & T. Stephens (Eds.), *Physical activity, fitness, and health: International proceedings and consensus statement* (pp. 633-655). Champaign, IL: Human Kinetics.

Farley, R. (1996). *The new American reality.* New York: Russell Sage Foundation.

Farquhar, J. (1987). *The American way of life need not be hazardous to your health.* New York: Norton.

Faucette, N., McKenzie, T., & Patterson, P. (1990). Descriptive analysis of nonspecialist elementary physical education teachers' curricular choices and class organization. *Journal of Teaching in Physical Education, 9,* 284-293.

Feagin, J., & Sikes, M. (1994). *Living with racism: The black middle class experience.* Boston: Beacon Press.

Fee, E. (1987). *Disease and discovery: A history of the Johns Hopkins School of Hygiene and Public Health, 1916-1939.* Baltimore: Johns Hopkins University Press.

Feighery, E., & Rogers, T. (1989). *Building and maintaining effective coalitions.* Palo Alto, CA: Stanford Health Promotion Resource Center.

Feinleib, M. (1995). Trends in heart disease in the United States. *American Journal of the Medical Sciences, 310,* S8-S14.

Feldman, M. (1993). Shape up! Physicians prod patients to give up bad habits. *Minnesota Medicine, 76,* 14-20.

Fernandez-Balboa, J. (1993). Sociocultural characteristics of the hidden curriculum in physical education. *Quest, 45,* 230-254.

Ferrie, J., Shipley, M., Marmot, M., Stansfeld, S., & Smith, G. (1998). The health effects of major organisational change and job insecurity. *Social Science and Medicine, 46,* 243-254.

Feudtner, C. (1995). The want of control: Ideas, innovations, and ideals in the modern management of diabetes mellitus. *Bulletin of the History of Medicine, 69,* 66-90.

Fick, D., Goff, S., & Oppliger, R. (1996). Running and its effect on family life. *Archives of Family Medicine, 5,* 385-389.

Fielding, J. (1994). The Live for Life Program of Johnson & Johnson: Direct and indirect economic benefits. In J. Opatz (Ed.), *Economic impact of workplace health promotion* (pp. 209-228). Champaign, IL: Human Kinetics.

Fielding, J., & Piserchia, P. (1989). Frequency of worksite health promotion activities. *American Journal of Public Health, 79,* 16-20.

Finnegan, J., Meischke, H., Zapka, J., Leviton, L., Meshack, A., Benjamin-Garner, R., Estabrook, B., Johnston Hall, N., Schaeffer, S., Smith, C., Weitzman, E., Raczynski, J., & Stone, E. (2000). Patient delay in seeking care for heart attack symptoms: Findings from focus groups conducted in five U.S. regions. *Preventive Medicine, 31,* 205-213.

Fitzpatrick, T., & Bosse, R. (2000). Employment and health among older bereaved men in the normative aging study. *Social Work Health Care, 32,* 41-60.

Fixx, J. (1977). *The complete book of running.* New York: Random House.

Fletcher, G. (1983). The history of exercise in the practice of medicine. *Journal of the Medical Association of Georgia, 72,* 35-40.

Foo, M., Robinson, J., Rhodes, M., Lew, L., Chao, M., Sokhan, D., & Eir, W. (1999). Identifying policy opportunities to increase physical activity in the Southeastern Asian community in Long Beach, California. *Journal of Health Education, 30,* S58-S63.

Forbes, D. (1994). *False fixes: The cultural politics of drugs, alcohol, and addictive relations.* Albany: State University of New York Press.

Forbis, P. (1996). Managed care and the athletic trainer. *Athletic Therapy Today, 1,* 23-25.

Ford, E., Ahluwalia, I., & Galuska, D. (2000). Social relationships and cardiovascular disease risk factors: Findings from the third National Health and Nutrition Examination Survey. *Preventive Medicine, 30,* 83-92.

Fox, D. (1987). The politics of the NIH extramural program, 1937-1950. *Journal of the History of Medicine and Allied Sciences, 42,* 447-466.

Francis, K. (1999). Status of the year 2000 health goals for physical activity and fitness. *Physical Therapy, 79,* 405-414.

Francis, L. (1984). *Young and unemployed.* London: Costello.

Frantzich, S. (1999). *Citizen democracy: Political activists in a cynical age.* Lanham, MD: Rowman and Littlefield.

Freedson, P., & Evenson, S. (1991). Familial aggregation and physical activity. *Research Quarterly for Exercise and Sport, 62,* 384-389.

Freire, P. (1973). *Education for critical consciousness.* New York: Seabury Press.

Freudenberg, N. (1998). Community-based health education for urban populations: An overview. *Health Education and Behavior, 25,* 11-23.

Freudenberg, N., & Manoncourt, E. (1998). Urban health promotion: Current practices and new directions. *Health Education and Behavior, 25,* 138-145.

Friedman, C., Brownson, R., & Peterson, D. (1994). Physician advice to reduce chronic disease risk factors. *American Journal of Preventive Medicine, 10,* 367-371.

Fuchs, V. (1988). *Women's quest for economic equality*. Cambridge, MA: Harvard University Press.

Fuchs, V. (1996). Overview. In V. Fuchs (Ed.), *Individual and social responsibility: Child care, education, medical care, and long-term care in America* (pp. 3-29). Chicago: University of Chicago Press.

Fukuyama, F. (1995). *Trust: The social virtues and the creation of prosperity*. New York: Free Press.

Fukuyama, F. (1999). *The great disruption: Human nature and the reconstitution of social order*. New York: Free Press.

Fuller-Thomson, E., & Minkler, M. (2000). African American grandparents raising grandchildren: A national profile of demographic and health characteristics. *Health and Social Work, 25*, 109-118.

Fullerton, H. (1993, November). Another look at the labor force. *Monthly Labor Review*, 31-40.

Furstenburg, F., Morgan, P., & Allison, P. (1987). Paternal participation and children's well-being after marital dissolution. *American Sociological Review, 48*, 695-701.

Gabelnick, F. (1997). Educating a committed citizenry. *Change, 29*, 30-35.

Gaesser, G. (1996). *Big fat lies: The truth about your weight and health*. New York: Fawcett Books.

Galen. (1951). *Hygiene* (R. Green, Trans.). Springfield, IL: Charles C Thomas.

Gans, H. (1962). Urbanism and suburbanism as ways of life: A re-evaluation of definitions. In A. Rose, *Human behavior and social processes: An interactionist approach* (pp. 70-85). Boston: Houghton Mifflin.

Gans, H. (1988). *Middle American individualism: The future of liberal democracy*. New York: Free Press.

Garg, A., & Moore, J. (1992). Prevention strategies and the low back in industry. *Occupational Medicine, 7*, 629-640.

Gass, K. (1989). Health of older widowers: Role of appraisal, coping, resources, and types of spouses' death. In D. Lund (Ed.), *Older bereaved spouses: Research with practical applications* (pp. 95-108). New York: Hemisphere.

Gerson, K. (1991). Coping with commitment: Dilemmas and conflicts of family life. In M. Wolfe, *America at century's end* (pp. 35-57). Berkeley: University of California Press.

Gettleman, T., & Thompson, J. (1993). Actual differences versus stereotypical perceptions of body image and eating disturbance: A comparison of male and female heterosexual and homosexual samples. *Sex Roles, 29*, 545-562.

Giddens, A. (1990). *The consequences of modernity*. Stanford, CA: Stanford University Press.

Giddens, A. (1991). *Modernity and self-identity: Self and society in the late modern age*. Cambridge: Polity Press/Basil Blackwell.

Gillick, M. (1984). Health promotion, jogging, and the pursuit of the moral life. *Journal of Health Politics, 3*, 369-387.

Glaser, W. (1976). *Positive addiction*. New York: Harper and Row.

Glassner, B. (1989). Fitness and the postmodern self. *Journal of Health and Social Behavior, 30,* 180-191.

Glyptis, S. (1994). Leisure provision for the unemployed: Imperative or irrelevant? *World Leisure and Recreation, 36,* 34-39.

Goldberg, P. (1978). *Executive health.* New York: McGraw Hill.

Goldfarb, M. (1991). *The cynical society: The culture of politics and the politics of culture in American life.* Chicago: University of Chicago Press.

Goldfine, B., & Nahas, M. (1993). Incorporating health-related fitness concepts in secondary school physical education curricula. *Journal of School Health, 63,* 142-146.

Goldstein, M. (1991). *The health movement: Promoting fitness in America.* New York: Twayne.

Goodman, R., Steckler, A., Hoover, S., & Schwartz, R. (1993). A critique of contemporary community health promotion approaches: based on a qualitative review of six programs in Maine. *American Journal of Health Promotion, 7,* 208-220.

Gordon, P., Heath, G., Holmes, A., & Christy, D. (2000). The quantity and quality of physical activity among those trying to lose weight. *American Journal of Preventive Medicine, 18,* 83-86.

Gove, W., & Umberson, D. (1985). *Marriage and the well-being of men and women.* Paper presented at the annual meeting of the American Sociological Association, Washington, DC.

Govier, T. (1997). *Social trust and human communities.* Montreal: McGill-Queens University Press.

Grayson, P. (1993). Health, physical activity level, and employment status in Canada. *International Journal of Health Services, 23,* 743-761.

Green, E., & Hebron, S. (1988). Leisure and male partners. In E. Wimbush & M. Talbot (Eds.), *Relative freedoms: Women and leisure* (pp. 37-47). Milton Keynes, UK: Open University Press.

Green, H. (1986). *Fit for America: Health, fitness, sport, and American society.* New York: Pantheon Books.

Green, K. (1988). Issues of control and responsibility in worker's health. *Health Education Quarterly, 15,* 473-486.

Green, L., & Kreuter, M. (1990). Health promotion as a public health strategy for the 1990s. *Annual Review of Public Health, 11,* 319-334.

Green, R., Mandel, J., Hotvedt, M., Gray, J., & Smith, L. (1987). Lesbian mothers and their children: A comparison with solo heterosexual mothers and their children. *Archives of Sexual Behavior, 7,* 175-181.

Griffin, P. (1985). Teaching in an urban, multiracial physical education program: The power of context. *Quest, 37,* 154-165.

Grosch, J., Alterman, T., Petersen, M., & Murphy, L. (1998). Worksite health promotion programs in the U.S.: Factors associated with availability and participation. *American Journal of Health Promotion, 13,* 36-45.

Grossman, A., & Wughalter, E. (1983). Leisure and fitness: Beliefs and practices of predominantly gay male members of a gymnasium. *Leisure Information Quarterly, 11,* 7-11.

Grunbaum, J., Kann, L., Kinchen, S., Ross, J., Gowda, V., Collins, J., & Kolbe, L. (1999). Youth Risk Behavior Surveillance—National Alternative High School Youth Risk Behavior Survey, United States, 1998 [CDC Surveillance Summaries]. *Morbidity and Mortality Weekly Report, 48,* 1-44.

Grzywacz, J., & Marks, N. (2000). Reconceptualizing the work-family interface: An ecological perspective on the correlates of positive and negative spillover between work and family. *Journal of Occupational Health Psychology, 5,* 111-126.

Hackett, T., & Cassem, N. (1983). Factors contributing to delay in responding to the signs and symptoms of acute myocardial infarction. *American Journal of Cardiology, 24,* 651-658.

Hahn, A., & Craythorn, E. (1994). Inactivity and physical activity in two regional centres. *Health Promotion Journal of Australia, 4,* 43-45.

Hahn, D., & Berger, M. (1990). Implementation of a systematic health maintenance protocol in a private practice. *Journal of Family Practice, 31,* 492-504.

Hahn, R., Teutsch, S., Rothenberg, R., & Marks, J. (1990). Excess deaths from nine chronic diseases in the United States. *Journal of the American Medical Association, 264,* 2654-2659.

Hanlon, J., & Pickett, G. (1984). *Public health: Administration and practice.* St. Louis: Times Mirror/Mosby.

Hanson, D., De Guire, M., Schinkel, A., & Kolterman, O. (1995). Empirical validation for a family-centered model of care. *Diabetes Care, 18,* 1347-1356.

Hardy, S. (1981). The city and the rise of American sport: 1820-1920. *Journal of Sport History, 12,* 183-219.

Harms, C. (1998). First, do no harm. Retrieved from the World Wide Web: http://www.edweek.com.

Harris, J. (1998). Civil society, physical activity, and the involvement of sport sociologists in the preparation of physical activity professionals. *Sociology of Sport Journal, 15,* 138-153.

Harris, K., Richter, K., Paine-Andrews, A., Lewis, R., Johnston, J., James, V., Henke, L., & Fawcett, S. (1997). Community partnerships: Review of selected models and evaluation of two case studies. *Journal of Nutrition Education, 29,* 190-195.

Harter, S. (1987). The determinants and mediational role of global self-worth in children. In N. Eisenberg (Ed.), *Contemporary topics in developmental psychology* (pp. 219-242). New York: Wiley.

Hartvigsen, J., Leboeuf-Yde, C., Lings, S., & Corder, E. (2000). Is sitting while at work associated with low back pain? A systematic, critical literature review. *Scandinavian Journal of Public Health, 28,* 230-239.

Haskell, W. (1994). The efficacy and safety of exercise programs in cardiac rehabilitation. *Medicine and Science in Sports and Exercise, 26,* 815-823.

Hawks, S., & Gast, J. (1998). Weight loss management: A path lit darkly. *Health Education and Behavior, 25,* 371-382.

Heinzelman, D., & Bagley, R. (1970). Response to physical activity programs and their effects on health behavior. *Public Health Reports, 85,* 905-911.

Hellison, D. (1995). *Teaching personal and social responsibility through physical activity.* Champaign, IL: Human Kinetics.

Henderson, A. (1987). Developing a credentialing system for health educators. In W. Ward (Ed.), *Advances in health education and promotion* (pp. 59-91). Greenwich, CT: JAI Press.

Henderson, K., Stalnaker, D., & Taylor, G. (1988). The relationship between barriers to recreation and gender role personality traits for women. *Journal of Leisure Research, 20,* 69-80.

Herrick, J. (1912). Clinical features of sudden obstruction of the coronary arteries. *Journal of the American Medical Association, 59,* 2115-2020.

Herzog, D., Newman, K., Yeh, C., & Warshaw, M. (1992). Body image satisfaction in homosexual and heterosexual women. *International Journal of Eating Disorders, 11,* 391-396.

Hetherington, E.M. (1992). *Coping with marital transitions: A family systems approach.* New York: Society for Research in Child Development.

Higgins, C. (1988). The economics of health promotion. *Health Values, 12,* 39-45.

Hill, J., & Trowbridge, F. (1998). Childhood obesity: Future directions and research priorities. *Pediatrics, 101,* 570-574.

Hochschild, A. (1989). *The second shift.* New York: Avon Books.

Homans, G. (1961). *Social behavior: Its elementary form.* New York: Harcourt Brace Jovanovich.

Horne, T. (1994). Predictors of physical activity intentions and behaviour for rural homemakers. *Canadian Journal of Public Health, 85,* 132-135.

House, J., Landis, K., & Umberson, D. (1988). Social relationships and health. *Science, 241,* 540-545.

House, J., & Mortimer, J. (1990). Social structure and the individual: Emerging themes and new directions. *Social Psychology Quarterly, 53,* 123-140.

House, J., Robbins, C., & Metzner, H. (1982). The association of social relationships and activities with mortality: Prospective evidence from the Tecumseh Community Health Study. *American Journal of Epidemiology, 116,* 123-140.

Hovell, M., Bursick, J., Sharkey, R., & McClure, J. (1978). An evaluation of elementary students' voluntary physical activity during recess. *Research Quarterly, 49,* 460-474.

Hovell, M., Kaplan, R., & Howell, F. (1990). Preventive medical services in the United States. In P. Lamal (Ed.), *Behavioral analysis of societies and cultural practices* (pp. 181-200). New York: Hemisphere.

Howard, D. (1943). *The WPA and federal relief policy.* New York: Russell Sage Foundation.

Howard, D. (1992). Participation rates in selected sport and fitness activities. *Journal of Sport Management, 6,* 191-205.

Howell, J. (1984). Early perceptions of the electrocardiogram: From arrhythmia to infarction. *Bulletin of Historical Medicine, 58,* 99-102.

Hughes, D., & Dodge, M. (1997). African American women in the workplace: Relationships between job conditions, racial bias at work, and perceived job quality. *American Journal of Community Psychology, 25*, 581-599.

Hunter, J. (1991). *Culture wars: The struggle to define America*. New York: Basic Books.

Iezzoni, L. (1996). When walking fails. *Journal of the American Medical Association, 276*, 1609-1613.

Increase in deaths from heart disease [Editorial]. (1903). *Boston Medical and Surgical Journal, 163*, 702.

Ingham, A. (1985). From public issue to personal trouble. Well-being and the fiscal crisis of the state. *Sociology of Sport Journal, 2*, 43-55.

Institute of Medicine. (1988). *The future of public health*. Washington, DC: National Academy Press.

International Food Information Council and American Dietetic Association. (1990). *How are Americans making food choices? Results of a Gallup survey*. Washington, DC: American Dietetic Association.

Jackson, J. (1990). Institutions in American society. In J. Jackson (Ed.), *Institutions in American society*. Ann Arbor: University of Michigan Press.

Jahoda, M. (1982). *Employment and unemployment: A social-psychological analysis*. Cambridge, MA: Cambridge University Press.

Janis, I., & Mann, L. (1977). *Decision making: A psychological analysis of conflict, choice, and commitment*. London: Cassel and Collier Macmillan.

Johansson, G., Johnson, J., & Hall, E. (1991). Smoking and sedentary behavior as related to work organization. *Social Science and Medicine, 32*, 837-846.

Jones, J. (1996). The origin of personal training. In S. Roberts (Ed.), *The business of personal training* (pp. 7-11). Champaign, IL: Human Kinetics.

Judy, R., & D'Amico, C. (1997). *Work and workers in the 21st century*. Indianapolis: Hudson Institute.

Kannel, W., & Sorlie, P. (1979). Some health benefits of physical activity: The Framingham Study. *Archives of Internal Medicine, 139*, 857-961.

Kanter, D., & Mirvis, P. (1989). *The cynical Americans: Living and working in an age of discontent and disillusion*. San Francisco: Jossey-Bass.

Kaplan, G., Lazarus, N., Cohen, R., & Leu, D. (1991). Psychosocial factors in the natural history of physical activity. *American Journal of Preventive Medicine, 7*, 12-17.

Karasek, R., & Theorell, T. (1990). *Healthy work: Stress, productivity and the reconstruction of working life*. New York: Basic Books.

Karper, W. (1995). Problems with inclusive elementary school physical education taught by classroom teachers. *Palaestra, 11*, 32-36.

Karvonen, M., Kentala, E., & Mustala, D. (1957). The effects of training heart rate: A longitudinal study. *Annales Medicinae Experimentalis et Biologiae Fenniae, 35*, 307-315.

Kavussanu, M., & McAuley, E. (1995). Exercise and optimism: Are highly active individuals more optimistic? *Journal of Sport and Exercise Psychology, 17*, 246-258.

Kawachi, I., Colditz, G., Ascherio, A., Rimm, E., Giovannucci, E., Stamp, M., & Willett, W. (1996). A prospective study of social networks in relation to total mortality and cardiovascular disease in men in the USA. *Journal of Epidemiology Community Health, 50,* 245-251.

Kawachi, I., Kennedy, B., & Glass, R. (1999). Social capital and self-rated health: A contextual analysis. *American Journal of Public Health, 89,* 1187-1193.

Kawachi, I., Kennedy, B., Lochner, K., & Prothrow-Stith, D. (1997). Social capital, income inequality and mortality. *American Journal of Public Health, 50,* 245-251.

Kelley, S., Brownwell, C., & Campbell, S. (2000). Mastery motivation and self-evaluative affect in toddlers: Longitudinal relations with maternal behavior. *Child Development, 71,* 1061-1071.

Kelly, J. (1983). *Leisure identities and interactions.* London: Allen and Unwin.

Kennedy, B., Kawachi, I., Lochner, K., Jones, C., Prothrow-Stith, D. (1997). Disrespect and black mortality. *Ethnicity and Disease, 7,* 207-214.

Kerr, M. (2000). The importance of psychosocial risk factors in injury. In T. Sullivan (Ed.), *Injury and the new world of work.* Toronto: UBC Press.

Kickbusch, I. (1989). Approaches to an ecological base for public health. *Health Promotion, 4,* 265-268.

Kiefhaber, A., Weinberg, A., & Goldbeck, W. (1979). *A survey of industry sponsored health promotion, prevention, and education programs.* Washington, DC: Washington Business Group for Health.

Kimiecik, J., & Lawson, H. (1996). Toward new approaches for exercise behavior change and health promotion. *Quest, 48,* 102-125.

King, A. (1994). Community and public health approaches to the promotion of physical activity. *Medicine and Science in Sports and Exercise, 26,* 1405-1412.

King, A., & Brassington, M. (1997). Enhancing physical and psychological functioning in older family care givers: The role of regular physical activity. *Annals of Behavioral Medicine, 19,* 91-100.

King, A., Carl, F., Birkel, L., & Haskell, W. (1988). Increasing exercise among blue-collar employees. The tailoring of workplace programs to meet specific needs. *Preventive Medicine, 17,* 357-365.

King, A., Haskell, C., Taylor, B., Kraemer, H., & DeBusk, R. (1991). Group vs. home-based exercise training in healthy older men and women: A community-based clinical trial. *Journal of the American Medical Association, 266,* 1535-1542.

King, A., Kiernan, M., Ahn, D., & Wilcox, S. (1998). The effects of marital transitions on changes in physical activity: Results from a 10-year community study. *Annals of Behavioral Medicine, 20,* 64-69.

King, A., Sallis, J., Dunn, A., Simons-Morton, D., Albright, C., Cohen, S., Rejeskis, J., Marcus, B., & Coday, M. (1998). Overview of the Activity Counseling Trial (ACT) intervention for promoting physical activity in primary health care settings. *Medicine and Science in Sports and Exercise, 30,* 1086-1096.

King, A., Taylor, C., Haskell, W., & DeBusk, R. (1990). Identifying strategies for increasing employee physical activity levels: Findings from the Stanford/Lockheed Exercise Survey. *Health Education Quarterly, 17,* 269-285.

Kirk, D. (1992). *Defining physical education*. Lewes, UK: Falmer Press.

Kirshenbaum, J., & Sullivan, R. (1983). Hold on there, America. *Sports Illustrated, 58*, 60-74.

Kizer, K., Pelletier, K., & Fielding, J. (1995). Work-site health promotion programs and health care reform. *Western Journal of Medicine, 162*, 467-469.

Klitzner, M. (1993). *Final evaluation report on the planning phase of fighting back: Community initiatives to reduce the demand for illegal drugs and alcohol*. Rockville, MD: Pacific Institute for Research and Evaluation.

Knight, J. (1992). *Institutions and social conflict*. Cambridge, MA: Cambridge University Press.

Knowles, J. (1977). The responsibility of the individual. *Daedalus, 106, 57-80*.

Kolata, G. (1993, May 3). Family aid to elderly is very strong, study shows. *New York Times*, p. A16.

Kottke, T., Brekke, M., & Solberg, L. (1993). Making "time" for preventive services. *Mayo Clinic Proceedings, 68*, 785-791.

Kraus, H., & Hirschland, R. (1953). Muscular fitness and health. *Journal of Health, Physical Education, Recreation and Dance, 24*, 17-19.

Kreuter, M., Scharff, D., & Brennan, L. (1997). Physician recommendations for diet and physical activity: Which patients get advised to change? *Preventive Medicine, 26*, 825-833.

Krieger, N. (1994). Epidemiology and the web of causation: Has anyone seen the spider? *Social Science and Medicine, 39*, 887-903.

Krieger, N. (1999). Embodying inequality: A review of concepts, measures, and methods for studying health consequences of discrimination. *International Journal of Health Services, 29*, 295-352.

Krieger, N., & Sidney, S. (1996). Racial discrimination and blood pressure: The CARDIA study of young black and white adults. *American Journal of Public Health, 86*, 1370-1378.

Kulinna, P., & Silverman, S. (2000). Teachers' attitudes toward teaching physical activity and fitness. *Research Quarterly for Exercise and Sport, 71*, 80-84.

Kurdek, L., & Schmitt, J. (1987). Perceived emotional support from family and friends in members of homosexual, married, and heterosexual cohabiting couples. *Journal of Homosexuality, 14*, 57-68.

Lalonde, M. (1974). *A new perspective on the health of Canadians*. Ottawa: Government of Canada.

Lapidus, L., & Bengtsson, C. (1986). Socioeconomic factors and physical activity in relation to cardiovascular disease and death: A 12-year follow-up of participants in a population study of women in Gothenburg, Sweden. *British Heart Journal, 55*, 295.

Larson, R., Gillman, S., & Richards, M. (1997). Divergent experiences of family leisure: Fathers, mothers, and young adolescents. *Journal of Leisure Research, 29*, 78-97.

Lasby, C. (1997). *Eisenhower's heart attack: How Ike beat heart disease and held on to the presidency*. Lawrence, KS: University of Kansas Press.

Lawson, H. (1992). Toward a socioecological conception of health. *Quest, 44,* 105-121.

Lawson, H. (1993). School reform, families, and health in the emergent national agenda for economic and social improvement: Implications. *Quest, 45,* 289-307.

Lawson, H. (1997). Children in crisis, the helping professions, and the social responsibilities of universities. *Quest, 49,* 8-33.

Lawson, H. (1998). Rejuvenating, reconstituting, and transforming physical education to meet the needs of vulnerable children, youth, and families. *Journal of Teaching in Physical Education, 18,* 2-25.

Lee, C., Duxbury, L., & Higgins, C. (1994). *Employed mothers: Balancing work and family life.* Ottawa: Canadian Centre for Management Development.

Leibowitz, J. (1970). *The history of coronary heart disease.* Berkeley: University of California Press.

Leichter, H. (1991). *Free to be foolish.* Princeton, NJ: Princeton University Press.

Leon, A., & Connett, J. (1991). Physical activity and 10.5 year mortality in the Multiple Risk Factor Intervention Trial (MRFIT). *International Journal of Epidemiology, 20,* 690-697.

Lewis, C., Raczynski, J., Heath, G., Levinson, R., Hilyer, J., & Cutter, G. (1993). Promoting physical activity in low-income African-American communities: The PARR project. *Ethnicity and Disease, 3,* 106-118.

Lewis, D., & Weigert, A. (1985). Trust as a social reality. *Social Forces, 63,* 967-985.

Lieberson, S. (1985) Making it count: The improvement of social research and theory. Berkeley: University of California Press.

Lindquist, C., Reynolds, K., & Goran, M. (1999). Socio-cultural determinants of physical activity among children. *Preventive Medicine, 29,* 305-312.

Little, J. (1990). The persistence of privacy: Autonomy and initiative in teachers' professional relations. *Teachers College Record, 91,* 508-536.

Littler, G, & Tobin, J. (1976) *The real score.* Waco, TX: Word.

Lobo, F. (1996). Coping with bulk unobligated time: The case of unemployment. *Society and Leisure, 19,* 377-413.

Logsdon, D., Lazaro, C., & Meier, R. (1989). The feasibility of behavioral risk reduction in primary medical care. *American Journal of Preventive Medicine, 5,* 249-256.

Lott-Whitehead, L., & Tully, C. (1999). The family lives of lesbian mothers. In J. Laird (Ed.), *Lesbians and lesbian families* (pp. 243-259). New York: Columbia University Press.

Luhmann, N. (1970). *Trust and power.* New York: Wiley.

Luke, M., & Sinclair, G. (1991). Gender differences in adolescents' attitudes toward school physical education. *Journal of Teaching in Physical Education, 11,* 31-46.

Maddox, J. (1997). Habit, health, and happiness. *Journal of Sport and Exercise Psychology, 19,* 331-346.

Maddox, N. (1999). *Why invest in disease prevention? Results from the William M. Mercer survey of employer sponsored health plans.* Washington, DC: Partnership for Prevention.

Madlon-Kay, D., Harper, P., & Reif, C. (1994). Health promotion counseling in residency training. *Journal of General Internal Medicine, 9,* 465-467.

Magnusson, M., Pope, M., Wilder, D., & Areskoug, B. (1996). Are occupational drivers at an increased risk for developing musculoskeletal disorders? *Spine, 21,* 710-717.

Maguire, J. (1991). Human sciences, sport sciences, and the need to study people in the round. *Quest, 43,* 190-206.

Mancini, J., & Blieszner, R. (1994). Coping with aging. In P. McKenry & S. Price (Eds.), *Families and change: Coping with stressful events* (pp. 111-125). Thousand Oaks, CA: Sage.

Manning, W., & Smock, P. (1997). Children's living arrangements in unmarried-mother families. *Journal of Family Issues, 18,* 526-544.

Marcus, B., & Forsyth, L. (1999). How are we doing with physical activity? *American Journal of Health Promotion, 14,* 118-124.

Marcus, B., Owen, N., Forsyth, L., Cavill, N., & Fridinger, F. (1998). Physical activity interventions using mass media, print media, and information technology. *American Journal of Preventive Medicine, 15,* 362-379.

Marmot, M., Rose, G., Shipley, M., & Hamilton, P. (1978). Employment grade and coronary heart disease in British civil servants. *Journal of Epidemiology Community Health, 3,* 244-249.

Martens, R. (1996). Turning kids on to physical activity for a lifetime. *Quest, 48,* 303-310.

Martin, J., Dubbert, M., Katell, A., Thompson, J., Raczynski, J., Lake, M., Smith, P., Webster, J., Sikora, T., & Cohen, R. (1984). Behavioral control of exercise in sedentary adults: Studies 1 through 6. *Journal of Consulting and Clinical Psychology, 52,* 798-811.

Martinek, T., & Hellison, D. (1997). Fostering resiliency in underserved youth through physical activity. *Quest, 49,* 34-49.

Marx, K. (1986). A preface to a critique of political economy. In J. Elster (Ed.), *Karl Marx: A reader.* Cambridge, MA: Cambridge University Press.

Mathews, W., Booth, M., & Turner, J. (1986). Physicians' attitudes toward homosexuality: A survey of a California medical society. *Western Journal of Medicine, 144,* 106-110.

McAuley, E., & Blissmer, B. (1999). Self-efficacy determinants and consequences of physical activity. *Exercise and Sport Sciences Review, 28,* 85-88.

McElroy, M. (1991). Athletes displaying their lives: The emergence of the contemporary sports autobiography. In W. Umphlett (Ed.), *The achievement of American sport literature* (pp. 165-183). Rutherford, NJ: Associated University Presses.

McElroy, M. (2001). Work-family spillover and participation in physical activity. Unpublished paper.

McGinnis, J. (1993). 1992 national survey of worksite health promotion activities: Summary. *American Journal of Health Promotion, 7,* 452-464.

McGinnis, M., & Griffith, H. (1996). Put prevention into practice: A systematic approach to the delivery of clinical preventive services. *Archives of Internal Medicine, 156,* 130-133.

McInerney, W. (1989). Social and organizational effects of educational computing. *Journal of Educational Computing Research, 5,* 487-506.

McKenzie, T., Faucette, F., Sallis, J., Roby, J., & Kolody, B. (1997). Effects of a curriculum and in-service program on the quantity and quality of elementary physical education classes. *Research Quarterly for Exercise and Sport, 64,* 178-187.

McKenzie, T., Feldman, H., Woods, S., Romero, K., Dahlstrom, V., Stone, E., Strikmiller, P., Williston, J., & Harsha, D. (1995). Student activity levels and lesson context during third-grade physical education. *Research Quarterly for Exercise and Sport, 66,* 184-193.

McKenzie, T., Marshall, S., Sallis, J., & Conway, T. (2000). Leisure-time physical activity in school environments: An observational study using SOPLAY. *Preventive Medicine, 30,* 70-77.

McKenzie, T., Nader, P., Strikmiller, P., Yang, M., Sone, E., Perry, C., Taylor, W., Epping, J., Feldman, H., Luepker, R., & Kelder, S. (1996). School physical education: Effect of the child and adolescent trial for cardiovascular health. *Preventive Medicine, 25,* 423-431.

McKenzie, T., Sallis, J., Elder, J., Berry, C., Hoy, P., Nader, P., Zive, M., & Broyles, S. (1997). Physical activity levels and prompts in young children at recess: A two-year study of a bi-ethnic sample. *Research Quarterly for Exercise and Sport, 68,* 195-202.

McKenzie, T., Sallis, J., Nader, P., Broyles, S., & Nelson, J. (1992). Anglo- and Mexican-American preschoolers at home and at recess: Activity patterns and environmental influences. *Developmental and Behavioral Pediatrics, 13,* 173-180.

McLeroy, K., Bibeau, D., Steckler, A., & Glanz, K. (1988). An ecological perspective on health promotion programs. *Health Education Quarterly, 15,* 351-377.

McMillan, D., & Chavis, D. (1986). Sense of community: A definition and theory. *Journal of Community Psychology, 14,* 6-23.

McMillen, M., Kaufman, P., & Klein, S. (1997). *Dropout rates in the United States, 1995.* Washington, DC: U.S. Government Printing Office.

Meaning of Work International Research Team. (1987). *The meaning of work.* New York: Academic Press.

Mechanic, D. (1995). Sociological dimensions of illness behavior. *Social Science and Medicine, 41,* 1207-1216.

Mein, S., & Winkleby, M. (1998). Concerns and misconceptions about cardiovascular disease risk factors: A focus group evaluation with low-income Hispanic women. *Hispanic Journal of Behavioral Sciences, 20,* 192-211.

Merry, U. (1995). *Coping with uncertainty.* Westport, CT: Praeger.

Messner, M. (1992). *Power at play and the problem of masculinity.* Boston: Beacon Press.

Mill, J. (1939). On liberty. In E. Burtt (Ed.), *The English philosophers from Bacon to Mill.* New York: Modern Library.

Miller, D., & Allen, T. (1994). *Fitness: A lifetime commitment.* Minneapolis: Burgess.

Mills, C. (1959). *The sociological imagination.* New York: Oxford University Press.

Milo, N. (1988). The profitization of health promotion. *International Journal of Health Services, 18,* 573-585.

Minkler, M. (1997). Introduction and overview. In M. Minkler (Ed.), *Community organizing and community building for health* (p. 6). New Brunswick, NJ: Rutgers University Press.

Minkler, M. (2000). Personal responsibility for health: Contexts and controversies. In D. Callahan (Ed.), *Promoting healthy behavior: How much freedom? Whose responsibility?* Washington, DC: Georgetown University Press.

Miracle, A., & Rees, R. (1994). *Lessons of the locker room: The myth of school sports.* Amherst, NY: Prometheus Books.

Mirowsky, J., & Ross, C. (1989). *Social causes of psychological distress.* New York: Aldine de Gruyter.

Mirvis, P., & Kanter, D. (1992). Beyond demographics: A psycho-graphic profile of the workforce. *Human Resource Management, 30,* 45-68.

Misztal, B.A. (1996). *Trust in modern societies.* Cambridge, UK: Polity Press.

Mittelmark, M., Hunt, M., Heath, G., & Schmid, T. (1993, winter). Realistic outcomes: Lessons from community-based research and demonstration programs for the prevention of cardiovascular diseases. *Journal of Public Health Policy, 14,* 436-462.

Mokdad, A., Serdula, M., & Dietz, W. (1998). The spread of the obesity epidemic in the U.S., 1991-1998. *Journal of the American Medical Association, 282,* 1519-1522.

Mokdad, A., Ford, E., Bowman, B., Nelson, D., Engelau, N., Vinicor, F., & Marks, J. (2000). Diabetes trends in the U.S.: 1990-1998. *Diabetes Care, 23,* 1278-1283.

Mooney, V., Kenny, K., & Leggett, S. (1996). Relationship of lumbar strength in shipyard workers to workplace injury claims. *Spine, 21,* 2001-2005.

Moore, L., Lombardi, D., White, M., Campbell, J., Oliveria, S., & Ellison, C. (1991). Influence of parents' physical activity levels on activity levels of young children. *Journal of Pediatrics, 118,* 215-219.

Morgan, W. (1986). Athletes and non-athletes in the middle years of life. In B. McPherson (Ed.), *Sport and aging* (pp. 167-186). Champaign, IL: Human Kinetics.

Morris, J., Heady, J., Raffle, P., Roberts, C., & Parks, J. (1953). Coronary heart disease and physical activity at work. *Lancet, 2,* 1053-1057, 1111-1120.

Morris, W., Conrad, K., Marcantonio, R., Marks, B., Ribisl, K. (1999). Do blue-collar workers perceive the worksite health climate differently than white-collar workers? *American Journal of Health Promotion, 13,* 319-324.

Morrison, J., Sprecher, D., McMahon, R., Simon, J., Schreiber, G., & Khoury, P. (1996). Obesity and high density lipoprotein cholesterol in black and white 9- and 10-year-old girls: The National Heart, Lung and Blood Institute Growth Study. *Metabolism, 45,* 469-474.

Moskowitz, D. (1999). The bucks behind the wellness boom. *Business and Health, 17,* 43-45.

Mothers Against Drunk Driving. (2000). MADD announces campaign against high risk drivers. *Alcoholism and Drug Abuse Weekly, 12,* 5-7.

Mrozek, D. (1987). The scientific quest for physical culture and the persistent appeal of quackery. *Journal of Sport History, 14*, 76-86.

Mudrack, P. (1992). "Work" or "leisure"? The Protestant work ethic and participation in an employee fitness program. *Journal of Organizational Behavior, 13*, 81-88.

Mulcahy, C. (1994). Working against the odds: Josephine Roche, the New Deal, and the drive for national health insurance. *Bulletin of the History of Medicine, 25*, 1-21.

Nader, P., Sallis, J., Patterson, T., Abramson, I., Rupp, J., Senn, K., Atkins, C., Roppe, B., Morris, J., Wallace, J., & Vega, W. (1989). A family approach to cardiovascular risk reduction: Results from the San Diego Family Health Project. *Health Education Quarterly, 16*, 229-244.

National Association for Sport and Physical Education. (1993). *Shape of the nation: A survey of state physical education requirements.* Reston, VA: American Alliance for Health, Physical Education, Recreation and Dance.

National Association for Sport and Physical Education. (1997). *Shape of the nation, 1997.* Reston, VA: American Alliance for Health, Physical Education, Recreation and Dance.

National Association for Sport and Physical Education. (1998). Physical activity for young people. *President's Council on Physical Fitness and Sports Research Digest, 3*, 1-7.

National Center for Health Statistics. (1991). New from NCHS. *American Journal of Public Health, 81*, 1526-1528.

National Center for Health Statistics. (1996). *Healthy people 2000 midcourse review and 1995 revisions.* Hyattsville, MD: Public Health Service.

National Commission of Excellence in Education. (1983). *A nation at risk: The imperative for educational reform.* Washington, DC: U.S. Government Printing Office.

National Commission on Working Women. (1990). *Women and work.* Washington, DC: National Commission on Working Women.

National Family Caregivers Association. (1997). Retrieved from the World Wide Web: http://www.nfcacares.org.

National Heart, Lung and Blood Institute. (1995). *Report of the conference on socioeconomic status and cardiovascular health and disease.* Bethesda, MD: U.S. Department of Health and Human Services.

National Institutes of Health Consensus Development Panel on Physical Activity and Cardiovascular Health. (1996). Consensus development conference statement to physical activity and cardiovascular health. *Journal of the American Medical Association, 276*, 241-246.

Navarro, V. (1993). *Dangerous to your health: Capitalism in health care.* New York: Monthly Review Press.

Nee, V. (1998). Sources of the new institutionalism. In M. Brinton & V. Nee (Eds.), *The new institutionalism in sociology* (pp. 1-16). New York: Russell Sage Foundation.

Nordhaus-Bike, A. (1997). Raising the bar: If employees join the fitness programs. *Hospitals and Health Networks, 71*, 80-81.

O'Brien Cousins, S. (2000). "My heart couldn't take it": Older women's beliefs about exercise benefits and risks. *Journal of Gerontology, 55*, 238-294.

O'Brien Cousins, S., & Keating, N. (1995). Life cycle patterns of physical activity among sedentary and active older women. *Journal of Aging and Physical Activity, 3*, 340-359.

O'Campo, P., & Rojas-Smith, L. (1998). Welfare reform and women's health: Review of the literature and implications for state policy. *Journal of Public Health Policy, 19*, 420-446.

O'Donnell, M., & Ainsworth, T. (1984). *Health promotion in the workplace.* New York: Wiley.

O'Hare, T., Williams, C., & Ezoviski, A. (1996). Fear of AIDS and homophobia: Implications for direct practice and advocacy. *Social Work, 41*, 51-58.

O'Neil, E. (1995). *Critical challenges: Revitalizing the health professions for the twenty-first century.* San Franciso: Pew Health Professions Commission.

O'Reilly, J., & Fagan, C. (1998). *Part-time prospects: An international comparison of part-time work in Europe, North America and the Pacific Rim.* London: Routledge.

O'Sullivan, M. (1989). Failing gym is like failing lunch or recess: Two beginning teachers' struggle for legitimacy. *Journal of Teaching in Physical Education, 8*, 227-242.

Oldridge, N., & Streiner, D. (1990). The health belief model: Predicting compliance and dropout in cardiac rehabilitation. *Medicine and Science in Sports and Exercise, 22*, 678-683.

Osler, W. (1910). The Lumleian lectures on angina pectoris, lecture I. *Lancet, 1*, 697-702, 839-844, 973-977.

Pacific Mutual Life Insurance. (1978). *Health maintenance.* San Francisco: Pacific Mutual Life Insurance.

Paffenbarger, R., Hyde, R., Wing, A., & Hsieh, C. (1986). Physical activity, all-cause mortality, and longevity of college alumni. *New England Journal of Medicine, 314*, 605-613.

Paffenbarger, R., Hyde, R., Wing, A., & Steinmetz, C. (1984). A natural history of athleticism and cardiovascular health. *Journal of the American Medical Association, 252*, 491-495.

Paffenbarger, R., Wing, A., & Hyde, R. (1978). Chronic disease in former college students: Physical activity as an index of heart attack risk in college alumni. *American Journal of Epidemiology, 117*, 161-175.

Panel on High Risk Youth. (1993). *Losing generations: Adolescents in high-risk settings.* Washington, DC: National Academy Press.

Pangrazi, R., & Darst, P. (1991). *Dynamic physical education for secondary school students: Curriculum and instruction.* New York: Macmillan.

Parcel, G., Simons-Morton, B., & O'Hara, N. (1987). School promotion of healthful diet and exercise behavior: An integration of organizational change and social learning theory interventions. *Journal of School Health, 57*, 150-156.

Park, R. (1997). High-protein diets, "damaged hearts," and rowing men: Antecedents of modern sports medicine and exercise science, 1867-1928. *Exercise and Sport Sciences Review, 25*, 137-169.

Parsons, T. (1951). *The social system.* New York: Free Press.

Pate, R., Pratt, M., Blair, S., Haskell, W., et al. (1995). Physical activity and public health. A recommendation from the Centers for Disease Control and Prevention and the American College of Sports Medicine. *Journal of the American Medical Association, 273,* 402-407.

Pate, R., Small, M., Ross, J., Young, J., Flint, K., & Warren, C. (1995). School physical education. *Journal of School Health, 65,* 312-318.

Patterson, J., Garwick, A., Bennett, F., & Blum, R. (1997). Social support in families of children with chronic conditions: Supportive and non-supportive behaviors. *Developmental and Behavioral Pediatrics, 18,* 383-391.

Paul, J. (1983). The health reformers: George Barker Windship and Boston's strength seekers. *Journal of Sport History, 10,* 41-57.

Paxton, P. (1999). Is social capital declining in the United States? A multiple indicator assessment. *American Journal of Sociology, 105,* 88-127.

Pearlin, L., Mullan, J., Semple, S., & Skaff, M. (1990). Caregiving and the stress process: An overview of concepts and their measures. *Gerontologist, 30,* 583-593.

Pechter, K. (1986). Corporate fitness and blue collar fears. *Across the Board, 23,* 14-21.

Pelletier, K. (1993). A review and analysis of the health and cost-effective outcome studies of comprehensive health promotion and disease prevention programs at the worksite: 1991-1993 update. *American Journal of Health Promotion, 8,* 50-62.

Pencak, M. (1991). Workplace health promotion programs: An overview. *Nursing Clinics of North America, 26,* 233-240.

Pew Health Professions Commission. (1995). *Critical challenges: Revitalizing the health professions for the twenty-first century.* San Francisco: Pew Health Professions Commission.

Pew Health Professions Commission. (1998). *Recreating health professional practice for a new century.* San Francisco: Pew Health Professions Commission.

Pitter, R., & Andrews, D. (1997). Serving America's underserved youth: Reflections on sport and recreation in an emerging social problems industry. *Quest, 49,* 85-98.

Poduri, A., & Grisso, J. (1998). Cardiovascular risk factors in economically disadvantaged women: A study of prevalence and awareness. *Journal of the National Medical Association, 90,* 531-536.

Popewitz, T., & Myrdal, S. (1991). *Case studies of the urban mathematics collaborative project. A report to the Ford Foundation.* Madison, Wisconsin, School of Education, Wisconsin Center for Education Research (ED343810).

Poponoe, D. (1988). *Disturbing the nest: Family change and decline in modern societies.* New York: Aldine de Gruyter.

Porter, D. (1999). *Health, civilization and the state.* London: Routledge.

Portman, P. (1995). Who is having fun in physical education classes? Experiences of sixth-grade students in elementary and middle schools. *Journal of Teaching in Physical Education. 14,* 445-454.

Powell, K., & Blair, S. (1994). The public health burdens of sedentary living habits: Theoretical but realistic estimates. *Medicine and Science in Sports and Exercise, 26,* 851-856.

Powell, K., & Dysinger, W. (1987). Childhood participation in organized school sports and physical education as precursors of adult physical activity. *American Journal of Preventive Medicine, 3,* 276-281.

President's Council on Physical Fitness. (1998). *American attitudes toward physical activity and fitness.* Washington, DC: President's Council on Physical Fitness.

Presley, J. (1991). *A history of diabetes mellitus in the United States, 1880-1990.* Unpublished dissertation, University of Texas, Austin.

Priester, R. (1992). Are financial incentives for wellness fair? *Employee Benefits Journal, 17,* 38-40.

Prochaska, J., & DiClemente, C. (1983). States and processes of self change in smoking: Towards an integrative model of change. *Journal of Consulting and Clinical Psychology, 51,* 390-395.

Prochaska, J., & DiClemente, C. (1984). *The transtheoretical approach: Crossing traditional boundaries of change.* Homewood, IL: Dorsey Press.

Pronger, B. (1990). *The arena of masculinity: Sports, homosexuality, and the meaning of sex.* New York: St. Martin's Press.

Pultorak, E. (1994, March). Teacher assessment: A dimensional change. *Journal of Physical Education, Recreation and Dance,* pp. 70-73.

Putnam, R. (1995). Bowling alone: America's declining social capital. *Journal of Democracy, 6,* 65-78.

Putnam, R. (1996). The strange disappearance of civic America. *American Prospect, 24,* 34-48.

Putnam, R. (2000). *Bowling alone: The collapse and revival of American community.* New York: Simon and Schuster.

Quality Counts. (1998). The urban challenge. Retrieved from the World Wide Web: http://www.edweek.com/sreports.

Raber, M., & Richter, J. (1999). Bringing social action back into the social work curriculum: A model for "hands-on" learning. *Journal of Teaching Social Work, 19,* 77-91.

Rader, B. (1991). The quest for self-sufficiency and the new strenuosity: Reflections on the strenuous life of the 1970s and the 1980s. *Journal of Sport History, 18,* 255-266.

Radley, A. (1989). Style, discourse and constraint in adjustment to chronic illness. *Sociology of Health and Illness, 11,* 230-252.

Rahim, M., & Marriner, R. (1997). Students' attitudes toward physical activity: Specialist versus nonspecialist. *Alberta Journal of Educational Research, 43,* 161-164.

Randall, C. (1989). Lesbian phobia among BSN educators: A survey. *Journal of Nursing Education, 28,* 302-306.

Reardon, J. (1998). The history and impact of worksite wellness. *Nursing Economics, 16,* 117-123.

Reiser, S. (1978). The emergence of the concept of screening for disease. *Milbank Memorial Fund Quarterly, 56,* 403-425.

Reiser, S. (1985). Responsibility for personal health: A historical perspective. *Journal of Medicine and Philosophy, 10,* 7-17.

Remington, R. (1988). *The future of public health*. Washington, DC: National Academy Press.

Richardson, B. (1895). Cycling and heart disease. *Medical Society Transactions, 18*, 98-99.

Roberts, K., Lamb, K., Dench, S., & Brodie, D. (1989). Leisure patterns, health status and employment status. *Leisure Studies, 8*, 229-235.

Robertson, B. (1999). Leisure and family: Perspectives of male adolescents who engage in delinquent activity as leisure. *Journal of Leisure Research, 31*, 335-358.

Robinson, D. (1990). An attributional analysis of student demoralization in physical education settings. *Quest, 42*, 27-39.

Robinson, J., & Godbey, G. (1997). *Time for life: The surprising ways Americans use their time*. University Park: Penn State University Press.

Roe, K., & Minkler, M. (1998/1999). Grandparents raising grandchildren: Challenges and responses. *Generations, 22*, 25-32.

Rogers, N. (1997). Centrality of caregiving roles and integration of leisure in everyday life: Naturalistic study of older wife caregivers. *Therapeutic Recreation Journal, 31*, 230-243.

Rose, M., & Robbins, B. (1993). Psychosocial recovery issues and strategies in cardiac rehabilitation. In F. Pashkow & W.A. Dafoe (Eds.), *Clinical cardiac rehabilitation: A cardiologist's guide* (pp. 248-261). Baltimore: Williams and Wilkins.

Rose, S. (1990). Advocacy/empowerment: An approach to clinical practical social work. *Journal of Sociology and Social Welfare, 17*, 41-51.

Rosin, H. (1999, December 21). Same-sex couples win rights in Vermont. *Washington Post*, p. A1.

Ross, C. (1993). Fear of victimization. *Journal of Quantitative Criminology, 9*, 159-175.

Ross, C. (2000). Walking, exercise, and smoking: Does neighborhood matter? *Social Science and Medicine, 51*, 265-274.

Ross, J., & Gilbert, G. (1985). The national children and youth fitness study: A summary of findings. *Journal of Physical Education, Recreation and Dance, 56*, 45-50.

Ross, J., Pate, R., Caspersen, C., Damberg, C., & Svilar, M. (1987). The National Children and Youth Fitness Study II: Home and community in children's exercise habits. *Journal of Physical Education, Recreation and Dance 58*, 85-92.

Rovner, J. (1997). The uninsured: An American time bomb. *Business and Health, 15*, 55-59.

Rudman, W. (1988). Sport and exercise in work culture. *Fitness in Business, 2*, 220-226.

Rudy, E., & Estok, P. (1990). Running addiction and dyadic adjustment. *Research in Nursing and Health, 13*, 219-225.

Russell, W., Dzewaltowski, D., & Ryan, G. (1999). The effectiveness of a point-of-decision prompt in deterring sedentary behavior. *American Journal of Health Promotion, 13*, 257-259.

Ryan, W. (1976). *Blaming the victim*. New York: Vintage Books.

Sacks, M. (1981). Running addiction: A clinical report. In M. Sacks & M. Sachs (Eds.). *Psychology of running.* Champaign, IL: Human Kinetics.

Sallis, J., Bauman, A., & Pratt, M. (1998). Environmental and policy interventions to promote physical activity. *American Journal of Preventive Medicine, 15,* 379-397.

Sallis, J., Hovell, M., Hofstetter, C., Elder, J., Faucher, P., Spry, V., Barrington, E., & Hackley, M. (1990a). Lifetime history of relapse from exercise. *Addictive Behaviors, 15,* 573-579.

Sallis, J., Hovell, M., Hofstetter, C., Elder, J., Hackley, M., Caspersen, C., & Powell, K. (1990b). Distance between homes and exercise facilities related to frequency of exercise among San Diego residents. *Public Health Reports, 105,* 179-185.

Sallis, J., Hovell, M., Hofstetter, C., Faucher, P., Elder, J., Blanchard, J., Caspersen, C., Powell, K., & Christenson, G. (1989). A multivariate study of determinants of vigorous exercise in a community sample. *Preventive Medicine, 18,* 20-34.

Sallis, J., & McKenzie, T. (1991). Physical education's role in public health. *Research Quarterly for Exercise and Sport, 62,* 124-137.

Sallis, J., McKenzie, T., Alcaraz, J., Kolody, B., Faucette, N., & Hovell, M. (1997). Effects of a two-year health-related physical education program on physical activity and fitness in elementary school students: SPARK. *American Journal of Public Health, 87,* 1328-1334.

Sallis, J., McKenzie, T., Elder, J., Broyles, S., & Nader, P. (1997). Factors parents use in selecting play spaces for young children. *Archives of Pediatric Adolescent Medicine, 151,* 414-417.

Sallis, J., McKenzie, T., Kolody, B., & Curtis, P. (1996). Assessing district administrators' perceptions of elementary school physical education. *Journal of Health, Physical Education and Dance, 67,* 25-29.

Samuels, S. (1990). Project LEAN: A national campaign to reduce dietary fat consumption. *American Journal of Health Promotion, 4,* 435-440.

Sarason, S. (1990). *The predictable failure of educational reform.* San Francisco: Jossey-Bass.

Scantling, E. (1995). An analysis of physical education avoidance. *Physical Educator, 52,* 197-202.

Schatz, B., & O'Hanlan, K. (1994). *Anti-gay discrimination in medicine: Results of a national survey of lesbian, gay and bisexual physicians.* San Francisco: American Association of Physicians for Human Rights.

Schauffler, H. (1993). Disease prevention policy under Medicare: A historical and political analysis. *American Journal of Preventive Medicine, 9,* 71-77.

Schauffler, H., & Chapman, S. (1998). Health promotion and managed care: Surveys of California's health plans and population. *American Journal of Preventive Medicine, 14,* 161-167.

Schenk, J., & Lewis, C. (1999). Credentialing: A paradox for the 21st century. *Nursing Leadership Forum, 4,* 14-17.

Schlechty, P. (1997). *Inventing better schools: An action plan for educational reform.* San Francisco: Jossey-Bass.

Schor, J. (1991). *The overworked American.* New York: Basic Books.

Schwartz, J., & Cohen, S. (1990). Changing physician behavior. In J. Mayfield & M. Grady (Eds.), *Conference proceedings, primary care research: An agenda for the 90s.* Washington, DC: U.S. Department of Health and Human Services.

Scutchfield, F. (1989). Point–counterpoint: The public health versus medical model of prevention. *American Journal of Preventive Medicine, 5,* 113-119.

Searle, M., & Jackson, E. (1985). Socioeconomic variations in perceived barriers to recreation participation among would-be participants. *Leisure Sciences, 7,* 227-249.

Shephard, R. (1994). Work-site exercise, physical fitness, and lost workdays. *Medicine, Exercise, Nutrition and Health, 3,* 268-284.

Shephard, R. (1996). Worksite fitness and exercise programs: A review of methodology and health impact. *American Journal of Health Promotion, 10,* 436-452.

Shepherd, G. (1998). Health care costs rise 4.8% in 1997. *Tampa Bay Business Journal, 18,* 4.

Shor, I. (1992). *Empowering education: Critical teaching for social change.* Chicago: University of Chicago Press.

Siedentop, D. (1998). *Introduction to physical education, fitness, and sport.* Mountain View, CA: Mayfield.

Siegrist, J. (1996). Adverse health effects of high-effort/low-reward conditions. *Journal of Occupational Health Psychology, 1,* 27-41.

Siever, M. (1994). Sexual orientation and gender as factors in socioculturally acquired vulnerability to body dissatisfaction and eating disorders. *Journal of Consulting and Clinical Psychology, 62,* 252-260.

Simkin, L., & Gross, A. (1994). Assessment of coping with high-risk situations for exercise relapse among healthy women. *Health Psychology, 13,* 274-277.

Simmel, G. (1964). *The sociology of Georg Simmel.* (K. Wolff, Trans.). New York: Free Press.

Simons-Morton, B., & Small, M. (1999). School physical education: Secondary analysis of the school health policies and programs study. *Journal of Health Education, 30,* S21-S27.

Simons-Morton, B., O'Hara, N., & Parcel, G. (1987). Children and fitness: A public health perspective. *Research Quarterly for Exercise and Sport, 58,* 295-302.

Simons-Morton, B., Taylor, W., Snider, S., & Huang, I. (1993). The physical activity of fifth-grade students during physical education. *American Journal of Public Health, 83,* 262-265.

Sleap, M., & Waburton, P. (1992). Physical activity levels of 5- to 11-year-old children in England as determined by continuous observation. *Research Quarterly for Exercise and Sport, 63,* 238-245.

Sleeper, S., Wholey, D., Hamer, R., Schwartz, S., & Inoferio, V. (1998). Trust me: Technical and institutional determinants of health maintenance organizations shifting risk to physicians. *Journal of Health and Social Behavior, 39,* 189-200.

Smith, A. (1999). Perceptions of peer relationships and physical activity participation in early adolescence. *Journal of Sport and Exercise Psychology, 21,* 329-350.

Snijders, T., & Bosker, R. (1999). *Multilevel analysis: An introduction to basic and advanced multilevel modeling.* London: Sage.

Sotile, W. (1996). *Psychosocial interventions for cardiopulmonary patients.* Champaign, IL: Human Kinetics.

Speers, M., & Lancaster, B. (1998). Disease prevention and health promotion in urban areas: CDC's perspective. *Health Education and Behavior, 25,* 226-233.

Stacey, J. (1991). Backward toward the postmodern family: Reflections on gender, kinship, and class in the Silicon Valley. In A. Wolfe (Ed.), *America at century's end.* Berkeley: University of California Press.

Statistics Canada. (1990). *Women in Canada.* Ottawa: Government of Canada.

Steckler, A., & Goodman, R. (1989). How to institutionalize health promotion programs. *American Journal of Health Promotion, 3,* 34-44.

Steenland, K., Johnson, J., & Nowlin, S. (1997). A follow-up study of job strain and heart disease among males in the NHANES1 population. *American Journal of Industrial Medicine, 31,* 256-260.

Stephens, T. (1987). Secular trends in adult physical activity: Exercise boom or bust? *Research Quarterly for Exercise and Sport, 58,* 94-105.

Stephens, T., & Craig, C. (1990). *The well-being of Canadians: Highlights of the 1988 Campbell Survey.* Ottawa: Canadian Fitness and Lifestyle Research Institute.

Steuart, G. (1993). Social and behavioral changes strategies. *Health Education Quarterly, 1,* S113-S135.

Stevens, P & Hall, J. (1991). Critical, historical, analysis of the medical construction of lesbianism. *International Journal of Health Sciences, 2,* 291-307.

Stokols, D. (1992). Establishing and maintaining healthy environments. *American Psychologist, 47,* 6-22.

Stokols, D. (1996). Translating social ecological theory into guidelines for community health promotion. *American Journal of Health Promotion, 10,* 282-298.

Stokols, D., Pelletier, K., & Fielding, J. (1995). Integration of medical care and worksite health promotion. *Journal of the American Medical Association, 273,* 1136-1142.

Stokols, D., Pelletier, K., & Fielding, J. (1996). The ecology of work and health: Research and policy directions for the promotion of employee health. *Health Education Quarterly, 23,* 137-158.

Stone, A. (1982). *Regulation and its alternatives.* Washington, DC: Congressional Quarterly Press.

Stone, D. (1986). The resistible rise of preventive medicine. *Journal of Health Politics, Policy and Law, 11,* 671-695.

Suen, J., Christenson, G., Cooper, A., & Taylor, M. (1995). Analysis of the current status of public health practice in local health departments. *American Journal of Preventive Medicine, 11* (Suppl), 51-54.

Susser, M., & Susser, E. (1996). Choosing a future for epidemiology: II. From black box to Chinese boxes and eco-epidemiology. *American Journal of Public Health, 86,* 674-677.

Syme, S. & Balfour, J. (1998). Social determinants of disease. In Wallace, R. (Ed.). *Maxcy-Rosenau-Last Public Health and Preventive Medicine* (pp. 795-810). Stamford, CT: Appleton & Lange.

Taira, D., Safran, D., Seto, T., Rogers, W., & Tarlov, A. (1997). The relationship between patient income and physician discussion of health risk behaviors. *Journal of the American Medical Association, 278,* 1412-1417.

Tannehill, D., Romar, J., O'Sullivan, M., England, K., & Rosenberg, D. (1994). Attitudes toward physical education: Their impact on how physical education teachers make sense of their work. *Journal of Teaching Physical Education, 13,* 406-420.

Taylor, C., Bandura, A., & Ewart, C. (1985). Exercise testing to enhance wives' confidence in their husbands' cardial capacity soon after clinically uncomplicated acute myocardial infarction. *American Journal of Cardiology, 55,* 635-638.

Taylor, R. (2000, June 29). A friendly touch: The increase of women in the U.S. labour market has spurred a call for family oriented employee programmes. *London Times,* p 13.

Tesh, S. (1981). Disease causality and politics. *Journal of Health Politics and Law, 6,* 369-390.

Thomas, G., Lee, P., Franks, L., & Paffenbarger, R. (1981). *Exercise and health: The evidence and implications.* Cambridge, MA: Oelgeschlager, Gunn and Hain.

Thompson, B., Wallack, L., Lichenstein, E., & Pechacek, T. (1990-91). Principles of community organization and partnership for smoking cessation in the Community Intervention Trial for Smoking Cessation (COMMIT). *International Quarterly of Community Health Education, 11,* 187-203.

Thompson, D., & Fowler, B. (1976). *The diary of a major league shortstop.* Minneapolis, MN: Dillon.

Thompson, J. (1994). Social workers and politics beyond the Hatch Act. *Social Work, 39,* 457-465.

Thompson, P., Funk, E., & Carelton, R. (1982). Incidence of death during jogging in Rhode Island from 1975 through 1980. *Journal of American Medical Association, 247,* 2535-2569.

Thorpe, K. (1997). Incremental strategies for providing health insurance for the uninsured. *Journal of the American Medical Association, 278,* 329-333.

Tocqueville, A. de. (1835). *Democracy in America* (H. Reeve, Trans.; P. Bradley, Ed.). New York: Vantage Books. (Original work published 1835).

Toffler, A. (1980). *The third wave.* New York: William Morrow.

Toffler, A., & Toffler, H. (1995). *Creating a new civilization. The politics of the third wave.* Atlanta, GA: Turner.

Tonnies, F. (1957). *Community and society* (C. Loomis, Ed. and Trans.). East Lansing: Michigan State University Press. (Original work published as *Gemeinschaft und Gesellschaft,* 1877).

Troiano, R., & Flegal, K. (1998). Overweight children and adolescents: Description, epidemiology, and demographics. *Pediatrics, 101,* 497-505.

Trudeau, F., Laurencelle, L., & Shepard, R. (1999). Daily primary school physical education: Effects on physical activity during life. *Medicine and Science in Sports and Exercise, 31,* 111-117.

Tsouros, A. (1990). *World Health Organization Healthy Cities Project: A project becomes a movement.* Copenhagen: FADL.

Tudiver, F., Hilditch, J., & Permaul, J. (1992). Does mutual help facilitate newly bereaved widowers? *Evaluation and the Health Professions, 15,* 147-162.

Tumin, M. (1953). Some principles of stratification: A critical analysis. *American Sociological Review, 18,* 387-394.

U.S. Bureau of the Census. (1992a). *Poverty in the United States: 1991.* (Current Population Reports Series P-60, 181). Washington, DC: U.S. Government Printing Office.

U.S. Bureau of the Census. (1992b). *Statistical abstract of the United States.* Washington, DC: U.S. Department of Commerce.

U.S. Bureau of the Census. (1992c). *Statistical brief: Housing of single-parent families* (SB/91-15). Washington, DC: U.S. Dept. of Commerce, Economics and Statistics Administration.

U.S. Bureau of the Census. (2001). *Census 2000.* Retrieved from the World Wide Web: http://www.census.gov/dmd/www/2khome.htm.

U.S. Department of Health and Human Services. (1990). *Healthy people 2000: National health promotion and disease prevention objectives.* Washington, DC: U.S. Government Printing Office.

U.S. Department of Health and Human Services. (1994). *Preventing tobacco use among young people. A report of the surgeon general.* Atlanta, GA: U.S. Department of Health and Human Services.

U.S. Department of Health and Human Services. (1996a). *Consensus development conference statement on physical activity and cardiovascular health.* Bethesda, MD: U.S. Department of Health and Human Services.

U.S. Department of Health and Human Services. (1996b). *Physical activity and health: A report of the Surgeon General.* Atlanta, GA: Centers for Disease Control.

U.S. Department of Health and Human Services. (1997). *Guidelines for school and community programs to promote lifelong physical activity among young people.* Atlanta, GA: Centers for Disease Control.

U.S. Department of Health and Human Services. (1998). Youth risk behavior surveillance—US, 1997. *Morbidity and Mortality Weekly Report, 47,* 1-92.

U.S. Department of Health and Human Services. (1999a). *Promoting physical activity: A guide for community action.* Champaign, IL: Human Kinetics.

U.S. Department of Health and Human Services. (1999b). Neighborhood safety and the prevalence of physical inactivity, selected states, 1996. *Morbidity and Mortality Weekly Report, 48,* 143-146.

U.S. Department of Health and Human Services. (1999c). Physician advice and individual behaviors about cardiovascular disease risk reduction—seven states and Puerto Rico, 1997. *Morbidity and Mortality Weekly Report, 48,* 74-77.

U.S. Department of Health and Human Services. (1999d). *Youth Risk Behavior Surveillance System.* Washington, DC: U.S. Government Printing Office.

U.S. Department of Health and Human Services. (2000a). *Healthy people 2010.* Washington, DC: U.S. Government Printing Office.

U.S. Department of Health and Human Services. (2000b). Prevalence of leisure-time and occupational physical activity among employed adults, United States, 1990. *Morbidity and Mortality Weekly Report, 49,* 420-424.

U.S. Department of Health and Human Services. (2000c). Surveillance for characteristics of health education among secondary schools. School health education profiles, 1998. *Mortality and Morbidity Weekly Report, 49*, Part 8, 1-41.

U.S. Department of Health, Education, and Welfare. (1978). Exercise and participation in sports among persons twenty years of age and over: United States 1975. Washington, DC: Advance Data #19.

U.S. Department of Labor. (1993). *1993 handbook on women workers: Trends and issues.* Washington, DC: Washington Printing Office.

U.S. Department of Labor Commission on Family and Medical Leave. (1996). *A workable balance: Report to Congress on family and medical leave.* Washington, DC: U.S. Department of Labor.

U.S. National Health Survey. (1957-58). *Heart conditions and high blood pressure reported in interviews* (Series B-13). Washington, DC: U.S. Government Printing Office.

U.S. Preventive Services Task Force. (1996). *Guide to clinical preventive services.* Baltimore: Williams & Wilkins.

U.S. Public Health Service. (1980). *Promoting health/preventing disease: Objectives for the nation.* Washington, DC: Government Printing Office.

U.S. Public Health Service. (1979). *Healthy people: The Surgeon General's report on health promotion and disease prevention.* Washington, DC: Government Printing Office.

U.S. Public Health Service. (1980). *Promoting health/preventing disease: Objectives for the nation.* Washington, DC: U.S. Government Printing Office.

Uitenbroek, D. (1993). Relationship between changes in health and fitness and the perception of exercise. *Research Quarterly for Exercise and Sport, 64*, 343-347.

Umberson, D. (1992). Gender, marital status and the social control of health behavior. *Social Science and Medicine, 34*, 907-917.

Update: Prevalence of overweight among children, adolescents, and adults, United States, 1988-1994. (1997). *Morbidity and Mortality Weekly Report, 46*, 199-202.

Uusi-Rasi, K., Nugard, C., Oja, P., Pasanen, M., Sievanen, H., & Vuori, I. (1994). Walking at work and bone mineral density of premenopausal women. *Osteoporosis International, 4*, 336-340.

van Ryn, M., & Burke, J. (2000). The effect of patient race and socio-economic status on physicians' perceptions of patients. *Social Science and Medicine, 50*, 813-828.

Ventura, S., Martin, S., Curtin, S., & Mathews, T. (1999). Births: Final Data for 1997. *National Vital Statistics Reports, 47*(18).

Verbrugge, L. (1986). Role burdens and physical health of women and men. *Women and Health, 11*, 47-77.

Verhoef, M., & Love, E. (1992). Women's exercise participation: The relevance of social roles compared to non-role-related determinants. *Canadian Journal of Public Health, 83*, 367-370.

Verhoef, M., & Love, E. (1994). Women and exercise participation: The mixed blessings of motherhood. *Health Care for Women International, 15*, 297-306.

Vinick, B. (1983). *Loneliness among elderly widowers.* Paper presented at the annual meeting of the Gerontological Society of America, San Francisco, CA.

Wadsworth, M., Montgomery, S., & Barley, M. (1999). The persisting effect of unemployment on health and social well-being in men early in working life. *Social Science and Medicine, 48,* 1491-1499.

Waldon, I., & Jacobs, J. (1989). Effects of multiple roles on women's health: Evidence from a national longitudinal study. *Women and Health, 15,* 3-19.

Wallace, H., Green, G., & Jaros, K. (1999). *Health and welfare for families in the 21st century.* Sudbury, MA: Jones and Bartlett.

Wallack, L. (1994). Media advocacy: A strategy for empowering people and communities. *Journal of Public Health Policy, 15,* 420-436.

Wallack, L., Dorfman, L., & Jernigan, D. (1994). *Media advocacy and public health.* Newbury Park, CA: Sage.

Wallerstein, N., & Bernstein, E. (1988). Empowerment education: Freire's ideas adapted to health education. *Health Education Quarterly, 15,* 379-394.

Walz, T., & Gove, V. (1991). The mission of social work revisited: An agenda for the 1990s. *Social Work, 36,* 500-504.

Warr, P.B., Jackson, P., & Banks, M. (1988). Unemployment and mental health. *Journal of Social Issues, 44,* 47-68.

Watt, J. (1959). Exercise and heart disease: Related fields for research. In S. Staley (Ed.), *Exercise and fitness: A collection of papers presented at the Colloquium on Exercise and Fitness.* Champaign, IL: Athletic Institute.

Weed, L. (1997). New connections between medical knowledge and patient care. *British Medical Journal, 315,* 231-235.

Weiss, M., & Duncan, S. (1992). The relationship between physical competence and peer acceptance in the context of children's sports participation. *Journal of Sport and Exercise Psychology, 14,* 177-191.

Welch, B., & Vecsey, G. (1982). *Five o'clock comes early.* New York: Morrow.

Wells, K., Lewis, C., Leake, B., & Ware, J. (1984). Do physicians preach what they practice? *Journal of the American Medical Association, 252,* 2846-2848.

Weschler, H., Levine, S., Idelson, R., Rohman, M., & Taylor, J. (1983). The physician's role in health promotion: A survey of primary care physicians. *New England Journal of Medicine, 308,* 487-490.

Weschler, H., Levine, S., Idelson, R., Schor, E., & Coakley, E. (1996). The physician's role in health promotion revisited: A survey of primary care practitioners. *New England Journal of Medicine, 334,* 996-998.

White, K. (1999). No more monkey business. Education week on the Web. www.edweek.com.

White, P. (1947). *Heart disease.* New York: Macmillan.

White, P., Young, K., & Gillett, J. (1995). Bodywork as a moral imperative: Some critical notes on health and fitness. *Society and Leisure, 18,* 159-182.

Whorton, J. (1978). The hygiene of the wheel: An episode in Victorian sanitary science. *Bulletin of the History of Medicine, 52,* 61-88.

Whorton, J. (1982a). Athlete's heart: The medical debate over athleticism, 1870-1920. *Journal of Sport History, 9,* 30-52.

Whorton, J. (1982b). *Crusader's for fitness: The history of American health reformers.* Princeton, NJ: Princeton University Press.

Wickrama, K., Lorenz, F., & Conger, R. (1997). Marital quality and physical illness: A latent growth curve analysis. *Journal of Marriage and the Family, 59,* 143-155.

Wilbur, C. (1983). The Johnson & Johnson program. *Preventive Medicine, 12,* 672-681.

Wilbur, J., Naftzger-Kang, L., Miller, A., Chadler, P., & Montgomery, A. (1999). Women's occupations, energy expenditure, and cardiovascular risk factors. *Journal of Women's Health, 8,* 377-387.

Wilcox, R. (1987). The failing of high school physical education. *Journal of Physical Education, Recreation and Dance, 58,* 21-25.

Wiles, R. (1998). Patients' perceptions of their heart attack and recovery: The influence of epidemiological evidence and personal experience. *Social Science and Medicine, 46,* 1477-1486.

Wilkinson, R. (1996). *Unhealthy societies. The afflictions of inequality.* London: Routledge.

Wilkinson, R. (1997). Health inequalities: Relative or absolute material standards? *British Medical Journal, 314,* 591-595.

Williams, D. (1990). Socioeconomic differentials in health: A review and redirection. *Social Psychology Quarterly, 53,* 81-99.

Williams, D. (1999). Race, socioeconomic status, and health. The added effects of racism and discrimination. *Annals of the New York Academy of Sciences, 896,* 173-188.

Wilson, M. (1990). Factors associated with issues related to, and suggestions for increasing participation in workplace health promotion programs. *Health Values, 14,* 29-44.

Wilson, W. (1987). *The truly disadvantaged: The inner city, the underclass and public policy.* Chicago: University of Chicago Press.

Wilson, W. (1997). *When work disappears: The world of the new urban poor.* New York: Vintage Books.

Wirth, L. (1938). Urbanism as a way of life. *American Journal of Sociology, 40,* 1-24.

Wirth, L. (1970). Urbanism as a way of life. In R. Gutman, & D. Poponoe, D. (Eds.), *Neighborhood, city and metropolis* (pp. 54-68). New York: Random House. (Originally published in 1938).

Wise, D. (1995). Private matters. *Business & Health, 13,* 22-27.

Wolf, S., & Bruhn, J. (1993). *The power of clan.* New Brunswick, NJ: Transaction.

Wolfe, A. (1991). *America at century's end.* Berkeley: University of California Press.

Wong, J. (1998). FDR and the New Deal on sport and recreation. *Sport History Review, 29,* 173-191.

World Health Association. (1976). *Statistical indices of family health* (No. 589). New York: World Health Association.

World Health Organization. (1978). *Alma Alta 1978 primary health care*. Copenhagen: World Health Organization.

World Health Organization. (1985). *Health for all in Europe by the year 2000*. Copenhagen: World Health Organization.

World Health Organization. (1986). *Ottawa charter for health promotion: An international conference on health promotion*. Geneva: World Health Organization.

Wright, S. (1993). Blaming the victim, blaming society or blaming the discipline: Fixing responsibility for poverty and homelessness. *Sociological Quarterly, 34*, 1-16.

Wrist wrap. (1998). *U.S. News and World Report, 124*, 72.

Wuest, D., & Bucher, C. (1999). *Foundations of physical education and sport*. Boston: WCB/McGraw-Hill.

Yair, G. (1990). The commitments to long distance running and levels of activity: Personal or structural. *Journal of Leisure Research, 22*, 213-227.

Yang, A. (1998). *From wrongs to rights: Public opinion on gay and lesbian Americans moves toward equality*. New York: National Gay and Lesbian Task Force.

Yang, X., Telama, R., & Laakso, L. (1996). Parents' physical activity, socioeconomic status and education as predictors of physical activity and sport among children and youths: A 12-year follow-up study. *International Review for Sociology of Sport, 31*, 273-291.

Yen, I., & Kaplan, G. (1998). Poverty area residence and changes in physical activity level: Evidence from the Alameda County study. *American Journal of Public Health, 11*, 1709-1712.

Yen, I., & Syme, S. (1999). The social environment and health: A discussion of the epidemiologic literature. *Annual Review of Public Health, 20*, 287-308.

Ziegler, J. (1997). The worker's health: Whose business is it? *Business and Health, 15*, 26-30.

Ziff, M., Conrad, P., & Lachman, M. (1995). The relative effects of perceived personal control and responsibility on health and health-related behaviors in young and middle-aged adults. *Health Education Quarterly, 22*, 127-142.

Zijderveld, A. (2000). *The institutional imperative: The interface of institutions and networks*. Amsterdam: Amsterdam University Press.

Zimmerman, M. (1990). Taking aim on empowerment research: On the distinction between individual and psychological conceptions. *American Journal of Community Psychology, 18*, 169-177.

Index

Figures and tables are indicted with an italic *f* or *t*.

About the Author

Mary McElroy, PhD, is a professor of kinesiology and the kinesiology curriculum coordinator at Kansas State University. At the university she has also served as assistant department head and coordinator of graduate studies and research. In addition, she is the past President of the North American Society for the Sociology of Sport.

McElroy has written extensively on sociology of sport. She has authored, co-authored, or contributed to 14 books and has been published in numerous journals including the *International Journal of Sport History*, the *Journal of Sport and Social Issues*, and the *Journal of Sport and Exercise Psychology*.

A lifetime member of AAHPERD, McElroy holds a PhD in the sociology of sport and physical activity from the University of Maryland and is well known nationally and internationally for her distinguished work over the past 20 years. In her free time she likes to play golf and jog.

You'll find
other outstanding
sociology resources at

www.humankinetics.com

In the U.S. call

1-800-747-4457

Australia 08 8277 1555
Canada 1-800-465-7301
Europe .... +44 (0) 113 278 1708
New Zealand 09-523-3462

HUMAN KINETICS
The Information Leader in Physical Activity
P.O. Box 5076 • Champaign, IL 61825-5076 USA